VENTURE CAPITAL INVESTMENT: AN AGENCY ANALYSIS OF PRACTICE

Venture capital is a relatively new investment form, especially in the UK and Europe. However, there exists no systematic analysis of what drives investor–investee relations in venture capital markets using a unified and coherent framework. *Venture Capital Investment* fills this gap by employing a principal–agent framework to provide a contemporary, global analysis of contracting relations practice. By deploying this state of the art framework, Gavin Reid is able to develop a powerful organizing principle for viewing the bewildering complexity of real-world venture capital activity.

The principal–agent framework is simply and clearly expounded, and background information on the UK venture capital industry provided, before the reader is presented with the main body of the work. This utilizes in-depth case studies of investor–investee relations, based on extensive empirical research and organized around the principal–agent method, which provide valuable insights into contemporary UK venture capital practice. *Venture Capital Investment* also considers risk management from the perspective of both contracting parties, information system development post-contract, and the 'trading' of risk and information in pursuit of superior contracting between investors and investees. The author concludes by employing the principal–agent method both to anticipate trends in UK venture capital activity and prescribe better business practice.

Written in a clear and accessible fashion this volume will be an excellent resource for students and instructors of economics and business studies and for all those wanting to know more about the important area of venture capital investment.

Gavin C. Reid is Professor in Economics and Director of the Centre for Research into Industry, Enterprise, Finance and the Firm (CRIEFF) at the University of St Andrews. He is a graduate of the Universities of Aberdeen, Southampton, and Edinburgh, and at the latter was awarded his PhD for a thesis on industrial price leadership. Formerly Reader in Economics at the University of Edinburgh, he has held visiting professorships at Queen's University, Ontario, the University of Denver, Colorado, and the University of Nice, and has been a Visiting Scholar at Darwin College, University of Cambridge. He has published extensively in the academic journals on industrial organization, small firms, microeconomic theory, business ethics, venture capital and intellectual property. He is author of six previous books, including *Theories of Industrial Organization* (1987), *The Small Entrepreneurial Firm* (1988) (with L. R. Jacobsen), and *Small Business Enterprise* (1993). He has been a Leverhulme Trust Research Fellow, and completed this current book while holding a Nuffield Foundation Research Fellowship.

ROUTLEDGE STUDIES IN THE MODERN WORLD ECONOMY

1 INTEREST RATES AND BUDGET DEFICITS
A study of the advanced economies
Kanhaya L. Gupta and Bakhtiar Moazzami

2 WORLD TRADE AFTER THE URUGUAY ROUND
Prospects and policy options for the twenty-first century
Edited by Harald Sander and András Inotai

3 THE FLOW ANALYSIS OF LABOUR MARKETS
Edited by Ronald Schettkat

4 INFLATION AND UNEMPLOYMENT
Contributions to a new macroeconomic approach
Edited by Alvaro Cencini and Mauro Baranzini

5 MACROECONOMIC DIMENSIONS OF PUBLIC FINANCE
Essays in honour of Vito Tanzi
Edited by Mario I. Blejer and Teresa M. Ter-Minassian

6 FISCAL POLICY AND ECONOMIC REFORMS
Essays in honour of Vito Tanzi
Edited by Mario I. Blejer and Teresa M. Ter-Minassian

7 COMPETITION POLICY IN THE GLOBAL ECONOMY
Modalities for co-operation
Edited by Leonard Waverman, William S. Comanor and Akira Goto

8 WORKING IN THE MACROECONOMY
A Study of the US labor market
Martin F. J. Prachowny

9 HOW DOES PRIVATIZATION WORK?
Edited by Anthony Bennett

10 THE ECONOMICS AND POLITICS OF INTERNATIONAL TRADE
Freedom and Trade: Volume II
Edited by Gary Cook

11 THE LEGAL AND MORAL ASPECTS OF INTERNATIONAL TRADE
Freedom and Trade: Volume III
Edited by Asif Qureshi, Hillel Steiner and Geraint Parry

12 CAPITAL MARKETS AND CORPORATE GOVERNANCE IN JAPAN, GERMANY AND THE UNITED STATES
Organizational response to market inefficiencies
Helmut M. Dietl

13 COMPETITION AND TRADE POLICIES
Coherence or conflict
Edited by Einar Hope

14 RICE
The primary commodity
A. J. H. Latham

15 TRADE, THEORY AND ECONOMETRICS
Essays in honour of John S. Chipman
Edited by James C. Moore, Raymond Riezman and James R. Melvin

16 WHO BENEFITS FROM PRIVATISATION?
Edited by Moazzem Hossain and Justin Malbon

17 TOWARDS A FAIR GLOBAL LABOUR MARKET
Avoiding the New Slavery
Edited by Ozay Mehmet, Errol Mendes and Robert Sinding

18 MODELS OF FUTURES MARKETS
Edited by Barry Goss

19 VENTURE CAPITAL INVESTMENT
An agency analysis of practice
Gavin C. Reid

VENTURE CAPITAL INVESTMENT

An agency analysis of practice

Gavin C. Reid

ROUTLEDGE
London and New York

First published 1998
by Routledge
11 New Fetter Lane, London EC4P 4EE

Simultaneously published in the USA and Canada
by Routledge
29 West 35th Street, New York, NY 10001

Typeset in Galliard by RefineCatch Limited, Bungay, Suffolk
Printed and bound in Great Britain by
Mackays of Chatham PLC, Chatham, Kent

British Library Cataloguing in Publication Data
A catalogue record for this book is available from the British Library

Library of Congress Cataloging in Publication Data
Reid, Gavin C.
Venture capital investment : an agency analysis of practice /
Gavin C. Reid
p. cm.
Includes bibliographical references and index.
1. Venture capital – Great Britain. I. Title.
HG5441.R45 1998
332.66 – dc21 98–6504
CIP

ISBN 0–415–17969–6

TO KENNETH CLYDESDALE REID

Choice your Seeds from the high, streight, young and well thriving Trees; and the fairest, weyghtiest, and brightest thereon.

John Reid, *The Scots Gard'ner*, 1683

CONTENTS

PART 3
Cases

FIGURES

TABLES

PREFACE

BACKGROUND

This book is the product of a research project which involved several years' work on the UK venture capital industry. In undertaking this work, I have benefited from collaborating with several fellow workers. Most important of these have been Professor Falconer Mitchell and Mr Nicholas Terry, both of the University of Edinburgh. Also of significance have been Margo Anderson and Julia Smith, who provided research assistance on the project. While this volume is sole authored, my debts to all four are significant, and are gratefully acknowledged. Where joint work has contributed to the drafting of specific chapters, direct acknowledgements have been placed at the relevant chapter headings.

While initiated in Edinburgh University, much of the work reported upon in this book has been accomplished at the University of St Andrews. Of importance to this endeavour has been the happy home for research ideas and practice provided by the Centre for Research into Industry, Enterprise, Finance and the Firm (CRIEFF) at the University of St Andrews, which I founded shortly after my arrival here in 1991. The extensive qualitative analysis on which this work is based would not have been undertaken had not Tony Lawson of the University of Cambridge dared me to have the courage to write a serious, extended piece of original research in modern economics that *did not* involve mathematical economics or econometrics. His powerful advocacy, as expounded in Lawson (1985), for example, of a less formalistic approach to economics, took some time to filter through after a sabbatical year at Darwin College, Cambridge, in 1987–88. However, four books later, and ten years on, this is my response.

A final debt of thanks should be expressed to members of the UK venture capital industry, who gave generously of their time, despite the pressures of modern commerce under which they operated. The presumption behind the publishing of this book is that sufficient time has elapsed since the fieldwork that the data upon which I report have now ceased to have market sensitivity. As a further precaution, I should remark that the data were gathered upon the understanding that, in analysing them, specific company names, and their personnel, would not be identified, save by a code number or letter. I have respected that throughout the book, though I have referred to personnel by their correct gender in reporting upon their comments. Otherwise, the text aims to be gender neutral. In order to allow busy readers to dip into the book at points of their particular interest (e.g. case studies, risk management), I have tried to make each chapter reasonably self-contained. To this end, I have repeated a number of key definitions, and explained again some central concepts, at several points throughout the text.

AGENCY ANALYSIS

Principal–agent (or simply 'agency') analysis provides a powerful overarching framework for analysing contractual relations between parties in which both risk and incomplete knowledge of actions are involved. This book applies principal–agent analysis to contemporary evidence on venture capital investment. The experiences of the two parties to the venture capital relationship, investors and investees alike, are analysed in terms of risk management, information-handling and the trading of risk and information.

EVIDENCE

In this book I present evidence that provides support for the use of principal–agent analysis for understanding and explaining venture capital investor–investee relations. The typical investee analysed is a small firm with about fifty employees, a turnover of about £1m. and an age of less than ten years. As an investee, its chief interest is in achieving main market listing. Its investor is typically a venture capital fund with about £50m. at its disposal. The investor backs as few as ten new investees a year, because of the rigour of its screening process.

The empirical evidence upon which I report is based on an extended enquiry into practice in the UK venture capital industry, involving over three years of intensive fieldwork. The broader evidence on which it draws is based on a panel of some fifty investors for the years 1988–92; a cross-section of twenty paired investor–investee cases (i.e. dyads) for 1993; and a further cross-section of fourteen investees for 1993. There were basically three steps involved in this work. First, there was early fieldwork, in which contacts with key individuals, who could facilitate further contact with significant figures in the venture capital world, were cultivated. Second, a 'panel' database was created, providing detailed cross-section data on major UK venture capital funds for the years 1988, 1990 and 1992. Third, questionnaire instruments for conducting fieldwork and telephone interviews were designed, piloted and implemented.

Concerning the third phase, distinct semi-structured interview and administered questionnaire schedules were designed for face-to-face interviews with investors and investees, treating them as principal and agent respectively, and the investee schedule was further adapted for additional telephone interviews. All interviews were structured around the same agenda, involving the main headings of risk management, information-handling and the trading of risk and information. Empirical evidence on venture capital contracting is examined below from this perspective. The data gathered were both quantitative (numerical) and qualitative (textual) and the overall analysis of investor–investee risk management in this book is pursued under these headings. Where I report upon the direct speech of respondents, the convention adopted is to enclose comments they made in double quotation marks.

THEORY

The venture capitalist is a type of financial intermediary (see Chan 1983), typically handling funds for an upstream client who lacks the skills to be involved in high-risk/high-return investment opportunities. Without financial intermediaries, investees would flood the market with projects of dubious value, hoping to exploit the ultimate investors' ignorance. This would cause the market for venture capital to fail, denying financial backing to potentially good projects, because investors who experienced unhappy involvements with bad projects would withdraw from this funding arena. Venture capitalists act as relatively well-informed financial intermediaries who can limit this problem of adverse selection in the market for funds by using their skills in handling high-risk investments. Work by authors like Admati and Pfleiderer (1994) appropriately views the skills of the venture capitalist as lying in the ability to resolve information asymmetries. In acting for upstream clients, venture capitalists benefit the ultimate investor and the investee alike in keeping active the market for outside equity. In turn, they benefit from the existence of this market by pursuing their trade in a profit maximizing fashion.

Although this book is essentially empirical, my view is that sound applied work should always have a theoretical underpinning. To this end, the general framework I have adopted is that of principal–agent analysis. Previous work (see Sahlman 1990) using this framework has focused on the relationship between the upstream client and the venture capitalist. However, in my approach, the *venture capitalist* is thought of as the *principal*, providing a large injection of equity finance for specific investments by the *owner-manager* or *entrepreneur*, to be thought of as the *agent*.

In general principal–agent settings (see Sappington 1991), the agent is regarded as being liable to shirk on effort and to avoid risk, once a contract has been agreed with the principal. That is, the principal is confronted with the problem of moral hazard. Therefore, the principal seeks to agree a contract with the agent that will elicit an optimal level of effort and risk-sharing. In the specific context of venture capital investor–investee relations, principal–agent analysis typically assumes a risk-neutral principal (investor) and an effort- and risk-averse agent (investee) (see Chan *et al.* 1990). If there were no agency problems, the principal (investor) would absorb all the risk and the agent would receive a fixed payment (see Lambert 1986). In fact, in the venture capital world such arrangements are very uncommon, and the data also indicate that they are disliked. When investees were asked whether or not they would like a fixed sum on exit from the deal, 63 per cent said 'No'. Comments which they added when replying included: "We prefer to achieve the realization of the true value of the shares"; and "We would want the same potential for gain as the [venture capital] institutions".

Thus theory suggests agency problems will arise, and practice confirms their presence. Given that agency problems arise, the issue of how they are resolved, particularly as regards the handling of risk, is subtle. Theoretical work like that of Lambert (1986) suggests that if high risk is encouraging owner-managers to underinvest in the more profitable projects which the investor actually prefers, then improved communications will increase the willingness of the owner-manager to choose the risky projects.

The work that I am reporting on in this book provides a particularly detailed picture of this communication process between investor and investee, and its influence on risk management and information-handling. As well as providing a coherent framework for examining this process, it also provides case study 'tests' of the principal–agent approach, in the sense of confirming the relevance of categories used (for example, the form which communication takes, like the provision of management accounts) and the predicted relation between them (for example, the 'trading' of risk and information in the pursuit of contract optimality). The book as a whole provides striking confirmatory evidence of the applicability of the principal–agent model to the venture capital financing of mature firms. For example, venture capitalists appreciated the danger of moral hazard, the post-contract tendency to reduce effort, and sought safeguards against it, through bonding arrangements, to establish a sound supply of accounting information. They were also aware, pre-contract, of the danger of adverse selection, arising from the tendency for investees to overstate returns and understate risk; and they sought to limit this tendency by rigorous screening (only 30 per cent of proposals being reviewed) and by thorough 'due diligence' (only 3 per cent of proposals being backed).

ACKNOWLEDGEMENTS

The research upon which this book is based has been supported by seedcorn funding from the Centre for Financial Markets Research of the University of Edinburgh, by a travel grant from the Carnegie Trust, and by a major grant from the Esmée-Fairbairn Trust over the period 1990–94. To these sponsors my grateful acknowledgement is expressed, at the same time as absolving them from responsibility for the form which the analysis below takes. I should also like to express thanks to leading players in the UK venture capital industry for granting us interviews, and for providing detailed data; and to Margo Anderson (1990–93) and Julia Smith (1993–) for providing research assistance while working at the Centre for Research into Industry, Enterprise, Finance and the Firm (CRIEFF) at the University of St Andrews. Also of positive influence were participants at: two of the Scottish Economic Society Conferences, Dundee University (1992) and Heriot-Watt University, Edinburgh (1994); the Industrial Economics Study Group Conference, UMIST, Manchester (1993); the Third Global Workshop on Small Business Economics, Tinbergen Institute, Rotterdam (1994); the British Accounting Association Conference, University of Paisley (1994); the conference on 'Risk in Organizational Settings', The White House, Regent's Park, London (1995), sponsored by the ESRC under the *Risk and Human Behaviour Programme*; and the conference on 'Private Equity into the Next Millennium' (1996), held at the Centre for Management Buyout Research (CMBOR), University of Nottingham, sponsored by the Research Foundation of the Chartered Institute of Management Accountants (CIMA). Previous versions of some of the material used in this book have appeared in the journals *Small Business Economics*, *Accounting and Business Research*, *Entrepreneurship Theory and Practice*, and the *European Journal of Finance*. See Reid (1996a), Mitchell *et al.* (1995), Mitchell *et al.* (1998) and Reid *et al.* (1997). Gratitude is expressed to the publishers for permission to draw on this material. All errors of omission or commission that this book may yet contain, despite good advice, have an authorial attribution. The assistance of Julia Smith of CRIEFF, Department of Economics, University of St Andrews, in preparing the manuscript is gratefully acknowledged.

This book is dedicated to my young son Kenneth, now well past the seedcorn phase, and currently experiencing rapid growth and rising performance. The John Reid of the dedication page is not, to my knowledge, a relative. The quotation from his work, the first Scottish gardening book, reflects both my interest in gardening, in a personal sense, and, more relevantly, its apposite nature in the present context. John Reid left Scotland for America in 1683, the year of publication of his book. He enjoyed great success. Initially indentured as an overseer to proprietors of a settlement, he bought ten acres of 'boggy meadow' from the proprietors when his indenture expired. From this simple 'start-up' he carved out an extraordinary career, eventually becoming Surveyor-General of the province of New Jersey, and acquiring an estate of thousands of acres of, no doubt, well-cultivated land. If this volume contributes, in even small measure, directly or indirectly, to the better cultivation of business practice, where private equity is involved, I shall feel my self-imposed task has been well worth completing.

G.C.R.

Castlecliffe
CRIEFF, Department of Economics
University of St Andrews

ABBREVIATIONS

ABC	activity-based costing
ACS	accounting control systems
AIS	accounting information system
AQ	administered questionnaire (see Appendix B)
BES	business expansion scheme
BVCA	British Venture Capital Association
CAPM	Capital Asset Pricing Model
CIMA	Chartered Institute of Management Accountants
CMBOR	Centre for Management Buyout Research
DCF	discounted cash flow
EC	European Community
EPOS	electronic point of sale
ICFC	Industrial and Commercial Finance Corporation (*later* 3Ii)
IRR	internal rate of return
ISO	International Standards Organization
LBO	leveraged buyout
MAV	moving average volume
MBI	management buy-in
MBO	management buyout
MCS	management control system
MIS	management information system
MSF	mature small firm
NPV	net present value
NVCA	National Venture Capital Association
NVT	new venture team
NYSE	New York Stock Exchange
OEM	original equipment and manufacture
POS	point of sale
PR	public relations
R&D	research and development
SIC	standard industrial classification
SME	small or medium-sized enterprise

SSI	semi-structured interview schedule (see Appendix A)
TQ	telephone interview questionnaire (see Appendix C)
VC	venture capital
VCI	venture capital investor
VCR	Venture Capital Report
WACC	weighted average cost of capital

Part 1

BACKGROUND

1

THE ANALYSIS OF VENTURE CAPITAL PRACTICE

1.1 INTRODUCTION

This book reports upon an investigation into UK venture capital practice. The distinctive features of this investigation are that it was structured around a single analytical principle, agency analysis, and that it was solidly rooted in evidence. The agency approach, more fully characterized as principal–agent analysis, concentrates on two features of contracting relations between investors and investees, namely, risk and information. The use of evidence focuses on primary source data obtained by direct contact with investors and investees. Thus a *single principle*, with its two constituent elements of risk and information, is applied to a *well-grounded body of evidence* on investor–investee relations.

The conclusions reached, and the methods by which this was done, are, I believe, of significance to both the analyst (be she a specialist in economics, accountancy, or finance, etc.) and the practitioner (be he a venture capitalist, business angel, financier, or banker, etc.). Put briefly, they are that the considerable complexity of contracting relations between investors and investees can be simplified down to the principle that skills and knowledge in risk management are traded for skills and knowledge in business management until both parties have exhausted all opportunities for further exploiting skills and knowledge. This having been done, the relationship between investor and investee is, in a particular sense, best or optimal.[1] The methods by which these conclusions, and the implications thereof, were reached were complex, and involved a blend of analytical principles and empirical methods. In this book, both are extensively

1 The particular sense I have in mind here is optimal or 'constrained optimal' according to the Pareto criterion of economics. This says that an economic change is good if it makes at least one economic actor better off, without making any other worse off. Once such changes have all been exploited, assuming no impediments to so doing, an optimum is achieved. If certain distortions cannot be removed, then the achievement of the optimum is defined subject to the constraints imposed by those distortions. In this particular context, a constraint typically *does* arise, the so-called incentive constraint arising from the self-seeking effort allocating behaviour of the agent (see Reid 1987: ch. 9).

explored, in order that the conclusions reached may be fully substantiated by argument, convincingly supported by evidence, and extensively illuminated by example.

The book is made up of four parts: background, evidence, cases and analysis. *Background* covers the nature of venture capital, principles and methods of investor–investee analysis, and the theory of principal and agent (expressed geometrically). *Evidence* considers the devices used to gather data ('instrumentation') from investors and investees, the methods deployed in working 'in the field', and the main characteristics of investors and investees. *Cases* develops analytical case studies for three different types of principals: an independent, a banking subsidiary, and a public institution. The investees referred to were active in timber processing, point-of-sale (POS) technology, diagnostic testing and biotechnology. *Analysis* engages in a cross-site exploration of four topics: risk management, information demand, information development, and the exchange of risk and information. The book closes with an epilogue, tying together the main argument, followed by appendices detailing the full instrumentation used in the empirical work.

This chapter itself is designed to provide the reader with complete orientation for the book as a whole. As well as exploring its purpose, main argument and contents, as above, it introduces the full range of ideas that are to be treated in greater detail in the ensuing chapters. First, investee and investor are introduced. The former is typically a mature small firm (MSF)[2] in the UK context, with sales of about £12½m. The latter is a venture capital investor (VCI), investing about £1m. in each investee. Second, the key analytical concepts of principal–agent analysis are introduced, focusing on issues like moral hazard, bond posting, monitoring, and information asymmetry. Third, the empirical background and investigative methods are considered, covering the main statistical characteristics of investors and investees, and the use of interview techniques in the field. The chapter ends with a brief concluding section.

1.2 FAST-GROWING MATURE SMALL FIRMS (MSFs)

The available evidence on life-cycle effects in small firms (e.g. Reid 1993) suggests that something prevents rapidly growing mature small firms (MSFs) from maintaining their growth trajectories. A commonly cited reason for this is a shortage of finance capital (see Mason and Harrison 1991b). If an attempt is made to solve this problem by increasing the level of debt, a number of constraining influences come into play. Higher gearing increases exposure to risk, and may

2 Mature both because the average age was over fifteen years, and because most involvements of investors (about 90 per cent) were *not* start-ups.

create vulnerability to debt-servicing crises. Debt itself may only be advanced by the banks to the extent that the entrepreneur can demonstrate that collateral exists, and this may set an upper limit on the gearing ratio. Debt default may be dealt with severely by the bank, who may offer no option of debt-rescheduling in a time of debt-servicing crisis, but may simply call in the loan pre-emptively to stop collateral being dissipated, thus forcing liquidation. If debt finance is seen as a logical option, offering as it does the advantage of keeping the entrepreneur's property right in his business intact, it is an option which is exercised with prudence by the borrower, and is handled with caution by the bank. If the shortage of finance capital to prolong or sustain growth is not sought in the form of debt finance, outside equity finance becomes an attractive alternative.

It may come in the form of support from a 'business angel' in the local business community, who has seen a promising small firm growing vigorously before his very eyes, but who hears of problems of financial capital shortage which look likely to limit future growth prospects for it. In the UK, at least, it is not yet well understood how these 'business angels' or informal investors work, partly because it is difficult to identify them in the business community. What evidence is available so far (e.g. Mason and Harrison 1994) suggests they provide small packets of funding, to a limited number of local firms, investing only periodically, and requiring relatively little in the way of formal vetting of proposals. Finally, there is a more formal side to venture capital investment, arising when substantial levels of equity provision are provided to mature small firms (MSFs) from funds which are managed by financial and industrial experts, very often on behalf of an upstream client like a pension fund, multinational enterprise or merchant bank (see Sahlman (1990) for the US context).

It is this last named form of provision that is the focus in this book, with the UK venture capital industry over the period 1988–94 providing the empirical basis of the discussion. I will appeal largely to two specific bodies of evidence: first, a panel of the UK venture capital industry for the years 1988, 1990 and 1992; and secondly, a cross-section of twenty pairs (or 'dyads') of investors and investees in 1993.[3] The latter sample includes the principal investors in the UK venture capital industry (accounting for three-quarters of the total provision), each of which is paired with one or more typical investees. The panel data provide the evidence on trends in the industry, and enable us to characterize the average or typical venture capital investor and investee in Part 2 below. The cross-section data enable detailed individual case studies ('within site') to be reported upon, as in Part 3, as well as comparative analysis ('cross site'), as in Part 4.

3 This is augmented by a further sample of fourteen investees, investigated using telephone interviews.

1.3 VENTURE CAPITAL INVESTORS (VCIs)

Venture capital involves the provision of equity finance to firms which are typically small in size and unquoted. They provide an opportunity for 'gain through growth potential', contingent on acquiring finance to permit new investment. Normally, the investor will expect to earn an adequate investment return within a few years through one of a variety of exit routes, for example stock market flotation, sale to a trade buyer or sale to management. While the USA has been the major location for the development of venture capital, in recent years the growth in venture capital funds in the UK has been dramatic (see Table 1.1).

Growth of funds invested rapidly grew from £325m. in 1985 to a peak of £1,647m. in 1989. After a slight falling away of investment after that, it recovered well. Indeed, in the UK most of the leading financial institutions have created venture capital funds (see BVCA *Directory*) and a range of autonomous organizations has also emerged. It is also interesting to note that many of the staff managing these funds have trained as professional accountants.[4] Their demands for accounting information can therefore be expected to reflect a high level of expertise. Indeed previous studies have indicated that accounting information is a key component in any decision-making process whose purpose is to

Table 1.1 Total venture capital investment, 1985–93

Year	*Value (£m.)*
1985	325
1986	46
1987	1,029
1988	1,394
1989	1,647
1990	1,394
1991	989
1992	1,434
1993	1,422

Source: British Venture Capital Association (BVCA).

4 See Venture Economics (1986). To illustrate with four examples picked at random from the *Venture Capital Report* (Cary 1989): Abingworth Management Ltd. had 8 VC executives, of which 4 were accountants; Biotechnology Investments Ltd. had 5 VC executives, of which 2 were accountants; Syntech Information Technology Funds had 4 VC executives, of which 2 were accountants; and Oakland Investment Management had 8 VC executives, of which 3 were accountants.

commit funds (Tyebjee and Bruno 1984; Macmillan *et al.* 1985). It is therefore likely to be an important aspect of the ongoing assessment by venture capital investors (VCIs) of investment outcomes.

A number of researchers have shown that the post-investment relations between VCIs and investees can be close and constructive. They involve the VCI giving advice, utilizing business contacts and facilitating finance, in addition to monitoring performance in a variety of ways (Gorman and Sahlman 1989; Macmillan *et al.* 1988). Studies have shown that venture capitalists do vary in their interaction with investees, altering the extent of their involvement in response to their perception of the need for assistance (Macmillan *et al.* 1988; Sweeting 1991a). While differences in the VCI/investee relationship and in the extent of contact between them are apparent, the reasons for these variations have not been deeply explored. The agency approach to the study of external investor–investee relations has stimulated increasing interest, and as a basis for analysing small firms has already shown promise (Eisenhardt 1989a; Sapienza 1989). It has therefore been suggested that the VCI/MSF relationship would be amenable to this type of analysis (Harrison and Mason 1992; Mitchell *et al.* 1992).

1.4 PRINCIPAL–AGENT ANALYSIS

An applied version of principal–agent analysis has been adopted in this book to provide a framework for the analysis of the investor–investee relationship. In a principal–agent relationship, one party (the agent) acts on behalf of another party (the principal). The agent is not fully supervised, and has a measure of independence, which she may be tempted to exploit to avoid risk and to shirk on effort. The principal therefore tries to construct a contract which will give the agent an incentive to share risk efficiently and to optimize her effort (Reid 1987: ch. 9). The use of the principal–agent model in accounting research was initiated by the likes of Baiman (1982) and consolidated in textbook treatments like Strong and Walker (1987). Applied principal–agent analysis has been used on the client–VCI relationship by Sahlman (1990). Here, we take the analysis one step further down the tier of superior–subordinate relations, and look at the VCI's relation to the investee. Since the work of Chan *et al.* (1990) the established risk framework has been that the VCI can be treated as a risk-neutral principal, and the investee as a risk-averse agent. Much further work has since been accomplished along these lines (e.g. Gompers and Lerner 1994; Admati and Pfleiderer 1994). A special interest has also emerged in explicit modelling of information and communication, especially as regards its control implications (e.g. Gordon *et al.* 1990; Cohen *et al.* 1992).

Despite this flourishing of theoretical work, the empirical character of the VCI/MSF relationship is still very poorly understood. This cannot be resolved by the use of secondary source data: it requires paying deliberate attention to the details of real contracting practices. The purpose of this book is to provide the reader with exactly such detail, and to explore for him or her its practical implications for risk-sharing and incentive alignment.

At the post-investment stage a principal–agent (or 'agency') relationship exists between the VCI and the investee (MSF). The VCI assumes the role of principal and the investee firm's directors the role of agent. Their relationship places the principal in a position where the problem of *moral hazard* has to be addressed. The directors of the investee firm, acting in self-interest and having relinquished full ownership of the firm (perhaps subsequently retaining only a minority share), are motivated to consume perquisites ('perks') and to limit effort. They will obtain 100 per cent of the benefit from these acts but will bear only a proportion (based on their remaining ownership stake) of their cost. The principal may therefore, through the subscription agreement or by other less formal means, attempt to establish arrangements to attenuate the effects of this moral hazard. These can take the form of *bonding* or *bond posting* whereby the principal imposes penalties on the investees if certain levels of performance are not met and establishes performance boundaries (e.g. gearing ratio standards) and decision autonomy limits (asset disposals) for the agent. More positively, *incentives* may be provided through the reward package set for the agent (e.g. performance-linked pay).

Moreover, the principal may attempt to influence the agent by *monitoring* the effectiveness of his or her performance. Performance measurement (or monitoring) will also be needed to operationalize bonding and the incentivized reward structure. For a principal such as a VCI, monitoring by direct observation of the agent's actions is impractical and therefore a flow of information is required. This is usually focused on the outcomes or results of the agent's actions. The use of such information to assess and motivate the agent suffers from two disadvantages. First, it is difficult for a principal to identify the extent to which any outcome is due to good fortune rather than the agent's effort and ability. Second, the agent possesses a greater familiarity with business operations than the principal, as well as having control over the generation of information. There is therefore an imbalance or *asymmetry* of information. Given the pursuit of self-interest, the agent may misrepresent performance or provide information selectively in order to make outcomes appear more favourable. In response, the principal may react by establishing disclosure rules and a syntax to govern the information flows.

The agency theory model is thus heavily dependent on information flows between agent and principal. Accounting, which provides financial measurements of inputs and outcomes, constitutes an integral part of this flow. It certainly is an important influence on those *ex ante* expectations which drive investment decisions. Equally, it appears logical that accounting information will serve a purpose in the *ex post* assessment of performance. A complementary consequence of its use to this purpose can be to limit the effects of moral hazard, by providing a basis for bonding and for monitoring the agent. The problem of information asymmetry, however, is one which is not simply solved by information per se, but by consideration too of the agent's control over the accounting systems of the firm.

In consideration of this issue, Chapter 12 examines how VCIs, as principals, establish and use accounting information flows from their investee firms, as agents. It does this within a principal–agent (or agency) theory framework, utilizing the above concepts. It is therefore primarily concerned with monitoring behaviour. Within this context the views of these investors on moral hazard and information asymmetry are also investigated.

1.5 EMPIRICAL BACKGROUND

Over the period June 1992 to September 1993 pairs of investors and investees ('dyads') in the UK venture capital industry were interviewed. The sampling frame was provided by the alphabetic listing of venture capital funds in the *Venture Capital Report* (Cary 1989). Respondents to an initial postal enquiry constituted the sample of investors, and in each meeting with an investor a request was made that they facilitated contact with nominated investees. This was generally granted.[5] The core data on which this book reports are made up of twenty investors and sixteen investees, as they relate to these dyads.[6] Six investors were unwilling or unable (for example, start-up fund *I*) to provide access to investees, and two investors were willing to provide access to two investees. The latter offers were particularly warmly accepted, as multiple agents add another dimension to the study.

According to data provided by the British Venture Capital Association (BVCA) the total value of venture capital investments undertaken at the time of the fieldwork was about £1,400m. The sample of investors included the two largest players in the UK venture market, and the twenty investors in all accounted for about three-quarters of investment activity within this market during the period 1992–23. The average value of investments made in the sample was £0.98 million.

In Chapter 7 a careful comparison is drawn between this sample of investors and the larger population of investors in the UK, as specified in the *Venture Capital Report* (Cary 1991), the latter being the body of data relevant to our period of the fieldwork. It indicates a close correspondence between sample and population characteristics. The main difference between the two is that the average size (for example, by employment, total funds invested) is somewhat greater

5 Indeed, in some cases, more than one investee was nominated. See the treatment in Chapter 8, for example, where an independent VCI and two of his high-technology investees are examined in an explanatory case study.

6 In addition, data on fourteen investees, examined by telephone interview questionnaires, are available (see Chapter 7).

for the sample than for the population, this being explicable by the presence of the two largest UK venture capital investors in the sample. Table 1.2 provides a summary comparison of some key attributes of investors in the sample and in the population. The typical deal size is similar between sample and population, as are other deal characteristics like maxima and minima for size of equity stakes, and number of full-time venture capital executives. These data, allied to the fact that the sample is a high proportion of the population (53 per cent), suggest that conclusions based on the sample have general validity for the population of investors.[7]

Investees were obviously far more diverse than investors, and contacts were provided by investors on the basis that they were representative of the typical investment involvement. Data are complete for investees on the qualitative dimension, but are somewhat less complete, as compared to investors, on the quantitative dimension. In the nature of things, as no database of all UK investees exists, it is not possible to provide comparisons between the sample of investees and the population of investees.[8] However, this is of little importance to the study, where the focus of interest is on the ***relationship*** of the investor to the investee, rather than investee attributes per se. Key characteristics of investees are given in Table 1.3. This information has been obtained from summary data sheets relating to investees, which they completed in addition to their participating in interviews involving the completion of administered questionnaires.[9] The data are revealing, and display a number of important features of investee firms. First, they are not young. None was less than three years old, and the average age

Table 1.2 Comparison of sample and population characteristics of UK venture capital investors, 1992–93

Characteristics	*Average values*[a]	
	Sample[b]	*Population*
Average value of investments (£m.)	0.98 (1.12)	0.78 (0.65)
Minimum equity stake (%)	6.1 (8.2)	6.3 (6.7)
Maximum equity stake (%)	57.6 (19.6)	56.7 (18.7)
Number of full-time venture capital executives	7.0 (6.2)	6.5 (4.3)

Notes:
a Values given are arithmetic means; standard deviations are in brackets.
b Sample has 20 investors; population has 38 investors.

7 A fuller statement of this argument, by reference to a broader range of statistics, is given in Chapter 7.

8 However, comparisons can be made usefully between 'extraneous' samples of investees, gathered independently (see Chapter 7).

9 See Appendix B for the instrumentation used.

Table 1.3 Characteristics of typical investees of venture capital investors

Characteristics	*Average values*[a,b]
Age of investee firm (years)	16.6 (20.4)
Number of employees (full-time)	166.9 (253.7)
Annual sales (£000s)	12,446.9 (22,279.9)
Net profit after tax (£000s)	788.4 (1,368.4)
Proportion of share capital held (%)	38.9 (30.1)
Current rate of return (%)	32.7 (39.0)
Forecast rate of return at exit (%)	43.0 (21.6)

Notes
a Average values are the arithmetic mean; standard deviations are in brackets.
b Sample has sixteen investees, but there are incomplete returns on some characteristics.

was nearly seventeen years. Second, while technically 'small' (that is, less than 200 employees on average), they are by no means micro-firms. Rather, they are firms of substantial scale, and they may even have ambitions for main market listing.[10] Third, investees are willing to contemplate a considerable dilution of ownership in order to permit the injection of large amounts of outside equity into the firm. The average proportion of share capital owned by the investee is 39 per cent. The range is from close to zero to 78 per cent, and the median is exactly 50 per cent. Fourth, both the current and expected internal rates of return[11] (IRRs) are high, having average values of 33 per cent and 43 per cent respectively.

Overall, what the data of Table 1.3 suggest is that investors are averse to the high-risk exposure of seedcorn and start-up financing – indeed, are averse to what some might regard as the classical form of business venturing. They limit adverse selection by backing mature small firms (MSFs). However, even though the main investment involvement is with development capital,[12] investors seek from investees, and get, a relatively high rate of return. Thus, in relation to the complete

10 The investor data indicate that market listing/flotation is the preferred exit route in about 20 per cent of cases.

11 Annualized internal rates of return (per cent), typically as computed on a Lotus 123 spreadsheet at the time of this study. The IRR is that discount rate at which the present value of takedowns of capital equals the present value of disbursements plus the present value of the residual. To illustrate, a disbursement of D which occurs t time periods after the first takedown has, for an IRR of r, a present value of $D/(1+{}^{r}/_{100})^{t}$. Some significant problems arise in computing IRRs in venture capital contexts. If, as is often the case, the investee firm has no publicly traded shares, the value of the residual is not defined by reference to a market, but must be estimated by subjective judgement. On further issues of this sort, see Bygrave *et al.* (1988).

12 In the sample of investors, the modal investment (45 per cent) was in development capital. The other main investment forms were buyout (40 per cent), start-up (11 per cent) and other (4 per cent).

spectrum of all investment opportunities, although venture capital investment clearly remains active in high-risk areas (see Chapter 8), in the UK it falls short of the highest-risk involvements.

1.6 INTERVIEW INSTRUMENTATION

The instruments used for gathering data on investors and investees were semi-structured interview schedules and questionnaires for both face-to-face and telephone interviews. Distinct questionnaire designs were used for each case, with the investor questionnaire schedule being more qualitative than the investee schedule. Investors and investees were also asked to complete basic data sheets which required them to supply information of the sort displayed in Tables 1.2 and 1.3 above. Investors and investees were typically paired in 'dyads', with each party being subject to separate face-to-face interviews. A further sample of investees was interviewed by telephone interviews. The full instrumentation is too complex and extensive to be considered in this introductory chapter. It is discussed in detail in Part 3, and facsimiles of the instruments, and their accompanying documentation, are given in the Appendices on instrumentation at the end of the book. As far as the scope of this chapter is concerned, Table 1.4 illustrates how respondents were approached. In this case, it indicates how the investors were questioned, under four main headings.

Putting aside for the moment the details considered in Part 3, I have simply abbreviated these four main headings to: expected returns; portfolio balance; screening; and risk-sharing. The investee aspects of risk management and their

Table 1.4 Summary of interview agenda for investor

I *Chance outcomes and sure prospects*
- Role of chance
- Use of actuarial values
- Certainty equivalents

II *Offsetting good outcomes against bad*
- Actions that affect chance
- Irreducibility of chance
- Portfolio balance
- Investee numbers and diversification

III *Effects of new investees on risk management*
- Methods of screening investees
- Portfolio balance consequences (e.g. risk/return; by sectoral and regional composition)

IV *Sharing risk with the investee*
- Investee motivation for risk-sharing (consequences for portfolio balance; implications of differing degrees of risk aversion)
- Investor willingness to accept risk and consequences for investee effort

relation to those of the investor were explored under a similar set of categories, but in a more structured way, using dummy and categorical variables to support the qualitative evidence supplied.[13] In the discussion of results, these four headings, expected returns, portfolio balance, screening and risk-sharing, are used to examine risk and information management among and between investors and investees.

1.7 CONCLUSION

The main themes of this book have now been sketched. They explore the relationships between a venture capital investor (VCI), a provider of risk capital, and a mature small firm (MSF). The framework used, principal–agent analysis, emphasized the importance of risk and information to the relationship between VCI and MSF. The testing of this framework requires gathering data 'in the field' using appropriately designed instruments for interviews with investors and investees. The main themes having been established, I turn now to the substantive work of this book, which involves taking these themes and fully developing and exploring them.

13 In addition, wherever possible, accounting data, brochures, financial PR, etc., were collected to the extent that the respondent was willing.

2

VENTURE CAPITAL

2.1 INTRODUCTION

At the time of the fieldwork on which this book is based, an influential UK venture capitalist, Lucius Cary,[1] defined venture capital (VC) as a type of external financial capital provision, usually in equity form, which was invested in high-risk ventures (typically new companies and especially new technologies) and which offered the possibility of significant gains to compensate for the risks involved in such investments. In the UK context, this was perhaps an idealized picture to paint of venture capital activity, arguably being more influenced by perceptions of US industry characteristics than by the more conservative features of the UK industry.[2] Just a few years earlier, when Nicholas Stacey (1990) had asked, '*Should venture capitalists be more intrepid?*', he had already been drawn to the conclusion that there existed a shortage of true risk capital in the UK. He expressed the view that, overwhelmingly, venture capital investors (VCIs) expected their investees to have a sound commercial track record and a management team of proven ability. He pointed to the lack of interest in the UK in start-up and seedcorn provision, observing that most venture capitalists would only start getting seriously involved with investees at the development capital stage.[3] They were observed to prefer later-stage to early-stage development, and were apparently most keen on management buyouts (MBOs). Table 2.1 identifies the main categories of venture capital involvement, and the sorts of ranges which were typical for the provision of funds in each case at the time of this study.

1 Lucius Cary is both a venture capitalist and the founding editor of *The Venture Capital Report* and its *Guide to Venture Capital in the UK and Europe*. He expressed this view in the 6th edition (Cary 1993) of the *Guide*.

2 Though even in the US case there has been a tendency for VCIs to withdraw from seedcorn and early-stage involvements (see Bygrave and Timmons 1992: ch. 2).

3 This tendency is even more marked in some countries with relatively immature venture capital industries. For example, in commenting on the Swedish scene, Landström (1992: 345) refers to 'a reduced number of investments in start-ups and high technology'.

Probably only the first three stages (£5k–£1m.) typify true business venturing, yet it is only in the last two categories (£500k–£25m.) that most of the UK venture capital activity takes place. Thus one can be accused of using an oxymoron in applying the term 'venture capital' in the UK case, as the 'venturing' falls far short of its original connotation of 'adventuring'.[4]

A more cautious definition of venture capital, perhaps reflecting better the reality of practice today, has been provided by the British Venture Capital Association (BVCA) in their *Guide to Venture Capital* (BVCA 1996b), in which they explain that venture capital refers to financing the start-up, development, expansion or purchase of a firm, in the act of which the VCI acquires, by agreement, a proportion of the share capital in the business in return for providing funding.[5] Here, there is no reference to high risk or high technology. In the light of expressions of views of this sort, it is worth referring to the work of Murray and Lott (1995) who have asked whether UK venture capitalists have a bias against investments in new technology-based firms. They observe that, in comparing UK and US industry statistics, US investors place, *pro rata*, three times as much finance with technology-based, start-up and early-stage investments as compared with UK counterparts, if MBO and LBO investments are removed from the data.[6] It was found in the UK that, in reviewing high-technology proposals from potential investees, VCIs tended to use different and/or more rigorous criteria for assessing technology-based projects.[7] There appeared to be a perception that high-technology investments were relatively more risky than other investment

Table 2.1 Types of venture capital

Type of provision	*Typical level of provision*
Seed capital	£5k–£10k
Start-up capital	£100k–£5m.
Early-stage development capital	£300k–£1m.
Later-stage development capital	£500k–£2m.
Management buyout	£5m.–£25m.

Note: Figures are typical for 1993 as reported in *The Venture Capital Report Guide to Venture Capital in the UK and Europe* (Cary 1993).

4 As used by Masey (1993) in the title of her book on a UK venture capital fund.

5 This may be contrasted with the unqualified definition of Kozmetsky *et al.* (1985: 1) that: 'The venture capital industry is a branch of the investment community which specializes in high-risk equity investments.'

6 The management buyout (MBO) is a procedure by which existing managers buy the firm they work for. The leveraged buyout (LBO) is a procedure for purchasing a business largely using debt. In the USA, the terminology LBO is often used as a synonym for MBO.

7 Although the ratio of high-technology proposals accepted to proposals received did not differ significantly between general and technology-specialized funds, suggesting that both fund types applied similarly more demanding criteria to such proposals.

opportunities (notably, later-stage) and this was reflected in the setting of higher IRR thresholds[8] when evaluating new-technology projects.

It is clear that the functional purpose of venture capital – a matter that ultimately relates to its conceptualization as a form of finance capital – is not even widely understood, let alone its purpose being the object of unanimity, even by expert opinion. Further, practice as regards the application of categories of venture capital funding (e.g. start-up finance) may vary widely, for instance by country (Green 1991). The purpose of this chapter is to set out the principal features of venture capital in terms of industry characteristics, theoretical approaches, and empirical evidence, so that the reader may have a more finely tuned awareness of the context, nature and purpose of venture capital than is possible by making reference to only one view, be it even an expert view. The next section provides an overview of the structure of the UK venture capital industry, expanding upon the very brief introduction in section 1.3 of Chapter 1. This is followed by a consideration of the way in which theorists have conceptualized the role and purpose of venture capital. Then in section 2.4 a statistical characterization of UK venture capitalists is provided to underpin the previous discussion empirically. The concluding section 2.5 completes the chapter.

2.2 THE VENTURE CAPITAL INDUSTRY

The roots of the venture capital industry lie as far back as the fifteenth century with the activities of merchant venturers. They were active traders in the Far and Middle East, where they also set up commercial enterprises, sometimes backed up with armed authority. The great European capitals, including London, were their source of private finance, supplied by wealthy capitalists, and the merchant venturers who sailed the seas took the risks. Out of this grew the East India Company, founded at the end of the reign of Elizabeth I. By the late seventeenth century, it was increasingly governing the territories in which it traded, which proved even more profitable than commerce. It lost its monopoly of trade in India in 1813, then its monopoly of the China trade, and eventually became purely a governing body, shorn of commercial functions.[9]

During the nineteenth century the Scottish investment trusts were leaders in the provision of private funds for investment companies engaged in high-risk

8 For a technical definition, see Chapter 1, fn. 11. The internal rate of return is a measure of the total rate of return from an investment that takes account of capital redemptions, possible capital gains, and income from dividends. Its value depends on factors like risk, investment duration, ease of exit and competition for the deal. An average value of 20 per cent or more is typically sought. The hurdle level could be 40 per cent or more for high-technology projects.

9 See Webb (1980: 70–1, 223–4) for further historical details. The treatment in Lorenz (1989: 6–8) also provides a useful historical background.

ventures like railways and canals. But modern venture capital only emerged in the UK in the 1930s, when Charterhouse launched a specialist fund whose purpose was the provision of equity finance for fast-growing, new small businesses. The Industrial and Commercial Finance Corporation (ICFC) was launched in 1945, by the Bank of England and the main clearing banks, to provide finance for development to new and expanding UK companies. By the early 1980s it had become known as 3i and was providing the major part of the total volume of UK venture capital finance. However, 3i has always favoured loan finance, or a mix of loan and equity finance, so its activities, major though they are, do not entirely satisfy the attributes one would naturally associate with venture capital.[10]

The origins of the term 'venture capital' appear to lie with the American financier, Jock Whitney, one of the richest men in America after the Rockefellers, who had experienced mixed fortunes in backing entrepreneurs.[11] After World War II he set up a fund of $10m., whose purpose was to institutionalize the process of risk investment. The company, J.H. Whitney & Co., was to have been described as a 'private investment firm', but this conveyed little to the relevant players in financial markets. His partner Benno Schmidt suggested the term 'venture capital' over lunch, as best combining the sense of both risk and adventure, and Whitney approved it on the spot. His firm was to provide the organizational template for future US institutions going by the name of venture capital investors, and US practice, in turn, has been a major influence in stimulating and modifying UK practice. After the USA and Japan, the UK is now the largest provider of venture capital in the world.

Based on data provided by the British Venture Capital Association (BVCA) and National Venture Capital Association (NVCA), as summarized and evaluated by Murray (1995c) and Terry (1994), a conspectus of the industry, in the period leading up to the fieldwork, now follows. These writers are in agreement in suggesting that the UK venture capital market developed towards maturity over the 1980s into the 1990s. It is equally agreed that the level of venture capital activity is cyclically sensitive. In considering data over time, therefore, it will on occasion be useful to appeal to data that have been adjusted for business-cycle effects. For example, if annual investment data are adjusted for prices and the cycle (Murray 1995c: fig. 1), a steady rise in UK venture capital investment is noted until 1985, followed by a more marked rise between 1985 and 1989, and then by a sharp fall up to 1991. The effect of adjusting for prices and the cycle is to dampen the variation in investment, rather than to change the general picture.

10 3i themselves prefer to be characterized as providers of development rather than venture capital. However, they are the main provider of small amounts of equity in the UK, and also hold the largest portfolios of unquoted companies.

11 See Wilson (1985: ch. 2) for more detail on the beginning of the venture capital industry. It is of interest that the US government set up a Small Business Investment Company in the same way as the UK government had facilitated the launch of the ICFC.

This pattern of marked cyclicity is also characteristic of the US venture capital industry.[12] The failure of the industry in the UK to recover fully after 1991 has already been displayed in Table 1.1 in the previous chapter, in which the peak value invested of £1,647m. in 1989 had not been reached again by the year of the fieldwork (1993), at which point the figure stood at £1,422m. On other measures too, this cyclical sensitivity is evident.[13] For example, the number of companies in which the industry invested per annum rose sharply from 635 in 1985, rising to a peak of 1,569 in 1989, before falling away to 1,198 in 1993 (just below the earlier 1987 figure of 1,298).

The industrywide average value of investment[14] rose rapidly from £0.51m. in 1985 to £1.05m. in 1989. After that, it remained steady at just over £1m. (with the exception of a fall to £0.89m. in 1990), reaching a value of £1.19m. in 1993. However, while the number of investees was falling, the size of investment was holding steady, suggesting a withdrawal of VC interest from the smaller-deal end of the market, which inevitably means a withdrawal from seedcorn and start-up financing. Indeed, a decomposition of investments by financing stage confirms this picture quite strongly.[15] By percentage of amount invested, start-up financing fell from 15 per cent to just 3 per cent over the period 1986 to 1993, whereas MBO/MBI finance rose from 45 per cent to 62 per cent.[16] The average size of financing fell considerably for start-ups over this period (down from £0.5m. to £0.3m.) and rose markedly for MBO/MBIs (up from £1.3m. to £3.3m.). These trends are explained by Terry (1994: 5) largely by increased risk aversion on the part of investors who had been 'burned' by failures of new high-risk companies. They had sought refuge in an increasing supply of less risky MBOs; but also were averse to the proportionally higher transactions costs (including 'due diligence') incurred in considering smaller firms as potential investees.

Other critical aspects of the structure of the UK venture capital industry involve consideration of organizational type, source of funds, and of sectoral and regional involvement. The three basic organizational types of funds are: independents, either privately or publicly listed; captives, managed on behalf of parent institutions (e.g. banks, pension funds); and semi-captives, which both manage independent funds and parent's funds. The independents are the dominant type and, in the year of the fieldwork, accounted for 46 per cent of investment in the industry, compared to 20 per cent by captives and 28 per cent by

12 See Bygrave and Timmons (1992: ch.. 11).

13 See Terry (1994: table 1), which is based on BVCA figures.

14 This differs somewhat from the panel data figures of section 2.4 below, as the latter is somewhat less exhaustive in its coverage.

15 See Terry (1994: table 2), which is based on data provided by 3i and the BVCA.

16 In an MBI, a new group of managers takes over the running of the MSF, after a takeover which was either agreed or hostile.

semi-captives.[17] Captives account for a stable proportion of investments (around 25 per cent over the period 1989–90) and semi-captives a rising proportion (after 1991), at the same time as the proportions of investments by independents has fallen from 56 per cent in 1986 to 46 per cent in 1993. The increase in the semi-captive category seems to arise from new organizational trends like syndication[18] and the sharing of the costs of 'due diligence'. These developments have assisted semi-captives in both risk-spreading and in realizing superior returns.

By source, the total amount of funding raised increased from £368m. in 1991 to £479m. in 1993. Of this, the major contribution was made by the pension funds, though their proportion had fallen (from 68 per cent in 1991 to 48 per cent in 1993) as that of banks and insurance companies had risen (from 4 per cent and 10 per cent respectively in 1991, to 9 per cent and 22 per cent respectively in 1993). By sector, both amounts invested and numbers of investees were widely spread across sectors, with the exception that consumer-related business was consistently the favoured sector. About a quarter of companies which received venture capital funds were in this sector, both in 1986 and in 1993. By percentage investment, the proportion invested in consumer-related business had risen significantly, from about one-fifth in 1986 to about one-third in 1993.

By region, London and the South East enjoyed the lion's share of venture capital activity, by companies receiving funding (46 per cent and 36 per cent in 1986 and 1993 respectively) and by percentage of amounts invested (64 per cent and 53 per cent in 1986 and 1993 respectively). The only other regions showing comparable vigour were the North West and Scotland. Scotland, for example, had a rising proportion of companies in which VCs were investing (9 per cent in 1986 and 14 per cent in 1993) and a corresponding rise in proportions of amounts invested (up from 7 per cent in 1986 to 10 per cent in 1993). One has to be cautious in interpreting these statistics, because the business density in London and the South East, for example, is considerably greater than in Scotland. If one considers the companies which received investment per one thousand of VAT registered businesses, then in 1993, London and the South East had a proportional involvement (0.68) which was close to that predicted by business density (0.67); whereas Scotland had a proportional involvement (1.28) which was considerably higher than that predicted by business density (0.83), which suggests that VC activity in Scotland in 1993 was relatively intense.[19]

17 Among the independents, 3i is the largest, and may have contributed as much as 30 per cent in that year.

18 Syndication involves several VC funds in the deal, each putting in proportions of equity, often with one fund playing the lead role. As well as spreading risk, it has other advantages like pooling knowledge, diluting equity, accessing more funding, and facilitating staging of funding.

19 This is partially reflected in the representation of several Scottish investees in the 'dyads' analysed in Parts 3 and 4.

General features of the maturing of the UK venture capital industry which are noted by Terry (1994) include trends to closer monitoring of investees, longer investment holding by the VCIs, and support for larger (typically buyout) rather than smaller funding involvements. These trends reflect the marketplace experience of VCIs and their desire to manage risk and attenuate adverse selection and moral hazard (see Chapter 3). Unfortunately, their actions undermined support for the traditional venturing areas of seedcorn and start-up funding. Terry (1994: 12) argues that ways of remedying this situation, including syndication and alliances (e.g. with corporate partners), are more likely to be successful if co-investors share expertise and knowledge.

Murray (1995c) covers rather similar ground to the above, though unfortunately he does not appeal to data right up to the time of the fieldwork on which this book is based. The important extra dimension his work brings is to the business strategy aspects of behaviour in the UK venture capital industry. Whereas Terry (1994) argues simply that the industry is mature in the sense of being what he calls 'seasoned' by a full turn of the business cycle, Murray proceeds in terms of the industry maturity model of Porter (1980). He argues, by reference to two sets of factors – environmental changes and consequences, and/or firms' responses – that the UK venture capital industry has dynamics which closely fit Porter's model. By 1993, under the heading of environmental changes, the UK venture capital industry had experienced a decline in the rate of industry growth, an increase in market information, an increase in buyer/supplier power, but no increase in international competition. Under the heading of consequences and/or firm responses it had experienced a decline in industry profitability, some increase in industry leavers, increased concentration of market shares, a quest for new products and services and for new markets (including the international), some rationalization of existing financial products and services, and an increasing emphasis on costs and services. His predicted trends, based on this strategy analysis, included further increases in market concentration, more rigorous marketing of financial products and services (and increasing specialization and/or differentiation in their presentation and delivery), and increasing internationalization of the main market segments.

It is not easy to conclude neatly this section on the venture capital industry, as many themes have been pursued; but probably the following points are most noteworthy. First, venture capital in the UK has a history going back centuries, but its modern form dates from about 1980. Second, the demand for, and supply of, venture capital are cyclically sensitive. Third, there has been a secular trend away from early-stage provision of venture capital. Fourth, while independents remain the major organizational form of VCI, semi-captives are growing proportionately. Fifth, by sector and region, venture capital is widely dispersed, with 'local' predominance obtaining in consumer-related businesses by sector, and London and the South East by region. Sixth, by whatever definition one cares to use, the UK venture capital industry is mature. I turn now from evidence to theory.

2.3 THEORIES OF VENTURE CAPITAL

Venture capital may seem to the reader to be such a practical subject that there is no need to approach it from the standpoint of theory. Indeed, it may seem that such a theory may be impossible to create. Both views are faulty. A theory of venture capital would be both a good organizing principle for channelling thoughts along consistent, orderly lines of reasoning, and a considerable challenge to the intellect in terms of originality, as it is by no means obvious how one might construct such a relevant body of theory. Reflecting these views about the absence of need for theory, or even its impossibility, venture capital has traditionally been treated in an atheoretical fashion.

However, starting with the work of Cooper and Carleton (1979) and Chan (1983), this tradition has begun to change. Cooper and Carleton (1979) focused on the partitioning of the final payoff, arguing for a combined debt and equity position being used by venture capitalists seeking to minimize value loss. They show that pure equity contracts will not provide an ideal policy, but some debt helps rapidly to shift policy towards the ideal. Chan (1983) focused on the role of venture capitalists as well-informed financial intermediaries, preventing the collapse of the market for outside equity caused by adverse selection. Following the insight of Leland and Pyle (1977), that financial intermediation can solve problems of markets with asymmetric information, Chan (1983) shows how financial intermediaries play the role of informed agents that induce Pareto-superior allocations, thus raising the welfare of investors.[20] Chan *et al.* (1990) have provided a complete theory of venture capital contracting, emphasizing the revelation by experience of the investee's skill, and conditions determining the subsequent control of the investment. A development due to Admati and Pfleiderer (1994) looks at how the venture capitalist as an inside investor resolves conflicts of interest and information asymmetries. Similarly, Amit *et al.* (1990) have viewed the relationship between venture capitalist and entrepreneur in principal–agent terms. They find, in a framework which assumes a risk-neutral investor and risk-averse investee, that if the investee's ability is common knowledge, risk-sharing with the investor will inevitably follow. Thus it will be observed that increasingly the literature has used ideas of risk-bearing and information asymmetry to develop a principal–agent perspective on venture capital investor–investee relations.

Before delving into these specialist theories, it may be useful to consider the more general theoretical perspective of Lam (1991), which uses no more than the fundamental tools of economic analysis. Because this approach is simple and

20 Pareto-superior allocations are achieved by freely allowing economic agents to seek and implement changes which make at least some economic agents better off, without making any worse off.

revealing, it is considered here for two purposes: (a) as a backdrop to more general explorations of the theoretical literature throughout the book; and (b) as a preparation for Chapter 4 of this book, which is based on detailed geometry. To the latter end, I explore in detail in the Appendix to this chapter – and using geometrical rather than the less accessible algebraic methods – the basic economic tools of MSF value maximization. In so doing, I draw on the work of Lam (1991) which intends to explain how venture capitalists add value to the firm.

In this approach, the MSF is viewed as efficiently turning its investment to good use one time period ahead. It does so according to a 'production possibilities' relationship, which specifies how much output will be produced in the next time period. The rate at which it does so is known as the marginal rate of return on investment (i). This falls, the more the MSF invests. The VCI is considered to be a provider of finance capital to the MSF at a price which is known as the opportunity cost of funds (r). The value of the MSF is maximized when the marginal rate of return on investment is equal to the opportunity cost of funds. If i exceeds r, then value can be increased by investing more in the MSF; if i is less than r, the MSF has been subject to overinvestment, and the return on investment is less than the extra cost of funds, so the MSF's value can be increased by retrenching on investment.

With this simple framework, three interesting issues can be addressed: raising the MSF's productivity; enhancing the MSF's access to loanable funds; and reducing the MSF's cost of capital. These will be considered in turn. First, it is possible for a proactive VCI to increase the MSF's marginal rate of return at any given investment level by improving its operations. It may do so by frequent contact and open communications (see Sapienza 1992), as well as by more formal methods, like imposing post-investment requirements on reporting, by scope and frequency, as discussed in Chapter 12 below.[21] If the VCI is successful, the raising of the marginal rate of return thereby achieved can both increase the value of the MSF and raise the optimal level of investment. Second, if the VCI reaches an agreement with the MSF, involving a measure of provision of new equity, this will be perceived to raise the quality of the MSF and to enhance its credibility. It will therefore be less likely to have limited access to the market for loanable funds. If the commitment of wealth by the VCI achieves this, the 'opportunity loss' of forgone investment opportunities is avoided. Third, the credit risk of the MSF may be reduced by VCI involvement (e.g. by its monitoring and control activities). This will lower the cost of finance capital to the VCI, increase investment, lower the marginal rate of return on investment, and increase the value of the MSF.

21 It should also be remembered that proactivity on the part of the VCI should be apt and correctly targeted, otherwise it may lower, rather than raise, efficiency. See Barney *et al.* (1994) where the receptivity of the MSF to VCI advice is carefully considered. Cable and Shane (1997: 157) too emphasize 'high quality and frequent communication'.

Bowden (1994) too, like Lam (1991), sidesteps the agency issue, by arguing that optimal principal–agent rules have already been implemented in his examination of cooperative bargaining (between VCI and MSF) over the share of the amount financed, and the share of the associated stream of earnings. In Edgeworth box fashion, a contract curve of efficient contracts can be defined as a locus in the space of the shares of capital necessary for the project.[22]

Bowden's (1994) analysis is extended by showing that if investors and investees are symmetric (i.e. same expectations, same costs of capital) and risk neutral, then either contracts cannot exist or they are indeterminate. Intuitively, if each party is risk neutral, they are effectively fully diversified, and hence do not need to seek another party for contracting. If the investor is risk neutral, but the investee is risk averse, then Bowden (1994: 318) shows that the investor will provide all the finance, but will not receive all the proceeds. In this plausible case, the investee enjoys a pure rent arising from the ideas or inventions embodied in the MSF.

Cable and Shane (1997: 144–7) share Bowden's concern with cooperation, and claim that 'the agency perspective is actually a subset of the broader explanation of these relationships provided by the Prisoner's Dilemma'. Cable and Shane note that there are powerful motives for defecting by both VCI and MSF. Thus the VCI has high opportunity cost, because another good deal can always be drawn from the top of a deep pack. The MSF is tempted to defect because it is initially easy to manipulate information (e.g. overstating performance, understating problems) to short-term ends. Cable and Shane (1997: 151) note that the risk-diversifying strategies of VCIs can be interpreted as defection strategies by MSFs who have committed all their resources to a single venture. Given these motives for defection, Cable and Shane seek reasons for cooperation, and find that the probability of it occurring rises with payoffs and returns (relative to ownership stake). Thus venture capital investing, with its reputation for big payoffs and returns, appears to provide fertile grounds for cooperation. They point out that experimental evidence indicates that cooperation goes up with time pressure, and that such pressures are often acute in the early stages of the MSF's life cycle. A prerequisite to cooperation is information transfer and this is thought to be conditioned by communication and social relationships. Bond posting can work as a formal device for bringing about cooperation in the early stages, but social relationships based on concepts like trust and generosity may count for just as much.[23]

Despite the above cautionary arguments about the limited scope of agency, or principal–agent, analysis, none of the alternative perspectives is entirely in conflict with it. Thus Cable and Shane (1997) would embed it in a Prisoner's Dilemma

22 Compare the similar device used in Chapter 4 below, which is a modification of the historically earlier concept to which Bowden (1994) makes appeal.

23 See, for example, further support of these notions by Sapienza and Korsgaard (1996: 569) who say, 'our findings suggest trust can be fostered by sharing information and influence'.

framework, and Bowden (1994) would see optimal principal–agent rules as already having been implemented before cooperative bargaining occurs. Even the traditional economic approach of Lam (1991) is itself modified by the agency perspective, incorporating as it does concepts like adverse selection, reputation and quality signalling.

Principal–agent analysis has from its inception been a widely adopted modelling perspective in economics.[24] However, with the notable exception of writers like Sahlman (1990), its acceptance in areas like accounting and finance, which are logical areas of application, has been slower. This is a pity because the accounting and financial systems of firms provide a much more detailed information structure than economics can typically offer. Fortunately, this compartmentalization is breaking down, with economists showing a willingness to look at accounting (e.g. Fricke 1987) and auditing (e.g. Ballweiser 1987), from the standpoint of principal–agent analysis. This book aims to push this agenda further, and develops an applied principal–agent approach to investor–investee relations in the venture capital industry.

Principal–agent analysis is concerned, of course, with situations in which one party, the agent (A), acts on behalf of another party, the principal (P). The employer and employee, the manufacturer and the salesman, and, perhaps most familiarly for the economist,[25] the shareholder and the manager, are all in principal and agent roles respectively. Here, the venture capitalist is viewed as the principal and the owner-manager of a successful small firm as the agent (see Chan *et al.* 1990; Amit *et al.* 1990).

A key characteristic of principal–agent relations is that the agent has an incentive to shirk on effort and to avoid risk.[26] The principal desires to conclude a contract with the agent which will provide him with an incentive to optimize effort and to share risk. The payoff to the contractual relation between principal and agent depends on the agent's effort and exogenous random factors which can be captured by the term 'the state of the world'. The principal experiences utility which depends positively upon the payoff, less what he must pay the agent. The agent experiences utility which depends positively on the payment he receives from the principal and negatively upon his own effort. Both principal and agent are thought of as expected utility maximizers, subject, as appropriate, to constraints. The principal determines a fee schedule for remunerating the agent as a function of the size of the payoff. In the optimal agency relationship the fee and the effort level will be set in such a way that the principal's expected utility is maximized subject to the constraints that the agent's choice of effort maximizes his own expected utility

24 See Sappington (1991) for an up-to-date survey.

25 See especially Jensen and Meckling (1976).

26 In so-called reciprocal principal–agent relations, this may be true of the principal as well.

level, and does not leave him with an expected utility level less than that he could enjoy in his next best activity. Because the agent's effort is incompletely observed, contracting is not first-best. It is, however, Pareto-efficient, with a measure of risk-sharing benefits being sacrificed so as to maintain the incentive for effort.[27]

This, briefly, is the theoretical backdrop to the applied analysis of this book. It has been stated in its starkest form for the sake of brevity, but, as the writings of the likes of Pratt and Zeckhauser (1985a) and Arrow (1985) suggest, the framework is very rich and guided only by the twin principles of uncertainty and information asymmetry. In Chapters 3 and 4 we develop a detailed account of the way in which this wider literature can be used to develop an applied principal–agent approach to the venture capital investor–investee relationship. Briefly, it involves three categories of applied analysis: risk management; information-handling; and trading risk and information. Under risk management, one explores: chance outcomes and sure prospects; offsetting good outcomes against bad; effects of a new investee on overall risk management; and sharing risk with the investee. Under information-handling, one explores: information types relevant to the investee relationship; differences in information between investor and investee; ways of reducing information selection; the correspondence of information with reality; and the effects of costs on information acquisition. Finally, one explores the trading of risk and information, looking at: the extent of risk-sharing with the investee; the extent of information-sharing with the investee; the exchanging of information for a risk-bearing capability; the effects of risk-sharing on effort; the effects of the size of equity stake on effort; discriminating between investees on efficiency grounds; and designing the contract with the investee to achieve efficiency. In Chapters 5, 6 and 7 it is shown how these categories are explored by direct interviews with both investors and investees. Twenty pairs (or 'dyads') of investors and investees in the UK venture capital industry were examined in this way in 1993. Several of these dyads are reported on below fairly fully in 'within site' case study fashion. On all this, see Chapters 8, 9 and 10; these chapters use the extensions of the framework described above which are developed in Chapters 3 and 4.

27 A Pareto-efficient situation prevails when it is not possible to make any economic agent better off, within the constraints under which they function, without making other economic agents worse off. First-best contracting occurs when many agents, all fully informed, are free to seek best trades. When a situation is reached in which no further trades can be taken to make some agents better off, without making other agents worse off, a first-best outcome has been achieved. If there are constraints on trades, first-best outcomes may not be possible, but Pareto-efficiency can be satisfied by exhausting such gainful trades as may be made.

2.4 TRENDS FOR THE TYPICAL UK VENTURE CAPITAL FUND

In this section, we present a stylization of the typical venture capital investor in the UK. It is based on average values for a panel of all the major UK funds, as observed in the years 1988, 1990 and 1992. Mean values are referred to when continuous variables are used, but in the case of binary or categorical variables the modal value is used. It is in this sense that a fund is referred to as 'typical'. For comparative purposes, all monetary variables are expressed in 1988 prices.

The typical specialist UK venture capital fund over the period 1988 to 1992 had £57m. at its disposal. Of this, £27m. was invested and had a value of £37m. Over the period considered, real funds invested had grown by 11.4 per cent per annum, whereas fund size itself had grown at 14.2 per cent per annum. Thus fund growth had been about 3 per cent ahead of investment each year. This suggests a shortage of good investment opportunities, but that a generally favourable investment outlook prevailed, despite the recession, with both an increasing amount of funding becoming available, and the level of funds invested rising.

Between 1988 and 1990, there was a jump in the average minimum investment a fund would contemplate from £173k in 1988/90 to £316k in 1992. At the same time, the minimum equity stake contemplated rose from 6 per cent in 1988/90 to about 14 per cent in 1992. The maximum equity stake contemplated remained very stable over the period, at an average of 55 per cent. In practice, there was an increasing tendency to larger investments. Though we have no information on the average equity stake taken out, it almost certainly was rising, probably quite steeply. The largest investment which would be contemplated rose from £3.5m. in 1988 to £4.5m. in 1992, and the average actual investment rose from £0.54m. to £0.92m. over the same period. The smallest investment VC funds would contemplate was stable over 1988/90 (average of £160k) but jumped up in 1992 to £258k.

By clients, the trend is very clear. The typical VC fund was lessening its involvement in start-up finance (down from 27 per cent to 12 per cent) and development finance (down from 43 per cent to 38 per cent), and getting increasingly involved in buyouts (up from 21 per cent in 1990 to 32 per cent in 1992). This may be interpreted as a diminished willingness to be involved at the high-risk end of equity provision.[28] It also implies a desire on the part of VC investors to manage risk by an improved information flow. The categories of involvement increasingly pursued provide more evidence on the ability of the

28 This tendency is to be noted even in the US venture capital industry (see Bygrave and Timmons 1992), and is even more evident in countries like Sweden (see Landström 1992).

entrepreneur, the track record of his associates, and their previous business endeavours. The real value of funds invested (at cost) rose rapidly throughout the period 1988/92 at an average annual rate of 31 per cent. At the same time, the average number of employees in a fund rose from about a dozen in 1988/90 to twenty-seven in 1992. The average number of VC executives increased much less, from six in 1988/90 to eight in 1992. That is, the ratio of employees to executives rose from two to three, implying a marked increase in delegation in terms of managerial style. This corresponded to an increase in proposals received of 30 per cent over 1990/92 and of proposals reviewed of 40 per cent over the same period. The number of new investments actually made increased slightly from an average of ten in 1988/90 to an average of thirteen in 1993. These statistics are quite revealing. They suggest an increased demand for outside equity, and an increased intensity of scrutiny of proposals, as measured by the ratio of proposals received to investments made. Over the same time, the increase in new investments actually matched the increased demand, suggesting an increase in the average quality of projects finding venture capital support.[29] In view of the earlier evidence on changes in the composition of projects supported, this was also associated with a decrease of riskiness in project involvements. Overall, this suggests an increase in VC investors' *ex post* rates of return. Unfortunately, actual or realized rates of return are a particularly sensitive statistic, and are rarely available from VC investors. The larger staff is apparently used to handle the increased volume of proposals received and reviewed, and of course to assist in the monitoring of the increasing stock of investments within VC portfolios.

The style of VC portfolio investment appears relatively unchanged. Typically, fees are charged, and investors must return monthly accounts. The preferred timescale for investment is seven to eight years, with most funds realizing their investments in about five years. There is a recent tendency for VC investors to stay with investees longer. Between 1988 and 1992, fund age went up, implying an increase in age from five years to eleven years over a time span of just four years. This evidence suggests that venture capital investors are 'staying with' the more valuable investments. The patterns of single, lead and consortium investments raised changed little over the period 1988–92. There was a slight increase in the willingness to become sole investor (34 per cent in 1988, 43 per cent in 1990, 41 per cent in 1992). Lead investor involvement, and consortium

29 This is what the treatment of venture capital funds as financial intermediaries would suggest would happen. According to this view, as expounded by Chan (1983), such funds prevent market failure. In their absence as well-informed agents, when investors have positive search costs, entrepreneurs offer only poor projects ('lemons'), putting off investors. As informed intermediaries emerge, specializing in high-quality information acquisition, venture capitalists reduce information asymmetry between investor and entrepreneur, thus raising the quality of investment selection, and thereby preventing the failure of the venture capital market.

investment involvement, were very stable, at about 28 per cent and 32 per cent respectively.

The above evidence provides empirical support for recent work by Gifford (1995) which emphasizes the limited time that venture capital executives can allocate to their various involvements. To make the most of his limited attention span, the investor will tend to favour later, rather than early-stage investment (as this economizes on due diligence), larger rather than smaller investment involvements (exploiting scale economies), and longer rather than shorter investment involvements (economizing on switching). These stylized facts are all featured in the panel data.[30]

2.5 CONCLUSION

This chapter has provided an overview of venture capital, covering its own definition, forms, industrial context, theory, and statistical features. It was seen to involve equity provision to promising unquoted companies, quite often in packages involving debt, and the staging of finance. In the UK context, a preference for development capital was observed, and two dominant features of specialization by investee were noted: by sector (consumer-related business) and by region (London and the South East, and Scotland). A theoretical perspective on venture capital was expounded (and is developed more fully in this chapter's appendix) covering: first, the basic economic approach, emphasizing the maximization of company value, subject to production constraints; and second, the agency approach, emphasizing the consequences of risk and information asymmetry. In general terms, the VCI was viewed as a financial intermediary whose information-reconciling activities promoted superior resource allocation. Finally, a summary statistical picture was provided of the development of major UK venture capital funds in the period up to the time of the fieldwork. The general background having been established, the more detailed aspects of the research can now be developed, starting with its theoretical underpinning.

30 Gifford's model emphasizes the other side of the agency relationship, with the venture capitalist as agent and the entrepreneur as principal. This follows the logic of some principal–agent relationships (e.g. that between a doctor as agent and patient as principal), but is not the way it is usually analysed in the finance literature on principals and agents. In fact, the two approaches are not mutually exclusive, as reciprocal principal–agent relationships are possible. They are of course much more difficult to analyse. In the analysis that follows, the usual approach is adopted. A small bit of evidence conflicts with Gifford's (1995) approach (see Chapter 8 below). It is that the entrepreneur ($\mathbf{A}^1_J$) did not feel he was competing with others for the venture capitalist's attention. However, what is more important is the investor's rather than the investee's view; and the waters are somewhat muddied in this case by multiple-investor (as well as multiple-investee) involvements.

APPENDIX: THE IMPACT OF THE VCI ON THE MSF's VALUE AND RISK

This appendix amplifies some of the theoretical analysis of section 2.2 above, as it relates to the work of Lam (1991) on the MSF's value and the significance of the VCI's role in influencing it. There are three points to be established: that the VCI can turn a negative value MSF into a positive value MSF if it is pro-active; that the VCI can reduce the credit risk of the MSF through equity participation; and that the VCI can add value to an MSF by reducing its borrowing costs.

In this appendix three simple economics diagrams will be used to establish these propositions. A mathematical treatment would provide the definitive statement of these results, but would probably make them inaccessible to many readers. As a compromise, I develop the results using some standard diagrams from the economist's toolkit, as modified to suit the VCI/MSF relationship (see Lam 1991). These geometrical arguments should be accessible to all readers with some (and not necessarily much) background in economics. They also pave the way for a more thoroughgoing treatment of theoretical issues of principal–agent analysis, using geometrical methods, in Chapter 3.[31]

In Figure A2.1 the horizontal axis denotes current, or base period (0), resources (X_0), and the vertical axis denotes expected, future period (1), resources (X_1). For points to the right of the origin (the point 0) current resources are available for consumption; and for points to the left of the origin, they are being used for investment. The straight lines AV_H and BV_L indicate different values of the MSF (high and low respectively) for a given cost of funds; represented by the common slope of these lines $-(1 + r)$ where r is the (given) opportunity cost of funds.[32] For X_1 equal to zero, all the value of the MSF is derived from current resources, and is indicated by the intercept on the horizontal axis. So, for the value line AV_H, the value of the MSF is measured by the magnitude $0V_H$, or simply V_H.

The production possibility (PP) curves used in Figure A2.1 indicate the rate at which deferred current resource consumption (i.e. investment) is efficiently converted into expected future resources, using the existing production and organizational technology of the MSF. The marginal rate of return on investment (i) is measured by the slope $-(1 + i)$ of the production possibility curve (e.g. of PP_L or

31 For those lacking this background, the standard treatment of investment and consumption over time by Gravelle and Rees (1981: ch. 15) should provide adequate preparation.

32 If V denotes firm value; X_0, X_1 current and future resources; and r the rate of interest, the value of the firm is $V = X_1/(1 + r) + X_0$. For given V and r, this is a straight line relationship between X_1 and X_0. By choosing $X_1 = 0$, the value of the firm is given on the horizontal axis. Further, $X_1 = (V - X_0)(1 + r)$ implies $dX_1/dX_0 = -(1 + r)$, which is the slope of this value line. The higher is r, the steeper is the absolute slope of the value line in (X_0, X_1) space.

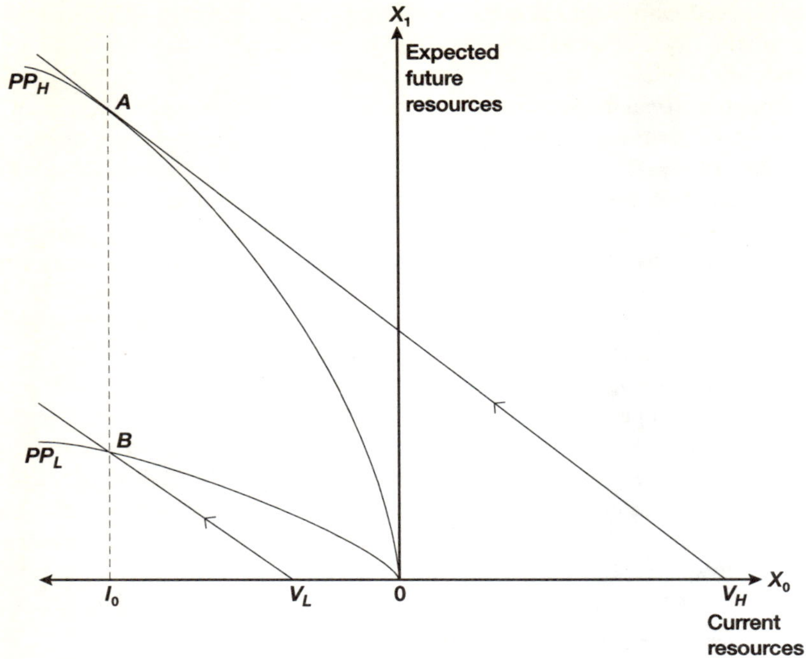

Figure A2.1 The consequences of VCI intervention in the MSF

PP_H).[33] This return is positive for positive increments in investment, but falls as investment increases. That is, there is a diminishing marginal rate of return on investment.

In Figure A2.1 the high-value firm, MSF_H, with production possibilities PP_H, would be backed by the VCI, given the opportunity cost of funds, r. At magnitude of investment $0I_0$, or simply I_0, the value of MSF_H is maximized, given PP_H. At A, the marginal rate of return on investment (i) is equal to the opportunity cost of funds (r).[34] The maximized value for the firm is given by V_H. At the same level of investment, I_0, the other firm, the low-value firm MSF_L, with production possibilities PP_L, does not have profitable investment opportunities. Its value, V_L, is negative, and its situation can be improved, as the opportunity cost of

33 If investment is increased by ΔI, this is equivalent to a decrease in X_0 of ΔX_0, that is $\Delta I = -\Delta X_0$. If the increase of expected future resources arising from this is ΔX_1, then the net return is $\Delta X_1 - \Delta X_0$ and the marginal rate of return is $(\Delta X_1 - \Delta X_0)/\Delta X_0 = i$. Rearranging gives $\Delta X_1/\Delta X_0 = -(1 + i)$, which says the slope of the PP curve is the negative of the marginal rate of return plus one.

34 The value line is tangent to PP_H at A, that is, the slope of PP_H equals the slope of AV_H, or $-(1 + i) = -(1 + r)$. This implies $i = r$, as in the main text.

funds exceeds the marginal rate of return on investment at *B*. A lower level of investment for this firm might raise the depressed marginal rate of return on investment sufficiently to bring it into equality with the opportunity cost of VCI funding, but from the shape of PP_L in Figure A2.1 this is going to be, if at all, for a lesser value than that of the V_H pertaining to MSF_H. One possibility suggested by Lam (1991: 140) is that the VCI might attempt a 'company turnaround' strategy on the MSF_L, transforming it into a business that creates more expected future resources for a given level of investment, perhaps by changing the organizational technology (e.g. by increasing the scope and frequency of monitoring). If MSF_L can be so transformed, to emulate the performance of MSF_H, efficient value-maximizing investment will be achieved at level I_0, and the company turnaround will have successfully raised the firm's value from V_L to V_H.

The next analytical point to be considered concerns the loss the MSF may incur if it fails to get access to loan finance. The argument can be demonstrated using Figure A2.2. The commitment of resources by the VCI to the MSF not only partially meets, in a direct fashion, the need for external finance by the growing firm, but also provides a signal of quality to providers of debt finance. Thus the 'value added' contribution of the VCI is the equity provision itself plus the opportunity cost avoided by failure of the MSF to get access to further loan finance through lack of credibility. In Figure A2.2, the MSF has a production

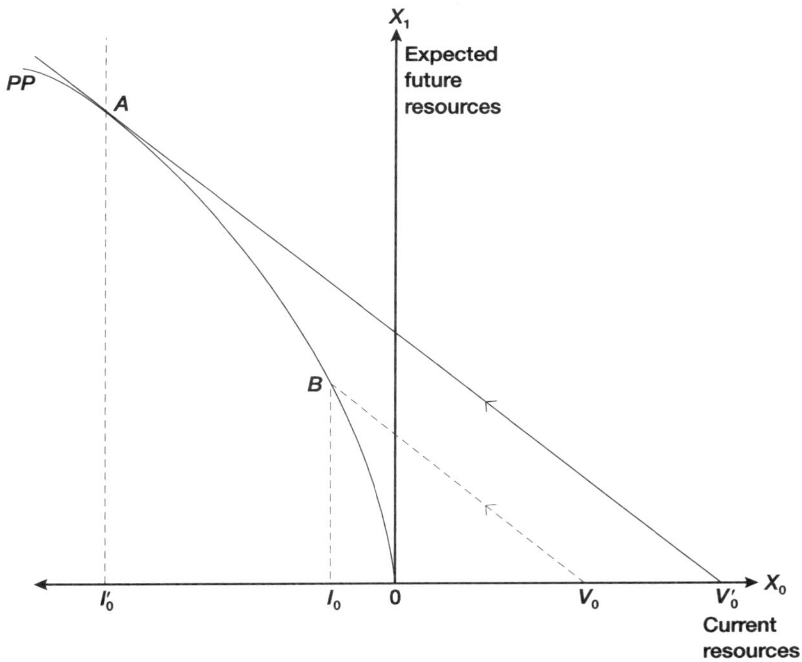

Figure A2.2 VCI intervention facilitates further finance

possibilities frontier of *PP*. If the firm's value is to be maximized, for a given opportunity cost of funds (indicated by the slope, $-(1 + r)$, of AV'_0), then, optimally, I'_0 should be invested in the firm so that at *A* the opportunity cost of funds equals the marginal rate of return on investment. When I'_0 is invested, the (maximal) value of the MSF is V'_0. However, if, through lack of reputation, the MSF were constrained in what it could invest, to a level I_0, then in terms of the same opportunity cost of capital the value of the firm would be the lesser one of V_0 (i.e. $V_0 < V'_0$).[35] In the absence of VCI intervention, the MSF is unable to exploit the fact that the marginal rate of return on investment exceeds the opportunity cost of finance. If the VCI's involvement prevents an investment magnitude of $I'_0 - I_0$ being forgone, a measure of the VCI's value added is the 'opportunity loss' in wealth of $V'_0 - V_0$.

Finally, the VCI may affect favourably not only the *value* of external finance for the MSF, but also its *price*. If the VCI involvement reduces the perceived risk of the MSF (and thus lowers, effectively, the opportunity cost of finance), and also raises the credit limit which suppliers of debt finance (like banks) are willing to

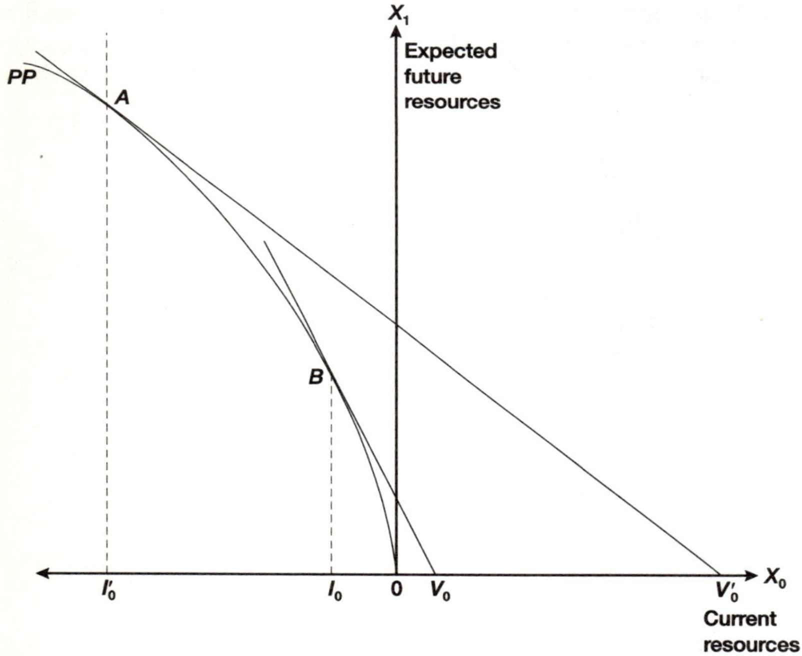

Figure A2.3 VCI intervention improves terms of offer of additional finance

35 Note the slopes of BV_0 and AV'_0 are the same, reflecting the same opportunity cost of finance.

advance,[36] a higher value for the firm will be generated. This is illustrated in Figure A2.3. Suppose the MSF initially has no track record, and lacks both credibility and security. It will only be able to get high-priced funding (with rate r_H). If a limited amount I_0 is invested, then the value of the firm is just V_0. True, the marginal return on investment equals the opportunity cost of funds at *B*, but the value of the firm is low. If, however, the intervention of the VCI raises the credibility of the MSF in terms of credit worthiness, a greater volume of finance becomes available at a lower price (with rate $r_L < r_H$). For this lower rate, the slope of the value line AV'_0 is less than that of BV_0. Then the lower opportunity cost of funds permits a higher level of investment (I'_0) to be made, at which the marginal return on investment (i) is pushed down from r_H to the lower r_L, which occurs at the point *A*. Then the maximum value of the MSF is now the higher value of V'_0 (i.e. $V_0 < V'_0$) because of the venture capital intervention.

Although these diagrams only suggest, be it all in a consistent and logical fashion, the nature of an entirely rigorous argument, it is possible to back them up with watertight mathematical developments. So far as they go, the diagrams provide an illuminating analysis of how VCIs add value to the MSF in several ways after their investment involvement: through raising efficiency, increasing funding, and lowering funding costs. Chapter 4 develops, in much greater geometrical detail, the finer points of contracting relations between the VCI and MSF.

36 Enlarging the 'line of credit', in US terminology.

3

INVESTIGATING INVESTOR–INVESTEE RELATIONS

with Falconer Mitchell and Nicholas G. Terry

3.1 INTRODUCTION

This chapter develops the core set of ideas, drawn from the literature of economics, accounting and finance, which underpin the research agenda on which this book is based. Building on this, instruments were designed to confront empirical evidence with the propositions suggested by this agenda. These propositions focus upon the nature, operation and significance of the relationship between a group of specialized funders and a specific type of unquoted company. The funders are venture capital investors (VCIs), and the venture capital fund itself is sometimes identified as the investor. The unquoted company is an investee with characteristics defined by a point in its life cycle. For example, the company may be contemplating expansion; or its owner-manager may wish to sell part of the business without either losing day-to-day control, or running the risk of that loss of independence which may attend public listing. Although a small firm may acquire investee standing at any stage in its life cycle, in a UK context it has typically been running successfully for some years before it attracts outside equity finance.

The construction of Chapter 3 is as follows. Section 3.2 sets the scene in terms of typical investor and investee attributes. Section 3.3 describes an approach to examining how the investee, typically a mature small firm (MSF), becomes involved with the venture capital investor (VCI). This emphasizes the terms and conditions of what constitutes a contractual relationship. Section 3.4 focuses on the use of information within the MSF, section 3.5 looks at VCI criteria for MSF selection and investment realization, and section 3.6 looks at the design of interview agenda. As a group, these three sections consider questions that arise from the writing of the contract, and the subsequent behaviour of the two parties. They indicate how these questions may be answered by deploying fieldwork methods to administer semi-structured interviews and questionnaires in face-to-face interviews. Section 3.7 briefly considers both the construction of an appropriate sampling frame, and the carrying out of fieldwork. The chapter concludes with a brief summary in section 3.8.

3.2 THE INVESTOR AND INVESTEE

It has been clear that there are two major players in the scene that will be presented in this book. They are: institutions which seek outlets for their investment (investors); and institutions which seek investment funds (investees). From these generic classes of investors and investees, two specialized types will emerge. The first is the venture capital investor (VCI), and the second is the mature small firm (MSF).[1] The investor, or venture capitalist, seeks to supply equity finance (the risk-bearing class of company shares) to an investee of the mature small firm variety.

One of the perceived advantages of venture capital[2] is that it provides to the promising MSF a large volume of relatively cheap funding at critical stages in its growth. Dividends may be delayed or suppressed until some future date, and the amounts raised may far exceed what would be possible with debt finance. The point at which the venture capital investor (VCI) can realize all or part of its claim in a firm is known as 'exit', and this typically occupies a more significant position in the mind of the VCI than dividend payments. Exit can take several forms, including: flotation of the MSF on a stock market; sale of the MSF to another company or 'trade buyer'; sale of the MSF to another venture capitalist; and sale of shares in the MSF back to managers (in the form of a management buyout, MBO, or management buy-in, MBI[3]). Some VCIs take a very close interest in their investee companies and provide them with advice, support and industry connections (known as 'hands-on' participation). Others only become involved directly in running the MSF when it encounters difficult trading conditions. In the literature on venture capital, as in Macmillan *et al.* (1988), such investors are described, respectively, as being 'close trackers' and 'laissez-faire' in style. While some experts like Sapienza (1992: 22) suggest that, in general, 'more involvement is better than less', it is also true that others, like Barney *et al.* (1994: 33), would caution that 'discernment should be used in the offering of advice' or else 'the chemistry of the relationship stands to be damaged'.

The return on unquoted equity invested in the MSF is often calculated using an internal rate of return (IRR) measure,[4] this being based upon any dividend

1 Its embodiments, following Barney *et al.* (1994), are the new venture team (NVT), these being the founders and/or managers who attract venture capital funding.

2 See Hoffman and Blakey (1987), and Bygrave and Timmons (1992: ch. 3).

3 The distinction between an MBO and an MBI is as follows. In an MBO there is no change in management, the incumbent managers being retained. In an MBI a new management group takes over, by either an agreed or a hostile takeover. In both cases, there are ownership changes to the management group. See Robbie and Wright (1995), who elaborate on the performance implications of these alternatives.

4 Formally, that discount rate which equates the present value of an investment's expected cash inflow to the present value of the investment's expected cost (see Brigham 1992: 349–51). It requires the solving of a polynomial expression by iteration. Standard software performs this task (e.g. the Lotus 123 software was popular for this purpose during this study). On limitations of the method, see Bygrave *et al.* (1988: 282–3).

distributions, profits from asset disposals, and valuation of the company at exit. Most VCIs set target rates of return[5] on their sets of investments of 25–40 per cent. Such investments constitute portfolios, these being combinations of investee firms selected on various criteria, including size of investment, industrial sector, geography, and perceived risk. In turn, these criteria are predicated on the stage at which the VCI becomes involved (e.g. seedcorn, development).

Unquoted companies seeking expansion finance may wish to use funds to increase productive capacity, to develop a new product or market, or to provide additional working capital. Even a company experiencing difficulties might attract investment if the VCI were to perceive an opportunity for strengthening its management or changing its company strategy in order to improve its financial performance or to achieve 'company turnaround', in the terminology of business strategy (see Grinyer *et al.* 1988). For companies at other points in their life cycles there could be a need for refinancing. This could be for reasons of both relative failure or success. If a company does poorly, it may need an extra injection of funds. Equally, if it does well, the owner-manager may wish to refinance the business on more favourable terms, either with the original VCI or with a new team of financiers.

The distinguishing features of firms displaying these needs in any of the above circumstances are typically that it is mature, with an established product or market presence (or both), and that it is small, in the sense of having its key decisions made by one or few individuals who have an ownership stake in the enterprise. So defined, the mature small firm (MSF) is the typical, if not only, investor in the context of this book.[6]

3.3 PRINCIPALS, AGENTS AND INVESTMENTS

It will be clear from the earlier developments in this book that the relationship between a VCI and an investee firm is considered to be amenable to the analytical approach suggested by principal–agent theory.[7] At its most simplified, the VCI

5 There is evidence, reported in Bygrave *et al.* (1988) in the US context, that these targets are rarely met. While boom conditions may temporarily put returns at very high levels (of over 100 per cent), overall rates of return have usually been below 20 per cent. Quoting a venture capital veteran (ibid. 288), it has been said that 'venture capital funds have oversold their ability'.

6 Other forms of company involvement for the VCI may include: start-up financing (sometimes called 'seed capital' or 'cornerstone financing'); early-stage financing; management buyouts and buy-ins; and secondary purchasing (involving company shares being traded among a group of VCIs). The management buyout (MBO) is the other main form of investment by VCIs considered in this book.

7 For an advanced treatment, see Holmström and Tirole (1989); and for a more accessible treatment, using only geometry, see Ricketts (1986), upon which the treatment in Chapter 4

would be seen as the principal, who controls contractual details and assigns tasks, and the investee firm as the agent, who accepts this authority and performs certain tasks on behalf of the VCI. The dominant motive for the VCI who seeks such a relationship is to provide a better financial rate of return than might otherwise be available to him or her. This is to state the argument in its starkest form, shorn of refinement or qualification, but it provides a useful reference point.[8]

The typical VCI involvement considered here possesses the following characteristics:[9]

1 the equity stake taken is a minority one in a high performing, mature small firm (MSF)[10] that is not currently listed on any formal stock market;
2 the investment agreed has a strictly finite life, with an expected duration of just a few years; and
3 the exit route anticipated for the VCI comprises either a stock market listing or some other form of change of ownership that would enable the principal to realize their equity stake (for example, a 'trade sale' or some variant of a 'buyout').

Typically, the principal can only judge the effectiveness with which the agent completes the assigned tasks in an indirect way. Most obviously, the principal will judge effectiveness in terms of outcomes or payoffs (e.g. measured in terms of a rate of return), but effort (measured by some sort of monitoring system, for example as a component of management accounts) may also be considered.

Conceived of as a principal,[11] the VCI may approach MSFs with a view to

below, appropriately modified to the investor–investee context, is based. One of the earliest attempts to view VCI and MSF relations in a principal–agent framework is the PhD thesis of Harry Sapienza (1989) at the University of Maryland. However, Sapienza interprets the model very much along the lines of the 'positive theory of agency' approach initiated by Jensen and Meckling (1976), which emphasizes monitoring (e.g. frequency) to the neglect of risk-bearing. Indeed, surprisingly in a venture capital context, Sapienza's work is almost entirely innocent of risk analysis.

8 It is also not totally unrealistic. In the illuminating practitioner paper by Hoffman and Blakey (1987), which insists 'you *can* negotiate with venture capitalists', it is clear that the power is very much in the hands of the venture capitalist, and they candidly admit (ibid.16) that, from the MSF standpoint, 'you'll have to give ground on many issues when you come to the bargaining table'.

9 In comparison to the average data reported in Chapter 1, these are seen as representative characteristics, but they should not limit the ambit of discourse. Much of the discussion below would apply equally well to overall venture capital investment activity.

10 See Chapter 1, sections 1.1, 1.2 and 1.5, for more on the type of firm being considered. Although small, it may be thought of as mature, in that rapid growth has taken it beyond early stages of the life cycle (e.g. beyond inception and start-up).

11 One of the aims of this study is to establish the efficacy of treating the VCI as the principal, rather than the MSF.

including equity stakes in its investment portfolio. As such, the VCI will aim to maximize his or her expected return, while holding down the return of the MSF to the minimum necessary to keep it in the contract. Here, the VCI may be viewed as the residual claimant, with a minority equity stake, who monitors the performance of the MSF. If the MSF were to be seen as the principal, then the firm would approach the VCI with a view to hiring the financier's venturing expertise. The owner-manager would then attempt to maximize return in the MSF while restricting the VCI's return to that level which is just necessary to conclude the contract. While the above depicts a strict and polar alternative to the distinctive roles of VCI and MSF, as principal and agent respectively, the possibility of mixed or reciprocal agency relationships too cannot be excluded, though this may be neither plausible nor illuminating in the present context.

Without marginalizing the potential significance of alternative uses of the principal–agent framework in these other contexts, the discussion here will emphasize the writing of a contract between the VCI as principal, in possession of an existing, fully diversified portfolio, and the MSF as agent, as a potential new entrant to this portfolio. The VCI may be assumed, plausibly, to be risk neutral because its portfolio is large and diversified in terms of investments in MSFs.[12] The MSF may be assumed plausibly to be risk averse because all of the owner-manager's wealth, including 'goodwill', is tied up in the firm. There appear to be two obvious reasons why the MSF would wish to be drawn into a contractual relationship with the VCI. These are:

1 to gain additional equity-based funding; and
2 to spread risk, by involving the VCI in the operation of the business.

The VCI may wish to offer and conclude a contract because:

1 this represents a supply of potentially profitable investment opportunities that might not otherwise be available (say, through a formal stock exchange, or a traditional bank lending market); and
2 this represents a skill- or knowledge-sharing arrangement that, again, may be unique.

12 Work by Statman (1990: 468–85) suggests that a fully diversified portfolio should include at least thirty investments. This is somewhat bigger than the figure of fifteen investments typically mentioned in the finance literature. A relatively extreme view is taken by Fama (1976), who reported, based on portfolios constructed from NYSE stocks, that the reduction of risk was substantial when the number of assets increased from just four to five; but that the further reduction in risk was merely marginal as the number of assets increased from thirty-four to thirty-five.

Thus the MSF offers the VCI an ownership and a knowledge share, in exchange for which the VCI offers the MSF an opportunity to spread risk, and to acquire additional capital. Payoffs may be defined in terms of the split in the value of the MSF at the time of exit from the contract. How this value is defined, the form this exit may take, and the manner in which the split between VCI and MSF is undertaken are issues that will be considered throughout this book. However these payoffs are defined, one feature is intrinsic: they are subject to uncertainty.

The simplest way to handle payoff uncertainty is in terms of two possible outcomes: a good state of the world; and a bad state of the world.[13] The VCI as a principal has some difficulty in disentangling the consequences of high skill and/or high effort by the MSF from mere good fortune: that is, the fortuitous occurrence of a good state of the world. Similarly, low skill and effort may be hard to disentangle from chance misfortune: that is, the fortuitous occurrence of a bad state of the world.

In facing such problems of performance evaluation, there are two important effects which the VCI must consider, namely, 'moral hazard' and 'adverse selection'. If the VCI does not attend board meetings or participate in strategic decision-making, 'moral hazard' may arise once the MSF has concluded a contract which involves the VCI in risk-sharing. Having private access to daily information plans within the firm, the MSF can act 'out of sight' of the VCI to its own benefit, in this sense creating a moral hazard. On the other hand, before the conclusion of a contract between the VCI and the MSF, the MSF has an incentive to misrepresent its likely profitability to the VCI, in order to enhance its prospect of a risk-sharing deal. The VCI will try to mitigate this 'adverse selection' by using a systematic appraisal device such as a screening mechanism (e.g. the scrutiny of business plans) in the pre-investment phase.

One purpose of the contract between the VCI and the MSF is to share risk. If the VCI is risk neutral, he or she will bear all the risk if the MSF's effort is observable. If the MSF's effort is not fully observable, it may be difficult to know whether high profitability, for example, is attributable to great effort, or to a good state of the world. This provides the MSF with an incentive to reduce effort. If a highly profitable outcome arises, the MSF may claim high effort without having actually made it, while the VCI may wish to claim a favourable state of the world. If a relatively unprofitable outcome arises, the MSF may claim an unfavourable state of nature, whereas the VCI may claim that the MSF put forth insufficient effort. Lack of perfect observability of the MSF (leading, for example, to possibilities of moral hazard) may mean that the MSF will be required to agree

13 See Chapter 4 below, where outcomes in these two states are modelled by the two dimensions of a box diagram.

to a contract in which he bears at least some risk, in order to provide him or her with an incentive for effort. This arises even if the MSF is risk averse and the VCI is risk neutral.

3.4 MANAGEMENT ACCOUNTING AND THE VCI/ MSF RELATIONSHIP

Management accounting is concerned with the accounting information which is generated within an organization to support management activity.[14] The establishment of a management accounting system is usually seen as being contingent upon a set of situational factors (Otley 1980: 413–28), including: environment (e.g. competitiveness of the market); technology (e.g. the nature of the production system); and organizational structure (e.g. the degree of centralization). As such, the accounting system chosen will vary considerably in nature and coverage according to circumstances. There is no standardization of practice such as exists in, say, financial accounting for company shareholders. The information available for the support of monitoring by the principal will therefore be largely determined by the nature of the management accounting system existing in the MSF. Given the nature of the relationship between a venture capital investor and the investee firm, the accounting information flows will be designed to suit particular needs and will be specified in the contract agreed between the parties. As the composition of the accounting information will be dependent on the nature of management accounting within the MSF, it is a management accounting methodology that will provide the most appropriate means of analysing the types of accounting information which pass between the VCI and MSF.

The essence of management accounting can be captured by an analysis[15] that highlights the uses of accounting information within the firm. It may be seen as serving three basic functions:

1 *problem-solving:* deciding which course of action is better (e.g. using discounted cash flows and marginal costing);
2 *attention-directing:* deciding which problems should be investigated (e.g. using variance analysis and ratio analysis); and
3 *score-carding:* assessing performance (e.g. using profitability and liquidity reports).

Problem-solving may utilize the type of systematic information which the VCI would wish to have available as a tool for management of the investee firm, but

14 See Ezzamel and Hart (1987) for advanced papers on this topic.
15 See the now classical treatment of March and Simon (1958: 161).

which may not currently play a prominent part in the information flow between the two parties. Conversely, the investigation of problems, and the assessment of performance, relate to the monitoring function of the VCI. They provide a basis for the design of stewardship-oriented reports from the MSF to the VCI. The VCI will also be interested in attention-directing information where this indicates potential future problems, or deviation from expected performance.

In designing such a reporting procedure the VCI is going to be concerned with overcoming (or mitigating) the difficulties arising from moral hazard and adverse selection. In particular, the VCI may worry about the MSF limiting effort, taking on other work, engaging in excessive business expenses, and presenting a flattering but artificial business picture. In short, there can be a problem of incomplete compliance. The solution can be seen to involve:

1 monitoring both the management effort and quality of the MSF and the outcome according to a mutually agreed yardstick that satisfies the criterion of transparency;
2 bonding[16] the VCI and MSF by imposing penalties on the MSF if certain levels of performance are not achieved, or covenants about such things as gearing levels and the disposal of assets, or both; and
3 providing incentives to management which could compromise increased discretion in decision-taking, or financial reward, or both.

3.5 VCI CRITERIA FOR FIRM SELECTION AND REALIZATION OF INVESTMENT

The characteristics of VCI involvement with MSFs described in section 3.3 above are capable of generating several questions about investment appraisal and review, but two issues will be emphasized initially:[17]

1 the basis upon which VCIs calculate entry value in order to determine both the amount and structure of finance (i.e. the mix of equity, secured debt and unsecured debt) that they are prepared to supply (or participate in supplying), and the equity stake that this would represent; and
2 the basis upon which VCIs calculate exit value in order to determine the performance targets for management, and the ultimate anticipated selling price of their shareholding.

16 Including so-called bond-posting. The bond has a value which is forfeited in the case of performance default (see Ricketts 1987: 150–1).

17 Other matters related to such things as the appraisal process and pre-selection for assessment based on industry sector, size and geographical location will be raised in section 3.6, which deals with instrument design. For an analysis of VCIs' preferences regarding the industry diversity and geographic scope of investments, see Gupta and Sapienza (1992).

Clearly, the entry value and the expected exit value for performance-setting will be connected by virtue of the rate of return demanded by the VCI. The pricing of the firm at disposal will be a function both of the extent to which the MSF has fulfilled its potential, and of capital and product market conditions ruling at the preferred time of sale.

In the absence of perfect foresight, the VCI faces the prospect of a divergence between the expected and actual realized values. The extent of this divergence represents the main source of risk for the VCI. Therefore, the investor will attempt to ensure that the expected return calculation reflects not only risk, time-horizon and liquidity (governed, for example, by the lack of a ready secondary market for unquoted shares), but also contractual impediments like adverse selection and moral hazard mentioned earlier. This means that the VCI will want to determine an entry value that captures these different influences upon exit value. At its simplest, the greater the perceived risk, the greater the incentive the VCI will have to suppress the initial equity value, to insist upon performance measurement, and to establish a mechanism for changing management behaviour.

There are two main approaches to attempting to answer the valuation question. The first of these determines the value of ordinary shares (or any financial asset) by reference to the present expected value of the prospective stream of net returns. For a VCI, the yield comprises any dividend receipts plus the net proceeds from exiting the investment. According to this – the Discounted Growth approach – any particular equity stake would have to demonstrate a discounted sum of returns equal to, or greater than, the cost of funds faced by the VCI, see Appendix, Chapter 2. Therefore, this method requires: robust estimates of the expected returns; an appropriate cost of capital; and an adjustment for the tax position of the VCI. Financial theory proposes solutions to these operational concerns based upon three devices: the application of the Capital Asset Pricing Model (CAPM)[18] in order to produce an appropriate risk-adjusted discount rate; the use of an implied ('target' or 'hurdle') rate of return employing qualitative as well as quantitative forecast returns; and the introduction of tax parameters in the Weighted Average Cost of Capital (WACC) calculation.[19]

Another way of determining value, taking account of the risk-return relationship, is to use financial accounting statements. Accounting information does not deal directly with those factors of principal interests to the VCI, namely, expected future cash flows and risk. However, some of the objective data in financial accounting statements may contain useful information about such matters. Those accounting measures most frequently associated with risk are: current ratio; dividend payout ratio; financial leverage; asset size; asset growth;

18 See Rees (1990: 223–32).

19 See Brealey and Myers (1991: 407–9, 465–6).

earnings variability; and earnings covariability. However, there are problems which the VCI encounters in attempting to apply fundamental ratio analysis, arising from the incomplete availability and variable quality of data. These will be a function of: the financing stage at which the VCI becomes involved; the legal status and trading history of the MSF; the MSF's approach to record-keeping; and the existence of comparator firms.[20] At a practical level, the best solution to incomplete or variable quality in financial accounting data may be for the VCI to attempt to replicate those ratios considered crucial to their assessment, using, for example, proxy or hybrid measures for such things as earnings or asset value.

The most important difference between the two valuation approaches described above is that the discounting procedure is an *ex ante* measure, while fundamental ratio analysis provides an *ex post* measure of value. It is not easy to see if, or when, one approach would be considered superior to the other, either for the VCI in general or across different financing stages. In addition, it is not clear what the relationship between the two techniques might be in terms of calculating entry and exit values. What can be said is that each VCI is likely to have developed a procedure for assessment based upon a combination of factual information, and a subjective feel for risk. The latter represents a type of cognition that is based more on intuitive insight and experience than on objective measures of risk.[21] The exact nature and application of these procedures for both assessment and valuation will be largely responsible for establishing the internal investment philosophy and the external image of individual VCIs.

3.6 DESIGNING THE INTERVIEW AGENDA

The previous sections have described briefly the nature and likely outline specification of the relationship that can exist between an MSF and its provider of equity finance. To better understand how these components are combined to produce a particular MSF–VCI contract, several questions can be put

20 For start-ups and early stages of financing, accounting data are likely to be very limited. At the buyout and secondary purchase stages, more meaningful data should be available. This chapter is concerned with the expansion stage, and firms here could have a range of information on offer to the VCI.

21 This arises because precise actuarial calculation requires large numbers of independent trials to establish probabilities as limits of relative frequencies of events. To the extent that each business situation is unique, however, use of this method is limited from the perspective of the entrepreneur. However, the entrepreneur may still assign probabilities subjectively to uncertain events, based on judgements of riskiness, and such probabilities will satisfy the usual statistical properties (e.g. they lie between zero and unity, and for mutually exclusive events the sum of their probabilities is unity).

to the two parties within the framework of an interview agenda (as suggested in section 1.5 in Chapter 1). Such an interview agenda should comprise three parts, each of which corresponds roughly to the sections so far considered in this chapter. Section 3.3 looked at the roles of the VCI and the MSF, as principal and agent respectively, and the rationale behind their sharing risk and information. This gives rise to the need to establish the various attitudes to risk that will influence the extent to which risk is shared. Section 3.4 examined the use of management accounting information in monitoring the performance of the contract. This gives rise to the need to establish the various ways in which information is handled by both parties. Lastly, consideration was given (in section 3.5) to the valuation question and to how, ultimately, risk management and information-handling interact. There is also a need to draw up separate interview agenda for the two parties, the investor and the investee, because of their different concerns. Here, however, for simplicity, attention will be focused upon the investor, the VCI, and the design of a semi-structured interview agenda for face-to-face use with VCIs (see Sweeting 1991b), utilizing the broad headings of: attitudes to risk; information-handling; and sharing risk and information. A fuller account will be provided in Chapter 5 of the rationale behind the instrumentation for both investor and investee.

Attitudes to risk

This involves both a narrow investigation of risk aversion by presenting the investor with choices between lotteries or gambles[22] and sure prospects, and a broader evaluation of risk management. For example:

1 Which does the VCI prefer: (a) the sum of £1m. with the chance nine in ten, or the sum of £3m. with the chance one in ten; or (b) the sure prospect of £1.2m., of £1.5m. etc.?
2 In selecting investee firms for portfolio construction does the VCI attempt to offset lucky good outcomes against unlucky bad ones?
3 Does the VCI consider how additional investments may affect the overall level of risk?
4 Does the VCI perceive that one of the motivations of the MSF in agreeing a contract is to share the risk with the VCI?

22 A simple gamble involves two possible outcomes (π_1, π_2) with probabilities p_1 and $p_2 \equiv 1 - p_1$ respectively. Formally, it may be represented by $G = (p_1, \pi_1; 1 - p_1, \pi_2)$. See Ricketts (1987: ch.5 app.), and the use of these ideas in a venture capital context in Chapter 4 below.

Information-handling

Part of this establishes a classification of information types, such as: financial and management accounts; market research; personnel details; and technical specification of product. There is also a need to know how these information types are utilized. Finally, evidence is sought on how information, in a generic sense, is managed. For example:

1 Does the VCI perceive itself to be less well informed about the MSF than its directors?
2 Does the VCI gather information from the MSF to make itself better informed *vis-à-vis* its directors?
3 Does the VCI feel that the directors of the MSF may have a rational motivation to misrepresent or bias information which is channelled through?
4 What action does the VCI take, if any, to guard against possible biases in information received from the MSF?
5 Does the VCI regard the information received from the MSF to be highly variable as an indicator of the actual state of affairs?

Sharing risk and information

The way in which views on riskiness and monitoring are brought together will shape the procedures used by the VCI for investment selection, management and review. An understanding of the stages of assessment and the techniques used will, therefore, be required. For example:

1 Does the VCI perceive itself as conferring risk-sharing benefits on the MSF, in exchange for the MSF conferring information-sharing benefits on itself?
2 Is there a relationship between the amount of risk accepted by the VCI and the amount of effort exercised by MSF directors?
3 What is the relationship between the size of the equity stake and the amount of risk the VCI is prepared to accept?
4 On what bases are entry and exit values calculated and predicted?

A particular way in which these points can be translated into a semi-structured interview agenda, to be addressed to VCIs, is indicated in Table 3.1. A more detailed account of the instrumentation by which this agenda was implemented, and a consideration of similar design issues for an administered questionnaire addressed to MSFs, is given in Chapter 5. Briefly, these three headings allow major features of agency analysis to be considered in face-to-face interviews.

All three sections explore issues at both the quantitative and qualitative level, be these of risk management, information-handling, or the relationship between the two. In the first part of the agenda, attitude to risk is examined in both a

Table 3.1 Outline of semi-structured interview (SSI) agenda for VCI

1	*Risk management*
1.1	Chance outcomes and sure prospects
1.2	Offsetting good outcomes against bad
1.3	Effects of new MSF on overall risk management
1.4	Sharing risk with MSF
2	*Information-handling*
2.1	Information types relevant to MSF relationship
2.2	Differences in information between investor and MSF
2.3	Ways of aligning information of investor and MSF
2.4	Ways of reducing bias in information
2.5	Correspondence of information with reality
2.6	Effects of costs on information acquisition
3	*Trading risk and information*
3.1	Extent of risk-sharing with MSF
3.2	Extent of information-sharing with MSF
3.3	Exchanging information for risk-bearing
3.4	Effects of risk-sharing on effort
3.5	Effects of size of equity stake on effort
3.6	Discriminating between MSFs on efficiency grounds
3.7	Designing contract with MSF to achieve efficiency

classical sense (based on probability distributions) and a qualitative sense (based on judgements about the role or significance of events, risk class, etc.). Formal and informal methods of hedging in portfolio composition are addressed, so that the extent to which diversification is consciously or unconsciously achieved may be gauged. Formal and informal risk-spreading strategies between investor and investee are examined, in terms of both their insurance function and their incentive properties, including effort elicitation.

In the second part of the agenda, a primary aim is to get a quantitative and qualitative grip on what is meant by information in an agency setting. A wide set of information types is examined and their properties explored, including the purpose to which they are put, their 'noisiness' as signals of underlying properties, and their incentive properties (e.g. as performance indicators). The way in which information systems become modified, post-investment as compared to pre-investment, is examined in terms of breadth and frequency of information provision.

Finally, in the third part of the agenda, risk and information are viewed together, as part of the contracting nexus between investor and investee. Specialization in skills for dealing with risk and information is a primary focus of this section, which aims to discover how free contracting between the parties concerned brings about something like a best or optimal relationship, drawing most heavily on parties' greatest skills, and augmenting their weakest skills. Implications for effort and risk distribution are drawn out.

The instrument designs for the investee are similar in terms of the basic categories of analysis, but differ considerably in detail. Thus the face-to-face administered questionnaire (AQ) is more highly structured, and has a greater quantitative emphasis. The telephone administered questionnaire involved further pruning down to allow the interview to be accomplished in a limited period of time.[23] This inevitably implied a further emphasis on quantitative as opposed to qualitative factors. In all cases, a significant body of collateral or auxiliary evidence was gathered in terms of accounting data, product descriptors, price lists, etc.

3.7 GOING INTO THE FIELD

To anticipate the narrative of Chapter 5, it should be said here that fieldwork was conducted with the aim of addressing the issues raised above by face-to-face interviews with the owner-managers of MSFs and their VC investors. Three phases to the fieldwork were involved: unstructured qualitative fieldwork; piloting of the instruments; and the administration of instruments. Owing to the presumed asymmetry of information between the VCI and the MSF, and their differing capabilities (e.g. in risk management), a pair of instruments was required to capture each side of the relationship. This allowed investor and investee to report independently on their perceptions of the contractual relationship in which they were involved, both implicit and explicit. In turn, the analysis of this evidence is better able to treat investor and investee as possessing distinct preferences, with each seeking most preferred positions within the contracting nexus.

The purpose of unstructured fieldwork is to collect evidence, free of preconceptions,[24] from VC funds and investee firms about: the received wisdom among investor practitioners as to how they undertake their tasks (described earlier as comprising investment selection, management and disposal); the awareness small firms have about the availability of venture capital, and their expectations, generally, when dealing with equity providers; and the reaction by both to issues covered in the previous section. Discussions took place with leading players in financial markets, various quangos and lobby groups, and several public bodies concerned with enterprise policy.

Draft versions of the semi-structured interview instrument, based on the agenda given in Table 3.1, were tried out with VCIs on site, and a similar procedure was used to pilot the administered questionnaire with MSFs, both by face-to-face and by telephone interviews. The initial approach to the VCI was

23 Typically, about 20 minutes was spent on each telephone interview.

24 For comparable methodologies which have also been applied in venture capital contexts, see Sapienza (1989), Sweeting (1991b), and Steier and Greenwood (1995).

with a pre-letter, accompanied by a summary of the proposed interview agenda and a list of basic data requirements (see Appendix A to this book). Piloting resulted in slight changes to the questionnaire. A similar procedure was used to test the instrumentation for the MSF, both by telephone and in person. Given the need to access MSFs through their equity finance providers, it proved necessary to modify the initial approach to them, which had to be facilitated according to the wishes of the 'gate-keeper' funders.

3.8 CONCLUSION

The contractual relationship between the MSF and VCI can be complex in an empirical sense, but the general principle governing its form is that the MSF offers the VCI benefits of ownership and knowledge-sharing, in exchange for which the VCI offers the MSF an opportunity to spread risk and to acquire additional finance. On this basis, a contract is written between the VCI and the MSF. Generally, this contract will be second-best, in a welfare sense. However, to the extent that agency costs are held down by contractual arrangements, outcomes may be produced which are close to those which would occur if information and monitoring were costless (that is, close to first-best contracting, in a welfare sense).[25]

The process of making, choosing and realizing equity investments described here is claimed to be dependent upon a particular treatment of the risk-return relationship. In the absence of a well-developed secondary market, providing a reference price for valuation and marketability for investment substitutability, a modified version of portfolio theory is required. The propositions emerging from this are then 'tested' using qualitative and quantitative evidence so as to offer an insightful view of UK venture capital investment behaviour.

25 First-best outcomes arise in conditions of free trade between many fully informed economic actors, when all opportunities for making at least one economic actor better off, without making another worse off, are exhausted. A second-best outcome aims to maximize welfare in a similar way, but subject to a distortion that cannot be removed.

4

PRINCIPLES OF AGENCY ANALYSIS

4.1 INTRODUCTION

The empirical context within which venture capital functions has been established. So too have the broad analytical principles which may be brought to bear on the relationship between the venture capital investor (VCI) and the mature small firm (MSF). However, the detailed ways in which investor and investee, in this sense, interact, especially as regards their handling of information and management of risk, have remained unexplored. This is a matter of fairly intricate analysis in terms of economic theory, and the lines of reasoning now to be developed to fill this gap in the structure of the book may not be accessible to all readers. However, the main points established are both important and, if mastered, highly illuminating.[1] If these lines of reasoning cannot be followed in detail by the reader, then a beneficial and pragmatic alternative, from the viewpoint of understanding the broad thrust of argument upon which this book's research is based, is to note the content of the sequence of propositions laid out in the development of material below.

Essentially two types of technique are to be expounded in this chapter. The first concerns a formalization of uncertainty that has been very influential in economics, accounting and finance, as well as in numerous cognate fields. This formalization is a theory of choice about decisions that may lead to a number of possible outcomes rather than one single, sure outcome. Thus a decision-taker, a good example of which is an entrepreneur, faces chance outcomes rather than

1 The methods expounded in this chapter are a part of standard economic analysis, as developed in advanced textbooks like Gravelle and Rees (1981: chs 19, 20). A more modern but less accessible account than this, of choice under uncertainty and principal–agent analysis, is contained in Kreps (1990: chs 3, 16). Particular acknowledgement should be made to the pedagogic journal article of Ricketts (1986) and especially to his textbook treatment in Ricketts (1994: ch. 5), both of which have been highly influential in the formulating of the ideas expressed below in box diagram form. Another useful account, written by an accountant and an economist, focusing as here on uncertainty and information, but using no geometry and little mathematics, is Strong and Waterson (1987).

certain outcomes arising from his or her decisions. To the extent that these outcomes are beyond the control of the decision-taker, they are said to depend upon 'states of the world'. The theory of choice under uncertainty assumes decision-takers can assign probabilities to these states of the world, and that they can attach these probabilities to specific values, like profits or income, that occur as outcomes in specific states of the world. Such pairings of probabilities and incomes or profits are termed 'prospects'. The central principle of the theory of choice under uncertainty is that economic agents have rational and consistent preferences over prospects which obey certain axioms. Section 4.2 shows briefly how preferences satisfying these axioms can be mapped geometrically using the device of indifference curves.

The second technique expounded in this chapter is also geometrical. It concerns what is known as an Edgeworth box diagram.[2] The dimensions of this box are defined by total incomes or profits arising in two states of the world. Opposite corners of the box relate to each of two decision-takers, of which the chosen examples are the venture capitalist and the entrepreneur. Because claims on income or profit are not certain, depending as they do on the state of the world, they are said to be 'state-contingent'. The theory expounded in section 4.3 shows how these decision-takers exchange, to their best advantage, these state-contingent claims.

These techniques having been established, they are then used to develop some fundamental results in principal–agent analysis. This type of analysis has its roots in the work of Mirlees (1971, 1976) on the optimal structure of incentives and authority within an organization. However, this work, and all that followed from it, is highly technical, and requires a knowledge of advanced mathematics. The approach adopted here is to expound some of the key results developed by principal–agent theorists like Holmström (1979) and his followers using no more than the geometrical device of the box diagram. I start by taking efficient contracting under full information as a reference point, move on to incentives for the entrepreneur as agent to put out effort, and conclude by considering how risk-sharing benefits can be enhanced by an information system if the entrepreneur's actions cannot be fully observed.

4.2 CHANCE OUTCOMES

This section is concerned with providing a simple development of the theory of choice under uncertainty in a form that can be assimilated into the box diagram treatment of subsequent sections. Here, the economic agent in question is the

2 Francis Edgeworth (1845–1926) was a well-known economist who held a professorship at Oxford University and popularized this technique in a book called *Mathematical Psychics* (1881).

entrepreneur, and the key issue is how her preferences are defined over chance outcomes. This leads into a consideration of indifference curves, and of how the shape of these curves conveys information about attitude to risk. The starting point for the analysis is that an economic agent, like an entrepreneur, having made a decision in an uncertain world, finds that several outcomes may arise, depending on the state of the world. For simplicity, just two states of the world, good and bad, will be considered.

In Figure 4.1 good (or favourable) outcomes give rise to a value or profit y_1 on the horizontal axis. Bad (or unfavourable) outcomes give rise to a value or profit y_2 on the vertical axis. Probabilities of good or bad outcomes are given by P and $1 - P$ with the property that $P + (1 - P) = 1$. For example, if an outcome which is good has a probability of 0.8, then if the only alternative is an outcome which is bad, this outcome has a probability $1 - 0.8 = 0.2$. These probabilities can be thought of as 'chances' in a gambling sense. For example, should a horse have a one in ten chance of winning a race, the 'good outcome', its probability of winning would be $\frac{1}{10} = 0.1$. By implication, the chance of losing the race, the bad outcome, would be 9 in 10 or $1 - 0.1 = 0.9$. Let me amplify the point with another example. Consider a commercial context, in which an entrepreneur knows from years of experience that a certain type of deal is concluded in just five out of a hundred cases. Then the probability of the 'good outcome' of concluding a deal is $\frac{5}{100} = 0.05$. Alternatively, it may be said that there is a 5 per cent

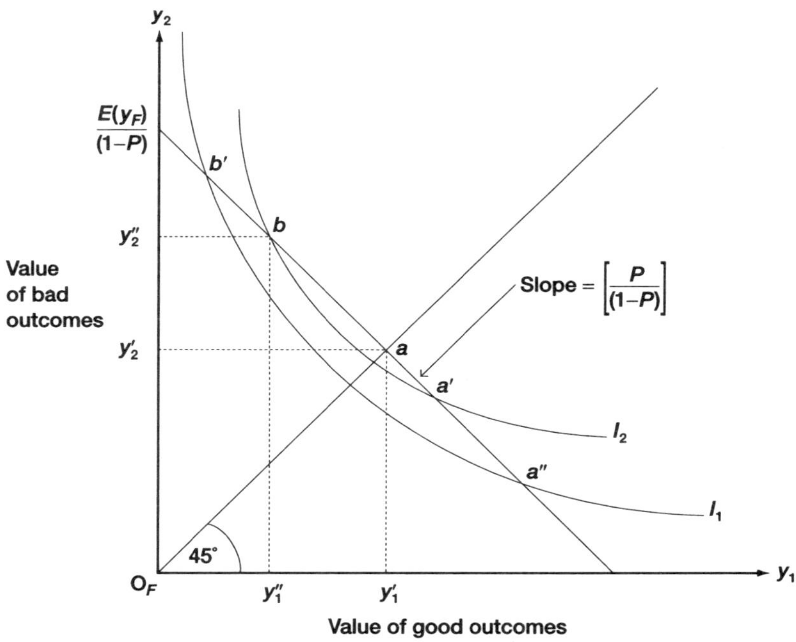

Figure 4.1 Indifference curves and attitude to risk

chance of the deal being concluded. By implication, the probability of the deal not being concluded, the 'bad outcome', is 1 – 0.05 = 0.95. Expressed another way, there is a 95 per cent chance of the deal not working out, that is, of the bad outcome occurring.

The probabilities of outcomes can be used to create 'expected' or 'actuarial' values for outcomes, which can be thought of as average values were the same chance situations to be confronted repeatedly under essentially unchanged conditions. So, if a profit of £10m. were to occur with probability 0.7 (i.e. chance of 70 per cent or 7 in 10) the expected value of profit would be (0.7)(£10m.) = £7m. If the entrepreneur (F), for example, were to have invested in a project from which she would receive a profit of £3m. in the good outcome (which has a chance of 25 per cent) and £1m. in the bad outcome (which has a chance of 75 per cent) her expected profit would be (0.25)(£3m.) + (0.75)(£1m.) = £0.75m. + £0.75m. = £1.50m. This can be thought of as the average profit she would get from her investment, were she repeatedly to invest in it under the same conditions. More generally, her ***expected*** profit from profits y_{1F} and y_{2F}, with probabilities P and $(1 - P)$ respectively, is $Py_{1F} + (1 - P)y_{2F} = E(y_F)$, where the symbol E denotes 'expected'. This can be rewritten as:

$$y_{2F} = \frac{1}{(1-P)} E(y_F) - \left[\frac{P}{(1-P)}\right] y_{1F}$$

which is the expected profit equation expressed in the normal form for a straight line.[3] It has a negative slope of $P/(1 - P)$, and an intercept on the vertical axis of $E(y_F)/(1 - P)$, as illustrated by the straight-line equation of expected profit going through ***a*** and ***b*** in Figure 4.1. Also drawn on this figure is a 45° line, which goes through the origin O_F. Because y_1 equals y_2 all along this 45° line, outcomes along it represent a set of risk-free situations. For these, whatever the probabilities, the entrepreneur always gets the same outcome. Point ***a***, for example, has this property, for $y_1'(= y_2')$ profit is received whether the 'good' or 'bad' outcome occurs. However, if one moves to ***b*** along the expected profit line, the situation is different. Compared to ***a***, the entrepreneurs will gain $y_2'' - y_2'$ if the bad outcome occurs and lose $y_1' - y_1''$ if the good outcome occurs. However, as ***b*** and ***a*** lie on the same expected profit line, ***on average*** the entrepreneur still gets $E(y_F)$. In this sense a gamble which would take the entrepreneur from ***a*** to ***b*** is 'fair'. However, if the entrepreneur prefers ***a*** to ***b*** she is said to be ***risk averse***, in the sense that she would rather always get the sure thing than its equivalent value,

3 From high-school algebra, this would have the form $y = e + fx$, where e and f are constants, with e the intercept on the vertical axis (when $x = 0$) and f being the slope dy/dx. For the expected profit equation, when y_{1F} is zero, y_{2F} is $E(y_F)/(1 - P)$, the intercept on the vertical axis. The slope of it, $dy_{2F}/dy_{1F} = -P/(1 - P)$.

on average. This sort of reasoning is used in posing questions about risk in Chapter 5 below.

To say that preferences can be expressed over outcomes, as above, is to admit that utility can be regarded as deriving from outcomes. If *a* is preferred to *b*, utility can be said to be higher for *a* than for *b*. In the theory of choice under uncertainty, a risk-averse individual enjoys lesser utility the greater is the disparity between outcomes (i.e. the greater the deviation from the risk-free 45° line). So *b* would be preferred to *b′*, *a* to *b*, and indeed *a* to *a′*. Thus curves which represent equal levels of utility for different combinations of outcomes, called ***indifference curves***, will be convex when viewed from the origin O_F for risk-averse individuals. The symbol *I* will be used for an indifference curve. Two such indifference curves are drawn in Figure 4.1, I_1 and I_2, with I_2 tracing out outcomes which provide a higher level of utility than does I_1. Moving out along the certainty line through O_F, higher values of outcomes pertain to higher levels of utility. Utilities are equal along each indifference curve: equal at *b′* and *a″* on I_1; and equal at *b* and *a′* on I_2, for example.

4.3 EFFICIENT CONTRACTING

The analysis developed in the previous section focused on the entrepreneur's attitude to risk, but a similar treatment could have been given to the venture capitalist's attitude to risk. He too can be considered to have preferences over chance outcomes, which can be captured by the shape of his indifference curves. As it turns out, if the venture capitalist is risk neutral, his indifference curves assume a very simple shape, namely, straight lines, so it was helpful to develop first a more general case, as above in section 4.2.

The concern here is with how two parties, the venture capitalist and the entrepreneur, engage in a shared relationship, which can be thought of as a contract, that involves decisions which lead to uncertain outcomes. For simplicity, just two outcomes, good and bad, will be considered, as previously.

The values or profits attached to outcomes, be they good or bad, are assumed to be shared, to a greater or lesser degree, by the venture capitalist (*V*) and the firm or entrepreneur (*F*).[4] If a good outcome occurs, giving rise to profit *y*, this

4 I have simplified the notation to *V* for the venture capital investor (VCI) and to *F* for the mature small firm (MSF) to make the use of subscripts, $_V$ and $_F$, less clumsy. Again, for simplification, I have tended in this chapter to talk of the venture capitalist and entrepreneur as being synonymous with the investor and investee, because it seems to help to convey to the reader issues about attitude to risk. For example it is easier to think in terms of the entrepreneur's attitude to risk, rather than the firm's attitude to risk. I trust it will be understood by the reader that, in the general context of this book, the firm, the investee and the entrepreneur are all of a piece, as are the fund, the investor and the venture capitalist.

split between the profit for the venture capitalist (y_{1V}) and profit for the mature small firm or its entrepreneur (y_{1F}) may be represented as (y_{1V}, y_{1F}) with the property that $y_{1V} + y_{1F} = y_1$. For example, if a deal is worth £10m. provided things work out well (the good outcome y_1), and entitlements to portions of this have been established (e.g. by proportion of equity in a business) at £6m. for the entrepreneur ($y_{1F} = 6$) and £4m. for the venture capitalist ($y_{1V} = 4$), then the expression $y_{1V} + y_{1F} = y_1$ would be written $4 + 6 = 10$, in units of £1 million. It will be seen that y_1 defines the horizontal dimension of a box diagram of the sort displayed in Figure 4.2. Similarly, if a bad outcome (y_2) occurred, with $y_2 < y_1$, and the value of the deal were only £1m. (i.e. £1m. < £10m.), and the split between venture capitalist (y_{2V}) and entrepreneur (y_{2F}) were determined on the same proportional basis (not a necessary restriction, but an illustration), the notation $y_{2V} + y_{2F} = y_2$ pertains, and the corresponding numerical values would be $0.4 + 0.6 = 1.0$, with units again measured in £ millions. It will be seen that y_2 defines the vertical dimension of a box diagram of the sort displayed in Figure 4.2.

Sufficient background argument has now been developed to make detailed reference to Figure 4.2, which displays a type of Edgeworth box diagram. As before, the horizontal axis represents values from good outcomes (y_1), and the vertical axis represents values from bad outcomes ($y_2 < y_1$). The origin for the mature small firm or entrepreneur is O_F and the origin for the venture capitalist is at the opposite corner of the box at O_V. The lines of certainty for the entrepreneur and venture capitalist are the 45° lines through O_F and O_V, respectively. Points within the box represent allocations of good and bad outcomes between the firm and venture capitalist. These allocations (i.e. *a*, *b*, and *c*) may be thought

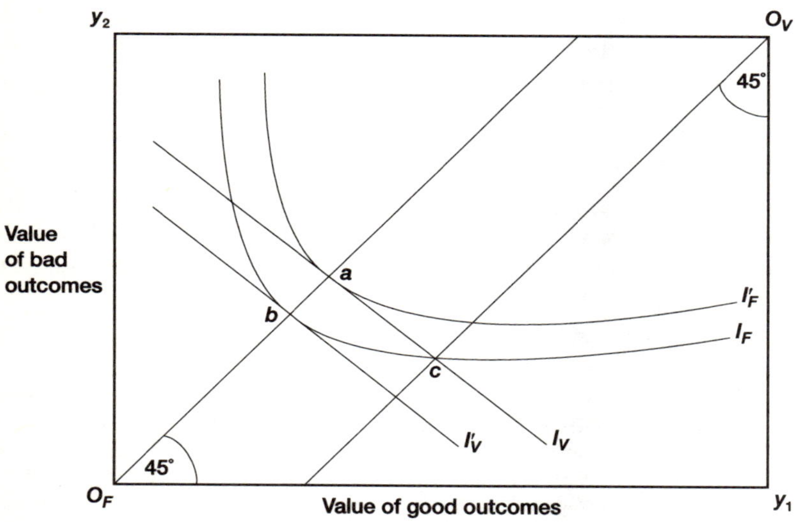

Figure 4.2 The contract curve of efficient allocations

of as potential contracts between the two parties. Convex indifference curves for the entrepreneur are given by I_F and I'_F, where I'_F represents a higher level of utility for the entrepreneur than I_F. These indifference curves are drawn to display risk aversion, suggesting the entrepreneur finds it hard to diversify away her risk, which is plausible if she is only involved with one mature small firm. The straight lines I_V and I'_V of Figure 4.2 are also types of indifference curves with I'_V representing a higher utility for the venture capitalist than I_V. They are constructed for a venture capitalist who displays risk neutrality, in the sense that, being straight lines, they suggest the venture capitalist is sufficiently diversified that he is indifferent between fair bets, as represented by points along a straight line like I_V.

The point *c* does not represent an efficient allocation of outcomes between venture capital investor and entrepreneur because, for example, a shift to point *a* would make the venture capitalist no worse off (utility remaining at I_V) but the entrepreneur better off (utility being raised from I_F to I'_F). Indeed, given the venture capitalist's utility of I_V, the best or optimal contract is at *a*, where I'_F is tangential to I_V. The movement along I_V from *c* towards *a* involves progressive steps which are said to be 'Pareto-superior' moves.[5] They are available until point *a*, where I'_F is tangential to I_V, implying I'_F is the entrepreneur's maximum utility, given the venture capitalist's utility is I_V. Then no further Pareto-superior moves are available and the contract is said to be Pareto-optimal.[6] All such tangency points have this optimal property, and the segment *ba* is a set of such efficient points, or contracts, as indeed is the whole length of the 45° line through O_F. This full set of efficient points is sometimes called the contract curve.

It is worth noting that in the move from *c* to *a* the venture capitalist, as principal, is providing the entrepreneur or firm, as agent, with fair insurance (thus relocating the entrepreneur's contract onto his risk-free 45° line). This is

5 Named after the Italian mathematical economist Vilfredo Pareto, who proposed the now widely adopted criterion that an economic change is good (that is, superior) if it makes at least one economic actor 'better off', without making any worse off.

6 Both indifference curves have slopes of $P/(1 - P)$ at this point. To amplify the analysis of the main text, suppose that both the venture capitalist and the entrepreneur have a utility function of the form $U(y) = m - n \exp[-Ry]$ where 'exp' denotes the exponential function, m and n are arbitrary constants, and R is a constant which measures absolute risk aversion. Risk aversion for the VCI and MSF are denoted R_V and R_F respectively. For outcomes y_1 and y_2 occurring, with probabilities P and $(1 - P)$, the expected utility is $E(U) = PU(y_1) + (1 - P)U(y_2)$. Then the slope of an indifference curve (which denotes constant expected utility) is dy_2/dy_1. For the chosen form of $U(y)$, this has the expression $-[P/(1 - P)]\exp[-R(y_1 - y_2)]$. Now, distinguishing between VCI and MSF, points of tangency between their indifference curves (like *a* and *b* in Figure 4.2) have a common slope of $P/(1 - P)$. Thus the following condition holds: $\exp[-R_V(y_{1V} - y_{2V})] = \exp[-R_F(y_{1F} - y_{2F})]$. Therefore, $y_{1V} - y_{2V} = (R_F/R_V)(y_{1F} - y_{2F})$. That is, the form this tangency takes hinges on the risk aversion of VCI and MSF. The measures of risk aversion R_F and R_V are related directly to the convexity of indifference curves.

because, in moving from *c* to *a*, the venture capitalist gives up claims to y_2 in exchange for claims to y_1 at a ratio which equals that of the outcome probabilities (that is, the slope of I_V, $P/(1-P)$). This occurs while the venture capitalist is increasing his own risk, because movement is off the certainty line through O_V. But as the principal is risk neutral, with straight-line indifference curves like I_V, this increasing risk does not lower utility, as *c* and *a* are on the same indifference curve, I_V. While the entrepreneur's expected return falls in moving from *c* to *a*, his actual utility rises because of a more than compensating decrease in uncertainty. In the case illustrated in Figure 4.2 an important point emerges under full information:

> *Proposition 1*
> If the venture capitalist is risk neutral and the entrepreneur is risk averse, then efficient contracting requires the venture capitalist to bear all risk, thus providing the entrepreneur with complete insurance.

4.4 INCENTIVES FOR ENTREPRENEURIAL EFFORT

The above assumes that the state of the world (e.g. good or bad trade) is completely observable, and that the effort of the entrepreneur is not at issue. However, if this is not the case, which is the concern of this section, new considerations affect the form of efficient contracting. These focus on the incentives which contracts provide for the entrepreneur to put forth effort within the firm. Such effort may be thought of as discretionary from the entrepreneur's standpoint.

In Figure 4.3, I'_F is the relevant indifference curve when the entrepreneur within the firm undertakes effort, and I_F pertains when the effort is zero. The sense in which I talk about the application of effort is that by applying it, the entrepreneur raises the probability of good outcomes occurring from P to P'. Therefore, the slope of the entrepreneur's indifference curve with effort I'_F has a higher absolute slope of $P'/(1-P')$ at *b*, along the entrepreneur's certainty line, compared to the lower slope of $P/(1-P)$ at *a* on the certainty line for the slope of the indifference curve without effort, I_F. A measure of the effort made by the entrepreneur to enhance the chance of good outcomes is the distance *ab* along the entrepreneur's certainty line.

I now come to an important construction. At point *c* in Figure 4.3, the indifference curves I_F and I'_F intersect, implying that the associated combination of outcomes provides a utility level which is equal, whether or not the entrepreneur makes an effort to raise the probability of the good outcome.[7] The locus of a

7 Similarly, if $\bar{I}_F$ is a higher indifference curve than I_F with no effort, and $\bar{I}'_F$ *is the corresponding* higher indifference curve with effort, their intersection point *c′* is another one at which the entrepreneur is indifferent between effort and no effort.

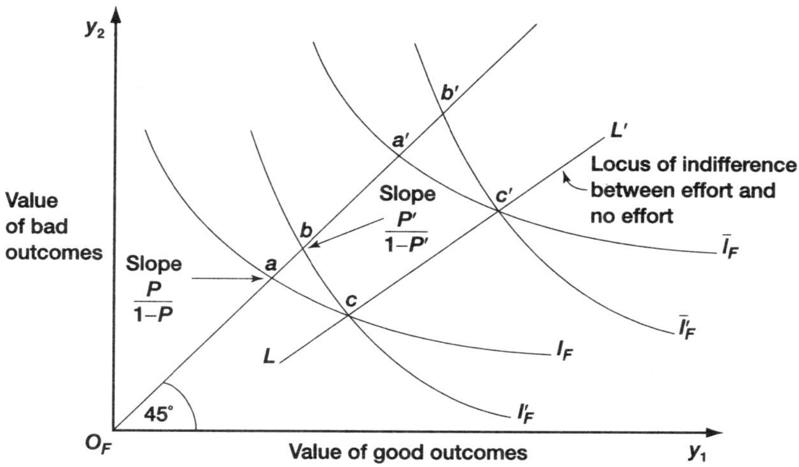

Figure 4.3 The implications of effort for indifference curves

point such as *c* is the line *LL′*, going through *c* and *c′*, which traces out all points such that there is indifference between effort and no effort on the part of the entrepreneur. To the right of this locus the claims on outcomes are sufficiently good that the entrepreneur is willing to put forth effort to raise the probability of achieving these desired outcomes, even though there is a disutility associated with effort. On the other hand, to the left of this *LL′* locus the entrepreneur has no incentive for effort. Therefore, to induce the entrepreneur to prefer effort, the contract offered must lie to the right of the *LL′* locus. It is now necessary to consider the venture capitalist and how he is affected by the entrepreneur's effort. The implications of such effort for efficient contracting can then be analysed.

The effect of the effort applied by the entrepreneur within the firm influences the indifference curves of the venture capitalist, as principal, as well as those of the entrepreneur, as agent. The indifference curve for the venture capitalist, like that for the entrepreneur, will now also have a slope of $P'/(1 - P')$. One such new indifference curve for the venture capitalist is denoted by I'_V in Figure 4.4. It intersects the indifference curve for the venture capitalist when the entrepreneur exerts no effort, I_V, at the point *e* on the 45° certainty line for the venture capitalist, VO_V. I now turn to contractual efficiency. At point ***a*** in Figure 4.4 risk is efficiently shared between venture capitalist (principal) and entrepreneur (agent) in the situation without effort, as illustrated earlier (e.g. in Figure 4.2 and Proposition 1 above). It occurs when the indifference curves for the entrepreneur (I_F) and the venture capitalist (I_V) are tangent at point ***a*** on the entrepreneur's certainty line, FO_F. However, when effort is undertaken by the entrepreneur, the relevant indifference curves are I'_V for the venture capitalist and I'_F for the firm. They intersect at ***d***, and the shaded area of ***bcd*** indicates the

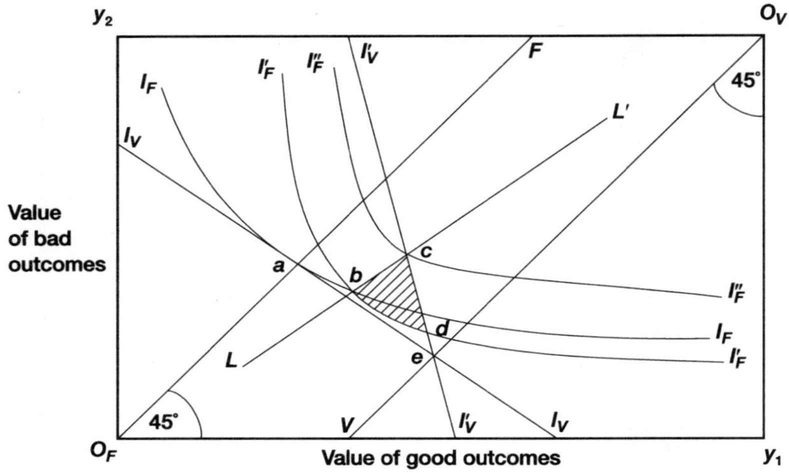

Figure 4.4 The implications of effort for efficient contracting

set of contracts which are a Pareto-improvement on the contract at *a*. All moves in *bcd* which are Pareto-improving are exhausted along the boundary *bc*, and therefore this segment *bc* contains the set of Pareto-efficient contracts. A movement from *c*, within the set *bcd*, would harm the entrepreneur, and a movement from *b*, again within *bcd*, would harm the venture capitalist. It is important to note that while *a* provides what is sometimes called a 'first-best' efficient sharing of risk, with the risk-neutral principal bearing all the risk, and the risk-averse agent bearing no risk at all, this feature is not true of segment *bc*. For example, at *c* the slopes of I''_F and I'_V are not equal, so utility-enhancing possibilities exist, in terms of contracts between these indifference curves, in a direction which is towards the entrepreneur's risk-free 45° line FO_F. Another proposition is therefore illustrated here:

Proposition 2

Pareto-efficient contracts, struck under circumstances of unobservable effort and state, will generally not be first-best, and will require the entrepreneur to bear some risk.

The reason for this is that gains from more efficient risk-bearing are sacrificed to those gains from providing incentives for effort which raise the probability of good outcomes. This sacrifice of efficient risk-sharing benefits in order to stimulate effort will occur only if effort is neither too costly nor lacking in sufficient leverage over the probability of good outcomes occurring. Although the entrepreneur, as agent, bears some risk in the set of contracts along *bc*, rather than no risk, as at *a*, and choices in *bc* are Pareto-superior to *a*, it will never be optimal for the risk-averse entrepreneur to bear all the risk and, by implication, for the venture capitalist to bear none of the risk. This would require efficient contracting to occur along the 45° line of certainty VO_V for the venture capitalist, in which case he would indeed bear no risk. In terms of Figure 4.4 this would require the locus *bc* to cut the venture capitalist's 45° certainty line. Point *b* must lie to the right of I_V as I_F is convex, because the entrepreneur is risk averse. However, were such a point to be on VO_V it would clearly leave the venture capitalist with lower utility than at *a*, so this could not lead to an efficient contract which is Pareto-superior to *a*. A further proposition is therefore illustrated:

Proposition 3
A risk-averse entrepreneur will never bear all the risk.

4.5 INFORMATION AND MONITORING

This section aims to consider how risk-sharing benefits can be better captured, by an information system, should the entrepreneur's activities within her firm not be fully observable. Such a system uses information to provide a signal of activity. Typically, this signal will be 'noisy' in the sense that while it does not fully capture what is going on in the firm, it does at least provide some indication of what the entrepreneur is doing.

Returning to the case of a risk-neutral venture capital investor and a risk-averse entrepreneur (illustrated in Figure 4.4 of the previous section), if no information were available on the entrepreneur's effort within the firm, efficient contracts would be along the locus *LL'*. Taking the efficient contract at *b* to extend the argument, recall that for this contract the entrepreneur is just indifferent between exerting or not exerting effort (indeed, this defines the locus *LL'*).

Suppose the venture capitalist drops in on the entrepreneur now and then to check what is going on in the firm. If he visits repeatedly, and never finds the entrepreneur, he may conclude that no effort is being made. This may be wrong, of course. Perhaps the entrepreneur is visiting a laboratory to check out some new technological development which may help the firm's performance, rather than out playing a round of golf. Equally, if the investor always finds the entrepreneur on the phone in her office when he visits, this does not mean that she never skips away to the golf course, nor does it rule out that she frequently phones the golf course to check course conditions or to confirm an updating of her handicap. One way of proceeding might be to raise the entrepreneurial reward by an increment (say, by K'), if she is hard at work when the venture capitalist drops in, or to penalise her by a decrement (say, by $-K$) if she is absent.

Given the behaviour of the venture capitalist, the entrepreneur is able to compute the chance that she is observed hard at work, when in fact she has just returned from the golf course or is phoning the club secretary; and the chance that she is observed absent, when actually she is visiting a laboratory on the firm's business. These calculations allow a 'monitoring gamble' to be constructed that takes account of the increments and decrements K' and $-K$ that modify the usual good and bad outcomes y_1 and y_2. If the venture capitalist is more likely than not to observe correctly what the entrepreneur is doing, then if the entrepreneur is indeed at the golf course, this is more likely to be observed than that she is at work. This expresses the minimal requirement for the venture capitalist's observation system to be 'informative'. If, further, the penalty for being observed absent from work (K) exceeded the reward (K') from being observed putting forth effort at work, the entrepreneur who neglected the business would wish not to be monitored by the venture capitalist in the way described. However, the more committed entrepreneur, who did put forth effort, again subject to informative monitoring, would be indifferent between the monitored gamble and the unmonitored gamble.[8] This argument appeals to the analytical principle that the entrepreneur is risk neutral, in the limit.[9]

Without monitoring, we have seen previously (section 4.4) that at a point such as *b* in Figure 4.4, the entrepreneur is indifferent between effort and no effort. However, if the entrepreneur is monitored in an informative way, she prefers exerting effort at *b* to not exerting effort, and does not perceive herself to be worse off than when there was no monitoring. The impact of signalling and monitoring (assumed costless), from the standpoint of the venture capitalist, is clear. If confronted with fair monitoring gambles, he would be prepared to offer them to the entrepreneur, whatever the absolute size of K and K'. In the limit, neither the venture capitalist nor the entrepreneur would be worse off in terms of risk-bearing because of the introduction of monitoring gambles.

Figure 4.5 can be used to summarize the above argument. The locus LL' can be compared to the locus LL' in Figure 4.4 above. Along it, here, as earlier, the entrepreneur is indifferent between making or not making effort, when contracting does not set out conditions concerning effort. When monitoring is introduced, using noisy but informative signalling, effort is preferred to no effort for the contract represented by *b*. It follows that a point such as *g* exists for which the entrepreneur is again indifferent between effort and no effort, this time when there is monitoring. The curve MM' represents the locus of a point such as *g*. At *g* the entrepreneur's utility is the same as at *b*, but the venture capitalist's

8 This holds for K' and K vanishingly small (see next footnote), maintaining a ratio equal to the probability that the investor observes the investee absent when she has been checking out a lab, divided by the probability that he sees her at work when she has not been golfing but devoting all effort to the firm.

9 I.e. risk neutral close to the 45° line through O_F; with 'close' implying vanishingly small K' and K which nevertheless bear the same ratio, the one to the other, of K'/K. This ratio, in turn, is set equal to the probability ratio of the previous footnote.

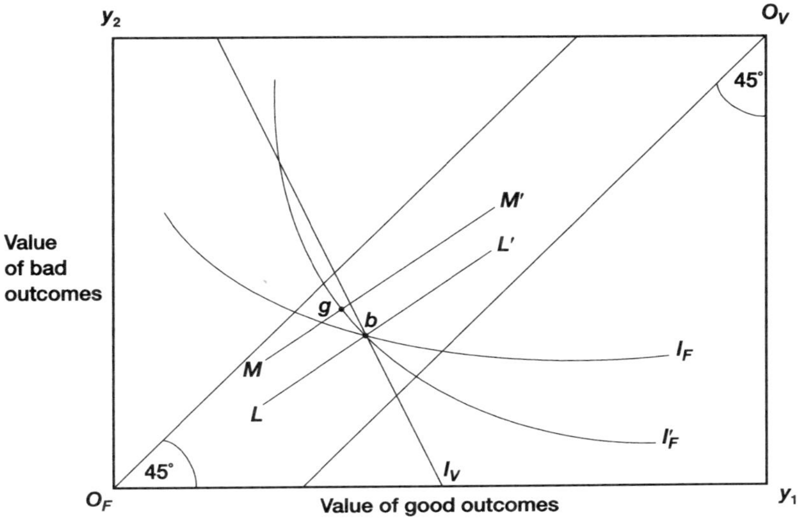

Figure 4.5 The implications of monitoring

utility exceeds that at *b*. To see this, consider a higher indifference curve for the venture capitalist than I_V. The intuition of what is happening here is that monitoring is being used to induce further effort as a substitute for the more inefficient distribution of risk. The key result of this section may therefore now be stated:

Proposition 4
Monitoring permits the realizing of risk-sharing benefits without the sacrificing of effort.

To conclude, it is necessary to consider the reliability of the information at the venture capitalist's disposal. In Figure 4.6, $E(y)$ denotes the expected outcome line with zero effort, and $E'(y)$ the expected outcome line with positive effort.[10] The horizontal and vertical axes represent payments when observed effort is positive (with reward K'), or when observed effort is zero (with penalty K), respectively. I_F and I'_F are the entrepreneur's indifference curves without and with effort respectively. The distance *ab* along the 45° certainty line O_FF represents the 'cost of effort' (see *ab* in Figure 4.3 above). Risk-bearing costs are represented by the distance *bc* in Figure 4.6, in the sense that it shows the cost to the

10 As a reminder on the straight line $E(y)$ relationship, refer to section 4.2 above and the line through *ab* in Figure 4.1.

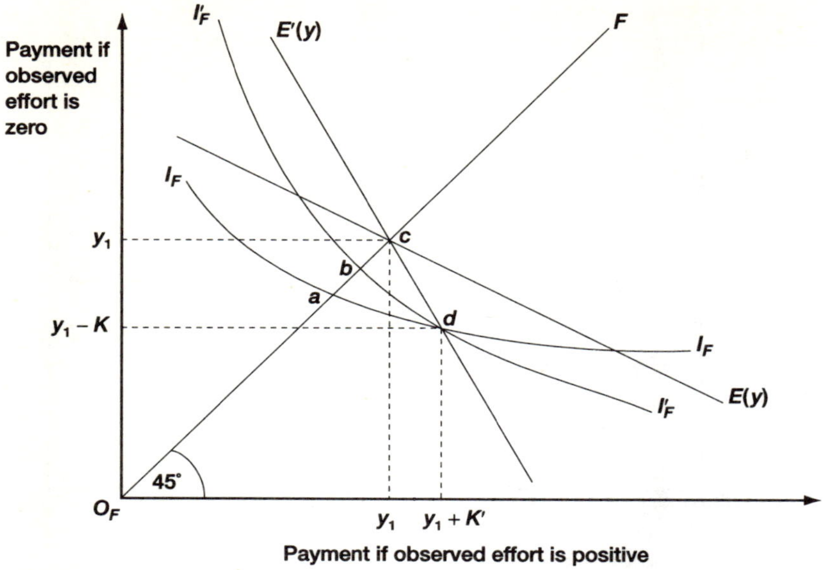

Figure 4.6 Monitoring gambles and the reliability of information

entrepreneur of taking a fair monitoring bet. At *c*, the entrepreneur will certainly receive y_1, but this provides no incentive for effort. If the entrepreneur is offered the monitoring gamble of $y_1 + K'$ if she is observed working and $y_1 - K$ if she is not, and this monitoring gamble is fair to entrepreneurs who make effort,[11] then she will be worse off at ***d*** compared to *c*. For the entrepreneur who puts forth no effort, fair gambles occur along the line $E(y)$, so ***d*** is obviously unfavourable. The zero effort indifference curve I_F cuts $O_F F$ at ***a***. If ***ab*** is the cost of effort, the entrepreneur will be indifferent between effort and no effort at ***d***. Thus ***d*** is the least costly monitoring gamble which is fair for an entrepreneur who makes effort, and it just manages to induce effort on her part.

If information were made more reliable (e.g. by improving the management accounting system) and it better detected entrepreneurs who made no effort, this would make I_F less steep at ***a***. Then, at ***d*** the entrepreneur's utility would be less than before, should she be a shirker, so making effort would be preferred, and a less costly monitoring gamble would exist between ***d*** and *c*. Even if information were perfect about the entrepreneur who made no effort, this would not entirely eliminate risk-bearing costs if there were still a chance of observing no effort from an entrepreneur who actually made effort (e.g. if she were absent from the

11 Fair in the sense that $p_1 K' = p_2 K$, with $p_1 > p_2$. Here, p_1 is the probability of observing no effort when it is actually undertaken.

office, but visiting a laboratory).[12] One therefore completes the analysis of this chapter with:

> *Proposition 5*
> As information becomes more reliable, an entrepreneur previously not producing effort can be induced to prefer to produce effort.

The intuition behind this is that as the venture capitalist's information improves, the monitoring gamble of the entrepreneur who makes no effort becomes more adverse, and thus the smaller are the magnitudes of K' and K required to induce the entrepreneur to prefer to put forth effort.[13]

4.6 CONCLUSION

The purpose of this chapter has been largely expository. It aimed to lay bare some of the basic analytical principles of principal–agent analysis without recourse to advanced mathematics. In doing so, it appealed to a number of devices from the economist's tool kit, including theories of choice under uncertainty and of the efficient exchange of state contingent claims. This required the use of indifference curve analysis and a variant of the Edgeworth box diagram. Five key results were expounded:

1. For a risk-neutral venture capitalist and a risk-averse entrepreneur, under fully informed conditions, efficient risk-sharing requires the venture capitalist to bear all the risk, thus providing the entrepreneur with complete insurance.
2. Under conditions in which effort and states are unobservable, efficient outcomes will not be first-best, and will require the entrepreneur to bear some risk.

12 To get zero risk-bearing costs would also require perfect information about the entrepreneur who made effort. In this case, the ratio of the probability of the venture capitalist observing no effort when it was actually being made, to the probability of his indeed observing effort when she actually made it, would be zero. Perfect information would require the slope of $E'(y)$ to be zero.

13 Therefore, the more reliable is information, the shorter is the distance *bc*: i.e. the lower is the cost to the entrepreneur of accepting a fair monitoring gamble. It may be that the reliability of information itself depends upon the venture capitalist's monitoring costs. For further analytical examination of this point, see Ricketts (1994: 128). There it is indicated that at high levels of monitoring, the monitoring costs may be large enough to absorb potential benefits; but also that at low levels of monitoring, information may become so unreliable that no Pareto-improvement is possible. This suggests that the venture capitalist may have an efficient level of monitoring between these two extremes, in which in effect the marginal benefit of monitoring is brought into equality with the marginal cost of monitoring.

3 A risk-averse entrepreneur will not bear all the risk.
4 Monitoring allows risk-sharing benefits between venture capitalist and entrepreneur, without the sacrifice of entrepreneurial effort.
5 More reliable information induces a greater preference for effort on the part of the entrepreneur.

While these principles by no means exhaust the content of principal–agent analysis, as regards relations between the venture capital investor and the entrepreneur's firm in which he invests they are rather central and will inform much of subsequent discussion. Other broader considerations of risk and information will also be introduced, but these too are influenced, if not entirely governed, by such aspects of principal–agent analysis. Referring to the work of Ricketts (1994: 131) himself, whose pedagogic devices have inspired the exposition of much of this chapter:

> Impressions about risk preferences; judgements about what can be observed, how, and at what costs; guesses about the probability distribution of various states of the world: these are the forces which mould contractual relations, and in so doing throw up the institutional structures which are observed at any one time.

It is to these impressions, judgements, and indeed even guesses sometimes, that this book now turns.

Part 2

EVIDENCE

5

INSTRUMENTATION

5.1 INTRODUCTION

In approaching any field of scientific enquiry one utilizes one or more instruments. They measure features and characteristics of the universe explored. Thus the meteorologist uses barometers and thermometers to measure climatic conditions. In the case under consideration in this book, the methodology adopted was conceived within a social sciences, rather than physical sciences, context. So, rather than being the likes of electronic sensors or pressure gauges, the instruments used here were those which are typical of the fieldworker, like interview agenda, semi-structured interviews and questionnaires. Instrumentation refers to the design and utilization of such instruments, and it is with this process that this chapter is concerned.

The instruments in question are: a semi-structured interviews schedule (SSI); an administered questionnaire (AQ) schedule; and a telephone interviews questionnaire (TQ) schedule. The first two of these were applied to investors and investees respectively, conceived of in terms of pairs, in face-to-face interviews; the third was applied to investees only, using telephone rather than face-to-face interviews. Below, these three instruments will be considered in turn by reference to their design and to their intentions, in terms of the issues they aimed to explore in the field. Full details of the instrumentation are contained in Appendices A, B and C of this volume, which include pre-letters, administrators' and respondents' guidance, and show cards, as well as the schedules per se. Relatively little attention will be given here to physical aspects of constructing features of the instrumentation as displayed in the appendices. Rather, my concern is with the research issues the instruments aimed to address, and with why they were explored in the specific fashion adopted. Before the instruments are discussed seriatim, some background considerations of instrument design will be addressed.

5.2 DESIGNING INSTRUMENTS FOR THE FIELD

In their discussion of reliability and validity in qualitative research, Kirk and Miller (1985: 72) conclude that documenting procedures is important and that numerous parties (including even peer reviewers, and research funders) deserve to know 'exactly how the qualitative researcher prepares him- or herself for the endeavour, and how data are collected and analysed'. This chapter has been written to fulfil this purpose.

It has been observed since time immemorial that when fieldworkers engage in their labour they use instruments to perform certain tasks. The modern fieldworker is not labouring on the land, gathering wheat with a scythe, but labouring in a 'field' which is a set of sites of interest, like firms, and is gathering in evidence using instruments like questionnaires and interview agenda. Initially, the field of this study was the set of investors in the UK venture capital industry. Like much of modern industry, it is service based.[1] Through contacts with investors in this industry, the field was enlarged to their investees, which involved greatly extending the range of investigation across industrial sectors. To illustrate, investees were engaged in diverse activities like marine engineering, biotechnology, funeral services, fashion garments, retail computing systems, hotel services and timber products.

In investigating these sites for the fieldwork, the primary aim was to examine investors (VCIs) and investees (MSFs) in 'dyads' (i.e. natural pairs), as in the methodology adopted by the likes of Sapienza (1989). There were twenty investors in total, representing most of the major UK venture capital funds, not all of whom were willing to nominate investees for further enquiry. Sixteen investees were eventually approached through investor contacts, of which four came in two pairs, which were useful for exploring multiple-agent issues.[2] Thus fourteen dyads were available and, for these, all contracting partners, be they investors or investees, were interviewed face to face.[3]

Investors were interviewed using a semi-structured interview agenda (see Appendix A). While allowing quite a free rein in many areas of response, it was also rather detailed at points, in a fashion which was verging on to the questionnaire type of format. All investees in the dyads were interviewed using the more focused device of an administered questionnaire (see Appendix B). However, it was also quite open and flexible at points, verging on an interview format, which allowed greater discretion to be expressed by investees in formulating their responses. In order to extend knowledge on the investee front, an 'extraneous'

1 Technically, it has a two-digit standard industrial classification (SIC) number of 81 (banking and finance).

2 Further detail on the sampling procedures is contained in Chapter 6.

3 There was one exception to this. A single investee in one of the dyads was interviewed by telephone rather than face to face, because of problems of access.

random sample of sixteen investees was obtained.[4] For this sample, the instrument used was a modification of the administered questionnaire (AQ) for investees. This was developed in a compressed and more structured fashion, to be administered by telephone interview (see the TQ in Appendix C). The dictates of limited time, and the lack of social signalling over the telephone (which *is* possible in face-to-face interviews), suggested that this more closed and focused method was an appropriate way of proceeding for the extraneous sample of investees.

This chapter examines the rationale behind the construction and use of each of the instruments for which a thumbnail sketch has been provided above: the face-to-face semi-structured interview; the face-to-face administered questionnaire; and the telephone-administered questionnaire. Each instrument will be dealt with, in turn, in sections 5.3 and 5.4, and the emphasis will be on question formulation and the information which questions were designed to elicit.

It will be observed in the development below that the fieldwork instrumentation being deployed is of a considerably greater sophistication than has been attempted in the literature. For example, a contrast could be made between the instruments used here (Appendices A, B and C at end of book) and those used in the literature, from the beginnings of work in this area, as exemplified by the seminal work of Sapienza (1989) through to current practice, as exemplified by Fiet (1995), using contemporary techniques.

Sapienza's approach is sophisticated and uses distinct questionnaires for VCI and MSF, as well as distinct interview guides for both. However, both his forms of instrumentation are brief: the VCI questionnaire is four pages long, with twenty-nine questions; and the MSF questionnaire (which was administered over the telephone) was one page long, with twelve questions. Neither provided significant opportunity for qualitative, judgemental response, and, mostly, attitudes were measured using Likert scales,[5] with very little quantitative data being collected (e.g. fund size, numbers invested, timescale of involvement).

Sapienza's (1989) interview guides for VCI and MSF were also brief (one page in each case) with just fifteen and fourteen questions respectively in each. These guides have no filtering or probe structure and were often so broad that almost no constraint upon, or structuring of, response could have been possible. For example, the MSF is asked about her investment involvement by simply saying, 'Have you been satisfied with it?', and the VCI is asked about his implicit contracting by the direct query, 'What do you think the keys to an effective relationship with the entrepreneur are?' While simplicity remains a goal in the form of questions asked, their structuring can be considerably more complex than this, and this indeed was an important goal of the research upon which I report.

4 That is, this sample of investees was obtained by an independent procedure to that used in getting investees for the dyads (see Chapter 6 for further details).

5 A method of ranking options.

In the study of Fiet (1995), where mail survey methods were used, the focus was narrowly on market and agency risk, and just twenty-six questions on attitude to risk were posed, all responses being on a Likert scale. A prime aim of the work reported upon below is to take previous instrumentation as a starting point, and to considerably advance instrument design beyond it in terms of scale, scope, sophistication and complexity.

5.3 SEMI-STRUCTURED INTERVIEW (SSI) SCHEDULE

This schedule was prefaced by a pre-letter, which was sent out to investors after the qualitative fieldwork upon which instrument design was predicated (see Chapter 6 below) had been completed. This pre-letter was designed to meet standard criteria in terms of explaining to the respondent (the venture capital investor, VCI) what the research aimed to do, why it was of interest that they should cooperate, how long the interviewing process would take, and how considerations of confidentiality would be respected. At the same time, the sampling 'snowballs' further forward through the request to have access to investees (mature small firms, MSFs) so that dyads, of paired investors and investees, could be constructed. Two items were enclosed with the pre-letter. The first was an interview agenda of the sort given in Table 3.1 of Chapter 3 above, which gave the respondent early warning of the structure of the interview. The second was a basic data sheet which could be filled in by the respondent before the interview. These data concerned basic characteristics of the fund in terms of size, specialization, reviewing of proposals, commitment of funds, degree of involvement, exit route, rate of return and speed to completion. These data were useful to investor and interviewer alike for orientation purposes before the interview. Furthermore, they facilitated the undertaking of cross-section statistical analysis of the investors.

The design of the questionnaire itself aimed to reflect best practice as regards instrumentation, as expounded in writings like Ryan *et al.* (1992) and Sekaran (1992: ch. 7). Two general design principles will be evident in the appearance of the semi-structured interview (SSI). The first is that clear guidance is given throughout to both interviewer and interviewee, extending from the preliminary remarks to the concluding remarks. In that sense, the whole 'social transaction', which is the essence of the interview itself, is heavily scripted. Even though I conducted the great majority of the interviews myself, it was helpful to have a tightly structured interview that guided one clearly through the key issues, thus ensuring all respondents were treated on a similar basis.[6] The second

6 It was also necessary, as at least a few of the interviews had to be undertaken by co-workers who were not so practised in the instrument design.

principle is that the grouping and sequencing of questions was carefully conceived. The three main divisions by topic were risk, information and the trading of risk and information. Both interviewer and interviewee had a summary agenda, and variety was explicitly used as an organizing device for the questions in order to limit, or avoid entirely, the problem of 'respondent fatigue'. In seeking to achieve these two design goals, due attention was paid to ensuring the ease of administration of the questionnaire, and the clarity of its instrumentation.

The first section of the SSI was concerned with risk management, which was treated under four headings: chance outcomes, diversification of risk, portfolio balance, and risk-sharing. With the exception of work by Ruhnka and Young (1991), there has been scant attention paid to creating a theory of venture capital risk management. Although, from the eighteenth century on, risk theorists like Bernoulli have argued that individuals faced with different prospects or gambles select the one that maximizes expected utility or value, the behavioural analysis of decision-takers subject to risk in experimental situations provides some cautionary tales. In particular, Khaneman and Tversky (1979) have discovered that experimental subjects display conduct which leads to what have been called 'certainty' and 'reflection' effects. To understand the 'certainty' effect, consider the choice between (A) and (B), where for (A) you have an 80 per cent chance of winning £4k, and for (B) you have a 100 per cent chance of winning £3k. The expected value of (A) is £3.2k and this exceeds the expected value of (B) which is £3k, yet more subjects prefer (B) to (A). It seems that subjects attach especial importance to certainty, and that certainty seems to be given a higher weighting than even something quite close to it. To understand the 'reflection' effect, consider the choice between (A) and (B), where (A) involves a loss of £4k with a chance of 80 per cent and (B) involves a loss of £3k with a chance of 100 per cent. Although the expected loss of (A), which is £3.2k, exceeds the expected loss of (B), which is £3k, most experimental subjects prefer (A). It seems that, when losses are almost inevitably involved, subjects appear to weight rather highly the slim chance of avoiding any loss.

While being aware of the experimental anomalies, it still seemed useful to take a classical risk analysis framework as a starting point, if only to see what violations of expected utility maximization might arise. However, if truth be told, under risk management one is looking at attitude to risk not only in a narrow, classical probabilistic sense, but also in a broader qualitative sense. If an economic agent (e.g. an investor) prefers to have the expected value of a gamble, rather than the gamble itself, then he or she is said to be risk averse.[7] As expounded in Chapter 4, a common assumption made in economics is that economic agents are risk averse.

7 The expected value of an outcome is the product of the value of the outcome and the chance of it occurring.

Were they not, their risk-loving behaviour would suggest a preference for a gamble over its expected value. But as a long-run decision strategy in the face of risk, this would be ruled out by economists, because those agents who applied it would inevitably lose on average in the long term: that is, they would not survive in an economic sense (e.g. they would be bankrupted). An intermediate case of risk neutrality exists, in which the economic agent is unconcerned about the riskiness of the gamble, and is only interested in its expected value: indeed, the agent is indifferent between the gamble and the expected value. The first part of Section 1 of the SSI aims to elicit information on risk preference in this sense, as well as investigating qualitative senses of whether projects are, or are not, perceived to be more or less risky.

Later parts of the SSI are concerned with both qualitative and quantitative measures of, and attitudes to, risk aversion. In Section 1.2 of the SSI my concern was with portfolio balance and how it was achieved. Put simply, this asks how investors attempted to balance risk and return within a portfolio; and, expressed rather more formally, it considers strategies for risk diversification by the investor. Intuition can be slightly misleading in this area, witness the fact that opinions differ widely on how large a portfolio should be to achieve high-risk diversification.[8] For this reason, it is probably worth spelling out quite explicitly and simply how diversification works.

To illustrate, suppose the investor has £100k to invest in two companies which make sunglasses and umbrellas respectively.[9] Here 'due diligence' involves checking the long-range summer weather forecast on the Internet, and this indicates that wet and sunny weather spells this summer are equally probable (i.e. 50 per cent probability in each case). Suppose that a share in each company currently sells at £10k. Looking ahead, if the summer were wet, suppose the umbrella share would be forced up to a higher value of £20k and the sunglasses share would be priced down to a lower value of £5k. On the other hand, if the summer were sunny, the umbrella company's share would be forced down to £5k, and the sunglasses company's share would be bid up to £20k. If the investor were to put all of her £100k in the sunglasses company, there would be a 50 per cent chance of getting £200k (sunny case) and a 50 per cent chance of her getting £50k on her investment (wet case). The 'expected value' of her investment would be $(0.5)(200) + (0.5)(50) = 100 + 25 =$ £125k. Similarly, if she were to put all of her £100k in the umbrella company, she would have a 50 per cent chance of getting £50k (sunny case) and a 50 per cent chance of getting £200k (wet case). Now the expected value of her investment would be $(0.5)(50) + (0.5)(200) = 25 + 100 =$ £125k. In each case, the investor has an upside of £200k and a downside of

8 For example, Fama (1976) would put it at twenty investments, whereas Statman (1990) would put it at thirty.

9 This example of diversification is based on the textbook discussion in Varian (1990: ch. 12).

£50k. Which one will be received depends on the 'state of the world'; that is, on whether it is wet or sunny.[10]

The upshot of the above discussion is that, on average, over a run of summers, the investor could expect to get £125k. However, rather than having to gamble on what might happen in any one summer, be it sometimes good and sometimes bad, the investor could choose to 'diversify' by making her investments in *both* companies. If she were to put £50k into each company she would get: a value of £100k from the sunglasses company, and of £25k from the umbrella company, should it shine; and a value of £25k from the sunglasses company, and of £100k from the umbrella company, should it rain. That is, whether it rains or shines, she certainly gets £125k. Here, diversification has successfully eliminated all investment risk. In the argot of the market, she has successfully 'hedged' her investments. The case is deliberately simple, and constructed to make a point, but illustrates this important principle very clearly. The efficacy of the example hinges on the perfect (in this case, negative) correlation between the two assets. In reality, such examples, though very valuable, are not common. Indeed, there is a tendency for stock prices to move together.[11] Provided their price movements are not perfectly positively correlated, it can be shown that there will always be at least some gain from diversification.

In Section 1.3 of the SSI, the concern shifts to screening, and to the effects of new investees on risk management. It has been observed already (see Preface) that VCIs tend to screen potential investments rigorously, in the sense of letting few investment proposals proceed forward to full appraisal, and that even those which are subject to 'due diligence' are not likely to be backed. My interest is in the rationale behind these screening procedures in terms of both risk-return considerations and portfolio diversification. For example, does the investor aim to achieve a mix of lower-risk/lower-return investments along with higher-risk/higher-return investments in his portfolio? And does the investor deliberately seek investments with uncorrelated returns, for example by aiming for a mix of sectoral and regional involvements in a portfolio?[12]

10 Compare the similar use of the terminology 'state of the world' in Chapter 4 above.

11 Typically positively, rather than negatively, though inverse stock movements across sectors are not unknown, as the example suggests.

12 If $\mathrm{var}(P)$ is the portfolio risk (measured by the expected value of the squared deviations of the returns for the portfolio from its mean value), then it may be expressed as $\mathrm{var}(P) = (1/N)\overline{\mathrm{var}(i)} + (N-1)/N\,\overline{\mathrm{cov}(i,j)}$. In this formula, N refers to the number of investments in the portfolio, $\mathrm{var}(i)$ and $\mathrm{cov}(i, j)$ refer to the variance of return on investment i and the covariance of returns between investments i and j, and bars denote average values. Then if $\overline{\mathrm{cov}(i,j)}$ were zero, all risk would be investee specific, and the term $(1/N)\overline{\mathrm{var}(i)}$ would become vanishingly small as N became large. That is, risk could be almost eliminated by holding a large number of investments. However, common factors, like interest rates and the business cycle, tend to cause a positive covariance between returns, which sets a limit on the extent to which larger portfolios can reduce risk. Even so, it is worth exercising judgement, to try to make $\overline{\mathrm{cov}(i,j)}$ as small as possible. See e.g. Tucker *et al.* (1995: ch. 2).

Finally, in Section 1.4 of the SSI, the importance of risk-sharing to the concluding of contracting is examined, very much inspired by the principles laid out in Chapter 4. The attitude to risk of the investor is further examined, as well as his judgement of the investee's attitude to risk. Then the focus is on the extent to which risk is shared between VCI and MSF, perhaps even to the extent of the investor bearing all the risk. This section of the SSI concludes by inquiring into the relationship between risk-bearing and effort. Specifically, it asks whether the VCI would always want to maintain some tension in the contractual arrangement, forcing the MSF to bear at least some risk as an inducement to effort on her part.

Section 2 of the investor's SSI schedule is concerned with information. It is plain from the analysis in Chapter 4 that the information system at the command of the investor has a major impact on the form of contracting, and, in particular, on its efficiency and its ability to elicit effort from the MSF. Yet the type of information which agency theorists have in mind is rarely specified, and they take refuge in the mysteries of 'an information set', made the more arcane by using a capital Greek letter to denote it. Section 2 of the SSI aims to demystify this convention by looking in detail at the forms information may take in VCI/MSF relations, and teasing out the attributes and qualities of this information.

Section 2.1 of the SSI looks at information types, and includes a request for documentation. It enquires into the way this information changes over time, and the extent to which the VCI has rights over the form this information assumes, or even the framework within which it is created. In Section 2.2 it turns to issues of information asymmetry between VCI and MSF. Most obviously, given the 'core' principal–agent perspective, it enquires into the informational advantage the MSF has over the VCI, and what forms this advantage takes. Thus the scope for unseen or unobserved actions by the MSF, as agent, is explored. But, more generally, there may be reciprocal agency relationships in play, so the perceived informational advantage of the VCI is also examined. This leads on to questions about sharing of information between VCI and MSF. For example, are certain types of information always freely available, while other types of information are only provided on a reciprocal exchange or trading basis?

Chapter 4 has already introduced the idea of information being used to 'signal' the underlying reality of an MSF. The rest of Section 2 of the SSI enquires into ways in which information systems may be prone to imperfect or inadequate signalling. It certainly enquires about 'noisy' signals in a narrow sense, but goes well beyond this in terms of how it views imperfect information.[13] The SSI distinguishes, for example, between information selection and noisy signalling. Information may be accurate, insofar as it faithfully reflects the reality it measures

13 In a narrow sense, 'noisy' signalling would be treated as a high variance on the signalling variable. But clearly, information imperfections can go well beyond this.

(in this sense having no noise), but, because it is incomplete in essential aspects, may be relatively uninformative. For example, the logical content of the data may not be communicated, or certain sensitive forms of information may be suppressed. In Section 2.5 of the SSI more conventional aspects of information noisiness are considered, as well as subtler difficulties like getting a conceptual grip on performance, given a variety of indicators like cash flow and profitability, and coping with unfamiliar conventions, jargon and argot that may conceal what the information was intended to reveal. The extent to which the investor can play a role in directing and controlling information is also considered, both in terms of potential influence on audit procedures, and in terms of the costs of acquiring and processing information.

It has been indicated in Chapter 4 that if unobservability is present, it is typically efficient for the entrepreneur to bear some risk. Further, there are benefits to risk-sharing which arise from monitoring, and this is at no sacrifice of entrepreneurial effort. Indeed, more reliable information can encourage increased entrepreneurial effort. With these principles in mind, the SSI concludes by investigating risk and information simultaneously. In Section 3.1 it starts by enquiring into the effect diversification has on the VCI's willingness to bear risk, and seeks to find out whether wider skills of risk management are built upon this advantage of diversification by the VCI. Then it asks how much information is shared with the investee. Here, concern is with issues like confidentiality, access to information, and the desirability or otherwise of full and free information. Next, in Section 3.3, the possibility of exchanging information for risk-bearing is investigated, and the implications that this possibility may have for the form in which information is transmitted. This leads to an enquiry, in Section 3.4 of the SSI, into the effects of risk-sharing on effort. Does imposing some level of risk on the entrepreneur keep her sharp? Would bearing all risk make her reduce effort? Is there an optimal level of risk she should bear?

The next issue, regarding effort, that is addressed in the SSI concerns the size of the VCI's equity stake. There will be a natural tendency on the part of the MSF to want the VCI to share heavily in the downside, but to want to reap most of the benefits from the upside. As a consequence, the VCI may create performance-linked equity, which encourages the MSF to produce extra effort to bring about good states of the world, but might display reluctance to increase ownership if bad outcomes occur, and it is suspected that this could have been avoided by greater effort within the MSF.

An analogy between the investors and a certain music hall artiste has been cleverly cultivated by Sharon Gifford (1995). It is that the investor is a little like the artiste who tries to keep several plates spinning at once, each on the end of a cane. There must be just enough effort allocated to each cane to keep all plates spinning. In a similar way, different investees in a portfolio compete for an investor's attention, and the investor must be sure to allocate sufficient effort to each so that all are kept afloat. Inspired by this analogy, the SSI asks whether treatment varies across investees and, if so, how this affects their behaviour.

Finally, the SSI looks at how contracts are designed to achieve efficiency. It does so in a way which recognizes both implicit and explicit contracting. Where explicit contracting was involved, an attempt was made to obtain as much documentation on it as was possible. Case study G of Chapter 10 below illustrates well the extent to which explicit contracting may be important. The work of Jones (1995) emphasizes implicit contracting, and the possibility of a rival approach to that of agency analysis, emphazising trust rather than monitoring and control. A view is then sought from the investor of what he would see as being the ideal relationship (or even optimal relationship) with the investee. This could be narrowly interpreted in terms of the contract curves and efficiency loci of Chapter 4, but may also be viewed more widely, taking into account considerations like reputation. The SSI schedule ends by providing the investor with assurances on confidentiality, and by seeking access to one or more of their investees, chosen as representative of their investee base. It was in this way that the sample of investees, used to form dyads of investors and investees, was obtained.

5.4 ADMINISTERED QUESTIONNAIRE (AQ) SCHEDULE AND TELEPHONE INTERVIEW QUESTIONNAIRE (TQ)

Many of the major design features of the instrumentation have been covered in the previous section of this chapter, but significant new considerations arise in investigating the investee side of the relationship, in terms of the entrepreneur and the MSF she runs. These largely revolve around the nature of the monitoring and control systems to which the MSF is subject, either voluntarily or at the behest of the VCI. To define the key features of these systems it is necessary to appeal to many concepts, familiar to those who work in economics, finance and especially management accounting.[14] The administration of the questionnaire was face to face, as with the SSI, this time with investees rather than investors.[15] Access to investees was gained through the tailpiece to the SSI schedule. Though a plurality of investees was requested, typically only one investee was provided, and occasionally two. The facilitating of this contact with investees by the introductions of investors was crucial to the success of the chosen way of proceeding. In all cases, investees approached on the recommendations of investors agreed to grant interviews.

The pre-letter to investees, agenda outline, basic data sheet, administered

14 Such concepts are covered at a basic textbook level in Drury (1996), at a more difficult textbook level in Lynch (1967), and at an advanced or research level in Ezzamel and Hart (1987).

15 Reference will also be made to telephone interviews with investees, using an instrument design directly derived from the AQ.

questionnaire (AQ) schedule for the MSF and the associated show cards are all available in Appendix B of the book for detailed examination. In this section I aim to give a more discursive account of the key issues explored in the AQ, to which I add motivational comments, remarks and extensions, as appropriate, much along the lines of the previous section. Where similar ground to the SSI is covered in the AQ, I shall be very brief. *A fortiori*, when the telephone interview (see Appendix C) questionnaire is considered, overlapping as it does with the AQ, my treatment will be very brief.

In administering the AQ, the interviewee received, along with the pre-letter, an interview agenda and a basic data sheet, much as with the SSI. The data sheet was rather different, given the investee rather than the investor status of the respondent, and covered quantitative information-like age, size, performance and financial structure. The AQ schedule itself worked through an agenda which covered risk management, information-handling, trading risk and information (as with the investor's SSI) and, in addition, business characteristics. The latter reinforced and augmented the material of the basic data sheet for investees as regards size, financial structure, performance, and form of exit. A significant design feature of the AQ as an instrument, compared to the SSI, was that, as a consequence of the AQ being more focused (i.e. less open-ended), a more extensive use of showcards, numbering ten in all, was made in eliciting responses.

Turning to the AQ proper, in a preamble (Section A) the bona fides of the interviewer, typically myself, were described, followed by an account of the direction and purpose of the interview. At this point, the age and line of business of the MSF were established. The next Section (B) of the AQ examined risk management. Similar questions were asked of the investee as were asked of the investor in the SSI, as regards attitude to risk in a narrow sense. The respondent was asked in one showcard whether she preferred a gamble to a value which was equal to its mathematical expectation; in another she was asked what the value of a prospective order was, which would be worth £1m. if placed, but would only be placed with a probability of a half.

Then respondents were asked to answer yes or no to each of a set of questions about more qualitative aspects of risk management including perception of chance, risk discounting, risk class, conveying risk to the investor, and insuring completely against risk (including its effort consequences). Attitudes to risk were also plumbed more generally, using a Likert scale,[16] on topics concerned with: perceived accuracy of the investor's use of risk classes; attractiveness of the investor as a partner with whom risk could be shared; and post-contract motivation since beginning to have shared risk with the investor. On matters of

16 For more information on this device, which allows respondents to place items in rank order (e.g. by intensity of preference), see Sekaran (1992: ch. 6). The original use of this scale involved making a cross on a line of unit interval to indicate intensity of preference. Modern usage tends to use a set of boxes in a similar way.

risk management by the investee to limit or modify risk exposure, and perceptions of how the investor appraised the riskiness of the MSF, respondents were given the opportunity to elaborate their views in an open-ended way, and these comments were recorded verbatim.[17] These comments have been referred to extensively in Chapter 11 below. However, in keeping with the more focused design of the AQ, as compared with the SSI, the investigation of risk management involved less discretionary responses by the investee, compared with the investor.

The next part, Section C, of the AQ looked at information-handling, and was again concerned to enrich the lean discussion of information in much formal principal–agent analysis. This section differed very much from the corresponding section in the SSI, in that it appealed extensively to management accounting concepts. The rationale behind this way of proceeding was that monitoring and control systems were installed within the MSF itself, so even when this was done at the instigation of the VCI, which was very often the case, the proper source of knowledge of their scope and construction was with the MSF.

The respondent was asked how she assessed the performance of her MSF, using measures like profitability, sales and investment turnover.[18] Here, for the first time, a characteristic feature of later question designs in the AQ was deployed. This involved determining whether such measures, if used, had been implemented at the instigation of the VCI, and whether the VCI required them to be reported to him. In other words, the process of the MSF contracting with the VCI provided a useful controlled set of circumstances. One could not only use them to examine significant shifts in terms of risk-bearing, in the quest for contract optimality, but also to detect significant shifts in monitoring and control methods. This is because these devices themselves impinge upon MSF performance, and influence the willingness of both the VCI and MSF, as partners, to share risk. Other areas in which enquiries of this sort were used included: budget setting and their frequency; cost attribution to products; and capital investment appraisal techniques.[19] The last named covered: rules of thumb, like the payback method; discounting techniques, like NPV and IRR; and qualitative assessment.[20] The importance of these methods was also appraised by respondents using a Likert scale.

17 By 'recorded', I mean physically recorded, in the sense of a written record of utterances. For a variety of reasons discussed in Chapters 3 and 6, the tape recording of respondents was rejected as a research technique.

18 That is, the ratio of sales to investment.

19 Additional questions on costs were also asked about cost categories (e.g. actual/standard, fixed/variable) and the involvement of accountants in costing design.

20 NPV refers to net present value, and IRR to internal rate of return. The payback period is the time required to bring into equality with the cost of investment the cash return on the project. The NPV is the difference between the present value of estimated future cash flows at

The extent of information asymmetry between the VCI and MSF was also investigated, this time from the perspective of the latter. The distribution of knowledge between VCI and MSF was investigated over a dozen dimensions ranging from technology and markets to business strategy and financial accounts. The extent to which broadly based classes of information, like financial data or personnel data, were subject to distortion or error was investigated using a Likert scale. Respondents were also requested to make qualitative statements about imperfections in information if they were thought to be marked.

The penultimate part of the AQ, Section D, concerned the trading of risk and information. In design, the section was created to dovetail with the corresponding section (actually Section 3) of the SSI. It investigated the investee's perception of the relative ability of the VCI and MSF to handle risk, the variety and quality of information flows between VCI and MSF, the incentive properties of contracting, and the extent to which efficiency in contracting was sought and achieved. At about half a dozen points, respondents were able to make qualitative responses to augment quantitative replies. These concerned matters like: the desire for more or less information; areas in which confidentiality over information should be retained; the effects of equity share on commitment to the MSF; and advantages to be gained, if any, by the MSF becoming better informed about the VCI's operational capabilities. As in the SSI, attitudes to performance-linked equity schemes were examined, this time from the perspective of the MSF. This part of the AQ concluded by exploring trust and optimality in contracting, again in a way which paralleled the treatment in the SSI. The AQ as an instrument had a final part on business characteristics. While reinforcing part of the data requested in the basic data sheet that went out with the pre-letter, it also explored further issues like capital structure, rate of return and expected exit. The interview with the investor concluded by making requests for documentation, which were usually granted, and by providing both thanks and assurances on confidentiality.

To conclude this chapter on instrumentation, I turn to the questionnaire administered by telephone interview (TQ). I shall be brief, as essentially the TQ was created by pruning the content of the AQ, and by creating new design features that were better suited to a remote, rather than a face-to-face, interaction. The rationale for using telephone interviews has already been discussed in terms of the desire to create an extraneous sample of investees. Further sampling details are contained in Chapter 6. The investees were approached first by pre-letter. As well as requesting access, and providing the usual orientation, this letter asked respondents to complete three tables before the telephone interview. These

management's desired rate of return, less the cost of the project. The IRR is that rate of discount which equates the present value of future cash inflows with the cost of the project. The MSF was explicitly asked what discount rate was used in capital investment appraisals.

concerned: attitude to risk; the most important attributes of the VCI and the MSF in contracting; and the significance, measured by a Likert scale, of certain features conducive to best outcomes in contracting, including efficient risk-sharing, free sharing of information and the increasing of motivation. In piloting and role-playing with a test instrument, it was found that these three areas were particularly troublesome and time consuming to use in telephone interviews, hence the adoption of this novel, but useful, protocol.

As an examination of Appendix C to this book will confirm, the pattern of the TQ very much follows that of the AQ. As before, Sections B, C and D are on risk management, information-handling and the trading of risk and information respectively. Again, a final section dealt with business characteristics, including size, gearing, control and rate of return. By compression and rephrasing, much of the content of the AQ was retained in the TQ. The main economy in administration of this instrument was achieved by excising the material which allowed respondents to make open-ended responses. This was regrettable, but a necessary price to be paid for using this efficient alternative method for augmenting the sample size of investees. Of particular value to the research was the fact that where a similar topic is investigated in the TQ, the question format is virtually identical to the AQ, so that responses recorded are entirely compatible, in a sampling sense, with those made in the face-to-face interviews. This is useful when it comes to discussing investee attributes in Chapter 7, as the samples obtained from the AQ and TQ can be pooled whenever questions correspond. This significantly increases knowledge about investees' characteristics and behaviour.

5.5 CONCLUSION

This chapter has been about the 'tools of the trade' of fieldwork. Three instruments have been described, and their design features have been explained in terms of their use in exploring agency issues. The common general features of all three instruments, be it for investor or investee, were that issues were always explored under the headings of risk management, information-handling, and the trading of risk and information. This instrumentation having been described and explained, the task remains of showing in the next chapter how the fieldworkers' tools were put to work.

6

FIELDWORK

6.1 INTRODUCTION

Methods of investigation in economics, management and finance, of which this book provides an example, have become more pluralistic as time has progressed, as demonstrated by Ryan *et al.* (1992). Influences from other sciences, both natural and social, have been admitted, like positivism.[1] There has been a decreasing reliance on secondary source data. These data are to be criticized on the grounds that they are usually gathered for other purposes than the study at hand (e.g. for tax assessment). Further, it is common to proceed without adopting any conscious theoretical framework for data gathering.[2] At the same time, perhaps as a reaction to this, there has been an increasing enthusiasm for the acquisition of primary source data which are targeted at a particular research area. Venture capital investment has enjoyed some celebrity for attracting investigations which proceed in this way (e.g. Sapienza 1989). This method allows the investigator the luxury of utilizing a specific analytical perspective, like principal–agent analysis, for determining the way in which data are gathered. For example, such a perspective may run in terms of the interrelationships between variables and economic actors. To illustrate, who reports what, to whom, in VCI/MSF relationships? Alternatively, the analytical framework is allowed to emerge incrementally and inductively, as suggested by the data-acquisition process itself.[3] The study by

1 A conspectus of research methods and methodology as related to finance and accounting, though covering much that is also of interest to economists, is contained in the volume mentioned in the main text by Ryan *et al.* (1992). For more of a business studies emphasis on similar themes, see Sekaran (1992).

2 Though often implicit theoretical perspectives are taken, which makes the data difficult to use for exploring any alternative perspectives, thus further encouraging effort to obtain primary source data.

3 This is the so-called grounded theory approach of Glaser and Strauss (1967), which allows hypotheses to be constructed based on emerging evidence as the fieldwork progresses. It is these hypotheses, rather than the data themselves, which are 'the results' (or outcomes) of the research.

Steier and Greenwood (1995) provides an example of the use of this methodology in a venture capital context. Illustrative of this trend to pluralism is the plea by Lawson (1985) for the use of more case histories and personal histories, and the emphasis of Carlsson (1987) on the value of primary source data. Even specialists in economic theory like Flaherty (1984) have admitted the value of fieldwork in generating and stimulating hypotheses (in her case, concerning technological change and growth in the international semiconductor industry).

Primary source data collection takes many forms. It may use indirect methods, like postal questionnaires or surveys, as in Fiet's (1995) analysis of risk-avoidance strategies by investors. Alternatively, it may use direct methods. These may be highly intensive, involving participant observation, as in the study of a major UK venture capital firm by Masey (1993). Or they may be less extensive, ranging from unstructured interviews, through structured interviews, as in Sweeting's (1991b) analysis of venture capital funding of new technology-based business, to administered questionnaires, as in Dixon's (1991) interview-based study of thirty large UK venture capital funds. The investigator, in choosing a technique, has to bear in mind considerations of resource constraints, access to the field, participant consent, and data complexity.[4] To amplify: fieldwork methods are time intensive, and therefore constitute a relatively costly research technique; ports of entry to the field may be privileged, and may require a process of accreditation or legitimization before they can be accessed; participants in the field may be reluctant to contribute, and their willingness to be examined may require respect for, and sensitivity towards, areas of confidentiality, requiring the building up of trust before revealing information is forthcoming; and the data gathered are themselves potentially very complex, which makes them difficult (and costly) to store, analyse and interpret.

In the context of this study, the fieldwork necessitated travel throughout the UK regions. It involved meeting up directly both with venture capitalists (VCs) and with personnel (typically directors) of mature small firms (MSFs) in whom the VCs invested. Access to the field followed on from relationships built up during early unstructured fieldwork involving the meeting of key players in the venture capital world, to legitimize presence in this arena. Beyond that, the willingness of investors to provide referrals to their investees was necessary, which required building up both trust in the investigator and comfort with the method of investigation.

The willingness to participate on the part of VCs, and to provide referrals to MSFs, was facilitated by a protocol of confidentiality and a promised method of reporting that would mask identities and avoid exposing data when they were still

4 For a general account of fieldwork methods and strategies, see Schatzman and Strauss (1973), and Burgess (1982, 1984).

market sensitive. The data collected were of diverse forms, including: qualitative, textual evidence, based on respondents' responses to enquiries, structured around an itemized agenda; quantitative evidence (real, binary and categorical) obtained from respondents' completed data sheets about their operations; and documentary evidence, including accounts, brochures, product descriptions, price lists and company histories. The first two classes of information were entered into a database enabling analysis to proceed (e.g. cross-site analysis) in terms of both textual ('string') variables and quantitative variables.[5]

All these considerations came into play in the research being reported upon in this book, and the purpose of this brief chapter is to show how they were addressed, what problems were thereby generated, and how they were solved. It considers first what is involved in going into the field, in terms of frameworks adopted. Then fieldwork methods are examined with an emphasis on face-to-face interviewing techniques. Next, sampling methods and the implications they have for analysis are considered. The chapter ends with a conclusion which establishes a background for looking in further detail, in the next chapter, at the two main players examined in the fieldwork, namely, the investor and the investee.

6.2 IN THE FIELD

Fieldwork methods enable the investigator to seek an understanding of the universe which he or she is exploring (in this case, the venture capital world), in a way which takes account of the context of the situation. The relations between players in the financial community, as in a village community, a family or a sect, are governed by rules and a vocabulary. Thus there are rules like 'my word is my bond', and argot with phrases like 'burn rate' and 'down and dirty'.[6] Procedures that are adopted (e.g. concluding a contract) and the words used to describe them (e.g. 'we decided we were happy to go to bed together') are dependent on a cultural background which must be understood if the words used to describe and explain situations are to make proper sense. Often, academics have been regarded as rather ineffective when they first encounter new cultural contexts, hence perhaps their preference for secondary source data. It is dangerous, certainly, to suppose that what an academic regards as a well-defined word in a

5 See Reid (1992), where methodological and computing issues surrounding the construction of databases of this mixed quantitative/qualitative form are discussed. A more general account of database theory and practice is Frank (1984).

6 On the argot of the venture capital world, see Gladstone (1988), though note also that it is constantly mutating. The 'burn rate' refers to the monthly rate at which a company spends cash, and 'down and dirty' refers to a round of equity, injected when a company is doing badly, which is highly diluting.

certain vocabulary (e.g. the word 'risk' in the vocabulary of financial analysts) assumes the same precision, or even same meaning at all, in a variety of contexts or situations (e.g. among entrepreneurs in a business start-up).

Pushing this argument to the limit, the gathering of data by actually speaking to people (preferably face to face, rather than over the telephone) has the greatest potential to generate insight into the object of analysis – in my case the investor/investee nexus in the venture capital world. However, speaking to people places special demands on the investigator. It requires one to think in a certain way, which involves sharing a vocabulary (e.g. as regards accounting, law and management), and accepting certain institutional constraints (e.g. the confidentiality of the investor/investee relationship). The natural desire to get as large a sample of primary source data as possible creates the temptation to use postal survey methods.[7] While this has clear advantages over the use of secondary source data (e.g. closer correspondence between theoretical terms, like 'portfolio balance', and its empirical equivalent, like the number and variety of investees), it still stops well short of harvesting the advantages of primary source data collection by going out in the field. However, the fieldwork involvement itself can vary considerably in intensity, from a brief ten-minute interview to participant observation, so its value too is variable rather than constant.

This study into venture capital investor/investee relations took an intermediate position. It eschewed participant observation of the sort that laid the basis for the TV documentary, and companion book, *The Adventurers* (Masey 1993), and instead scaled-up the interview method to something relatively detailed and complex. Briefly, the initial fieldwork was unstructured and involved familiarization with many aspects of the venture capital world (e.g. key players, physical locations, standard literature, leading institutions). This was followed, as described in Chapter 5, by the administration of distinct semi-structured interviews and questionnaires to pairs of investors and investees ('dyads').[8] Finally, further information on investees was obtained using two telephone interview schedules: one, a scaled-down version of the investee semi-structured interview schedule (see Chapter 5 above), and the other a custom-designed schedule for investigating the extent of funding shortages among mature small firms.[9]

In applying the method of 'grounded theory' (Glaser and Strauss 1967)

7 In the context of venture capital, see studies like those of Fiet (1995), Barney *et al.* (1994) and Landström (1992).

8 For other 'dyad' studies of investors and investees in the venture capital world, see the seminal work of Sapienza (1989), where twenty-seven investees were interviewed face to face, and fifteen investees by telephone. Also, see Steier and Greenwood (1995) which examines one such dyad relationship longitudinally; and Landström (1990) which looks at three investors and their (sometimes multiple) investees.

9 However, this latter study will not be reported upon here. It is fully considered in Reid (1996a), and the instrumentation is reported in Reid and Anderson (1992).

which involves the use of techniques like face-to-face interviews, data are recognized as creating or generating a narrative: they have a story to tell. Theory construction may proceed from an inductive base, to which is added deductive elements involving conceptualization, elaboration and formulation. While not slavishly adopting this approach, which has found its strongest advocates in areas like ethnography, sociology, social psychology and social anthropology, this study of venture capital has been influenced by it, especially in its use of early unstructured fieldwork to suggest an appropriate frame of reference and in its favouring of face-to-face interview methods. In the event, the theory utilized – that of principal–agent analysis – was one already available from work conducted in other areas (notably the insurance literature, where problems of moral hazard and adverse selection are ubiquitous). However, the choice of this general framework, and especially the particular, indeed unique, formulation of it for the investor/investee case, were very much dictated by 'grounded theory', that is, by 'the story' that the earliest collected data were telling.

The approach adopted in the early unstructured fieldwork was deliberately very open.[10] I spoke to a range of players with an interest in the venture capital world. They included both active players, and what might be called observers of play. The former category included people with personal duties or tasks of portfolio composition and monitoring, for a range of investment involvements. The latter category included people who had a duty of oversight over venture capital activity in general, or a wider interest in the funding nexus itself (e.g. from the standpoint of a public policy body, or a non-venture capital private financial institution). What emerged from this unstructured fieldwork was that: (a) venture capital investment was a potentially risky investment involvement, but that risk exposure was not passively accepted by the investor, it was 'managed'; and (b) information exchanges between investor and investee were rich and varied, and aimed both to improve the knowledge of each party, and to satisfy certain incentive criteria. It was apparent that how risk was managed varied greatly across investors, and that information systems had different designs and properties. But a common characteristic was that risk management and information-handling were central to investor–investee relations.

6.3 FIELDWORK METHODS

In carrying out the fieldwork, key players in the UK venture capital industry, including past Presidents of the BVCA, were interviewed personally, as well as

10 So-called focus interviews were carried out, which are highly unstructured and aimed at suggesting future approaches and frameworks.

the investors and investees of the sample. These interviews constituted a focus of cognitive and visual attention, ensuring a high quality and good volume of information. In this sense, they had considerable advantages over postal questionnaire methods.[11] Such interviews were in the nature of social encounters or interactions, and as no clear cut rules or norms existed these had to be established quickly and precisely. When it came to the structured fieldwork, as Chapter 5 has indicated, this was facilitated by the design of the instruments (SSI, AQ, TQ, respectively), which effected a standard introduction, and laid down ground rules and background information as the interviews progressed.

When the content of the questions was sensitive, as when it related to emotive issues (e.g. the effort level of the investee), or when there was a limited basis for trust between parties (e.g. when areas of confidentiality between investor and investee were probed), it was important to proceed with caution and discretion. A cardinal principle which I adopted in conducting the fieldwork was to ensure that interviews, as social encounters, did not collapse, either by the interviewee refusing to participate further or by only doing so in an unhelpful way, both being known problems of the fieldwork method. Fortunately, pre-testing of the instrumentation, through role-playing interviews within the research team, teased out such potential problem areas before encounters in the field proper; and this, allied to the good nature and long sufferance of interviewees, ensured all agreed interviews were successful social transactions. Another difficulty to be finessed, arising from the 'one-off' nature of the encounters, was that of ensuring that investors and investees, as interviewees, did not attempt to present themselves in unusually flattering ways. Here, one had to avoid being what is sometimes called 'the conspicuous listener', with my role being to listen to responses without denial, contradiction or competition. The role of the pre-letter, and the standard text used to guide the direction and progression of the interviews, was to motivate, through sense of duty, personal satisfaction and interest in the topic, the involvement of investors and investees alike in the interview process and its outcome.

It was established with respondents that the interviews were the subject of a legitimate academic need, which had importance to the construction of a general and useful body of knowledge about the venture capital industry and its functioning. Respondents were given assurances on selection, confidentiality and the form of the enquiry, and the extent of involvement required, and it was important that these assurances were honoured in the conduct of the fieldwork.[12] In

11 To contrast methods, consider the thorough work of Fiet (1995) in which, even after four rounds of mailed surveys of 245 subjects (US venture capitalists), only 141 usable responses were obtained (a response rate of 57 per cent).

12 For example, confidentiality was reinforced by only identifying respondents by code letters or numbers; and the deal sensitivity was respected by only reporting on activities after three or more years had elapsed since the fieldwork.

conducting interviews, my goal was to be visibly attentive, non-judgemental, communicative and empathetic, but always in control.

In terms of data collection within the field, questions were designed to elicit a steady flow of information from respondents, all directed towards illuminating key features of investor/investee interactions. Although respondents were allowed to be relatively unconstrained in expressing views and conveying information, the overall pattern adhered broadly to interview agenda, and the detailed pattern was related directly to the coded items in the instrumentation.[13]

For example, in the course of face-to-face interviews the main headings of the interview agenda, so far as 'information' was concerned, were: types of information, asymmetries of information, sharing and trading information, information selection, information error, and costs of information.[14] Interviews started in June 1992, gained tempo month by month, and were concluded by September 1993. In face-to-face interviews, two researchers were involved in each instance, one as interviewer, typically me, and one as recorder, typically a research assistant.

Early experience in the field had suggested that tape-recording interviews led to huge volumes of evidence which were expensive to transcribe, difficult to analyse, and were generally overlain with problems of redundancy, irrelevance, repetition and overdetermination. Earlier work (Reid *et al.* 1993) on small business strategy, involving the use of semi-structured interviews, suggested that note-taking was an efficient and economical way of being able to reconstruct the interview encounter. It permitted a natural and continuous sieving of information as the interview proceeded, which ensured salience and intelligibility in what was reported. The structure of the instruments, including the use of numerical 'layering' of responses, enabled the reported responses to be naturally coded, and then entered on a database as string variables. An important aspect of reporting was to capture apposite direct quotes. This protocol proved highly satisfactory, and produced a good quality of data, recorded in the same sequence, and on the same basis for each respondent, all in a framework which proved useful both for framing summaries of the data and for detecting patterns in, or suggesting insights from, the data. Interviews varied in duration from one-and-a-half hours to two-and-a-half hours, very much influenced by the personal style of the respondent. As well as interview material, accounting data, financial PR, brochures, etc., were also collected. The site visit typically also involved a tour of the office or production facility, and introductions to key personnel within the MSF were normal. In the case of VCIs, the interviewees' firms accounted for over three-quarters of UK venture capital provision. Based

13 See Appendices A, B and C at the end of the book, and also the discussion of instrumentation in Chapter 5.

14 Other areas of the agenda, relating to risk, and to the trading of risk and information, were similarly decomposed.

on available biographies,[15] venture capitalist interviewees (who were nominated by their firms) had, in general, considerable (typically, twelve years') experience in the venture capital industry, and were often familiar with accounting methods, for example through possessing a professional accounting qualification or having qualifications in finance, economics or business. Among the full-time executives of each VC fund there was almost inevitably an accountant, though this person was not always nominated as the interviewee for the study. In short, both the organizations examined and the personnel within them were very information oriented, which made this novel aspect of the investigation less daunting to conduct than I had initially anticipated. One naturally thought that venture capitalists and entrepreneurs would be thoughtful about, and able to express views upon, risk; but one was less confident that they could be equally engaged by discussions on information. Fortunately, this misgiving was ill-founded.

Finally, to conclude this section on fieldwork methods, I should mention that when it proved impossible to fund further face-to-face interviews with investees, particularly in the far-flung places in which some MSFs were located, a telephone interview procedure was adopted.[16] This required significant modifications to the administered questionnaire (AQ) instrument, essentially recasting and pruning, to produce the telephone interview administered questionnaire (TQ). This was both piloted with MSFs and pre-tested in simulated interviews, with different personnel playing the roles of investigators and investees according to different briefings. Each interview for the study proper took twenty to thirty minutes over the telephone. It was also possible in some cases to persuade the responding investee to post on further information about the MSF, like company accounts. In conducting these telephone interviews as adjuncts to the main fieldwork, the principles of best practice in the use of this method were followed.[17]

6.4 SAMPLING AND ANALYSIS

Essentially three types of sampling procedures lie behind the data collection and fieldwork aspects of the research. First, there was sampling of the investors,

15 Documented, for example, in all editions of the *Venture Capital Report Guide to Venture Capital in the UK and Europe*, which has been edited by venture capitalist Lucius Cary since 1983 (when attention was first on the UK alone).

16 The main motivation for doing so was the relative lack of information about investees. The investor case studies were augmented with a wider body of panel data on investors. Such evidence is not readily available for investees, hence the desire to conduct telephone interviews.

17 See, for example, the advice embodied in the work of Frey (1983), which was closely followed in terms of constructing the pre-letter, identifying oneself, explaining the purpose of the interview, conducting the interview, and achieving closure of the interview.

which was based on the two major financial centres in the UK, London (predominantly) and also Edinburgh.[18] Second, there was sampling of investees paired with investors (in so-called dyads), with choices being made by investees. Third, there was sampling from the wider body of investees, as reported in the *Venture Capital Guide* (Cary 1989).[19]

The first process involved establishing, through use of an alphabetic list of leading investors given in the *VCR Guide*, who would be available to participate in the study. This involved both mail and telephone contact, and some reference to earlier unstructured fieldwork to assist in legitimizing the enquiry. After some negotiating, a sample of twenty participating investors was composed, which included the main players on the UK venture capital scene, plus a number of emerging and new players. The total funds at their disposal, across all portfolios, made up the bulk of UK venture capital involvement.

Figure 6.1 displays the locations of the investors in the UK, indicating their concentration in and around London and Edinburgh, with very little provincial activity. This diagram might be usefully compared with the more general one provided by Mason and Harrison (1991a: 228) which shows even more clearly London and the South East, and Scotland as the dominant regions for total capital invested by the BVCA members.

The specific person who made access to the functioning of the fund possible (sometimes called 'the channel' in fieldwork argot) was asked to nominate one or more investees who were typical of their investment involvements, and in this way sixteen paired investees were obtained, four of which came in two pairs, each pair with the same investor.[20] In addition, a further fourteen investees were selected by random sampling from lists in the *VCR Guide*. While the investees nominated by the investors tended to have some proximity to them,[21] this is not an inevitable outcome, and is perhaps less likely the more VCI/MSF relations approximate to the laissez-faire, rather than to the 'close tracker', mould.[22] The

18 Outside London, Edinburgh is the dominant financial centre in the UK and, indeed, rivals other major European financial centres like Frankfurt. At the time of the fieldwork, more than 25,000 people were employed in financial services in Edinburgh. It was the home of two major independent banks, six major life assurance companies, including Europe's largest mutual fund, seven merchant banks, three security brokers and the full range of financial support services.

19 Specifically, the *Venture Capital Report Guide to Venture Capital in the UK* (Cary 1989).

20 Put another way, fourteen dyads were obtained, two of which involved multiple (specifically, two) investees.

21 This is known to be a common feature of VCI/MSF involvement. See Lerner (1995), where it is reported that 47 per cent of VCIs in his US sample were within five miles of their MSFs. In Landström's (1992) Swedish sample, the distance between VCI and MSF was less than 250 km in 79 per cent of cases, and less than 50 km in 60 per cent of cases. To emphazise the point, one notes that the coast-to-coast distance in many parts of the UK is less than 250 km.

22 On this distinction, see Macmillan *et al.* (1988).

former case is more likely, the less the VCI takes on seedcorn and start-up involvements, and the more the VCI takes on development capital involvements.

As Figure 6.2 indicates, the locations of investees were quite widely dispersed, compared to investors. While there is some approach to what Bygrave and Timmons (1992: 258) called an 'entrepreneurial metropolis' in the case of Edinburgh and, especially, London, the wide dispersion of investees suggests that in a compact nation like the UK, with excellent, rapid transportation networks, lack of physical proximity between investor and investee is usually not a complete impediment to contracting. In terms of the execution of the fieldwork, the division of territory for interview purposes was, roughly, Scotland, North East

Figure 6.1 Locations of investors in the UK
Note: + denotes investors' locations

Figure 6.2 Locations of investees in the UK
Note: * denotes investees' locations

England and London, with more outlying investees (e.g. in Cornwall, Devon, Norfolk) being approached through telephone rather than face-to-face interviews.

It will be observed that, in the sampling procedures used, the general desire was to appeal to ideas of representative or statistically random samples, rather than judgement, 'snowball' or theoretical samples. Despite being influenced by grounded theory, especially in its regard for the inductive approach, this study stops well short of methods which deliberately guide sample composition. Theoretical sampling seeks new evidence that will cast light on an emerging theory or hypothesis suggested by the data. The bare bones of a theory can emerge as data are being classified, very often by creating new categories which have potential theoretical significance (e.g. business angels). The method of theoretical sampling would say that once this process has been started, further evidence should be selectively gathered to 'saturate' these categories (i.e. to confirm fully their existence). Once created, such saturated categories, in which the investigator now has considerable confidence, become the building blocks of a new theory (e.g. of informal investment), and enable the investigator to generate hypotheses as the outcome of the process of data collection and analysis.

By contrast, with statistical sampling, because one is typically drawing from universal distributions of attributes where a lot of the 'weight' of the density function is around the average values, much of what one observes in statistical samples is around average in terms of attributes. The potentially highly informative, non-average data (being informative, just because they are *not* very average) are underrepresented in this approach, as compared to the theoretical sampling approach. In the work being reported upon here, the sample is sufficiently large[23] that less reliance needs to be placed on alternatives to statistical sampling; and the extensive use of case study methods, and all the insights into theory construction which they generate, is not thereby denied (see Part 3 below). While not generally using case studies to generate hypotheses, the approach in this book is to explore the 'fit' of case studies with a particular theoretical approach, principal–agent analysis. As Ryan *et al.* (1992: 117) point out, science is based on a logic of replication, and one can therefore regard case studies as being like experiments which ask whether observations comply with (i.e. 'fit') a particular theory. Thus case studies seek the basis for 'theoretical generalization' (i.e. how wide is the scope of applicability of this theory?) rather than 'statistical generalization' (i.e. how typical are certain relationships in the population as a whole?). The first approach focuses on explanation, and the second on regularity.

6.5 CONCLUSION

The purpose of this chapter has been to provide insight into the data-gathering process which lay behind this research. In itself, this raises significant methodological issues, of which the most important concerns the purpose of, and end served by, case studies constructed from this fieldwork. I would agree with the approach of Yin (1984) to case studies, which emphasizes their importance to theoretical generalization rather than their statistical representativeness. I believe the latter category has not been neglected in any way in the fieldwork design, but

23 E.g. twenty investors, as compared with the three investors in the analysis of Sweeting (1991).

always the greater emphasis was on gathering 'thick data' that have the potential of playing a large explanatory role in illuminating VCI/MSF relationships. However, before turning to explore the construction of specific cases (Part 3), and developing their cross-site implications (Part 4), I will now extend the brief statistical accounts of investor and investee characteristics sketched in Chapters 1 and 2. Given the sampling procedures adopted, as explained above, these accounts will provide reasonable insights into population characteristics, even though the main thrust of the research reported upon is explanatory.

7

INVESTOR AND INVESTEE CHARACTERISTICS

7.1 INTRODUCTION

The research on which this book is based has available to it several bodies of data, which are useful for description and characterization, case study treatment, and cross-site analysis. This material is deployed in such diverse fashions throughout the book that a single chapter devoted to laying out clearly what the evidence says about investors and investees seemed likely to perform a useful organizing function. If it also stimulates analytical insights, and enriches the case study evidence, so much the better. However, the more prosaic purpose of the chapter is simply to identify the main characteristics of the investors and investees who appear in manifold situations throughout the rest of the book.

7.2 EVIDENCE ON INVESTORS AND INVESTEES

The available evidence on investors and investees has been mentioned briefly in Chapters 1 and 2, and may be summarized as follows. Concerning venture capital investors (VCIs), there are three bodies of data. First, there is information from the semi-structured interviews (SSI) with twenty investors, based on the interviews per se. Second, there is information from the associated basic data sheets. Third, there is information from three cross-sections of data for the leading UK venture capital funds. These cross-sections relate to years leading up to the fieldwork, namely, 1988, 1990 and 1992, and there are 47, 48 and 38 funds, respectively, in each cross-section. These cross-sections take the form of a 'panel' in the sense that the same funds are tracked, cross-section by cross-section, if they are still functioning.[1] The data available on funds in this panel follow a format which

1 Because some funds may not stay in existence – and indeed do not over the period observed – the panel is known as 'unbalanced'. Features of this unbalanced panel have already been examined in Chapter 2.

is close to that described in Chapter 5 for the basic data sheets of the semi-structured interviews (SSI) conducted with VCIs.[2]

Turning now to the investees, a hint of their attributes has already been given in Chapter 1. They are mature small firms (MSFs) run by entrepreneurs and, again, there are three bodies of data, but this time they are of slightly different forms. First, there is information from the interviews with those MSFs which were in the dyads, conducted using an administered questionnaire (AQ). Second, there is evidence from the associated investees' basic data sheets.[3] Third, there is information obtained from conducting telephone interviews with an extraneous sample of fourteen investees, using a specially designed administered questionnaire (TQ).[4]

Generally, the SSI and AQ will be exploited in qualitative terms, this being a consequence of their intrinsic design features. Therefore, much of this chapter will be concerned with the second and third types of data for both VCIs and MSFs. However, as a matter of orientation, especially for Part 3 of this book on case studies, Table 7.1 displays the cases for which complete dyads are available, identifying the preference of the VCI by sectoral involvement with the investee and business type, and indicating the actual line of business for the investee (MSF) with which a contract was concluded. The most common business type among investors in the dyads table is an independent, followed by a bank (or its subsidiary). This is also true of the full sample of twenty VCIs for which the SSI was conducted. It will be observed that, generally, the VCI did not have strong industrial preference. But, to the extent that some preference was displayed, there appeared little difficulty in getting an investee to match this preference. This is no doubt a consequence of VCIs having a very wide field of potential investees upon which they can draw. The core businesses of the MSFs were diverse, but there was perhaps less involvement with services than might have been expected in a UK economy which is now predominantly service based. Manufacturing activity is generally well represented, very often in technically advanced areas. From funeral and hotel services, to combustion equipment, instrumentation, and speciality paper, one gets the impression of secure investment on the part of VCIs, rather than adventuring, confirming views expressed earlier in this volume, that there is a general reluctance for VCIs in the UK to get involved with high-technology MSFs. While Case J is a signal exception to this, and Case L a mild exception, this is the overall picture presented by the evidence.

2 For further details on the investors' basic sheet for the SSI, see Appendix A to this book.

3 For further detail on the investees' basic data sheet for the AQ, see Appendix B to this book. There were sixteen such investees, counting two extra distinct cases of multiple agents for single principles, and fourteen basic data sheets. Their basic data sheets covered size, monitoring, investment appraisal, performance, financial structure, rate of return and exit.

4 For further details of the telephone-administered questionnaire (TQ), see Appendix C to this book.

Table 7.1 Features of investor–investee (VCI–MSF) dyads

	Investor (VCI)		Investee (MSF)		
Case	*Industrial preference*	*Type*[1]	*Size*[2]	*Age*[3]	*Line of business*
D	None	1	8	4	Funeral directors
E	None	1	55	3	Manufacturer of studbolt and fastener products
F	Manufacturing	4	193	3	Manufacture of combustion equipment and refractories
G	Open; but liked media-related businesses	4	30	16	Computer systems for retailers
H	Generally open; some preference for high-tech	5	840	70	Speciality papers and boards
J	Generally open, but liked high-tech	1	50	7	(1) Pharmaceutical manufacture
			41	10	(2) *In vitro* diagnostic equipment
K	None	2	735	31	Manufacturer of electronic printed circuit boards
L	Innovative, engineering	1	7	4	Carbohydrate synthesis and analysis
M	Health care, IT, environment	1	35	10	Environmental services
P	None	5	97	7	(1) Oilfield operations, service and support
			80	3	(2) Hotel services
Q	None	5	35	60	Distribution of ladies' separates
R	None	5	270	17	Instrumentation and electrical engineering

Source: Basic data sheets for investors and investees (see Appendices A and B).

Notes:

1 *Type* denotes business type for the VCI, coded as follows:
1 independent, 2 subsidiary, 3 investment managers, 4 public sector, and 5 bank (or a subsidiary).

2 *Size* denotes MSF's number of employees.

3 *Age* denotes the number of years the MSF has been in business.

The MSFs can be very 'mature', with some long-lived firms being represented, two of which (Cases H and Q) extend over several generations. The mean age of MSFs in Table 7.1 is seventeen years, which is brought down from an undoubtedly higher modal age for this subsample by several very young MSFs. While a few of these (e.g. Cases L, J and D) are close to inception, some (e.g. Cases F and P2) involved businesses which had been relaunched. Even some of the most modern forms of enterprise (Cases J2 and M) had quite long track records before VCI involvement. On this evidence the characterization of 'mature' which has been adopted for the investees in this book is appropriate. The size of the MSFs, in terms of employment, ranges from the small to the medium.[5] Only Cases H, K and R in Table 7.1 are beyond the small-firm category, having employment sizes of over two hundred. There are even two micro-firms in the investee list (Cases D and L). The mean employment size for this group of investees is 167, clearly below the threshold of 200. Going beyond the MSFs involved in the dyads of Table 7.1 to the full set of investees, including the extraneous sample of fourteen which was analysed using the TQ, the average employment size of MSFs is just 185, and the average age is a full nine years. The latter is shorter than the seventeen year average for investees in Table 7.1, but still indicates a considerable maturity in the sample of investees. One concludes that the expression 'mature small firm' (MSF) generally provides an apt description for investees involved with UK venture capital funds. I turn now to treating investors and investees individually and in greater detail.

7.3 CHARACTERISTICS OF THE INVESTOR (VCI)

The sample frame of investors was given by the alphabetic listing of venture capital funds in the *Venture Capital Report* (Cary 1989), which provides a comprehensive listing of active venture capital investors in the UK. A simple random sample of twenty was selected, and the selected venture capitalists were approached by pre-letter, and subsequently by telephone, with a view to arranging a face-to-face semi-structured interview.[6] If it was not possible to conclude an interview, the next name on the list was selected. The original sample

5 Definitions vary. The European Commission definition of small and medium-sized enterprises (SME) is that the number of full-time employees in such firms should be less than 500. This is split up as follows: micro (0–9); small (10–99) and medium (100–499). See Storey (1994: ch. 2) for this and other definitions. Note that, in the UK, the Department of Trade and Industry (DTI) has recently released statistics on SMEs in the UK which adopt the convention, in terms of employees, of small (0–49), medium (50–249) and large (250+). On this definition, three of the investees in Table 7.1 are large (Cases H, K and R). The DTI definitions are in accord with the Companies Act 1985, which says: A company qualifies as a small company in a particular financial year if, for that year, two or more of the following conditions are satisfied: (a) the amount of its turnover for the year should not exceed £2.8m., and this amount must be adjusted proportionately in the case of an accounting period greater or less than twelve months; (b) its balance sheet total should not exceed £1.4m.; (c) its average number of employees should not exceed 50, calculated on a monthly basis. For a medium-sized company, the corresponding conditions are: (a) turnover not more than £11.2m.; (b) balance sheet total of not more than £5.6m.; (c) average number of employees not more than 250. Again, a minimum of two of these conditions must be satisfied. See BPP (1997), *Financial Reporting* text for CIMA.

6 For the busy reader who has started the book by dipping into this chapter, it should be remarked that complete details on instrumentation and sampling are given in Chapters 5 and 6 respectively.

frame had forty-seven funds in it, and the sample selected had twenty funds in it. Table 7.2 lists the main characteristics of the population and sample, giving mean values for each characteristic, with the standard deviations in brackets. There is a general similarity between the characteristics of the sample of funds and the population of funds. Thus the funds under management, average value of investment, minimum and maximum equity stakes and numbers of venture capital executives are similar between sample and population.

Table 7.2 Main characteristics of VCI for sample and population

	(1) *Sample values* (*n* = 20)	*(2)* *Population values* (*n* = 38)
Vcfund (£m.)	67.3	72.9
	(60.2)	(93.9)
Averg (£m.)	0.98	0.78
	(1.12)	(0.65)
Mineq	6.1	6.3
	(8.2)	(6.7)
Maxeq	57.6	56.7
	(19.6)	(18.2)
Freqin	15.5	11.4
	(6.1)	(2.2)
Employ	26.6	14.0
	(37.7)	(16.6)
Timescale	5.0	7.9
	(1.2)	(2.3)
Newinv	15.4	10.2
	(20.8)	(10.4)
Vcexec	7.0	6.5
	(6.2)	(4.3)
Tfunval (£m.)	66.0	32.6
	(80.6)	(17.2)

Notes:

(a) Mean values, with standard deviations in brackets.

(b) *Definitions of variables:*

Vcfund	Venture capital funds under management (£m.)
Averg	Average value of investments made (£m.)
Mineq	Minimum equity stake taken (per cent)
Maxeq	Maximum equity stake taken (per cent)
Freqin	Number of involvements per annum with investee
Employ	Total number of employees
Timescale	Timescale for investment (in years)
Newinv	Number of new investments made each year
Vcexec	Total number of full-time venture capital executives
Tfunval	Total value of funds invested at valuation (£m.)

(c) *Sampling frame* based on listing of 47 funds in Cary (1989), *Venture Capital Report: Guide to Venture Capital in the UK*, 4th edition. Sample values in column (1) are based on a random sample of twenty from this listing, with values obtained during interviews. Population values in column (2) are based on 6th edition of same work (Cary 1993), computed for 38 remaining funds from original sampling frame.

For example, venture capital funds under management were £67.3m. and £72.9m. in the sample and population respectively. The sampled VCIs tended to be more frequently involved with investees, to make more new investments per year, and to have a shorter timescale to exit, but none of these differences are marked. There are two notable exceptions to this, both size related: the total value of funds invested, and the total number of employees. The latter has a high sample standard deviation (37.6), mainly because two major VCIs had 106 and 150 employees respectively. With them excluded, the mean employment in the sample was just 13.8, which was similar to the population value. One VCI had a total value of funds invested which was over twice as large as the next investor by size. Thus while a useful feature of the sample is that it is representative in that it includes the two largest players in the UK venture capital market, in a sense, being the largest, these VCIs are not typical, and this has a large leverage on mean values. Subject to this caveat, the sample appears to provide a reasonably representative picture of the UK venture capital industry.

A useful device for providing a sense of what the sample is like is to present a statistical picture of the typical, average, or modal VCI in the sample. This generalizes the presentation of data in Table 7.2, and the next two paragraphs are based on calculations from the 'basic data sheets' which VCIs were requested to complete at the time of interview.[7] First, I will consider real variables for which means can be computed; then, in Table 7.3, more qualitative variables will be introduced. By business type, VCIs were: banks (35 per cent); independents (40 per cent); public (10 per cent); subsidiaries (10 per cent); investment managers (5 per cent). Thus, in the sample, the typical VCI was an independent. It had no strong positive industrial preference for its investments,[8] and a slight geographical preference for investment in the UK. It had been in existence for six years. About 550 proposals were received each year, of which some 165 (30 per cent) were reviewed, leading to fifteen new investment involvements (3 per cent). Typically, it took about fifteen weeks from proposal to the completion of investment.

In terms of size, the typical VCI of the sample had twenty-seven employees and seven venture capital executives. It had about £67m. funds under management, and £24m. available to invest. Total funds invested at cost were £45m., and at valuation £67m. The smallest and largest investments that would normally be contemplated were £0.3m. and £4.1m. respectively. In practice, the smallest investment made was £0.4m. The average investment size was £1m. By type of investment, the breakdown was: start-up (11 per cent); development (45 per cent); buyout (40 per cent); other (4 per cent). Thus the typical VCI involvement entailed the provision of development capital, with the 'pure' form of VCI investment accounting for 4 per cent or less.

7 They typically obliged, with the single exception of Case S.

8 Though there was a slight negative tendency to avoid high-technology firms – what is sometimes called, rather cynically, in the trade, the 'bleeding edge' of technology.

Table 7.3 Main characteristics of investors

Case	*Min/max equity stake*	*Management monitoring fees*	*Directors' fees*	*Preferred exit*	*Time-scale (yrs)*	*Frequency of reporting*	*Representation on board*	*Required IRR*
A	2/55	11.25k	5.75k	Repurchase	5	Monthly	Almost always	n.a.
B	19/80	Yes	Yes	Market listing/trade sale	5	Monthly	Always	50%
C	1/40	Low	Low	Market listing/trade sale	4	Monthly	>10%	35%
D	0/100	Yes	Yes	Various	6	At least monthly	Always	n.a.
E	1/49	n.a.	5k	Trade sale	6	High	Occasional	35%
F	3/75	Yes	No	Flotation/sale back/trade sale	5	At least monthly	Always	30%
G	25/50	4k	10k	Trade sale	5	At least monthly	Yes	40%
H	3/90	Yes	Yes	Flotation/trade sale	3.5	Monthly	Always	35%
I	5/40	2.5%	Yes	Trade sale	4	Monthly	Occasional	30%
J	5/49	No	No	Any	5	At least monthly	Almost always	n.a.
K	10/90	Linked to deal	Linked to deal	Trade sale/flotation	5	Monthly	Yes	38%
L	25/40	No	Yes	Many	7.5	At least monthly	Occasional	n.a.
M	10/100	No	No	Trade sale	3.5	Monthly/quarterly	Yes	20%
N	0/30	3%	7.5k	Trade sale	4	Monthly	Almost always	30%
O	1/49	2%/12.5k	n.a.	Many	n.a.	Monthly	Rarely	n.a.
P	1/49	No	No	Many	7.5	Monthly	Occasional	15%
Q	1/49	Yes	No	Many	n.a.	Monthly	Independent nominee	n.a.
R	1/49	20% value	Yes	Trade sale/market listing	4.5	Monthly	Yes	30%
S	n.a.	n.a.	n.a.	n.a.	n.a.	n.a.	n.a.	n.a.
T	1/49	n.a.	n.a.	Flotation/trade sale	n.a.	Monthly	n.a.	n.a.
Avg.	6/60	Yes	Yes	Trade sale	5	Monthly	Always/yes	32%

Notes:

(a) Where variables are real, arithmetic means are computed in the last row; otherwise modal values are the quoted averages, or else qualitative averages.

(b) In Case S, no basic data sheet was returned.

Next, I consider the more qualitative variables in Table 7.3. It shows that, on average, the minimum and maximum equity stakes contemplated were 6 per cent and 57 per cent respectively, although it was not normal to take a majority stake in the MSF.[9] However, typically, management/monitoring fees *were* charged, as were directors' fees.[10] The VCI's desired timescale for investment was five years. By preferred exit route the breakdown was: management repurchase (5 per cent); trade sale (47 per cent); market listing/flotation (19 per cent); other (28 per cent). Thus the typical preferred exit route was a trade sale. The breakdown by type of investment was: sole (35 per cent); lead (33 per cent); consortium (31 per cent). Thus sole investment was slightly the preferred investment involvement by the VCI, and exit was early, after about five years, typically by 'selling on' the firm.

In terms of monitoring, the average frequency of reporting was high at fifteen times per year, post-investment, in the sample. Representation on the board had frequencies: always (35 per cent); almost always (20 per cent); sometimes (30 per cent). Typically, the VCI always required representation on the board of directors, completing the picture of tight monitoring and control. The required internal rate of return (IRR) for investee involvements (i.e. 'hurdle rate') was 32 per cent, which is a fairly typical figure,[11] but one which certainly suggests an expectation that monitoring and control will embrace the MSF's performance. It is through these summary statistics that insights of this sort have been provided, giving the reader, it is hoped, a background feeling for the functioning of the VCIs examined throughout this book. I turn now to the other partner in contracting, namely, the investee.

7.4 CHARACTERISTICS OF THE INVESTEE (MSF)

The sample frame of investees was given by: (a) referrals from investors to the other partner in a dyad; and (b) a random sample of investees selected from investee listings within investor portfolios published in the *Venture Capital*

9 In 30 per cent of investment involvements the equity stake could be bought back.

10 Practice here was very varied. Some required no fees, or low fees, while some required fixed fees, and others percentages. Overall, monitoring fees were low or zero. Directors' fees, when charged, tended to exceed monitoring fees.

11 This is a measure of the rate of return on an investment which takes account of capital growth and dividend income (see footnotes to Chapters 1 and 2 for more technical details). Targets here are usually 20 per cent or more, and can be as high as 40 per cent or more for high-technology projects. Venture capitalists are notoriously coy about the actual rate of return, but the evidence is that it is often surprisingly low. Work by Bygrave *et al.* (1988) indicates that IRRs are both cyclically sensitive and subject to secular trends. They can be at, or even below, 10 per cent, but a modal figure of around 16 per cent is plausible.

Report (Cary 1989).[12] A concatenation of these data sets produces a combined body of evidence on thirty-one investees. By now the reader will be familiar with the investees of the dyads, so this section will emphasize the full data set of investees. In addition, I shall conclude by appealing to a certain amount of qualitative evidence on investees' attributes to motivate better the discussion. But, to begin with, it is to the numerical evidence that I turn.

In Table 7.4, key statistics for two subsamples of investees are presented, relating to size (by sales and employment), longevity, and capital structure (measured by gearing and equity share). One sample (column 1) relates to investees in the dyads (of VCIs/MSFs), and the other sample (column 2) relates to the extraneous sample of investees. In the first case, the investees were selected in a fashion which was meant to produce a 'representative investee'.[13] The advantage of the method used was that it guaranteed that *pairs* of investors could be obtained, and that both high response rates and a ready willingness to cooperate on the part of

Table 7.4 Comparison between investee attributes across samples

	(1) Dyad sample (n = 17)		*(2) Extraneous sample (n = 14)*	
	Mean	*Standard deviation*	*Mean*	*Standard deviation*
Employ	108.6	163.1	219.2[1]	312.7
Sales (£000)	2,912	11,576.4	14,500.0[2]	15,093.5
Gearnow	76.7	111.9	44.6	46.7
Equity	44.5	25.0	42.4	29.0
Inbusin	67.6	100.3	121.3	86.5

Notes:
(a) *Definitions:*

Employ	Number of employees
Sales (£000)	Turnover in £000
Gearnow	Current debt/equity ratio
Equity	Proportion of share capital owned
Inbusin	Number of months in business

1 Inflated by Case T12 (a major textile manufacturer of thread) having an employment size of 1,200. Without Case T12, the statistics are: mean = 143.8; standard deviation = 140.

2 Similarly, without Case T12, the statistics are: mean = 12,581.1; standard deviation = 12,410.3.

12 This was a difficult procedure, as only investee names and locations were given, not contact names and addresses. These had to be determined from various directories, including telephone directory enquiries.

13 In seeking a representative investee, the VCI may have selected randomly from his portfolio, or an element of judgement may have been applied. For example, he may have deliberately sought that investee which best typified the nature of the VCI/MSF *relationship*, rather than that which best represented statistical attributes like size, age and capital structure.

investees were likely. As regards the second sample, this was certainly obtained by a process of random sampling. However, there may have been an element of respondent bias intruding through the requirement that investees needed to be willing to grant an interview. For example, it may have been that larger, better-resourced MSFs were more willing to talk to me in an interview than smaller, more pressured MSFs.

The table seems to suggest there are differences between the MSFs in the two samples, at least in some respects. Certainly, the MSFs in the extraneous sample seem to be older and larger.[14] They are, on average, twice the size of those in the dyad sample by employment, and five times the size by sales, though these statistics are distorted by the presence of one exceptionally large investee, with 1,200 employees and a turnover of £50m. However, even if what is arguably an outlier is dropped, the size difference remains evident. In terms of capital structure, inside equity is a similar proportion between groups, and both have relatively low gearing, though the gearing of the dyad groups is almost double that for the extraneous sample. The main difference between the two samples, in terms of their collection, was that the response rate was very much higher for the dyad groups. The willingness of investees in the dyad group to cooperate was, in some measure, a matter of perceived obligation by the investee. It seems likely that this is largely the source of the disparity between the investee subsamples. There is sufficient division of labour in a larger MSF to allow at least some personnel time to be directed to general enquiries, of which this study is an example. In smaller MSFs such discretionary time is less likely to be available, and lacking any obligation to help, the investee may simply refuse an interview. However, though sample heterogeneity may be evident, it does at least allow a more far-ranging perspective on investee behaviour which, given that this is not a large sample study, is arguably advantageous in terms of better displaying the morphology of investees.

Proceeding therefore with an examination of the combined sample, having noted the caveats above, it is again possible to present a typical or modal picture, this time as it relates to the investee rather than to the investor.[15] The typical investee had been in business for nine years. It was certainly not a micro-firm, having 185 full-time employees, an annual turnover of £13m., net assets of £50m.[16] and net profits (after tax) of £265k. In terms of capital structure, it had a relatively low gearing, post-investment, of 62 per cent, but before the involvement of the venture capital investor it had been as highly geared as 199 per cent. The proportion of share capital in the MSF held by the investee was 44 per cent

14 One would, of course, generally expect age and size to be positively associated for relatively young firms such as these.

15 Figures given for the typical investee are average figures for continuous real variables and modal values for categorical variables.

16 Net assets measured as fixed assets plus current assets minus liabilities.

and this had not been determined with an eye to control of the company. The current rate of return on the business was just 7 per cent, and before venture capital involvement had been as low as 5 per cent. An optimistic rate of return of 73 per cent was expected at exit. The payback period on capital investments was three years and, when discounting techniques were used, the rather high discount rate of 14 per cent was set. Given the choice between a gamble and its actuarial value for sure, the investee preferred the sure thing, suggesting risk aversion.

Risk considerations will be treated in far greater detail in Chapter 12, but the last statistic quoted for the 'typical' investee is worth exploring further at this point. Rather than looking at the average or modal response over all investees, consider the responses noted in Table 7.5 for the extraneous sample. Investees were asked to choose between a gamble and receiving its expected value 'for sure', and most (64 per cent) chose the 'sure' thing. Though it is hinted at rather than proven, the younger investees (average age 9) seem to be more likely to choose the gamble than the older investees (average age 15). Three other points worth observing are: the considerable size of investees; their diversity by age; and their tendency to be involved in engineering, manufacturing, etc., rather than in services.

Table 7.5 Characteristics of investees in extraneous sample

Code	*MSF's trade*	*Main line of business*	*Size*[1]	*Age*[2]	*Risk*[3]
T01	Biotechnology	Drug research and development	1,300	2	G
T02	Radio	Independent local radio	260	9	S
T03	Radio	Local commercial radio	300	4	S
T04	Computers	Design and manufacture of computers	60	10	G
T05	Plastics	Plastic extrusion	65	22	G
T06	Manufacturer	Machine-vision manufacturer	30	12	S
T07	Computers	Provision of software products and services	360	12	S
T08	Engineering	Hydraulic engineering	41	16	S
T09	Construction	Manufacture of products for construction industry	7	2	G
T10	Distribution	Distribution of raw materials for glass fibre industry	46	9	S
T11	Engineering	Engineering	60	25	S
T12	Manufacturing	Manufacture of textile thread	1,200	212	N[4]
T13	Construction	Subcontractor for floor coverings	350	75	S
T14	Brewing	Contract-packaging of beer	140	2	S

Notes:
1 *Size* is number of full-time employees.
2 *Age* is years in business.
3 *Risk:* G denotes favoured gamble; S favoured sure thing; N no response.
4 No reply given, though MSF of Case T12 did agree that the relationship of the company to its VCI depended on pure chance for its success "to some degree".

It would be possible to say considerably more about investee characteristics on a statistical level, but the requirement for mere description now perhaps is spent, and the more urgent task of analysis beckons. Before leaving this section on investees, it is perhaps worth conveying what statistics cannot suggest – namely, the unique character of many investees who were investigated in this field – by taking a portion of a vignette for investee Case P2, an unusual one, involving a firm just two-and-a-half years old, with seventy-five employees, annual sales of £3.8m., assets of £1.7m. and profits of £240k. Of the hotelier trade, in which he was involved, the investee said:

> "We have four hotels, three in Scotland, one in the Lake District. We're a start-up, so we're low in staff numbers centrally. I do all the sales, finance and administration here in Central Scotland with one secretary. Our hotels have 135, 125, 70 and 70 rooms; so we are in the tourist category and cater predominantly for the coach tour business. This gives us block bookings: we are pre-contracted up to a year ahead. The need to do this stems from our location and seasonality. The hotels are very personalized. If we require new products we look at each situation. Our packages vary from month to month. Our 'Turkey and Tinsel' package attracts people from November onwards. This year is our first full year of trading. In the coming year we expect £4m. turnover and £1m. gross profit. We look at profit rather than rates of return, and will probably exit through flotation."[17]

How many attending 'Turkey and Tinsel' holiday breaks in the Lake District would imagine the whole control of their hotel – and three others – was managed by one man and a secretary in Central Scotland? How many would have seen that capacity utilization is the key to profitability, and that therefore targeted packages for block bookings were the way to make sure capital and equipment were used intensively and profitably? Even this extract from the vignette conveys, in a way that no statistics of economics, finance and accountancy could do, how much scope for imagination and lateral thinking there is within the MSF, even in those well-trodden areas where no scope for change at first may seem possible. Thus the enquiring mind of the entrepreneur can conceive of new possibilities and can create previously unseen opportunities, as if by a conjuring trick. Without diminishing the scope for such factors, nor denying their critical importance in the entrepreneurial process, I turn now to the task of analysis, by examining in the remaining chapters of this book the details of contracting practices between investor and investee.

17 In this quote, double quotation marks are used to indicate that direct speech of a respondent is being reported. The use of this convention is adopted throughout Part 3 on Cases, which follows this chapter.

7.5 CONCLUSION

The purpose of this chapter has been to establish a backdrop or mosaic of investor and investee attributes that prevents the reader from saying, 'Ah, that is all very well, but what are these guys really like that you are talking about?' In all attempts to convey meaning and illumination by developing new principles of reasoning, as in principal–agent analysis applied to investors and investees, a handle on reality through concrete evidence and example can be immensely useful in promoting understanding. But it is no substitute for analysis itself. Even though it is not a formal prerequisite to analysis, this chapter can serve perhaps as a facilitator of analysis. It is in this light that the evidence of this chapter has been presented. It is hoped that one is now better prepared than otherwise to experience illumination through the analysis of evidence that is to be conducted in the next seven chapters.

Part 3

CASES

8

CASE STUDY J: INDEPENDENT PRINCIPAL

8.1 INTRODUCTION

This chapter develops one of the three analytical case studies (Chapters 8, 9 and 10) which aim to display the fine detail of how risk management and information-handling proceed in the empirical setting of investor and investee as principal and agent. This, the first of these three chapters, is unusual in that it examines the multiple-agent case. It considers the applicability of principal–agent analysis to the relationship between a principal who is an 'independent' venture capitalist and two of his agents, who run entrepreneurial firms in high-technology areas. It does so using an 'explanatory case study'[1] whose purpose is to see whether the categories suggested by principal–agent analysis (e.g. the monitoring system) are indeed observed in practical venture capital settings, and whether the relations between these categories (e.g. between risk-bearing and effort) are as suggested by theory. The methodology adopted is close to that used by Steier and Greenwood (1995) in their examination of venture capital deal-structuring, and by Sweeting (1991b) in his analysis of new technology-based businesses. It will be shown that when this case study methodology is deployed in these three chapters, it provides striking confirmatory evidence of the applicability of the principal–agent model to the problem of venture capital financing of high-performing business ventures.

The purpose of Part 3 as a whole is to show that the approach expounded earlier (Chapter 4) of treating the venture capitalist as principal ($\mathbf{P}_J$), and the entrepreneur as agent ($\mathbf{A}_J$), enables empirical evidence to be neatly mapped into theoretical categories. To illustrate by reference to case study J in this chapter, $\mathbf{P}_J$ showed awareness of the moral hazard and adverse selection problems created by information asymmetry and took steps to attenuate them.[2] For example,

1 For further information on this method see Ryan *et al.* (1992: ch. 7).

2 In the following three chapters, principal and agent will be denoted by bold letters, e.g. as **P** and **A**, with a subscript indicating the particular case, e.g. $\mathbf{P}_G$ for the principal in case G. In

although $\mathbf{A}_J$ was more exposed to risk than $\mathbf{P}_J$, being less diversified, $\mathbf{P}_J$ required $\mathbf{A}_J$ to continue to bear some risk post-contract to maintain the incentive for effort. Even with a subscription agreement that required detailed reporting by $\mathbf{A}_J$ to $\mathbf{P}_J$, private information remained in the hands of $\mathbf{A}_J$ regarding such matters as products and technological change. From the standpoint of the other side of the relationship, $\mathbf{P}_J$ was perceived by $\mathbf{A}_J$ to have an informational advantage in matters like capital structuring and flotation.

8.2 APPLIED PRINCIPAL–AGENT ANALYSIS: CASE STUDY J

Principal $\mathbf{P}_J$

The principal ($\mathbf{P}_J$), as a person, was a well-known player in the UK venture capital scene. The specific investor interviewed, who for convenience will also be called $\mathbf{P}_J$, had a very high profile in the venture capital industry. He was a graduate of an ancient university and a keen card player. He had been the president of a leading venture capital organization and had appeared frequently on television.

The principal ($\mathbf{P}_J$), as an institution, was an independent venture capital fund which had been in existence since 1982. $\mathbf{P}_J$ would contemplate any form of profitable industry involvement, but had a preference for the high-technology area. Its geographical preference was to make investments in the UK. It had eight full-time venture capital executives and sixteen employees, making it around the average size in terms of personnel. Typical skills of the executives involved degrees in law, economics or a science, with additional professional or academic credentials (e.g. CA, MBA). $\mathbf{P}_J$ managed about £50m. in value of venture capital funds, of which about £40m. (at cost) had been invested, which was thought to have a current value of £50m. At the time of interview, in 1993, £8m. of funds were regarded as available for investment. Average investment size was about £1m., and the largest undertaken had been £3m. There was a reluctance to get involved in investments of less than £250,000, though an investment as low as £100,000 had (exceptionally) been made. Investment style was highly flexible. $\mathbf{P}_J$ was involved in all the major categories of venture capital activity, with its commitments by percentage of funds being: 10 per cent start-up; 20 per cent early-stage; 20 per cent development; 30 per cent management buyouts (MBOs); and 20 per cent for the rest (replacement, follow-on, etc.). $\mathbf{P}_J$ would take an equity stake of anything from 5 per cent to 49 per cent, charged no fees, and had no preconceptions about the appropriate exit route. This flexibility of style was also apparent in his willingness to be involved with others in the joint funding of the same

this chapter the two agents are distinguished by a superscript. Thus $\mathbf{A}^1{}_J$ and $\mathbf{A}^2{}_J$ are the two agents. If only $\mathbf{A}_J$ is written, then the generic sense of agent for case J is intended.

investees. Its percentage involvements were as follows: sole (30 per cent), lead (40 per cent) and follower (30 per cent). $\mathbf{P_J}$ was keen on monitoring, and required a high frequency of reporting and a high level of involvement at the board of directors level.

About 600 proposals were received by $\mathbf{P_J}$ each year, of which only 100 were seriously received. Of these, about ten were accepted each year. This rigorous screening is typical of all successful venture capital involvements, but is especially so in the high-technology area. About 1.5 per cent of proposals were accepted (compared to 3 per cent for the sample as a whole). In discussing venture capital backing of high-technology firms, Roberts (1991) referred to this particularly rigorous screening, and also referred to other special features in such cases, such as a preference for mature firms, founder teams (rather than solo entrepreneurs), price inelastic product demand, and realistic team self-appraisal. These preferred qualities are expressed in relation to the broad range of investment involvements. Among the high-technology ventures themselves, high-quality and relatively low risk were also sought.

The time from proposal to completion of investment could vary from a week to a year, but was usually 6–8 weeks. The timescale of investment was flexible, and could be anything from 3 to 7 years. $\mathbf{P_J}$ did not believe in incorporating a 'buy back' exit route in the subscription agreement that would allow the investee to buy back the investor's equity stake; but, in practice, he could not think of a case in which this possibility was beyond negotiation. No formal hurdle rate was set for the internal rate of return (IRR)[3] on investments. $\mathbf{P_J}$ said that he wanted the complete probability distribution of IRRs for a particular investment, and compared investments by comparing these distributions. He emphasized that he would never compare them simply in terms of most likely outcomes for IRRs. The only clear indication he would give on desired IRRs was that realized values must be 'significant'.

Agent $\mathbf{A^1_J}$

The first agent ($\mathbf{A^1_J}$) to be considered in this chapter was one of two referrals from the principal, both of whom were active in the high-technology area.[4] The person to be identified with $\mathbf{A^1_J}$, again for convenience, had a doctoral degree and a distinguished research record. $\mathbf{A^1_J}$ was in a high-technology firm with an active R&D programme, which led it to be actively in collaboration with leading genetic research units. Their shared interest was the development of transgenic

3 The internal rate of return is the discount rate that equalizes the present value of cash outflows with the present value of cash inflows. See any practitioner-based manual on venture capital investment (e.g. Gladstone 1988: 384).

4 The first agent $\mathbf{A^1_J}$ produced large volumes of low-cost human therapeutic proteins. The second agent $\mathbf{A^2_J}$ developed and manufactured *in vitro* diagnostic tests.

technology. This involves the transfer of a gene from one animal species to another. $\mathbf{A}^1_J$ was also engaged in contract development and manufacturing activities. Contract services were offered to the pharmaceutical and biotechnology industries to develop transgenic production processes. This process can be fully specified right through from the R&D stage to full-scale manufacturing at specified volumes.

The investee, who will be treated as the agent ($\mathbf{A}^1_J$) in the context of this case study, had been in the business of pharmaceutical manufacturing for six-and-a-half years. Key budgets were computed annually and reviewed half-yearly. $\mathbf{A}^1_J$ had annual sales of £1.7m. and fifty full-time employees. In undertaking investment appraisals of new investment, a 30 per cent risk premium was added to the discount rate. Net profits after tax were just £20,000 and the current rate of return was –10 per cent. Considering $\mathbf{A}^1_J$ collectively as the executive directors, they held less than 1 per cent of the equity. Essentially, the company had been set up by venture capitalists who initially held 100 per cent of the equity. The gearing ratio was low (<10 per cent). The company was to be floated within a year, with the general assumption being that typically the venture capital investors would want to exit thereafter. However, it was thought that some might feel 'locked-in' by their previously high level of commitment.[5] $\mathbf{P}_J$ was only one of the several major investors in this MSF, half of whom were from overseas (two from the USA, one from France, one from Japan).[6]

Agent $\mathbf{A}^2_J$

The second agent ($\mathbf{A}^2_J$) of this case was also active in the high-technology area. The person to be identified with $\mathbf{A}^2_J$ was an accounting graduate of a leading Scottish ancient university who had obtained a first-class honours degree. He was a noted prize winner when he qualified as a chartered accountant, and had obtained an MBA with distinction. After experience in a major UK accounting partnership, he had been appointed as an accountant and business analyst for an enterprise board. Through the involvement of the enterprise board with the company, he had been appointed finance director, and also acted as company secretary.

5 If commitment were high in terms of magnitude of equity stake, the over-rapid selling of shares after flotation might adversely affect the share price. It is not uncommon for the prospectus released at issue to state which investors will stay in after flotation. Typically, packages of shares would be sold at various dates after flotation, and these sales may be coordinated by investors.

6 In the development of the case that follows, it should be borne in mind that the principal was only one of several investors, and that the investee was only one of several investees. Thus many statements about $\mathbf{P}_J$'s relation to $\mathbf{A}^1_J$ and $\mathbf{A}^1_J$'s relation to $\mathbf{P}_J$ are generic, and not tied to these particular principals and agents.

His company specialized in the development, manufacturing and marketing of *in vitro* tests for human diseases. It worked closely with leading academic research centres to foster the commercialization of promising products. Examples included predictive assessment of cardiovascular disease, and early identification of osteoporosis. $\mathbf{A}^2_J$ also developed and manufactured products for major companies with international sales operations under their own labels.

Considering $\mathbf{A}^2_J$ as the company itself, it had been in business for ten years at the time of being examined for this study. Like $\mathbf{A}^1_J$, which was over six years old, $\mathbf{A}^2_J$ was also a mature firm (see Roberts 1991: 15). It was initially set up to exploit research emerging from a Scottish university with a major medical research reputation. Having raised £4m. of equity finance six years after inception, it quickly relocated within a year to purpose-built premises on a new technology park not far from the university.

Having been in business ten years, $\mathbf{A}^2_J$ had forty-one full-time employees, sales of £1.7m. and net assets of £335k. Key budgets were calculated quarterly, and discount rates and payback periods were thought to be irrelevant to capital investment appraisal. Being a development company, its net profits after tax were a loss of £653k. It held no debt, and historically had tended to have very low levels of debt before the venture capital investor became involved. $\mathbf{A}^2_J$ said the company had “always been equity driven”. He held no share capital in the business, and control of the company was an irrelevance to him. There was no ‘sweat equity’ in the business arising from the effort involved in getting it up and running.

The rate of return was zero at the time of interview, but $\mathbf{A}^2_J$ hoped that it would be an overall 80 per cent on an IRR basis by the time of exit from the relationship with $\mathbf{P}_J$. $\mathbf{A}^2_J$ pointed out that different investment interests would enjoy different rates of return. The enterprise board would make £500k on a £225k investment; and some would make as much as £2.8m. on a £800k investment over two years. The most favoured would make as much as 500 per cent on their investments, but others would make losses. As $\mathbf{A}^2_J$ said, “It’s all through capital growth” that a return was made. The desired form of exit was by main market listing, and $\mathbf{A}^2_J$ thought that the venture capital investor was very important to the fortunes of the business.

8.3 PRINCIPAL ($\mathbf{P}_J$): RISK MANAGEMENT

In his role as an investor, $\mathbf{P}_J$ believed that chance, luck, odds or probability played a major role in determining outcomes. However, as agency theory suggests, he thought that risk could be managed, and that success in the face of it depended, first, on investment management and, secondly, on the structuring of the deal with the investee (e.g. by classes of share). $\mathbf{P}_J$ thought that actual outcomes of investee–investor involvements were due to financial judgement in about a third of cases, to management in slightly less than a third of cases, and to pure luck in slightly more than a third of cases. In other words, luck was still a predominant determining factor. Unusually, the style of fund management to which $\mathbf{P_J}$ subscribed embraced the full set of involvements noted in Table 2.1 above, from seed capital through to MBO. In his portfolio management, $\mathbf{P_J}$ attempted to diversify away risk. He believed in attempting to offset good outcomes against bad, and held that this was helped by good judgement in assessing the quality of management possessed by investees. To achieve full risk-spreading or diversification advantages, $\mathbf{P_J}$ felt that at least twenty investees should be included in a portfolio, but would go as high as fifty investees for high-risk portfolios. There is an element of overkill in this diversification strategy, in that risk-spreading is thought to be achievable with rather fewer investees (see Tucker *et al.* 1995: ch. 2). There was no unique annualized internal rate of return (IRR) that came to mind in $\mathbf{P_J}$'s appraisals of investees, as he claimed to think more in terms of a distribution of IRRs rather than point values. From other evidence, it seems that expected IRRs from such distributions could be as high as 80 per cent. In contemplating taking on a new investee, a clear view was always taken of the risk/reward balance in the portfolio. Timescale was considered important also, as part of fund management involved closing funds as well as opening them. $\mathbf{P_J}$ said it was important to keep investees exposed to risk, and thought this affected effort positively. He felt it was important to remind investees that they were in some sense partners, sharing gains and losses together, as "otherwise they see you as a banker". To achieve this, the deal had to be properly structured, both at the outset and as it evolved.[7] If this were not done, in his experience, "a very successful business becomes as hard to manage as a very bad business". Three points of interest to applied principal–agent analysis emerge from this. First, $\mathbf{P_J}$ functioned in a risky environment, and felt his own conduct could mitigate risk exposure. Secondly, $\mathbf{P_J}$ engaged in portfolio management to diversify away part of his risk. Thirdly, $\mathbf{P_J}$ favoured shifting some part of the risk onto the investee in order to maintain the investee's incentive for effort.

8.4 INFORMATION-HANDLING ($\mathbf{P_J}$)

$\mathbf{P_J}$ required considerably more information from $\mathbf{A_J}$ than was strictly necessary.[8] Monthly management accounts were typically required. Only with reluctance would $\mathbf{P_J}$ contemplate reducing this frequency, it being more likely to be reduced as the longevity of the relationship with $\mathbf{A_J}$ increased. In other words,

7 For further insight into deal-structuring with UK high-technology ventures, see Sweeting (1991b: 614). Sweeting particularly emphasizes the tendency to customize deals, which fits well with the evolutionary approach advocated by $\mathbf{P_J}$ in the text.

8 According to the requirements for provision of accounting information to shareholder in the Companies Act 1985.

reputation, established by successful repeated contracting, could reduce the monitoring requirements. Because $\mathbf{P_J}$ had a nominee director on the board of directors, he had full access to accounts month by month, and was committed to vetting them. He admitted that he knew less than $\mathbf{A_J}$ both immediately before and after the deal was concluded. He was aware that at the time of investing "there is an incentive for them not to share all" (see Lerner 1994b). For example, in a management buyout (MBO) he said, "It's in their interest to sell the worst story". Even then, he continued, some go in the reverse direction and end up overinvesting. $\mathbf{P_J}$ felt that his experience with many investments made him less likely to be fooled by anomalous and misleading accounting than inexperienced entrepreneurs. He said of the MBO that, "Management might think a firm is worth £x, but you think it is only worth £$\frac{1}{2}$x. They fall out with you, buy it for £x, finance it elsewhere, find they have overinvested, and it all goes wrong". While they know a lot more about some aspects of the company than $\mathbf{P_J}$, and may even be holding back part of this knowledge for strategic reasons, they may nevertheless lack skill in investment evaluation of the sort possessed by $\mathbf{P_J}$.

As well as investees not always handling information correctly, $\mathbf{P_J}$ thought they selected information to favour their bargaining positions. The extent to which this was done was thought to vary by type of deal. $\mathbf{P_J}$ categorized 'openness' of deals as follows: start-up, 'pretty open'; buyout, 'open'; buy-in, 'very open'; and development, 'less open'. In the last case, he said, "They want us in at the highest price possible". An attempt was made to mitigate information disadvantage both before and after the deal. $\mathbf{P_J}$ admitted that before the deal was struck, "They know all the good and bad things about the company", and that, "Once they have conned you at the outset, they are likely to want to carry on doing so for as long as possible".

$\mathbf{P_J}$ thought that controlling his information flow in terms of the day-to-day running of the investee's business depended on the quality of his relationship with $\mathbf{A_J}$. He sought openness, ample data, and information with content. He found that investees usually conveyed what they intended, especially on an accounting level. Simple systems, with an emphasis on numerical data, were what he favoured.[9] Management and audited accounts were mainly used to keep information and reality aligned, but monthly meetings played a part as well. If there were any doubt, influence would be brought to bear, exceptionally, on the audit of accounts. Usually the cost of information acquisition was low because "it all goes through board meetings on which our paid director sits". Costs of requesting extra information from $\mathbf{A_J}$ were perceived to fall on $\mathbf{A_J}$ alone. In extreme cases, $\mathbf{P_J}$ would bear the cost: "We'd put money in if we didn't believe

9 This confirms the finding of Macmillan *et al.* (1988) that venture capitalists were mostly involved in the financial aspects of their investees.

something, for example bring in an accountant to do the work". If an unreasonable degree of distortion of information were detected, the cost would be severe for the investee. $\mathbf{P_J}$ spoke of a case in which he discovered a deliberate selection of information by an investee which involved changing the basis of disclosure in an unnotified fashion. A fraudulent director was found to be at the root of it; he was dismissed, and the company collapsed.

So far as information possessed by the VC fund itself was concerned, it was felt by $\mathbf{P_J}$ that selection of information did occur with regard to $\mathbf{A_J}$'s performance. Thus $\mathbf{A_J}$ would not necessarily note all upside aspects of performance, though he would report to $\mathbf{P_J}$ what he did know; but $\mathbf{P_J}$ might not retort with what had been missed. Regarding the downside of performance, should $\mathbf{A_J}$ not report all aspects, $\mathbf{P_J}$ would "expose them and get $\mathbf{A_J}$ to comment". In commenting upon, or exposing, downside aspects of performance, $\mathbf{P_J}$ had a preference for providing all factual information on the performance default. However, qualitative information on the performance of individuals might not be conveyed. $\mathbf{P_J}$ said that he "wouldn't say to $\mathbf{A_J}$, 'you're hopeless'", and even stronger views formed on individuals over time would not be fully expressed. Such comments were thought to have poor or perverse incentive consequences.

Three aspects of applied agency analysis are highlighted by this evidence on information management. First, information asymmetry was present both before and after conclusion of contract. $\mathbf{P_J}$ acted in a way which displayed awareness of this, both in terms of problems of adverse selection (e.g. by $\mathbf{A_J}$ overstating the investment potential of a project before conclusion of the deal) and moral hazard (e.g. by $\mathbf{A_J}$ easing up on performance after being in the contract for a while, but reporting this incompletely). Secondly, information could be used not only to inform decisions better, but also to modify and change $\mathbf{A_J}$'s effort: that is, it had incentive properties. Thus if $\mathbf{P_J}$ exposed $\mathbf{A_J}$'s concealed performance default by skilled use of his information system (e.g. management accounts) this enhanced $\mathbf{A_J}$'s future performance. Thirdly, information itself could be more or less 'noisy'. It could be enhanced if gathered more frequently (e.g. by monthly rather than quarterly accounts) and/or in different forms (e.g. by representation on the board, as well as monthly management accounts), and also by audit. However, some 'noise' always remained.

8.5 TRADING RISK AND INFORMATION ($\mathbf{P_J}$)

$\mathbf{P_J}$ thought that as a venture capitalist he was able to "take a higher probability of failure" than $\mathbf{A_J}$ as investee. He thought the entrepreneur had to be a risk-taker by definition, and was more exposed to risk: "He loses sleep, we don't." However, he thought there was an optimal level of risk that $\mathbf{A_J}$ should be allowed to bear: "It shouldn't be extreme; they become dysfunctional." He thought that, properly determined, this level of risk which $\mathbf{A_J}$ was allowed to bear should stimulate his effort "to work hard for success, and, above all, to *avoid* failure".

P$_J$ thought there was a trade-off between his risk-bearing and **A**$_J$'s provision of information. He felt he would go further with bearing risk for a company if there had been a full disclosure of information than if there had not. He said, "If you know the worst aspects, you'll bail them out". He thought that as investor he would share most information with **A**$_J$, but admitted to some areas of confidentiality. He estimated that 95 per cent of information was full and free, and 5 per cent was not.

The contract agreed with **A**$_J$ was thought to be 90 per cent formal and 10 per cent implicit. However, it was felt that explicit conditions were often broken in practice, and the implicit areas grew as the relationship with **A**$_J$ became more prolonged. In agreeing a contract, he preferred an equity stake of 15 per cent to 35 per cent, but for a big fast-growing company he might let this drop to 5 per cent. He was an advocate of using performance-linked equity and used ratchets "all the time".

P$_J$ found it difficult to characterize the best form of contract. He did not think this was unique. When asked if he aimed for an optimum he said, "There are many optima". He used return on capital employed, gross margins and sales to distinguish between investees on efficiency grounds, but was concerned not to overfocus on internal rates of return (IRRs). In the ideal contractual relationship he thought that reputation was valuable (for him).

This last section on **P**$_J$ was concerned with his contracting with **A**$_J$. Three aspects of contractual arrangements sharpen further the 'fit' of the principal–agent framework in this context. First, part of the purpose of contracting was risk-sharing, with **P**$_J$ being the bearer of the greater burden, but **A**$_J$ remaining subject to such risk as best stimulated performance. Secondly, contracting involved an exchange of information, and in some measure there was a trade-off between information exchange and risk-bearing. Thirdly, contracting embodied performance evaluation components (e.g. returns, margins, sales) and incentives linked to performance (e.g. ratchets).

We turn now to the view of the first investee (**A**^1_J) to be considered in terms of its relationship with **P**$_J$. It must be borne in mind that, from a generic standpoint, while **P**$_J$'s views were typically based on many investee involvements, this was not typically true of **A**$_J$. In Case J which is being considered in this chapter, the first investee, **A**^1_J, did have multiple involvements with investors, but this was not always the case.

8.6 INVESTEE (A^1_J): RISK MANAGEMENT

The first investee, regarded here as an agent (**A**^1_J), had been running his firm in Scotland for four years, and had been a founder investor two years earlier. **A**^1_J had a strong scientific background, including publication and research of recognized international standing.[10] His view, therefore, was based on both experience and analytical capability. Intellectually, he was well matched in these aspects with $\mathbf{P}_J$. In the view of $\mathbf{A}^1{}_J$, chance played a significant, if not dominant, role in determining outcomes. For example, he was prepared to admit that the net profit of a project was partly a matter of chance, and would use a risk discount to adjust this figure. Given the choice between a risky alternative with an actuarial (expected) value of £1.2m. (with high probability ($\frac{9}{10}$) of £1m., and low probability ($\frac{1}{10}$) of £3m.), as against a sure prospect of £1.2m., $\mathbf{A}^1{}_J$ rejected the sure prospect and chose the risky alternative, confirming $\mathbf{P}_J$'s view (expressed in 3.5 above) that entrepreneurs had to be risk-takers. $\mathbf{A}^1{}_J$ did say, however, that, "There's a devil of a difference between £1m. and £1.2m.", suggesting a feeling for some qualitative risk-discounting.[11] In another question on risk, concerning a random customer order, which only had a $\frac{1}{10}$ probability of being filled, he valued the order at the actuarial equivalent, but with the proviso that the random experiment was to have numerous repetitions, which was presumably perceived to reduce risk exposure and hence the need for risk-discounting. Like $\mathbf{P}_J$, he felt that there were steps he could take to modify his exposure to risk. One device $\mathbf{A}^1{}_J$ used was in his experimental work. He would 'scale-down' experiments on larger animals, to smaller animals. This enabled many more trials to be conducted on smaller rather than larger animals, at any given cost, and he felt scientists within his firm had a good enough grasp of the 'scaling-up' biological methodology (e.g. scaling-up from mice to sheep) to ensure that the results obtained were useful. $\mathbf{A}^1{}_J$ did not feel any responsibility to represent the riskiness of his projects to $\mathbf{P}_J$, barring giving the facts. He said, "They work it out", but felt that there was a tendency for $\mathbf{P}_J$ to overestimate the risk inherent in the business. In agreeing to become an investee of $\mathbf{P}_J$, $\mathbf{A}^1{}_J$ said it was important to him that $\mathbf{P}_J$ shared some of the business risk. He did not feel that this diminished his own motivation or commitment to the business. Indeed, $\mathbf{A}^1{}_J$ seemed to be unswerving in his commitment and pointed out that, "Every year I've taken my bonus in shares rather than cash". $\mathbf{A}^1{}_J$ did not express a preference for a fixed sum on exit, which implies rejection of the

10 The investor had both high human capital (studies up to PhD level) and wide knowledge of the new transgenic technology. As a founder inventor he satisfied the criteria suggested by Wozniak (1987) for identifying entrepreneurs who would be 'early adopters' of a new technology.

11 The behaviour of $\mathbf{A}^1{}_J$ does not meet the strict terms of the principal–agent model adopted, possibly because the downside is probable but safe, and the upside, while improbable, is exciting. On such biased heuristics in risk assessment see Khaneman and Tversky (1979). The risky order question led to a reply suggesting risk neutrality if a sufficient number of independent trials were available. Finally, the qualitative remark, "There's a devil of a . . .", suggested a tendency to risk aversion. It is clear that for this agent, the attitude to risk was highly sensitive to the form of gamble.

risk-free option.[12] While $\mathbf{A}^1{}_J$ claimed that his motivation had not slackened since concluding a contract with $\mathbf{P}_J$, saying that it had "stayed the same", this does not mean that $\mathbf{P}_J$'s influence had been unimportant. In the absence of appropriate incentives, one would expect the problem of moral hazard to arise, and the apparent absence of it indicates effective contractual design and execution.

Three points of importance to applied principal–agent analysis emerge from this discussion of $\mathbf{A}^1{}_J$'s risk management. First, $\mathbf{A}^1{}_J$ was relatively more exposed to risk than $\mathbf{P}_J$, lacking options for diversifying away the risk. In the face of this, $\mathbf{A}^1{}_J$ displayed a propensity to bear risk, even given the option of an attractive risk-free alternative, provided the risky alternative has some reasonable chance of a very high return. Secondly, $\mathbf{A}^1{}_J$ was motivated by his high-risk exposure to enter into a contract with $\mathbf{P}_J$ which offered risk-sharing benefits.[13] Thirdly, the tendency for $\mathbf{A}^1{}_J$ to be subject to moral hazard in the post-contract situation was attenuated by his remaining subject to a significantly risky environment, albeit less risky than in the pre-contract situation.

8.7 INFORMATION-HANDLING ($\mathbf{A}^1{}_J$)

In order to assess his firm's performance $\mathbf{A}^1{}_J$ used sales, net profit and cash flow in his quantitative appraisals. These were reported to $\mathbf{P}_J$ (see Macmillan *et al.* 1988), as was the wage bill, but the latter was felt to be of little significance. Quantitative appraisal used performance against budget, the 'variance analysis' of management accounting control methods (see Ezzamel and Hart 1987: ch.14). In addition, a non-quantitative approach to performance was used, described as 'technical milestones'. Within certain timescales, like a year or eighteen months, $\mathbf{A}^1{}_J$ asked whether a piece of research was working out, in the sense of achieving technological goals within budget.

The key activities of management under $\mathbf{A}^1{}_J$ were setting financial budgets, costing the output produced, producing information to monitor the business, producing information for strategic decisions, and taking 'head counts'. None of this was said to have been done at the instigation of $\mathbf{P}_J$, but certainly all of it was reported to $\mathbf{P}_J$. In comparing the state of knowledge of $\mathbf{P}_J$ to $\mathbf{A}^1{}_J$, it was thought that $\mathbf{A}^1{}_J$ had superior knowledge of technology, markets, managerial staff, technical staff and supply sources. On matters of budgets, capital structure, business strategy, management accounts, financial accounts and capital investment it was felt that $\mathbf{P}_J$ and $\mathbf{A}^1{}_J$ were equally well informed. In only one category, but a crucial

12 The argument being that otherwise there would be some sum which would at least compensate for the probability of high return, if nominating a risky outcome per se were not favoured.

13 This suggested that the qualitative risk assessment put the MSF into a risk-averse category.

one, was it thought that $\mathbf{P}_J$ had a clear information advantage over $\mathbf{A}^1{}_J$, namely, that of 'going public', especially should the flotation be done in the USA.

Budgets (profit and loss, cash flow, balance sheet, capital, head count) were set annually. Costs were actual, rather than standard, and could be directly attributed to materials, labour and production overheads. Even though $\mathbf{A}^1{}_J$'s firm was highly technological in orientation, when a new project was being set up accountants were involved in costing at the design stage. For example, a new project was being considered which involved investigating the suitability of pigs' hearts for human heart transplants. As well as being of great technical interest, with a clear research agenda, this was regarded as a new product area. The financial director, who was also an accountant, was involved in the detailed costing of this research, right through to the point at which the new product would come out in the marketplace.

In contemplating new projects which involved capital investments a net present value criterion was used. However, qualitative assessment was also very important. It was said that prospective returns on many projects were so high, should a new project successfully come to market, that most capital investment decisions which were required to be made for technical reasons would in fact be carried out. To illustrate, $\mathbf{A}^1{}_J$ said that, "If flying-in sheep from New Zealand is necessary, we would do it – indeed, we've done it". Once in place, investments would be monitored against both technical and financial budgets.

All classes of information reported back to $\mathbf{P}_J$ were said to be subject to error or distortion in reporting. In the case of products, production, financial and personnel data, this distortion was slight. In the case of markets, it was significant. To illustrate market uncertainty, $\mathbf{A}^1{}_J$ gave the example of therapeutics that his firm was developing. For such products, he thought the percentage of the market that could be acquired was often unknown, even unknowable, because in some cases the market had not even been created, and because actions and reactions of competitors were so hard to anticipate. As a consequence, $\mathbf{A}^1{}_J$ said that a deliberate mixture of high- and low-risk projects was run within the firm: "We don't put all our eggs in one basket. We have a number of different products. We are risk-diversified." [14]

From the viewpoint of applied principal–agent analysis, three points are noteworthy in this section on $\mathbf{A}^1{}_J$'s handling of information. First, there was a rich information flow from $\mathbf{A}^1{}_J$ to $\mathbf{P}_J$. $\mathbf{A}^1{}_J$ made a wide range of technical, managerial and financial data available. Secondly, and not independently of the first point, there was only limited information asymmetry between $\mathbf{A}^1{}_J$ and $\mathbf{P}_J$. However, this apparent transparency of the information system slightly masked difficulties $\mathbf{P}_J$

14 Although $\mathbf{A}^1{}_J$ attempted to spread risk across high- and low-risk projects, as all were nevertheless in a fairly narrow area of biomedical research, there could only be a limited extent to which this could genuinely diversify risk.

might have in interpreting technical data, and in dealing with large volumes of other information, much of which might not be decision-sensitive. Thirdly, there was an inherent 'noisiness' in much information. $\mathbf{A}^1{}_J$ was involved in a leading-edge technological venture in which high risk was intrinsic. Only to a limited extent could this be diversified across projects. From a market standpoint, which was what most influenced the shared pay-off between $\mathbf{P}_J$ and $\mathbf{A}^1{}_J$, most information 'noisiness' was irreducible.

8.8 TRADING RISK AND INFORMATION ($\mathbf{A}^1{}_J$)

The flow of information from $\mathbf{A}^1{}_J$ to $\mathbf{P}_J$ was extensive (i.e. full and detailed). Indeed, it was felt that a problem of 'data reduction' arose, and that from a decision standpoint, lesser information might, strictly speaking, be more useful. $\mathbf{A}^1{}_J$ had a right of information control which was exercised over personnel matters, new technology before filing for patents, and some customer identities. It was felt that $\mathbf{P}_J$'s own information system could be 'leaky' out of a lack of awareness of the potential market sensitivity of some data.

$\mathbf{A}^1{}_J$ was party to a share option scheme which had been agreed with $\mathbf{P}_J$ in place of a previous bonus scheme, and it was thought to have superior incentive properties. The bonus scheme was thought to encourage short-termism, whereas "both management and venture capitalists are interested in increasing the value of shares". Options were to buy at a fixed price, and the number of shares was variable, with up to 5 per cent going to executive directors and up to 5 per cent to staff. It was thought by $\mathbf{A}^1{}_J$ that there would be yet more motivation if these limits were raised, saying: "It would certainly motivate senior management, and would 'tie people in'."

In terms of the contractual relationship with $\mathbf{P}_J$, $\mathbf{A}^1{}_J$ thought that his own knowledge of products, markets and riskiness was important, and of effort, financial expertise and commitment, crucial. In evaluating the attributes of $\mathbf{P}_J$, it was felt by $\mathbf{A}^1{}_J$ that only the supply of finance capital was crucial, and that in other areas $\mathbf{P}_J$'s attributes were either on a par with $\mathbf{A}^1{}_J$ or even (e.g. as regards financial expertise, effort) irrelevant. Despite $\mathbf{A}^1{}_J$'s confidence in his abilities over a wide range of technical areas, scientific and financial, he felt that the single most important attribute he brought to the contractual agreement with $\mathbf{P}_J$ was commitment to the business. Not surprisingly, $\mathbf{A}^1{}_J$ thought that $\mathbf{P}_J$'s most important attribute was the supplying of finance capital. $\mathbf{A}^1{}_J$ felt no sense of having to compete with other investees for more favourable treatment from $\mathbf{P}_J$, but was unusual in having multiple investor involvements.[15] This would tend to increase

15 This turned out to be a general finding, as discussed in Chapter 14. In expounding Case J, this greatly diminishes the need to consider investee interactions.

his bargaining power *vis-à-vis* $\mathbf{P}_J$. The contractual relationship with $\mathbf{P}_J$ was thought to be tightly defined in theory, but based on trust and understanding in practice. The main area in which scope for more satisfactory contracting lay was thought by $\mathbf{A}^1{}_J$ to be with a wider vision by $\mathbf{P}_J$ of the well-being of the company as a whole, rather than a narrow concern for the investor's immediate advantage. Ideally, it was thought to be important that contractual arrangements led to an appropriate capital structure, efficient risk-sharing, the free sharing of information, and the maximization of the rate of return. But above all, it was felt that contractual arrangements should increase motivation. $\mathbf{A}^1{}_J$ was confident that even with his 1 per cent of the share capital he had control of the business. He said: "Venture capitalists can't run the business – I have control because of my specialist knowledge."[16]

Recurring again to the 'fit' of the observations to the categories of principal–agent analysis, the following points are suggested. First, risk was so high that the trade-off between risk and information led to the adoption of very full and complex information flows from $\mathbf{A}^1{}_J$ to $\mathbf{P}_J$. This did not entirely remove information asymmetries, but certainly attenuated them. Secondly, the incentive properties of the contract were important, with a share option scheme being favoured over a bonus scheme from a motivational standpoint. Thirdly, the contractual relationship itself was largely implicit, complex, and almost continuously renegotiated.

8.9 INVESTEE ($\mathbf{A}^2{}_J$): RISK MANAGEMENT

The second investee ($\mathbf{A}^2{}_J$), regarded here as an agent in relation to $\mathbf{P}_J$ as a principal, had been involved with the firm for six months. He had a strong financial background, having been an outstandingly well-qualified accountant, and knew the development capital field well through his previous involvement with the enterprise board which had played a major role in this MSF's business launch eleven years earlier. He was both highly experienced and of great intellectual ability. While not a technologist in the relevant area,[17] the manufacture of *in vitro* diagnostic kits, he was familiar with a broad range of operational issues within the company.

16 This kind of statement explains the finding of Siskos and Zopounidis (1987) that venture capital evaluation criteria do not usually include R&D. The main criterion appears to be 'management quality', which no doubt is displayed in abundance by this investee. A corollary of this is that the investor severely limits his control capability through his lack of specialist technological knowledge.

17 This deficiency was remedied within the company by the background of its chairman. He had been vice-president of R&D of a high-technology company for eighteen years, and held non-executive directorships of a number of high-growth development companies in the biotechnology field.

When asked whether the outcome of his relationship with the investor involved some chance elements, $\mathbf{A}^2_J$ replied affirmatively. When given the choice between what was effectively a lottery, or gamble, in which you received either (a) £1m. nine times out of ten, on average, and £3m. once out of ten; or (b) £1.2m. with certainty, he chose the former. Thus he was willing to go for the risky alternative, presumably because the probable downside was not much worse than £1.2m. and the not improbable upside was quite superior to £1.2m. This is described as risk-loving behaviour. Significantly, he did not display indifference between the alternatives (risk-neutral behaviour), despite the fact that the actuarial value of the lottery was equal to the value of the sure thing. When asked about a significantly more risky situation, in which a customer may or may not place an order for £1m. with 50 per cent probability (e.g. by the toss of a coin), $\mathbf{A}^2_J$ said the value of the customer's prospective order was zero.[18] This suggests that orders of this sort were very much a matter of one-off deals, so no 'frequency limit' principle could be appealed to in computing expected value.[19]

When asked whether his exposure to risk could be modified by his actions (a consideration explored in Chapter 4), $\mathbf{A}^2_J$ replied "yes" and proceeded to elaborate in some detail. He felt that, "Any modifications would just reduce it from very high to moderate risk", that is, you could not manage away, by diversification or any other means, all of the risk in a commercial setting. On the business risk aspect he said, "We look at the marketing side – try to get effective distributorships and OEM[20] alliances". An alliance had been formed with [Y], a prominent local foodstuffs manufacturer that had global market operations. $\mathbf{A}^2_J$'s company determined the specification, but it met the quality requirements of [Y] and was also branded by [Y]. This piggyback arrangement, which originated in car manufacturing (e.g. a company would make car seats to Ford's specification), significantly reduced market risk for $\mathbf{A}^2_J$.

When asked whether an attempt was made to communicate to investors the level of risk to which the business was subjected, $\mathbf{A}^2_J$ replied "no". His reply was equivocal when he was asked whether potential investors tended to *over-* or ***under***estimate the risk involved in the business. He said that, "It depends who you are talking to". If it were an institutional investor, then "They know pretty well what the risk in bio-tech is". This is because institutional investors who get involved in high-technology ventures quite often have team members with considerable scientific knowledge, as well as financial expertise (e.g. a first-class

18 This suggests quite risk-averse behaviour. Thus attitude to risk is quite sensitive to the form of the gamble offered. See Khaneman and Tversky (1979) and the discussion in Chapter 5.

19 The frequency limit principle would assign a probability of success or failure according to observed outcomes in a set of trials that were, in principle, indefinite in number. In repeated coin tossing, the expected value for the order would be $(\frac{1}{2})$ £1m. = £$\frac{1}{2}$m., not zero.

20 OEM means 'original equipment and manufacture', which allows the company to benefit from established trade names and connections.

honours graduate from Cambridge in microbiology, who took an MBA with business finance specialization after graduation at Warwick[21]). On the other hand, when faced with high-technology ventures of this sort, $\mathbf{A}^2_J$ thought that, "Private investors find it more difficult to contemplate". This appeared to be through lack of knowledge rather than through faulty risk assessment.

$\mathbf{A}^2_J$ thought that in seeking a venture capital investor, an "extremely important" aspect of the relationship was that it involved sharing some of the business risk. The prospect of receiving a fixed sum from the venture capitalist at exit, rather than sharing a proportion of the value of the firm, was found unattractive. The firm was essentially a development company, with currently low profits but enormous potential for generating future value, so this response was understandable.

Concerning motivation, $\mathbf{A}^2_J$ thought that this had decreased since the venture capital investor started sharing the business risk, which is a standard prediction of agency theory. However, the drive and professionalism apparently remained undimmed, for he thought that he was still no more relaxed in running the business.

8.10 INFORMATION-HANDLING ($\mathbf{A}^2_J$)

When asked which methods were used to appraise the performance of his firm, $\mathbf{A}^2_J$ replied that there were four methods of assessment: sales, net profit, cash flow, and performance against budget. The latter is, of course, known as 'variance analysis', and for this company, net profit had been negative. None of these methods of assessment was new since the investor had become involved with the business, and all four were reported to $\mathbf{P}_J$.

The range of managerial actions taken within the business was extensive, including setting financial budgets, costing the output produced, making appraisals of capital investment, and producing information for operating decisions. All of these actions were reported back to the investors, but not as a consequence of investor involvement. Further managerial actions involved producing information to monitor the business and controlling staff numbers. Both of these were actions which had been newly encouraged after $\mathbf{P}_J$ became involved, but they were for internal monitoring and control purposes and were not reported to him. Another action which had been instigated by $\mathbf{P}_J$ was the production of financial information for strategic decisions. Here, $\mathbf{P}_J$ had a significant interest, and required this information to be reported back to him.

In trying to gauge the extent of $\mathbf{P}_J$'s knowledge compared to the investee, $\mathbf{A}^2_J$ was asked about all the categories of information which were relevant to the

21 This is an invented example, but not atypical, as a perusal of various editions of the *Venture Capital Report* will reveal.

running of the firm. In effect, this was a way of pinning down empirically what is described by agency theorists as the agent's 'information set'. So defined, $\mathbf{A^2}_J$ had an information set whose elements included technology, managerial staff, technical staff, budgets, management accounts and supply sources, all of which were thought to be better understood by $\mathbf{A^2}_J$ compared to $\mathbf{P}_J$. Only as regards business strategy did $\mathbf{A^2}_J$ think $\mathbf{P}_J$ was more knowledgeable. For the remaining elements of the information set – markets, capital structure, financial accounts and capital investment – $\mathbf{A^2}_J$ thought $\mathbf{P}_J$ was equally knowledgeable. On balance, the perception of this investee was that for most classes of information he was certainly no less well informed than the investor, and indeed he was generally better informed than him. That is, information asymmetry was acute, and the balance of knowledge was strongly in favour of the agent rather than the principal.

The forms of budget within $\mathbf{A^2}_J$ were diverse, and were originally set at disparate intervals. Thus, before the venture capital investor was involved, the profit and loss account and capital budget were set annually, and the cash flow and balance sheet, monthly. Head count did not need close attention at that point, as fewer than ten people were originally employed within the firm. After venture capital involvement, these intervals all became monthly, for all forms of budget. That is, venture capital intervention was associated with a higher frequency of monitoring. There was also evidence that the intensity of the monitoring, in this sense of probing more deeply, had gone up. For example, in commenting on the capital budget, $\mathbf{A^2}_J$ said, "It is set annually, and we spend and phase it month by month". To illustrate, he said, "We decided to spend £160k this year and review it monthly". This review process 'had teeth' in that $\mathbf{A^2}_J$ said, "We might reset the budget depending on the circumstances prevailing at the time". Making reference to a prospective new manufacturing system, by way of example, he said, "At the moment, we're discussing an automated system which we can either do in modules, four each at £25k, or all in one go, at £90k". The issue here was presumably to stick to budget in the short period, and start installing the modular system; or to reset the budget to permit an initially larger capital expenditure, in order that a long-run saving could thereby be achieved.

The costing procedures used within the company were in their infancy. An attempt had been made to attribute direct labour costs to products since the venture capital investor had become involved, but the system had not been perfected, although $\mathbf{A^2}_J$ said, "We're working on it". While admitting that there was "nothing being done at the moment", $\mathbf{A^2}_J$ wished to express the view that attributing costs to products was "being addressed". He had been in touch with a professor at his former university, who was an expert on activity-based costing (ABC), to discover, in this way, "whether as a company we can handle the information".

The product costs used were standard (rather than actual) and, while $\mathbf{A^2}_J$ could distinguish between fixed and variable costs, he said, "We ignore fixed costs". He continued, "The system at the moment is almost marginal costing" (which of course would force out of view the role of fixed costs) and "margins are extremely high". Accountants were not involved in costing at the design stage.

Possibly because of the company development context in which this firm functioned, involving a number of relatively long-shot projects, formal techniques of appraisal of capital investments were not used, not even the payback period.[22] $\mathbf{A}^2{}_J$ said of the qualitative assessment procedure, which he regarded as highly important, that, "Any prior capital investment is by its very nature qualitative", and "We're always talking about it, and trying to improve what's already there". In other words, given that much of the required plant was already installed, the main issue in terms of capital investment was the enhancement of the quality of an existing stock, and this was by its nature a qualitative procedure.

In terms of reporting back to the venture capital investor, $\mathbf{A}^2{}_J$ felt that *no* classes of information were free from distortion or error in reporting. Thus data were generally what agency theorists would call 'noisy'.[23] This 'noisiness' was thought to be slight for data on products, production, finance and personnel, but marked for data on markets. Part of the problem in estimating markets is that the technologies used are new, and there is little prior evidence on customer demands. Further, marketing is subject to quite strict institutional vetting and constraints. For example, in Europe the EC IVD Directive requires tight quality control, like ISO 9001; and there are demanding product-testing and validation procedures required by the US Food and Drug Administration. $\mathbf{A}^2{}_J$ admitted that he was only "going historically by what [the company] have done in terms of achieving sales budgets – which can only be set on market knowledge". However, there was undoubtedly "distortion" which "suggests error on the market knowledge". The implication of market errors was expressed bluntly: "[The company] runs out of money." There was evidence of 'hubris' in the evaluation of market prospects. This is perhaps to be expected, given the signs of some tendency for risk-loving behaviour noted in section 8.9 above. $\mathbf{A}^2{}_J$ talked positively of his company being "entrepreneurial" and "market orientated", and having "an optimistic view of what can be achieved". However, he confessed that there was a downside to this, saying, "One of [the company's] fundamental problems is that they have always overestimated the level of turnover".

8.11 TRADING RISK AND INFORMATION ($\mathbf{A}^2{}_J$)

The agent, $\mathbf{A}^2{}_J$, thought the principal, his venture capital investor, $\mathbf{P}_J$, was better equipped to handle risk than himself. His reason for this amounted to the prin-

22 A point made explicitly by $\mathbf{A}^2{}_J$, with respect to this most basic of techniques.

23 This terminology is borrowed from communications theory, in which a pure signal is fully informative but a noisy signal has random variations added to it, thus diminishing the informativeness of the signal.

cipal's ability to diversify away his risk. Thus $\mathbf{A}^2_J$ said, "He's got greater breadth of exposure to risk" and had what he described as a "broader perspective" on risk than himself. He described the flow of information which he provided to the venture capital investor as being 'measured' in the sense of related to requests. So far as the extent of information requested went, $\mathbf{A}^2_J$ thought it was reasonable.

In his relationship with $\mathbf{P}_J$, $\mathbf{A}^2_J$ felt that he did retain the right of confidentiality over certain aspects of running the business. He said that although "venture capitalists are given a wide range of information", he wished that areas of confidentiality could be more extensive. Two examples of this were licence and distributorship agreements. On the other hand, $\mathbf{A}^2_J$ did not think it would be advantageous to the running of the company to be better informed about $\mathbf{P}_J$'s operations. One suspects that $\mathbf{A}^2_J$'s main motivation in wishing to extend his own areas of confidentiality was trade secrecy in a competitive, high-technology area, rather than the masking of intrinsic efficiency. In this sense, the desired information asymmetry was not simply an agency effect.

When asked what attributes of his were most important in terms of what he brought to the relationship with $\mathbf{P}_J$, $\mathbf{A}^2_J$ identified effort and knowledge of the products as being very important. Also thought to be important were risk-bearing, knowledge of markets, financial expertise and commitment to the business. The supply of finance capital was thought to be unimportant. *Per contra*, the attributes which were thought to be very important in terms of what $\mathbf{P}_J$ brought to the relationship were the supply of finance capital and risk-bearing. Other important attributes of $\mathbf{P}_J$ were thought to be the knowledge of products and markets, effort and commitment to the business, and financial expertise. The perceived relationship between $\mathbf{A}^2_J$ and $\mathbf{P}_J$ was therefore complementary, with $\mathbf{A}^2_J$ bringing to it market knowledge and effort, and $\mathbf{P}_J$ bringing to it risk-bearing skills and finance capital. Indeed, when asked to identify the *single* most important attribute which each brought to the relationship, $\mathbf{A}^2_J$ identified it as knowledge of the products from his perspective, and the supply of finance capital from $\mathbf{P}_J$'s perspective. Thus the basis of the potential for a trading relationship between principal ($\mathbf{P}_J$) and agent ($\mathbf{A}^2_J$) is sharply delineated.

The level of equity held in the firm by $\mathbf{A}^2_J$ had always been low. Its level was not thought to influence commitment to the business. Briefly, he thought this was because going from a zero equity holding, to holding two thousand shares, was a "negligible change". $\mathbf{A}^2_J$ was party to a performance-linked equity scheme with $\mathbf{P}_J$, and up to 7 per cent of the authorized share capital, which had not been issued, could be held. From the standpoint of the managing director, who was not the respondent, the acquiring of additional shares was not strictly performance related, but rather arose because when he was bought into the company he did so "at rock bottom" and "was promised a number of options to fulfil contractual obligations". Performance-linked equity was thought to be a good motivator from his own standpoint, according to $\mathbf{A}^2_J$.

In his relationship with other investees of $\mathbf{P}_J$, $\mathbf{A}^2_J$ felt he had to compete in some measure for more favoured treatment. In multiple-agent contexts (see Chapter 4 above) one might indeed expect the principal to use comparisons between agents to draw relative efficiency conclusions, and thereby to influence his allocation of attention across agents. Though $\mathbf{A}^2{}_J$ was aware of being in some kind of "beauty parade" in front of $\mathbf{P}_J$, this did not encourage him to attempt to "put on a good show". Rather, he would "let the facts speak for themselves". It was apparent that the implicit contract was perceived to be more important than the explicit contract by $\mathbf{A}^2{}_J$. He thought his relationship with $\mathbf{P}_J$ was based largely on trust and understanding, and felt that this was developing "on an ongoing basis". This need not imply the absence of intrinsic problems of agency in the contracting between $\mathbf{A}^2{}_J$ and $\mathbf{P}_J$, but rather that they were generally satisfactorily resolved, permitting a larger role for trust.

When asked whether there was scope for moving further towards an optimum in his relationship with $\mathbf{P}_J$, $\mathbf{A}^2{}_J$ replied that this was not the case, as he felt their relationship was already "close to optimum". This reinforces the positive view of the contracting mentioned above, where technical issues of information, incentives, skills and risk-bearing had been resolved to an extent that trust predominated. Indeed, $\mathbf{A}^2{}_J$ mentioned that this kind of relationship had emerged "because of the level of support the venture capitalists have provided to the company". In determining the ideal relationship with his investor, $\mathbf{A}^2{}_J$ identified capital structure as being of paramount importance. Also important were efficient risk-sharing, a maximum rate of return and the increasing of motivation. $\mathbf{A}^2{}_J$ rated the enhancement of reputation and the free sharing of information as unimportant. The latter view was noteworthy as it reinforced the view that a chief concern of $\mathbf{A}^2{}_J$ was to retain some areas of information confidentiality. This did not appear to be motivated by a desire to obtain contractual advantage through exploiting information asymmetry in this case. Rather, it was driven by a desire to maintain trade secrecy in an area where competitive advantage was very much governed by superior technological capability.

8.12 CONCLUSION

A framework for analysing case study evidence on investor–investee relations was deployed using applied principal–agent analysis. The three main categories of analysis used were identified as risk management, information-handling, and the trading of risk and information. This was then applied to a detailed case study of a major UK venture capital fund and two of its high-technology investees.

The following conclusions emerged. First, both $\mathbf{P}_J$ and $\mathbf{A}_J$ were exposed to risk, but $\mathbf{P}_J$ had greater risk management options, notably by portfolio diversification. $\mathbf{A}_J$ attempted to spread risk by project diversification, but ultimately remained exposed to risk and displayed relatively low-risk aversion.[24] $\mathbf{P}_J$ and $\mathbf{A}_J$ agreed to contract in a way which involved risk-sharing, the greater burden being borne by $\mathbf{P}_J$, but some remaining on $\mathbf{A}_J$ for incentive reasons (that is, maintenance of $\mathbf{A}_J$'s motivation in the face of moral hazard temptations). Second, information asymmetry was intrinsic to the relation between $\mathbf{P}_J$ and $\mathbf{A}_J$ and means were sought to reduce it in order to improve the efficiency of contracting. Information flows were improved pre-contract to attenuate adverse selection, and were required to be rich and full post-contract to limit moral hazard. The information structure was used by $\mathbf{P}_J$ not just to improve decision-making, but also better to align incentives for $\mathbf{A}_J$ with his own. Despite the large volume and diversity of information exchanged, an irreducible 'noisiness' remained which left the outcome of the relation between $\mathbf{P}_J$ and $\mathbf{A}_J$ subject to considerable uncertainty. Third, there was a trade-off between risk and information which could not be removed, even with a rich information flow, especially from $\mathbf{A}_J$ to $\mathbf{P}_J$. Such information was used for performance evaluation, and the designing of incentives linked to performance. The reduction of information asymmetries, the sharing of risk and the negotiation of incentives were achieved largely through a continuously renegotiated implicit contract.

In this type of empirical analysis, one is not engaging in empirical testing of the econometric type, but checking the extent to which actual observations 'fit' the categories, and relations between them, suggested by theory. In the case of venture capital investor–investee relations examined here, the 'fit' with many features of principal–agent analysis appears to be good. It therefore provides confirmatory evidence for this type of economic theorizing.

24 Though this was probably because qualitative considerations were underplayed in considering his attitude to risk. When taken seriously, a more risk-averse mentality on the part of $\mathbf{A}_J$ is evident.

9

CASE STUDY H: PRINCIPAL A BANKING SUBSIDIARY

9.1 INTRODUCTION

The previous chapter considered the case of a relatively small independent venture capital fund, and two of its investees. There, concern was with the smaller end of the market, and high-risk, high-technology, early-stage involvements would be contemplated. By contrast, this chapter considers the case in which the principal (**P_H**) is a subsidiary of a well-known UK investment bank. In this case, there was an aversion to high-risk, high-technology, early-stage involvement on the part of **P_H**, and an almost exclusive preference for large-scale development capital involvement.

P_J of Chapter 8 managed about £50m. of venture capital funds, from which investments of £1m. were typically made, but deals down to values of £250k were not unusual, and even deals of as low values as £100k were contemplated in exceptional circumstances. By contrast, **P_H** of this chapter managed funds of £175m., and would not contemplate a deal with a value of less than £2m. Thus this chapter's concern is with the problems of larger fund management by a venture capital company which is backed by 'big money' and can draw upon a deep financial tradition.

9.2 APPLIED PRINCIPAL–AGENT ANALYSIS: CASE STUDY H

Principal P_H

The principal (**P_H**) had as its parent company a long-established international merchant bank. In turn, this merchant bank was a member of a large international banking group. Merchant banks were the traditional source of outside equity provision for promising, fast-growing firms before the growth of the UK venture capital industry. As this industry has developed, so merchant banks have created subsidiary undertakings, of which the principal (**P_H**) of this chapter is an example. This subsidiary (**P_H**) is wholly owned by the merchant bank, with fully paid-up share capital which is held by the merchant bank. The reason for creating $\mathbf{P_H}$ was to establish offices in London and Scotland that could call on the broader experience and capabilities of the group (e.g. in buyout lending) to pursue a specialization in the provision of development capital, and to facilitate management buyouts (MBOs) by appropriate equity funding deals.

At the time of the study, the principal ($\mathbf{P_H}$) managed £175m. of venture capital funding, of which £86m. were available to invest. The minimum investment size to be contemplated was £2m., and the main goal was to seek any quality businesses in the UK, rest of Europe, USA, Canada and Japan, subject to certain caveats, based on experience. These were: (a) that no consideration would be given to start-up and early-stage businesses, emphasizing the specialization of $\mathbf{P_H}$ in development capital rather than classical venture capital; and (b) that certain industrial areas were excluded, notably high-technology companies[1] and property-related investments (e.g. hotels). These caveats emphasize two goals of the principal: avoidance of high-risk involvements (e.g. 'long-shot' development companies), and specialization in chosen areas of specific competence. The latter implies, for example, the avoidance of undesired areas like property involvements, which are dealt with by other specialized venture capital investors through devices like the business expansion scheme (BES).[2]

The typical practice of the principal was to acquire part ownership of the investee, in order to profit from growth, without unnecessarily pressing forward its pace, and to sell its stake at the same time as management shareholders did when the investee company was floated on the Stock Exchange or transferred to a third party by trade sale. Less typically, if very large amounts of equity were required, the principal ($\mathbf{P_H}$) would lead and represent a syndicate composed of a variety of financial intermediaries with interests in the financing of businesses at the development stage. While specialist providers of development capital do not have a great reputation for proactive involvement with investees (this being more characteristic of seedcorn or start-up investment specialists), this principal ($\mathbf{P_H}$) had cultivated a reputation for working closely with management and displaying high levels of commitment towards the investee. On the other hand, it should be observed that the closeness of the investor–investee relationship in an MBO might be quite short-lived. For example, one major buyout deal, valued at £42m., for a UK company which was a household name, took only six weeks to

1 This did not exclude involvement with companies using leading-edge technology. Indeed **P** had been involved in creating a development finance package for an aviation company of £200m.

2 The business expansion scheme (BES) provided tax relief to individual taxpayers who invested in new ordinary shares of a new company. The scheme aimed to encourage investment in unquoted companies who engaged in high-risk business and had experienced difficulties in raising equity finance. While eligible businesses could be in almost any trading sector, a common abuse of the scheme has been for 'asset-backed' venturing to fund investments in property development, fine wines, etc. After 1988, BES investment in businesses specializing in letting residential property were encouraged.

conclude, after which the principal's only involvement was at arm's length, through a non-executive directorship on the part of one of its directors.

The principal ($\mathbf{P_H}$) received about 250 proposals a year, of which fifty were reviewed, and just two on average were accepted (i.e. invested in) per year. The time from proposal to completion of investment was short, ranging from six to seven months. The number of employees was sixteen, with five full-time venture capital executives. This puts the principal in the medium-size category. By investee type, $\mathbf{P_H}$ was involved largely with MBOs (94 per cent) and strictly on a minority basis with development capital (6 per cent). The range on minimum and maximum equity stake was 3 per cent to 90 per cent with a normal minimum of at least 10 per cent. In less than 5 per cent of investments could this equity stake be bought back. Fees arose from arrangement and underwriting, and the preferred exit routes were by flotation and trade sale. The timescale for investment was typically 2–5 years, though, as indicated above, the period of intensely proactive involvement was often much shorter. During the investment involvement, $\mathbf{P_H}$ required monthly reporting by the investee. In 72 per cent of investments, $\mathbf{P_H}$ was the lead investor. In all such cases, representation on the investee's board of directors was required. The required internal rate of return (IRR) was high, though not atypical, as it lay in the range of 30 per cent to 39 per cent.[3] Of course, as noted below, this IRR was not necessarily realized, nor did it accord with investee's expectations.

The initial field contact for this investor was through an office in Scotland which provided a wide range of banking services across all industrial sectors, with some emphasis on arranging export and project finance. Scotland, as a prospective area of investment involvement, has the advantage of having Edinburgh as a major financial centre, as well as possessing an economic base which has become considerably diversified (e.g. scotch whisky, North Sea oil, 'Silicon glen', financial services) since its domination by the massive industries of coal, steel, shipbuilding, etc., ceased. Personnel based in the office in Scotland had many years of experience in investing in unquoted companies in Scotland, and could also appeal to wider experience in handling large European MBOs and MBIs.

Agent $\mathbf{A_H}$

The agent ($\mathbf{A_H}$) was located in Scotland and was a speciality paper and board manufacturer. The company had deep historical roots, having been founded in the 1920s. A USA-based company had acquired the firm in 1981 and by 1984 had downsized the agent's company to just four paper mills, three in Scotland

3 The venture capital executive interviewed said: "I wouldn't like to say what our IRR is, but it's got to be a number with a three in front of it." Ruling out 3 per cent and 300 per cent as implausible, I assume 30–39 per cent is suggested.

and one in England. Following further acquisition activity, the American parent decided to divest the agent's company, to refocus on its core business in North America.[4] By late 1990 the managing director of $\mathbf{A_H}$ had assembled a buyout team which included himself and the general managers of the four mills. This team conducted a so-called beauty contest for providers of development capital. They reached terms with this particular principal ($\mathbf{P_H}$) because they were convinced that $\mathbf{P_H}$ would be able to bargain hard with the American parent and had the skill and acumen to deliver on the deal contemplated. This 'beauty contest' hints at something of a reciprocal principal–agent relationship, in that the management team of $\mathbf{A_H}$ perceived itself as having a choice concerning which potential **P** with which to conclude a contract. However, looked at from the principal's standpoint, considering the very small number of deals they concluded from the wide variety of choices open to them, this reciprocity was limited. By contrast, the extent to which $\mathbf{A_H}$ had a wide variety of choices was severely limited. This arose because $\mathbf{A_H}$ was something of an unknown quantity. As part of a Delaware-registered company, $\mathbf{A_H}$ had been free of any legal requirement to return audited accounts from 1981. A representative of $\mathbf{P_H}$ voiced the view that: "To buy a business when there had been no audited accounts for the last ten years takes either an unusual degree of recklessness or an unshakeable belief that the price is justified by future potential." In other words, the principal was very much in the driving seat in terms of risk-taking and pricing of the deal.

In the event, the complexity of concluding the deal was given a further twist by overriding background features like the Gulf War and recession in the UK economy. In more than one sense, these provide rather good examples of bad states of the world. The main features of the deal were that the principal ($\mathbf{P_H}$) contributed £10.3m. in the form of equity investment (with some contribution too from the management buyout team) and, further, provided access to the banking resources of its own parent. This facilitated debt and mezzanine finance[5] of a further £29m. Finally, an additional facility of £8.9m. was negotiated for working capital and capital expenditure, this being thought important to permitting the management of $\mathbf{A_H}$ a measure of financial flexibility.

In terms of this management of $\mathbf{A_H}$, its characteristics were as follows. Key budgets were set annually and updated quarterly. $\mathbf{A_H}$ aimed for a 28 per cent return on capital employed, which was above the current rate of return at the time of interview, but below the perceived target of 35 per cent rate of return set

4 A motivation for wanting to shed subsidiary business was to reduce its borrowings.

5 Mezzanine finance is: 'A term which has caused confusion because it has been used by different people to mean different things. Originally it was used to describe bridging finance which companies would raise for working capital shortly before raising capital on a stock market. Latterly it has been used to describe a financing instrument which has elements of both debt and equity, e.g. debt with rights to convert to equity, or a share in profits' (Cary and Mallinson 1997).

for the time of exit of the venture capital investor. In terms of capital investment appraisal, $\mathbf{A_H}$ used simple payback and discounted cash flow (DCF) methods. There were 840 full-time employees in the firm, the bulk of whom (660) were involved in production. The net assets of $\mathbf{A_H}$ were £38m., and the most recent figure available for net profits after tax, at the time of interview, was £5.7m. The equity holding of $\mathbf{A_H}$ was 25 per cent, of which 5 per cent was personally held by the managing director. This 25 per cent holding was maintained after flotation. The gearing ratio was 40 per cent before venture capital intervention, and the aim was to get it close to zero after conclusion of the deal.

Considering $\mathbf{A_H}$ as a collectivity, the management buyout team members were previous paper mill managers within the company. The managing director had led the buyout and was a well-qualified engineer and manager. He was well respected within the industry, being a council member of its Federation, and chairman of its environmental committee. The other managers in the MBO all had twenty to thirty years' experience in the industry, within and without the company, and were seasoned in the holding of high levels of responsibility.

9.3 PRINCIPAL ($\mathbf{P_H}$): RISK MANAGEMENT

When asked the extent to which possible outcomes of investment involvements were subject to uncertainty, $\mathbf{P_H}$ replied that while no numerical odds were attached to outcomes, "any investments we make are more likely than less likely to be successful". This suggests a decision rule like 'seek better than even odds' to invest. It appeared that greater certainty could lower the required or hurdle rate of return. Thus, although a target internal rate of return of 30–39 per cent was set (with 35 per cent often being the 'point' target), $\mathbf{P_H}$ mentioned that, "In a recent case we had a company with a prospective IRR touching 30 per cent" [suggesting ≥ 30 per cent as target], but nevertheless, "We thought it was a good business, so we invested".

In considering the example of a risky project in which there is just a 1 in 10 chance of gaining £10m., the $\mathbf{P_H}$ explained that in evaluating the worth of this project the risk level would be very relevant. Indeed, in view of the high risk, the project was evaluated as worthless. In a less risky situation, with a 9 in 10 chance of getting £1m., and a 1 in 10 chance of getting £3m., compared to getting £1.2m. for sure, $\mathbf{P_H}$ indicated indifference between these alternatives. In this case, $\mathbf{P_H}$ appears to be risk neutral, in that $1.2 = (0.9 \times 1) + (0.1 \times 3)$ is the actuarial value of the uncertain prospect, and indifference was expressed between this and the sure prospect of £1.2m. This sort of risk evaluation would be expected for a fully diversified $\mathbf{P_H}$. Indeed, in expanding on how chance outcomes for investment involvements were handled, $\mathbf{P_H}$ said explicitly, "We work out expected return and spread the risk equally over the portfolio". The interviewer had not prompted the use of terminology like 'expected return', 'spread the risk' and 'portfolio': rather, the more general heading for this line of enquiry was the non-technical expression 'offsetting good outcomes against bad' (see Appendix B, Q.1.2). It seems certain, therefore, that $\mathbf{P_H}$ was implementing risk-diversifying methods. $\mathbf{P_H}$ held that good chance outcomes could be balanced against bad, saying, "This is inevitably going to happen", and was explicit that, "We are looking to maximize return on a portfolio". The latter statement is close to the role of traditional portfolio analysis which says agents maximize expected return for a given level of risk. When asked if systematic methods were deployed to offset good outcomes against bad, $\mathbf{P_H}$ replied affirmatively. He said, "It's very risky to put all your money in one technology", and argued further that he had a preference for companies which themselves diversified risk.

In considering the effects of a new investee on overall risk management, $\mathbf{P_H}$ was asked whether, in contemplating a new investment, the chances of doing it well or badly were weighed against its prospective return. $\mathbf{P_H}$ did show an awareness of this issue and, in his reply, tended to emphasize downside risk and the need to keep it under control. He argued that, "The higher the projected returns, the higher the chance of them doing badly, as there is greater variability". The desire to attenuate downside risk was expressed by the phrase "the key criterion is that you don't want to lose money", which is clearly a markedly different phrase from one giving primacy to the making of money. $\mathbf{P_H}$ said that in screening potential new investees, consideration was given to how they would fit in with the existing portfolio of investees. From the perspective of the enquiry being pursued in this book, one was looking for reference to the sectoral and/or regional composition of the portfolio, and the mix of risk/return ratios in a portfolio. $\mathbf{P_H}$ said explicitly, "We would balance high risk and low risk within a portfolio", adding the caveat that this would imply mostly low-risk investees, mixed with a few high-risk investees. Again, reference was made to the desirability of firms themselves being diversified, for $\mathbf{P_H}$ said, "We try and be in companies dependent upon different sectors/different influences in the economy".

When asked about sharing risk with the investee, $\mathbf{P_H}$ gave rather full responses. The emphasis in the line of enquiry was on whether investees were highly motivated to share risk with $\mathbf{P_H}$. It was felt by $\mathbf{P_H}$ that shifting the financial risk towards him was not necessarily a prime motive of $\mathbf{A_H}$. In $\mathbf{P_H}$'s opinion the investee was mainly thinking: (a) that his job was unsatisfactory or likely to vanish; (b) that business ownership would be a fulfilling alternative; and (c) that to judge from a friend's company that had just gone public, by going this route they "could get seriously rich". This is to emphasize that the payoff motive may dominate the risk-sharing motive, though risk is still a consideration. For example, it has an effect on effort. $\mathbf{P_H}$ suggested that the risk left for $\mathbf{A_H}$ to bear should be neither too great nor too small: "If he bears no risk, the incentive for effort decreases. When risk is high, he becomes dysfunctional – like rabbits staring into the headlights." The principal ($\mathbf{P_H}$) was aware that sharing in the (risky) payoff involved sharing in the risk. He was categorical that, "We cut management in for a stake", implying a desire for risk-sharing. Typically, the stake of $\mathbf{P_H}$ was large, indeed "so large that we have technical control over the business". The extent to which

$\mathbf{A_H}$ could get performance-related equity was readily negotiable, and certainly flexible upwards.

9.4 INFORMATION-HANDLING ($\mathbf{P_H}$)

While no standard was laid down for how $\mathbf{A_H}$ reported to $\mathbf{P_H}$, the information required was extensive and frequent. This extended to monthly reporting in the form of accounting data on profit and loss, balance sheet, and cash flow, and included a commentary or narrative on how the business was performing. Though it might be expected that information would vary over time and across investees, $\mathbf{P_H}$ maintained that they were "all broadly of similar quality, [and] not differentiated by efficiency". This may say more about the severity of the screening of investees adopted by $\mathbf{P_H}$ than about the actual efficiency variation across potential and actual investees. Unusually, given the historical lack of audited accounts for the previous decade, $\mathbf{P_H}$ did not have direct access to $\mathbf{A_H}$'s accounting system. However, there was initial vetting of $\mathbf{A_H}$'s accounting system by $\mathbf{P_H}$ in that "at the time of making the investment, we sat on the audit committee". This arrangement suggests a coalition between investor (principal) and auditor, in contrast to the analysis of Ballweiser (1987), which suggests the possibility of a coalition between investee (agent) and auditor. Arguments against Ballweiser include, first, the loss of reputation the auditor might suffer if found to be in collusion with the party it is auditing (that is, the investee); and second, the desire by the investee to be independently audited, because otherwise costs of opportunistic behaviour would have to be borne.

As the central tenet of agency analysis suggests, $\mathbf{P_H}$ perceived there to be an asymmetry of information between investor and investee (described in the semi-structured interview using terminology like 'differences in information' and 'informational advantage'[6]). $\mathbf{P_H}$ admitted candidly of $\mathbf{A_H}$ that: "On *all* aspects the management ***in situ*** knows more." They [$\mathbf{A_H}$] were close to the daily operations and knew what data related to: "They know what's going on in the business. If you're producing the numbers, you always know more than the person who's reading them." On the other hand, the principal also perceived an informational advantage for the investor: "We are familiar with bank margins, fee norms for investment, as well as methods of capital restructuring and investment appraisal." This knowledge was not merely passive ('know what') as in the beginning of the last quote, but also active ('know how')[7] as in the end of the quote. $\mathbf{P_H}$ mentioned financial appraisal expertise as an important part of 'know how', expanding upon this informational advantage over $\mathbf{A_H}$ by saying he himself had

6 See Appendix B: Q.2.2.

7 See the work of Loasby (1995) on this distinction.

"the ability to do, structure and appraise, which you wouldn't find within an investee company".

$\mathbf{P_H}$ elaborated on the way in which, when meeting with $\mathbf{A_H}$, a discussion developed which considered what types of information could usefully be shared. In terms of agency analysis, this is probing the extent to which, and methods by which, the information of investor and investee becomes aligned to enhance contractual efficiency.[8] $\mathbf{P_H}$ explained that performance, budgets and the business plan were freely shared. It was also expected that $\mathbf{A_H}$ would contact $\mathbf{P_H}$ if they were approached by a third party with a view to a trade sale. Although $\mathbf{P_H}$ did not appear to think explicitly in terms of trading his knowledge with investees' knowledge (saying, "We don't see it like that"), he provided an example of a buyout which hinged exactly on this device ("I give him my knowledge . . . [he] gives me the deal").

It was felt by $\mathbf{P_H}$ that no attempt was made to select information presented to the investee. The information was "pretty upfront" and "appears in the mould which we show the investee company". On the other hand $\mathbf{P_H}$ was sharply aware of the tendency for the investee to be selective in the information supplied. This happens "all the time", there being the general tendency for management teams to "try and keep some information to themselves". In selecting information, investees "always tend to make the picture more rosy than it is". Labour relations and market prospects were areas where the investees "normally put on a positive gloss". The evidence of this tendency to hidden or unseen actions by investees confirms the basic framework of agency analysis, which says that reporting and monitoring systems will be put into place to attenuate this effect, but that its existence is naturally to be expected, in that some advantage may accrue to the agent from having an information advantage over the principal.

$\mathbf{P_H}$ was asked whether problems arose in getting information that enabled him to get to grips with the reality that governed the relationship with the investee. This struck a resonant chord with $\mathbf{P_H}$ who said that this was a major concern, and that, "We examine it in such detail that we beat it completely to death". In seeking to improve the information flow and quality, $\mathbf{P_H}$ was willing to "go back to school" and said, "People are always talking about things we haven't got a clue about, so we put up our hands and ask them". He gave as an example an investee firm which was a brewing company. A presentation was given by the company that appeared to hinge on the central notion of an MAV. Unfortunately, the investors had no idea what an MAV was! They were not too embarrassed to ask, discovered MAV meant 'moving average volume', and were much the wiser for this useful nugget of information. While admitting that events like this were not the norm, for "if they use jargon, they generally seek to explain it to you", it was

8 The source of contractual efficiency arising as it does, in part, from an information asymmetry between investor and investee.

not uncommon – "It does happen". As regards auditing of the investees' accounting system, $\mathbf{P_H}$ again suggested that he exerted some influence here. He expected to sit on the audit committee and "would not have auditors from a company we weren't happy with". To reinforce a comment made at the beginning of this section on information-handling, if there were to be any coalition formed with the auditor, it would be with $\mathbf{P_H}$, not $\mathbf{A_H}$. Concerning the effects of costs on information acquisition, $\mathbf{P_H}$ took quite a sophisticated view, showing an awareness of the opportunity cost of information acquisition and an awareness of problems of "bounded rationality".[9] $\mathbf{P_H}$ said of information, "Processing it is the problem. You can only absorb so much data or information. We occasionally shout 'Stop!".' It is worth observing that the provision of excessive information in this way by $\mathbf{A_H}$ may amount to being uninformative. What one seeks is salience or relevance in information provision, rather than a large volume of information per se.

9.5 TRADING RISK AND INFORMATION ($\mathbf{P_H}$)

In interview, $\mathbf{P_H}$ was probed about the extent to which he shared risk with $\mathbf{A_H}$. A point of particular interest was whether the investor was better equipped to handle risk than the investee. $\mathbf{P_H}$ was aware of being far less risk exposed than the investee, saying, "It doesn't matter as much to us as to the investee if they go bust". The implication here is that not only does the principal have risk-spreading advantages ("We like our portfolio to be diversified"), but also that he has greater bargaining power in contractual relations because he can walk away from a deal with alacrity. Again, it was confirmed that the principal tried to run a transparent information policy for the agent $\mathbf{A_H}$, saying, "It's all pretty open". It was felt to be appropriate that $\mathbf{A_H}$ should retain the right of confidentiality over certain types of information. The extent of this was defined as "everything that isn't in the public domain". The safeguard on information provision which $\mathbf{P_H}$ had, and which no doubt played a part in this apparently permissive attitude on the part of $\mathbf{P_H}$, was that the banking nexus automatically conferred strong rights on the investee: "We always have the 'let out' of discussing the company's affairs with the bank." As a consequence, $\mathbf{P_H}$ was able to assert to all practical purposes that, "There is a full and free exchange of information". Given that $\mathbf{P_H}$ was aware of the strong and natural tendency of the agent to Balkanize information, it is a measure of the success of the principal–agent contracting nexus in this case that the information flow nevertheless ended up being "full and free".

9 In the sense of Herbert Simon (1982), according to which, economic agents are rational by intention, but they are 'bounded' by limitations to their cognitive ability (e.g. in computation and modelling).

It was felt that this approach to full and free information was facilitated by a willingness on the part of **P$_H$** to bear greater risk for the investee. **P$_H$** stated that, "Assimilation of information about what is going on in the business is our real problem".[10] On whether he were willing to bear more risk the more telling the information provided by **A$_H$**, **P$_H$** said: "Yes, you are. It influences our judgement if it [that is, information] can be more easily assimilated." The inference one draws here, given the context, is that the phrase "our judgement" refers to risk assessment by **P$_H$**. On whether there was a menu or trade-off between risk-bearing and investee information provision, **P$_H$** had a position which is less easy to interpret. He said "no" there was no trade-off, and that he would "just see what the risk is". Here the view being expressed was that there was some level of intrinsic risk in the investment involvement and that the goal of the investor, as the risk specialist, was to determine this. This was a different issue, however, from determining how risk was to be apportioned. In this sense, the investor saw little point in thinking in terms of a risk/information trade-off, as this was dominated by the larger consideration of estimating the absolute level of intrinsic risk.

However, **P$_H$** agreed that risk or uncertainty had a bearing on investees' effort. He was quite categorical that "lack of risk makes people lazy". He amplified this point in a more colourful fashion by saying: "If they're 'fat and happy' they don't make a lot of money – and we need to sharpen them up." It was felt that there were incentive advantages in keeping the investee risk-exposed. **P$_H$** said: "We are aware of the incentive of leverage. We like management to invest in the companies we're buying." Although there was no precise figure given for how much risk the investee should best bear,[11] **P$_H$** estimated that asking investees to put in about £20k–£50k would adequately incentivize effort, presumably bearing in mind the magnitude of the typical investee's net worth. It is of note that the sense of risk being conveyed by **P$_H$** here was risk exposure, rather than riskiness of outcome.

Concerning the relationship between equity stake and effort, **P$_H$** explained that he would not take less than 10 per cent of equity (on which he expected a greater than 30 per cent rate of return). He explained an insider acronym, TRFM, which can be read as 'too rich for management'. The implication of this is that if a deal is created which is very attractive, then the principal expects to be a prime beneficiary. It was made clear that performance-linked equity ('ratchets') were used, but the basis of their operations was one of the few areas in which **P$_H$** insisted that, "The documentation is confidential". One operating principle in equity involvement was said to be "start low and aim high", which was felt to have good motivational features. It was made clear that **P$_H$** felt any performance

10 See the notion of 'bounded rationality' mentioned above.

11 This should be interpreted in the light of previous remarks about risk being possibly too high or too low, which suggests some desired intermediate risk level or interval.

enhancement was likely to arise from venture capital intervention and that the investor should therefore be a major beneficiary. Hence he said, "We want to buy companies that are inefficient", but no doubt with company turnaround potential.

In terms of portfolio or fund building, $\mathbf{P_H}$ claimed that, in principle, no investee received more favourable treatment. He was categorical that, "We do the deal at the moment, rather than compare it to previous deals". This is an impressive commitment to independence in investment decision-making. At the same time, $\mathbf{P_H}$ was aware that in creating a portfolio with balance on the risk/return spectrum, "It's a sequential series of choices".

Finally, the investor was asked about how the contract was designed, with the investee in mind, to achieve efficiency. While the practice of investor/investee relations very much hinged on an evolving implicit contract, underlying it was a formal contract designed in what Americans would call 'boilerplate' terms – in other words, exactly and unforgivingly specified. The phrase $\mathbf{P_H}$ himself used was that contracts were "bolted to the ground". The formal contractual process involved a pre-completion legal check list and a formal subscription agreement. It was not felt that a best or optimal equity involvement with the investee could be conceived. $\mathbf{P_H}$ likened the investment process to creating art out of brute raw materials, saying: "It's pretty much hammer and chisel stuff." In some measure, as with art, the efficacy of the investment process was a matter of judgement. It was thought to be difficult clearly to rank investment as success or failure, though it was possible to identify bands of efficiency in investment. The ideal investor/investee relationship was thought to be one in which $\mathbf{P_H}$ had "a hugely profitable investment, the business prospered after our involvement, and it was perceived by the investee that we had offered value".

9.6 INVESTEE ($\mathbf{A_H}$): RISK MANAGEMENT

The investee, a producer of speciality paper and board, is represented here by the responses of the managing director of the group, and the leader of the management buyout group. He thought that there was "always an element of luck" in the investor/investee relationship, but continued, "I certainly don't rely on luck". In an uncertain situation, $\mathbf{A_H}$ thought, "You cut the odds as best you can". Given a choice between £1.2m. for sure or a gamble offering £1m. with 0.9 probability and £3m. with 0.1 probability, $\mathbf{A_H}$ categorically chose the sure prospect, saying, "We would never take anything on under these conditions". This clearly categorizes $\mathbf{A_H}$ as a risk-averse investee. This contrasts with the view of the investor, who expressed indifference between the certain and risky (but actuarially equivalent) prospects. This combination of a risk-neutral investor, with a risk-averse investee, is exactly what underpins the risk analysis of the principal–agent approach of this book.

Interestingly, $\mathbf{A_H}$ naturally thought in terms of shortening the odds on risky investment projects, saying: "If it's a capital investment that would make money for us, we could try to reduce the odds." To put the matter in the terminology of Chapter 4's formal developments, the investee would exert effort to increase the probability of the good state of the world occurring.

$\mathbf{A_H}$ agreed that an adjustment would be made to net profit figures to take account of chance elements. A computer model was used for individual investment appraisal and a grid was utilized for comparing one case with another. This computer model was used for sensitivity analysis, which extended to appraising the market implications of project delay, or the consequences of different rates of market development. This computer modelling very much emphasized the comparative advantage of the investee in market risk assessment. $\mathbf{A_H}$ appraised his own business venture, founded on a long-standing company, with an established set of markets, as "low-risk". In contemplating a high-risk project, with just a 50 per cent chance of success (valued at £1m.), $\mathbf{A_H}$ valued it at zero, saying, "I haven't got the order at that time". This is a similar type of evaluation to that of $\mathbf{P_H}$; that is, neither party displayed an inclination to think in expected value terms when chances were no better than even.

It has been noted above that $\mathbf{A_H}$ would attempt to improve the odds for an attractive project. He had said that "there always *are*" ways to limit or modify exposure to risk, and the procedures he adopted are worth considering. The basic trading policy of $\mathbf{A_H}$ was risk averse and included currency hedging. Consultants were used for advice on risk-handling. An attempt was made to tie in customers, especially in the USA, by branding and financial incentives, including bulk discounting. Despite these devices, it was still the case that "products and prices had to be right". $\mathbf{A_H}$ felt that his overall strategy for risk management was comprehensive, saying, "We're very diversified in terms of customers,[12] products, markets and geographical distribution", concluding therefore that, "We have a very high spread of risk".

Despite the investee's personal risk aversion, and detailed attention to risk-handling, $\mathbf{A_H}$ felt ("in my view") that potential investors tended to overestimate the risk inherent in the business. Although he said that he was "very aware of risk", he was somewhat surprised that, relatively speaking, $\mathbf{P_H}$ was "much more aware of risk". While $\mathbf{A_H}$ was inclined to think that $\mathbf{P_H}$ worried about risk "through ignorance", it transpired that the focus of their worry was, "We're very susceptible to world wood pulp prices". Essentially, "if world prices go up, then the product price goes up too", which, even if the competitive position *vis-à-vis* current rivals were unaffected (assuming no differential incidence of price increases), would disadvantage this firm as against substitute products. $\mathbf{A_H}$ was disappointed that volatility in world pulp prices was "all the investor wants to talk

12 Of customers, it was thought advantageous that "we are not dependent on government orders", presumably because of the danger of excessive customer concentration, and the consequent loss of bargaining power and increase in risk.

about", though in a sense he admitted the importance of risk by saying that, in seeking to agree a contract with a venture capitalist, it was "very important" that $\mathbf{P_H}$ would share some of the business risk.

$\mathbf{A_H}$ displayed confidence in estimates of the prospective value of his firm, and a willingness to bear risk (or a confidence in asserting low risk) by his rejecting the option of a fixed return on exit, rather than a proportion of the value of the firm. Although $\mathbf{A_H}$ said, "I don't think you're ever relaxed in running a business", even after venture capital intervention, he said that there was "no doubt about it" but that his motivation within the business had "greatly increased" since he started sharing the risk with $\mathbf{P_H}$. This again suggests that perhaps the investee's business was more risky than he was sometimes prepared to admit, even to himself.

9.7 INFORMATION-HANDLING ($\mathbf{A_H}$)

In terms of using information to assess the firm's performance $\mathbf{A_H}$ used a wide range of methods, including sales, return on investment, net profit, net profitability, cash flow and the wage bill. All of these data were required to be reported to $\mathbf{P_H}$, who insisted upon a very full flow of information. Only the cash flow measure of performance had not been used before venture capital intervention. In terms of taking managerial actions for monitoring and appraising the business, $\mathbf{A_H}$ was very active on a broad front. He took the actions of setting financial budgets, costing output produced, producing monitoring information, appraising capital investments, producing information for operating and strategic decisions, and controlling staff numbers (e.g. headcount). Since venture capital intervention, the only new class of information that was used as the basis for managerial actions was that financial information which was generated for strategic decision-making. Operating decisions were discussed informally at pre-board meetings. Strategic decisions – the new area of involvement in terms of the production of financial information – were now considered in the context of a three-year rolling plan, rather than on the simple annual budgetary basis which had been used under US control of the business.

Clearly, $\mathbf{P_H}$ was taking extensive steps to attenuate information asymmetry between himself and $\mathbf{A_H}$, as a great deal of information was being reported to him. However, for the two classes considered so far, much of it was already being generated in the investee firm. Over a much wider range of information types, extending well beyond the performance and managerial actions data considered so far, $\mathbf{A_H}$ was asked to rate the relative state of his knowledge compared to that of the investor $\mathbf{P_H}$. For most information types, $\mathbf{A_H}$ thought he was relatively more knowledgeable with regard to technology, markets, managerial staff, technical staff, business strategy, capital investment, supply sources and competition. The state of knowledge was thought to be the same for both $\mathbf{P_H}$ and $\mathbf{A_H}$ in just three areas, that is, budgets, management accounts and financial accounts. These are, of course, naturally classified as 'hard' data, compared to data on such matters as technology, competition and strategy, which involve estimation and judgement. In only one area, capital structure, was $\mathbf{P_H}$ thought to be more knowledgeable than $\mathbf{A_H}$, this being, arguably, $\mathbf{P_H}$'s key area of specialist skill.

Two clear points have emerged from this examination of the distribution of knowledge between $\mathbf{P_H}$ and $\mathbf{A_H}$. The first was that $\mathbf{P_H}$ desired as much hard information as it could have from $\mathbf{A_H}$, and was willing to identify new areas of hard information (e.g. cash flow) in which it would wish to be informed. Secondly, $\mathbf{P_H}$ remained relatively ignorant of many areas of company activity, even after intermediation, especially in those areas where information was soft rather than hard (e.g. competition, strategy). Forms of budget determined the frequency of budget setting, ranging initially from one month for the balance sheet, to three months for headcount and profit and loss, to six months for cash flow, and twelve months for promotional advertising. After venture capital intervention, no reporting frequency went down, and only for the profit and loss account and capital budget did they remain the same. Advertising budgets were set quarterly rather than annually, and all other budgets were set monthly. Change was particularly evident in the case of cash flow, with the new interval for budget setting being monthly rather than biannually. This reinforces the relative importance of cash flow to the business, as perceived by $\mathbf{P_H}$, which was noted above in the context of performance appraisal. The general result, that reporting frequency increased markedly post-investment, is amplified considerably in Chapter 13.[13]

Increased *frequency* of reporting is, like increased scope of reporting, an aspect of the generally greater *intensity* of post-investment reporting required by the venture capitalist. In terms of the agency approach this attenuates moral hazard, and further promotes contractual efficiency by more precise control of the investee's firm.

In deciding on capital investment, $\mathbf{A_H}$ used a wide variety of techniques, including payback, internal rate of return, net present value, accounting rate of return, and qualitative assessment methods. All were rated as highly important in the investment process, barring net present value and accounting rate of return, which were rated as being of moderate importance. The use of internal rate of return, net present value, and accounting rate of return were all new since the venture capital intervention occurred. This is what is to be expected more generally when the major goal of the venture capitalist investor is fully to protect him- or herself from agency risk by creating a complex of monitoring and control devices. This behaviour is thought by writers such as Fiet (1995) to be typical of venture capitalists who specialize in development capital, which is indeed the case with $\mathbf{P_H}$. Also, by encouragement from $\mathbf{P_H}$, sensitivity analysis of capital investment decisions, using discounted cash flow techniques, was undertaken by $\mathbf{A_H}$.

13 See, especially, Table 13.4 and associated discussion.

This was rated as a highly important technique. In using capital investment appraisal methods, which involved discounting, a discount rate of 25 per cent was used, which is significantly below the avowed rate of return figures of $\mathbf{P_H}$ of 30–39 per cent. The payback period was said by $\mathbf{A_H}$ to be, ideally, less than two years. This would seem to be very short, given the sorts of technologies used in the industry, and may reflect some earlier history within the company of cash-flow problems and short-termism.

$\mathbf{A_H}$ had considerable confidence in the accuracy of much of the information he transmitted back to $\mathbf{P_H}$. In particular, production, financial and personnel data were thought to be subject to no distortion or error in reporting; and product and market data were thought to be only slightly prone to distortion or error in reporting.

9.8 TRADING RISK AND INFORMATION ($\mathbf{A_H}$)

Although, within the framework developed here, one tends to think of the principal being skilled in risk management and the agent as skilled in running the firm, $\mathbf{A_H}$ regarded himself as better equipped to handle risk than $\mathbf{P_H}$. In fact, this makes sense if one distinguishes between market risk and agency risk, as does Fiet (1995). Arguably, the successful specialist investor in development capital is particularly skilled in dealing with agency risk (e.g. by organizational devices such as monitoring, control and incentives). On the other hand, the investee who has successfully survived, and even flourished, through 'growing on' his firm, has demonstrated a capability in handling market risk. This latter line of reasoning seems to be supported by the justification which $\mathbf{A_H}$ proffered for his own view: "I have the knowledge of the business, industry, market, product and competition." Put another way, $\mathbf{A_H}$ explained: "We're the players in our league; they're the players in theirs." Expressed yet another way, he is saying, "We handle market risk; they handle agency risk". This attitude helps to explain the earlier comments above (section 9.6) on the bewilderment $\mathbf{A_H}$ expressed when $\mathbf{P_H}$ regarded the investee company as prone to what we are describing as market risk: $\mathbf{A_H}$ is used to handling it, whereas $\mathbf{P_H}$ is not. They therefore have different perceptions of market risk.

The flow of information which $\mathbf{A_H}$ provided to $\mathbf{P_H}$ was characterized as extensive (i.e. 'full and detailed'). To put it categorically, $\mathbf{A_H}$ said: "We don't hold anything back." In terms of the volume of information provided $\mathbf{A_H}$ thought, "What we did was about right", and felt that, "We kept them well-informed on the state of the business". This is despite the earlier protest of $\mathbf{P_H}$ that he could be subject to information overload (see section 9.4 above). $\mathbf{A_H}$ may or may not have been aware that the information overload of $\mathbf{P_H}$ perpetuated information asymmetry between them.

$\mathbf{A_H}$ felt that it was proper to retain the right of confidentiality over aspects of running his business and mentioned the following: market statistics and information; product development; technology; and market positioning *vis-à-vis* competitors. This finding reinforces the point made above that these are all areas which involve market risk – precisely the areas in which $\mathbf{A_H}$ thought he had a comparative management skill advantage over $\mathbf{P_H}$. $\mathbf{A_H}$ thought that his area of confidentiality was neither too great nor too small, and had no desire, in terms of perceived potential gain in the running of his business, to become better informed about the operations of the venture capital investor $\mathbf{P_H}$.

As the diagrams of Chapter 4 emphasized, we can think of $\mathbf{P_H}$ and $\mathbf{A_H}$ as trying to devise 'best trades' in seeking to conclude a mutually agreeable contract. It is therefore of interest to know what special qualities each partner in the principal–agent relationship brings to the contractual agreement. $\mathbf{A_H}$ noted the following as being very important attributes that he brought to his relationship with $\mathbf{P_H}$: knowledge of the product or service; knowledge of markets; effort and commitment to the business. Risk-bearing and financial expertise were also thought to be important, though these are usually specialist attributes that one associates with the investor rather than investee. The supply of finance capital was rated as unimportant by $\mathbf{A_H}$ in terms of what he brought to this particular deal, because he "didn't have a lot to bring". However, he admitted, "It's important in principle". While his supply of equity was relatively 'small beer' in relationship to the size of the deal, this does not exclude it having important incentive properties and consequences within the agreed contractual framework.[14]

Using these same attributes to explain what the venture capitalist brought to the relationship, $\mathbf{A_H}$ identified the following as very important: risk-bearing; commitment to the business; and a new category – a networking relationship with the City. $\mathbf{A_H}$ felt that $\mathbf{P_H}$ provided valuable input to the deal-making process, by the City introductions that were facilitated. The value of this access to financial networks which the investor may facilitate has been emphasized by Steier and Greenwood (1995: 352) and Fried and Hisrich (1995: 103). Effort and financial expertise were also thought to be important attributes of $\mathbf{P_H}$. By contrast, knowledge of the product or service, and knowledge of markets, were thought to be unimportant attributes of $\mathbf{P_H}$.

There therefore seems to be a complementarity of skills between $\mathbf{P_H}$ and $\mathbf{A_H}$, with the one supplying what the other lacked, and certain common skills (e.g. financial expertise) and drives (e.g. commitment to the business) providing the bridge that linked these complementary skills together effectively. Simplifying this relatively complicated picture to one which emphasized single critical attributes on either side of the contractual nexus, $\mathbf{A_H}$ emphasized knowledge of the markets for himself, the investee; and supply of finance capital for $\mathbf{P_H}$, the investor. He also mentioned that the meshing together of these different skills would never work unless both parties, $\mathbf{P_H}$ and $\mathbf{A_H}$, displayed commitment to the

14 See below, in the discussion of the form which authorized share capital took.

business. Put another way, this simplified picture says the starting point must be a determination to contract, and the execution of the contract above all hinges on the market expertise of the agent and the financial resources of the principal.[15]

The highest proportion of equity that $\mathbf{A_H}$ had held in the firm, just before flotation, was 42 per cent; the lowest had been 20 per cent. While $\mathbf{A_H}$ said that his commitment to the firm did not vary whether his equity share was more or less, this needs careful interpretation. Clearly, $\mathbf{A_H}$ had been strongly driven by a desire for the success of his firm both pre- and post-investment. However, post-investment, this desire was buttressed by a quite highly incentivized scheme agreed with $\mathbf{P_H}$. There was a performance-linked equity scheme ("a ratchet, in other words", as $\mathbf{A_H}$ put it), which was described by him as follows: "Originally, we had 20 per cent of equity which, by ratchet, we could take to 37 per cent. The base line went up by a fixed 5 per cent; we repaid our preference shares earlier and went up to 42 per cent." The performance criterion which $\mathbf{A_H}$ had to satisfy to bring about this increase in equity share was based on both cumulative profit and capital value at exit, and it was the latter that put into play the main change in equity holding. While, as we have observed, $\mathbf{A_H}$ said that his commitment to the business did not depend on equity share, it is clear that he distinguished between commitment and motivation, for he was categorical that the performance-linked equity scheme had been a good motivator for him. Indeed, in his own words, "It was central".

Although span of control arguments, such as those proposed in sophisticated form by Gifford (1995), would tend to suggest rival needs by agents in multiple-agent/single-principal relationships, $\mathbf{A_H}$ did not feel he had to compete with other investee involvements of $\mathbf{P_H}$ for more favoured treatment. Putting on a 'good show' for the investor, $\mathbf{P_H}$, was thought to be irrelevant. While the contract which had been agreed with $\mathbf{P_H}$ was tightly legally defined, $\mathbf{A_H}$'s experience was that, "We put it in a drawer and got on with the business". This suggests an evolving implicit contract between $\mathbf{P_H}$ and $\mathbf{A_H}$ underpinned by a 'safety net', but strictly specified, explicit contract. The latter would typically only be referred to in crisis conditions,[16] which fortunately had not been encountered in the progression of this deal.

At the end of this process, $\mathbf{A_H}$ felt that the relationship between him and $\mathbf{P_H}$ had reached a kind of an optimum by conclusion of the deal, including exit arrangements.

15 Fried and Hisrich (1995) point out that the financial resources of the investor are a considerable source of power in the contracting process. Arguably, it consolidates the investor's role as principal, rather than agent.

16 As Fried and Hisrich (1995: 107) point out: 'VCs tend to avoid the use of formal power because it is highly confrontational, and managers may have some countervailing formal power as well.'

9.9 CONCLUSION

In many ways Case H even more clearly 'fits' the principal–agent framework than Case J in Chapter 8. In the analysis of risk in this chapter it was far more unambiguous that the investor ($\mathbf{P_H}$) was risk neutral, through skilful use of portfolio diversification techniques, and the investee ($\mathbf{A_H}$) was risk averse, though willing to confront business risk head on. The agreed contract left the investee risk exposed to moderate moral hazard.

Information asymmetries between investor and investee were marked. The investor responded by requesting a great deal of information from the investee, post-investment. Most of this had to be reported monthly, and the detail was considerable. Only in the areas of budgets, and management and financial accounts did the investor have a natural knowledge advantage over the investee. The main unique attributes that the investee brought to contracting were knowledge and effort; the main unique attributes that the investor brought were risk-bearing and network contacts. Both parties had in common financial expertise and commitment.

The incentives for effort were strong. A performance-linked equity scheme could take the investee's equity from about one-fifth to nearly one-half. This was a powerful motivator for the investee. Contracting relations between investor and investee were tightly legally defined, but explicit clauses were only usually referred to in crisis conditions. The parties were close to an optimum in their contracting.

10

CASE STUDY G: PRINCIPAL PUBLIC SECTOR OWNED

10.1 INTRODUCTION

For this case study, $\mathbf{P_G}$, the principal, was a financial institution owned by the public sector which managed about £10m. of venture capital funds. The public nature of its funding should be no surprise to those familiar with the roots of 3i in the ICFC.[1] There is indeed a long history of the public sector playing an active role in stimulating private investment. $\mathbf{P_G}$ supported smaller investments than did either $\mathbf{P_J}$ or $\mathbf{P_H}$, being willing to provide as small a financial package as £42k. The maximum contemplated was the relatively low threshold of £1.3m., and the average investment involvement was £300k. The agent, $\mathbf{A_G}$, produced or supplied a range of software services and products for retail computer users. The special attribute of this chapter's case study is that $\mathbf{P_G}$ managed funds on behalf of local authorities, rather than banks, financial intermediaries or corporations. The treatment makes explicit reference to the subscription agreement, as this appeared to have an unusually high influence on the form which investor–investee relations took.

Formally, $\mathbf{P_G}$ was an investment company owned by a consortium of London boroughs, which concentrated its activities in the Greater London area. Historically, it had invested its own funds, but at the time of this study it managed funds on behalf of institutional upstream investors, typically local authority superannuation funds. The agent $\mathbf{A_G}$ provided software and hardware packages to meet diverse demands in retail business management. These packages were designed for everything from accounting and merchandising to stock control and electronic 'point of sale' systems (EPOS). The latter were a major specialization of $\mathbf{A_G}$'s firm, with systems ranging from those that used low-cost PCs up to Unix

1 The roots of 3i (Investors In Industry) were in the Industrial and Commercial Finance Corporation (ICFC), established in 1945 by the leading public financial institution of its day, the Bank of England, along with the major clearing banks. Its role was (and is, as 3i) to provide venture and development capital to new and rapidly growing UK firms. It has remained the major player in the UK venture capital industry.

minicomputers. $\mathbf{A}_G$ had annual sales of £7.1m. and employed thirty full-time workers. The principal, $\mathbf{P}_G$, managed £10m. of venture capital funds, had five employees, and concentrated almost exclusively on the provision of venture capital.

This chapter proceeds, as do Chapters 8 and 9, by considering the principal and agent in turn, addressing issues under the headings of risk management, information-handling, and the trading of risk and information.

10.2 APPLIED PRINCIPAL–AGENT ANALYSIS: CASE STUDY G

Principal $\mathbf{P}_G$

The introduction to this chapter has sketched the main attributes of the principal, $\mathbf{P}_G$. As elsewhere in this book, $\mathbf{P}_G$ is also identified with the specific respondent in the semi-structured interview. In Case G, he was the chief executive of the group and had joined it seven years earlier to establish the venture capital side of its business. His early career had been with a large public enterprise and a multinational firm based in the UK. He had worked for six years as part of the management team of a venture capital start-up and had nearly a further decade of experience in a wide variety of subsidiary companies in printing, film, video production, advertising and retail financial services. He had two university degrees. In short, he brought to his role a high level of accumulated human capital, both in terms of experience and credentials.

The team which he headed included an economist, an accountant, and a company secretary. They all had strong commercial backgrounds and experience in various aspects of providing equity capital, including deal generation and appraisal, completion of new investments and management of portfolios of investee companies. As a collective entity, $\mathbf{P}_G$ had high levels of technical expertise and considerable practical experience upon which to draw.

The core business of $\mathbf{P}_G$ was venture capital, though it also was involved in activities such as training and property development. Although rooted in the public sector, it engaged in a number of joint ventures with partners from the private sector. In setting up $\mathbf{P}_G$ as a provider of venture capital, an early commitment was made to the enterprise economy in that an explicit operating criterion was that: "Rigorous commercial investment criteria are applied." From the start, $\mathbf{P}_G$ specialized in investing venture capital in small and medium-sized enterprises (SMEs).[2] The majority of this activity was in development finance and

2 This interpretation of SMEs may differ from that widely used in the applied microeconomic literature (e.g. Storey 1994). There, concern is with firms right down to the 'micro-firm' level (i.e. ten or fewer employees), to which considerable attention is given, and up to fairly low maximum employment sizes (e.g. 200 or fewer employees). The SMEs of concern to $\mathbf{P}_G$ were very much beyond the micro-firm range.

management buyouts (MBOs), with start-up and early-stage investment involvements only being contemplated if the relevant companies displayed exceptional promise.

$\mathbf{P_G}$ had no industrial preferences, though it had a specific interest in media companies, and by geographical commitment was firmly committed to Greater London, with some lesser involvements in South East England. It received about a thousand proposals a year, of which fifty were reviewed and, on average, about five were backed. The screening used had a fine filter, compared to US experience. For example, Roberts (1991), in his analysis of detailed review procedures used in venture capital funds, discovered two typical cases in which eight to twelve out of one thousand, and thirteen out of two thousand, proposals were eventually backed. Thus particularly stringent screening was used by $\mathbf{P_G}$ to attenuate adverse selection. An initial view of the proposal could be taken very rapidly (within days), but due diligence, if the matter were carried forward, took 1–3 months. After deal approval and letter of offer, which usually took 1–2 months, the investment was usually completed within a further month. Investments were realized over a 4–6 year time horizon, and exit was by trade sale or public listing, with a slight preference for the former. $\mathbf{P_G}$ required monthly management accounts from $\mathbf{A_G}$, and insisted that one of their full-time venture capital executives (of which there were three) should become a member of the board of $\mathbf{A_G}$, and should attend monthly. Thus the close frequency of reporting implied close monitoring, and membership of the boards, coupled to regular attendance, bestowed control.

$\mathbf{P_G}$ managed £10m. of venture capital funds, and had invested £7.2m. at the time of this study. The value of funds available to invest was just £2.4m. Investments as low as £40k would be considered, but the typical size was £300k and the maximum £1.3m. Most (60 per cent) of the investments were in developments and MBOs, but a significant minority (40 per cent) was in start-ups. If $\mathbf{P_G}$ was the sole investor (as he was in 90 per cent of cases), he sought a 25–50 per cent equity stake. The minimum equity stake could be as low as 10 per cent and the maximum as high as 100 per cent, but the average equity stake was a minority one, as discussed in the typical case of Chapter 3.

Agent $\mathbf{A_G}$

The agent $\mathbf{A_G}$ was a computer software house which traded within $\mathbf{P_G}$'s chosen geographical area, being located in Greater London. The firm had been created by a management buyout (MBO) five years before this enquiry (i.e. 1988). The administered questionnaire was conducted with a member of the board of directors who had daily 'hands-on' experience with his company's operations. He was the finance director, held a university degree and was a qualified accountant. The board of directors had five members, four of whom held interests in the shares of the company to a total value of £43k, with the distribution of interests being 38, 30, 21 and 12 per cent.

In terms of organizational and legal structure, $\mathbf{A}_G$ was a group, with a holding company and subsidiary company. The principal activity of the group was to supply, install and maintain computer systems for customers across most retail sectors. It had attained a secure user base of about one hundred customers at the time of enquiry, and this base was regarded as having growth potential, despite the sensitivity of retail sales to the phase of the business cycle. The firm had grown rapidly since the MBO of 1988.

Turnover grew at 52 per cent per annum, shareholders' funds at 19 per cent per annum, and fixed assets at 8 per cent per annum between 1989 and 1992. At the time of interview in 1993, $\mathbf{A}_G$ had thirty full-time employees, annual sales of £7.1m., net assets of £1m. and net profits (after tax) of £350k. The gearing ratio was zero, as $\mathbf{A}_G$ had a policy of holding no debt.[3] $\mathbf{A}_G$ held 67 per cent of the share capital, and this had been deliberately chosen at a level which conferred control over the company. At the time of the MBO the management team had "hired venture capital consultants" to act as financial 'deal-makers', who recommended this level of shareholding. This terminology is reminiscent of that used by Fried and Hisrich (1995) in which venture capitalists themselves are described as 'consultants with financial interests' in a company. In order actually to implement the MBO, a venture capitalist had to be found to invest in the company. Shares were split according to the importance (and salaries) of directors, with a maximum of £16k being put in by the managing director. The management team did not receive any 'sweat equity' (i.e. equity received for the work of getting the new form of the company launched). $\mathbf{A}_G$ provided an interval estimate[4] of the annual net rate of return earned by his company of 35–50 per cent, saying, "It all depends . . .". The rate of return before involvement with the venture capitalist was estimated as zero. The expected exit from the investor/investee relationship was by sale of the company. In interview, $\mathbf{A}_G$ was too cautious to commit himself to guessing at the expected rate of return at the time of exit from the relationship with the $\mathbf{P}_G$, saying, "I don't have any idea". This caution was more likely to have arisen from circumspection as opposed to ignorance, because certainly the business had enjoyed rates of return which were well above the realized rates typically achieved by venture capital investors, as opposed to their hurdle rates.

3 Here, preference shares are not treated as debt in the numerator of the gearing ratio. However, interpretations differ. For example, capital gearing = debt ÷ equity, where debt is all external borrowing and equity measures all shareholders' funds. A figure of unity may be regarded as the norm, although much higher figures may occur in practice, and also much lower figures (as with $\mathbf{A}_G$). If the latter, the aversion to debt usually arises from a desire to minimize risk exposure, and to avert debt-servicing costs, or even crises.

4 Interval estimates, indicating a likely range of outcomes, usually carry the connotation that most cases will fall within that range. They are to be distinguished from point estimates which provide a 'best guess' or most likely outcome estimate.

10.3 PRINCIPAL ($\mathbf{P_G}$): RISK MANAGEMENT

Confronted with an example of a risky project with just a 1 in 10 chance of netting £10m., $\mathbf{P_G}$ evaluated its risk element as being 'very relevant' to an evaluation of the worth of the project. Indeed, he simply valued the project at zero, so high was the perceived risk. This cautious attitude to risk was amplified by his later comment that, "Our job is to minimize chance outcomes". In a mixed situation, where the investor could either receive £1.2m. for certain or else would confront a lottery situation, or gamble, which involved receiving £1m. with chances 9 in 10 or £3m. with chances 1 in 10, $\mathbf{P_G}$ nominated the former. He did so even though the actuarial value of the latter is equal to that of the former,[5] and the latter gives the investor quite good odds of getting £3m. This suggests risk aversion on the part of $\mathbf{P_G}$. If $\mathbf{P_G}$ felt he could fully diversify away his risk, one might expect risk neutrality (indicated by indifference between the former and latter options). In fact, in answering a rather different question in the administered questionnaire (actually Q 1.3 on the effects of new investees on overall risk management[6]), $\mathbf{P_G}$ said something which was highly revealing about his attitude to risk: "We are pretty much risk averse and will only make an investment if we feel a very high level of confidence that the plan will succeed. We don't look at it if there is a small chance of it being mega-successful but there is something we're not sure about." The meaning which $\mathbf{P_G}$ attaches to risk aversion differs from that adopted in the main text, but his remark is telling in terms of his mode of risk management.

In commenting on his attitude to chance outcomes compared to sure prospects, $\mathbf{P_G}$ said: "We don't do an analysis of various outcomes; we are aiming for the best outcome." There was little reference made to handling chance outcomes, other than to say: "We look at the likely returns on exit, this being the best guess we can make, based on the information available today, about the best companies in the sector." Here, phrases such as "likely returns" and "best guess" are defined in relation to best performance in the sector. This seems illogical until the operating basis of $\mathbf{P_G}$ is mentioned, namely, "We invest on the basis that the investee company is going to do well", which is a credible policy statement, given the stringency of screening. In other words, $\mathbf{P_G}$ would only back best-practice companies, and it is against this yardstick of performance that investees were measured.

$\mathbf{P_G}$ was asked about the extent to which chance good outcomes were balanced against chance bad outcomes for a given set of investee involvements. While this did not represent the way he thought of investment, he proffered the reply, "They *can* be . . . with the benefit of hindsight, that's what happens in a port-

5 That is £1m.$(\frac{9}{10})$ + £3m.$(\frac{1}{10})$ = £1.2m.

6 See Appendix B, Section 1 on Risk Management.

folio". He agreed that proceeding in this way "makes sense to me, if we are doing it to affect the success of the portfolio".

In his approach to building a portfolio of investees, $\mathbf{P}_G$ was more structured in his approach than some of his initially offhand remarks would suggest. For example, he said, "We have three separate portfolios, with good and bad investments in each", and also, "Sectoral balance is something we do take into account, but it's not a high priority". The caveat in the last quote was a deliberate reminder that the overruling principle was "to maximize our commercial performance" and that "everything we do is directed towards maximizing outturn on any particular day". The goals of getting maximum performance and of achieving portfolio balance are, in fact, not contradictory.[7]

There were also other forms of evidence that $\mathbf{P}_G$ attempted to use to optimize his portfolio. When asked what the least number of investee firms was that he would wish to have in his portfolio, $\mathbf{P}_G$ initially responded, "There isn't one". But by the time he had gone through his argument about maximizing performance, and had indicated the ways in which quarter million pound 'packets' of funding were used to build a multimillion pound portfolio, he ended up saying, "We need not less than 8 or 10 companies to give reasonable returns". This view on portfolio composition is supported by expert opinion (e.g. Fama 1976). Further, in talking of screening new investees with a view to fitting them into an existing portfolio, he freely admitted, "We only invest in one region", which does not seem to fit a pattern of diversification.[8] However, as conversation progressed, he modified this picture by saying: "We look at each proposal that comes to us on its merits. Sector balance is something we do take into account, but it's not a high priority." He added: "We are relaxed about having two or three investments in one sector, but not in one niche." To summarize on risk assessment and portfolio balance, $\mathbf{P}_G$ appears to be among the more conservative of investors. He dislikes risk, preferring sure things, and is not convinced that portfolio balance exercises will diversify away all his risk. However, despite the occasional protest, he does indeed appear to take prudent steps to balance his portfolio by mixing high and low returns, by avoiding too many niche specialists and by spreading risk over eight or more investees per portfolio.

Turning now to risk-sharing with investees, $\mathbf{P}_G$ thought risk aspects were dominated by the investee's "desire to fulfil his dreams with our money". However, in

7 Optimality of the portfolio implies the maximizing of an index of performance, subject to various constraints. Just like the billiard player who achieves optimum performance (see Friedman 1953) without knowing the laws of physics (e.g. elasticities, rolling resistance, etc.), so the expert fund manager may achieve optimum performance without knowing how to solve a Markowitz (1959) quadratic programme. On the latter, see Williams (1985) for programming methods.

8 It does correspond, however, to the evidence noted by Gupta and Sapienza (1992) that small business investment companies, which are probably the US equivalent of $\mathbf{P}_G$, favour industry diversity, but narrow geographic scope.

discussing the effect of risk exposure on investee effort, he admitted that a consequence of risk reduction could be that "it might reduce motivation", but "it depends on the extent to which the investee is exposed". The motivating factor was what $\mathbf{P_G}$ called "hurt money",[9] which meant $\mathbf{A_G}$ had "something to lose, invested". What really 'hurt', and therefore created incentives, was thought to be hard to judge, and "depends on what really motivates who we're getting involved with. There is a great deal of personal evaluation." This is a clear recognition of the economist's hypothesis that attitudes to risk are unique to individuals (Hey 1979), rather than determined by some agreed technical procedure. On balance, $\mathbf{P_G}$ felt that, "Risk exposure and effort are related, a bit – but there's not that high a correlation between them". Motivating $\mathbf{A_G}$ was thought to be more related to equity participation; and this was said as though it were to minimize the influence of risk. However, if the payoff (e.g. at exit) is random, which is the only tenable assumption, this does not successfully put the role of risk in the back seat. Indeed, $\mathbf{P_G}$ seemed aware of this, because he said, "We would never offer a fixed payoff". However, the way in which he thought $\mathbf{A_G}$ was motivated was not primarily through bearing risk, but through the opportunity to share in (prospective) profit. $\mathbf{P_G}$ reasoned: "The essential basis of the deal is that we want the investee to be motivated to maximize our return, so it must be linked to equity. If the value achieved is X + something, we give more." Even this explanation does not avert the risk issue, because prospective profit is not certain, but uncertain, involving an element of risk. The actual picture one gets of $\mathbf{P_G}$ is of a risk-averse investor who ideally would like zero risk involvements, and adopts systematic methods so to limit risk that deals can be viewed in risk-free terms (e.g. using certainty equivalence), with an emphasis on profit incentivization for performance.

10.4 INFORMATION-HANDLING ($\mathbf{P_G}$)

The principal took a strict, almost contractual, view of what accounting information should be provided by the investee. He required "a minimum of monthly management accounts by the third week of the month following". He was clear that this was regarded as a formal obligation for $\mathbf{A_G}$, for he emphasized that: "It is written into the subscription agreement that they must provide this information." It was apparent that there was tight quality control on the return of this information, because shortcomings "might lead to additional supplementaries, depending on circumstances".

The subscription agreement ran to over twenty pages and it was clear that the relevant clause on accounting information provision was strictly interpreted. It

9 I interpret this slightly odd phrasing as meaning that what $\mathbf{A_G}$ had invested was sufficiently significant that the prospect of losing it would hurt him.

ran as follows: 'The Company shall maintain proper accounting records and promptly provide such management information, accounts, budgets and other documentation as [$\mathbf{P_G}$] may from time to time require.' It was also clear that the role of the board too was interpreted strictly in terms of the subscription agreement. According to it, the board is empowered to 'determine the general policy of the company . . . including the scope of their respective activities and operations', and 'the board will reserve to itself all matters involving major or unusual decisions'. $\mathbf{P_G}$ was determined that these explicit contractual powers would be fully implemented, plus more, in the evolving implicit contract with the investee as the deal progressed.

$\mathbf{P_G}$ said that his direct access to $\mathbf{A_G}$'s accounting system was, de facto, unlimited, because "at the dictates of the director we have rights to information". $\mathbf{P_G}$ was proactive as regards the investees' accounting system and said: "We do an accountant's report and insist necessary changes are made *prior* to investment. Afterwards we control, and put right, anything that may be wrong." In other words, close control is taken, both pre- and post-investment, of the quality of the investee's provision of accounting information. This point is considered in greater detail in Chapter 12 below.

Informational asymmetries, which can have an impact on both investors and investees, are known to reduce the efficiency of contracting. This is, of course, why a party to a contract like the principal, who has so much to gain from resolving information asymmetries, is inclined to pay keen attention to the quality and value of information flowing from investee to investor. $\mathbf{P_G}$ felt that the extent of information asymmetry could vary widely, saying, "Depending on the circumstances, we can have a lot or not very much". In view of the attention $\mathbf{P_G}$ paid to accounting information, as described above, it is unsurprising that he said of information asymmetry, "The accounting system should try to minimize this". However, he was at pains to point out that this did not mean the focus of his team's attention was on accounting alone, for such systems, and their data, were really only a means to an end. The true focus was on profit, and $\mathbf{P_G}$ emphasized, "We are all 'profit-responsible' people on the team".

Looking at the information asymmetry the other way around, $\mathbf{P_G}$ thought that his biggest advantage over the investee was that, "We are corporate finance specialists". The implications of this, $\mathbf{P_G}$ said, were that: "We understand how companies work, how profits are made, and which skills are often lacking in investee companies." These skills were thought to confer on him "very much an advantage over our investees on things such as capital restructuring and investment appraisal".

In seeking to align the information of investors and investees, $\mathbf{P_G}$ would meet with investees to discuss what types of information it would be useful for both to share. This was done "as part of the appraisal procedure". In carrying it out, "the underlying relationships tend to be close, especially with smaller companies such as ours". $\mathbf{P_G}$ was "not conscious" of trading his knowledge (e.g. on capital restructuring) with the investee's knowledge (e.g. on computer software markets), though in fact that is what seems to have been achieved, for he reported: "We work on an open system [with] open information. There is a close and open exchange of information at all times." Here, it is notable that $\mathbf{P}_G$ even used the word 'exchange' himself in describing information flows between investor and investee.

Of course, simply because information is exchanged does not, in and of itself, ensure its transparency. Information can be provided selectively, a feature described by Williamson (1975) as 'information impactedness'. If some parts of a set of information that are crucial to comprehension or logical structure are not transmitted, the remaining information can be useless, even if it is voluminous. However, there may be logic and efficiency behind the desire to provide information only on a 'need to know' basis, or to protect some classes of information because of a confidentiality clause. $\mathbf{P}_G$ admitted that "there *are* things" not conveyed to the investee. He said, "We do 'manage' the flow of information" because "we do have our confidential ideas of what we're going to do with an investee company". There were no constraints on doing this because what were involved were "usually informal things, rather than formal reporting". This does seem to suggest that a measure of 'information impactedness' is introduced deliberately by the principal in order better to maintain his seniority in the principal–agent relationship.

Looked at the other way around, it is clear that investees too might be motivated to provide information which is incomplete, biased or selective. However, the first reaction of the principal to this possibility was to say, "I don't know". If the sense intended here is that whatever is concealed is thereby unknown, then this is logical enough, but uninformative. As discussion proceeded, the principal backed off from this tautological position, to say that, in the context of information selection, "We do know these people very, very well". Having created an impression of generally rich information, he then seemed better able to discuss exceptions, that is, to identify areas in which he thought investees might be selective about information. $\mathbf{P}_G$ thought, on reflection, that these included "possibilities of outcomes on exit". The word 'possibilities' as applied to 'outcomes' is pregnant with meaning, and suggests both diverse forms of outcomes as well as magnitudes of outcomes. Beginning to warm to this theme that investees might seek to control information flows, $\mathbf{P}_G$ said, "On some occasions, investees want to set their own agenda, and not ours", but added, "I hope we're 'on top of the market' in each of these areas to minimize the effects of that". This clearly highlights the importance of monitoring (being 'on top') in limiting information asymmetry.

Finally, so far as information-handling goes, one has to consider the extent to which there is a correspondence between information and reality. A lack of such a correspondence presents itself initially as a measurement problem.[10] However, its

10 For example, what is the best way to measure stock holdings in the company?

roots may be partly organizational.[11] $\mathbf{P_G}$ admitted that he had encountered problems in using current information sources to get to grips with the reality that governed the relationship with the investee. He said: "It does happen from time to time. For example, in a recent case there was a stock control problem. The company was very profitable, but we weren't seeing the cash. We went in and sorted it out." As another example of such problems, $\mathbf{P_G}$ referred to a case in which "cash wasn't appearing". He said: "It turned out that there was a debtor problem that needed to be sorted out quite quickly." Here again, we see how a measurement problem (where is the cash?) led to an organizational modification (chasing up bad debtors).

Generally, $\mathbf{P_G}$ did not encounter problems of the sort that arose from the information which was returned by investees being inadequate at conveying what $\mathbf{A_G}$ intended. In one particular sector, however, there was a persistent problem: "A number of our media investments have trouble understanding turnover and profit and loss, and so on. They don't see the importance of it. It is a real conceptual difficulty." Here is a case of so-called creative enterprise finding it difficult to come down to earth and tackle the more humdrum aspects of running a business, like using accounting data knowledgeably.

$\mathbf{P_G}$ was willing to influence the audit of investees' accounting systems, saying he "almost certainly would" assert influence, this being achieved "through the board". He was not deterred from asking for information from investees by the costs of acquiring or processing it. He regarded such costs as being borne by the investees and said, "We take a very rough and ready view". This amounted to a presumed liability on the part of the investee to provide whatever information was required. $\mathbf{P_G}$ considered that for the investee: "The monthly reporting cycle is fundamental to managing any company. If you don't, or can't, do that, just get out of the business!" In short, $\mathbf{P_G}$ thought that efficient information management was an indispensable prerequisite to business success.

10.5 TRADING RISK AND INFORMATION ($\mathbf{P_G}$)

In considering the extent of risk-sharing with the investee, the $\mathbf{P_G}$ was asked whether he felt he was better equipped to handle risk than the investee. Although he answered this in the negative, it was evident that he distinguished between the types of risk that the principal and agent confronted. $\mathbf{P_G}$ was clear that both he and $\mathbf{A_G}$ shared a common goal of seeking profit within their relationship: "We have one objective in mind – to maximize our return from the portfolio. He wants to maximize the return from his business." In reaching this goal, each party to the contract had a different specialization in risk-handling: "We're very

11 For example, how does one evaluate, install and implement a new system of stock control?

good at assessing risks for them . . . but so are our investee companies at assessing risks for their type of business." This view, that the overall risk of an economic activity can be decomposed into various classes of risk, is sophisticated, and by no means isolated in terms of the firms examined (see section 9.8 above). It is a part of financial risk analysis that has already clearly been absorbed (or reinvented) within the venture capital world.[12]

When asked about the openness of information to investees, $\mathbf{P}_G$ replied: "We receive a very large amount of information that is confidential." For example, he said, "We don't release information about investee companies to other investee companies". As well as nominally preserving confidentiality, this procedure also prevents investees from using one another for yardstick purposes, and reduces their power to bargain for better deals with the principal on a comparability basis.

$\mathbf{P}_G$ perceived $\mathbf{A}_G$ as having very little reciprocal entitlement to confidentiality, saying: "It isn't a question of rights. Our rights to information are chiefly to do with performance of business." Yet $\mathbf{P}_G$ would push demands for information beyond this, even arguing, "He'd have to tell us about patentable ideas – it's within the ownership of the company". Within the venture capital world it would not be uncommon to take a fairly hands-off attitude to the specifics of intellectual property (e.g. in terms of details of the patent process) developed within the firm, provided a proper appreciation of its market implication were known, so here $\mathbf{P}_G$ goes further than most.

$\mathbf{P}_G$ thought that the full and free exchange of information was an unattainable ideal, saying, "Over all matters, it's impossible". More narrowly, he seemed to appreciate that, in specific contexts, it may be important to be particularly fully informed. Thus he felt that "in terms of the running of the business, we would want a free and full exchange of information", for example "for shareholders". Although full and free exchange of information may be unattainable, it was clear that $\mathbf{P}_G$ thought that the flow of information was itself negotiable. He said: "We would be prepared to increase our exposure if there were an opportunity offered by the company." Apparently such an opportunity might relate to a new investment proposal. He was aware that "like any other investment appraisal", if it were not openly available, in the sense of printed reports, presentations, or videos, it might yet usefully be "in a person's head". More openness about such ideas, in the sense of revealing more information about investment opportunity, would apparently encourage $\mathbf{P}_G$ to increase his risk exposure. Although $\mathbf{P}_G$ did not go so far as to agree that there was a menu of risk-bearing and information providing options – dismissing this by saying, "I don't think the minds of either party work in that way" – it is apparent that his description of circumstances under which he would increase his risk exposure as he became more informed about an investment amounted to something close to this.

12 See Fiet (1995) for venture capital examples.

Although P_G agreed that risk had some influence on the investee's effort, he thought its significance was "not very much". He did not feel sympathetic to the argument that there was a temptation for the investee to reduce his effort once a deal had been agreed that would spread his risk by sharing it with the investor. Of this effect – the well-known one of moral hazard in the post-contract phase[13] – he said, "Those circumstances only arise where, in terms of pre-investment appraisal, we get it wrong. For example, if we did a deal with someone who had a technical bias, but who turned out not to be interested in making or maximizing profits or returns." He was unconvinced by the notion of an ideal or optimal level of risk that the investee should bear, saying, "I don't know how I'd calculate it". In terms of a concept used earlier ('hurt money' in section 10.3), P_G explained: "We would not wish to have a level of 'hurt money' such that the person involved was too worried about the money and not about the business concerned." Thus, far from believing risk-bearing necessarily elicited greater effort (an effect he tended to understate), P_G felt excessive risk exposure could make A_G dysfunctional.

Overall, so far as P_G was concerned, the effect of risk on investee effort was not a major issue, compared to the incentives created by equity participation. It was the practice of P_G to take a stake in the investee up to a maximum of 50 per cent. He said, "It's a house negotiation guideline". Equity participation by the investee was used in a flexible way to affect effort by the device of ratchets.[14] These were not always successful. P_G noted that, "Ratchets frequently require changing, particularly if things have gone badly". In such circumstances he felt that, "Ratchets can have a negative impact", in which case, "we do negotiate". Here, P_G made reference to Clause 11 of the articles of association, which refer to 'Powers of Directors'. This clause refers to the business plan agreed by directors, and to the way in which the board can vote on resolutions relating to 'any material change in the nature of the business of the company' and other matters, including 'any profit sharing, profit related bonus or incentive schemes, and any variations or amendment to the terms or operations thereof'. It was clear that this Clause 11 was invoked through the board of directors by instigation of P_G in his role as director, and that other restrictions affecting A_G could be varied, including 'what kind of car could be used' under the heading of 'capital expenditure'. Venture capital investors as a class are particularly sensitive about vanities like company cars and company flagpoles or fountains. They feel, for example, that the purchasing of expensive sports cars displays frivolity on the part of the investee, and indicates a lack of prudence and commitment by him to his company.

There was some evidence that certain investees would enjoy more favoured treatment than others: "This would apply to further rounds of investments." P_G

13 See Chapter 4 for more formal development.

14 A device for offering an individual increased equity interest in a company, dependent on certain performance thresholds being achieved.

also noted that investees "would probably get more visits if they were not performing". It was not felt that this affected the behaviour of investees (e.g. by seeking extra attention) because, $\mathbf{P_G}$ maintained, "We are very close to our companies – even those that we are not happy with".

In considering the design of the investor/investee contract to achieve efficiency, $\mathbf{P_G}$ reluctantly agreed that formal legal documents were more important than understanding or trust. He said: "I think it's to do with enforcement and litigability. Any corporate financing needs a lot of paperwork." $\mathbf{P_G}$ felt this documentation was important, saying, "It's about protecting your rights". He referred frequently to the importance of standard documentation for such purposes, including articles of association, subscription agreements and contracts of employment. $\mathbf{P_G}$ felt that the best equity involvement with his investee was a minority one, saying, "49.9 per cent would be ideal, depending on circumstances and how the investee feels about it". Although this desire for no more than a minority stake is not necessarily common in the venture capital world,[15] $\mathbf{P_G}$ rationalized it by saying, "We are seeking to support, not to control".

When it came to considering whether there was an ideal relationship to be attained with the investee (e.g. in terms of information flows, risk distribution or capital structure), $\mathbf{P_G}$ was reluctant to generalize. Referring to investee companies, he said, "They are all so different". Specific features were important: "We look at the deal, its sector, and how the company's going to perform." Such special considerations were felt to govern the way deals were put together. To illustrate, $\mathbf{P_G}$ said: "We might decide we'd like cash or have loan-stock redeemed first." The overriding consideration remained the potential return on the deal. To emphasize this, $\mathbf{P_G}$ said: "We won't make an investment if the company shows less than 40 per cent IRR on the business plan we're backing" – even though the line of enquiry was about the ideal or optimal investor/investee relationship. The reason is clear: to $\mathbf{P_G}$ the best arrangement, no matter how idiosyncratic, was the one which delivered the highest return possible, given the circumstances.

10.6 INVESTEE ($\mathbf{A_G}$): RISK MANAGEMENT

The investee company ($\mathbf{A_G}$) had been a computer software house since 1977 and had been subject to a management buyout (MBO) in 1988. The main line of business for $\mathbf{A_G}$ was the provision of computer systems for retailers, with a specialization in POS ('point of sale') systems. To illustrate, the software that one sees being used to operate the tills at one of the retail outlets of a chain of department

15 For example, in Landström's (1990) study of venture capital in Sweden, a marked trend from minority to majority holdings in investee firms was noted. For his sample, venture capitalists held majority stakes in 59 per cent of portfolio firms (Landström 1990: 355).

stores will be a POS system. This might provide the management of each store with nominal and purchase ledgers, invoice payment and other 'back office' facilities. Link-ups between stores enable management to exert tight financial control over operations within stores, creating scope for cost saving and other efficiency benefits. The technical backbone of $\mathbf{A_G}$'s activities was a point of sale (POS) retailing system created by one of the world's greatest computer and software companies. What $\mathbf{A_G}$ did was install and support such systems, an activity which involved creativity and adaption, so that a customized or bespoke system was made available which best fitted the retailer's needs.

The respondent for $\mathbf{A_G}$ was a highly qualified financial director who had close knowledge of the firm's operations. As elsewhere in this book, the firm and the person will often be treated synonymously. $\mathbf{A_G}$ admitted that the outcome of his relationship with the investor had an element of chance in it, saying, "It's luck in some ways". He gave the example of AT&T's attempt to set up a group of companies in the UK, which had failed because of chance circumstances. Given the choice between (a) a risky situation or gamble in which £3m. was received in one out of ten cases, and £1m. in nine out of ten cases; and (b) a certain situation in which just £1.2m. was received (the expected value of the risky alternative in (a) above), $\mathbf{A_G}$ chose the risky alternative, suggesting a willingness to embrace risk when the downside is not too severe (i.e. only getting £1m. rather than £1.2m.). In a more risky situation in which a customer would place an order for £1m. in just one out of two cases, $\mathbf{A_G}$ valued this prospective order at zero, rather than at £$\frac{1}{2}$m. (its actuarial or expected value). Here, expected values are not considered, presumably because $\mathbf{A_G}$ regards every sales situation as a unique, or one-off, deal. This is understandable, given the 'bespoke' or 'customized' nature of services $\mathbf{A_G}$ supplied to retailers. In contemplating a new project, $\mathbf{A_G}$ said firmly that he did consider the chance nature of the net profit generated, but admitted that, "Investment decisions in this type of business are very difficult". Of new projects, he said: "It's hard to know how much money you'll make out of it. We try to work out how many customers will actually buy it. If you get the first customer to pay for development, anything more is profit." This suggests estimating the frequency of adoption, despite the answer to the earlier question about random customer uptake; and also indicates a type of 'expected breakeven point' analysis for new projects.[16]

$\mathbf{A_G}$ regarded his own business venture as being essentially low risk in nature. He used various devices to limit or modify risk, such as "getting customers to pay for development; modifying rather than rebuilding systems; taking existing products or what you've already got and developing it further rather than starting from first principles". $\mathbf{A_G}$ was aware of the risk-spreading advantages

16 See any standard accounting text for a treatment of breakeven analysis, usually discussed under the heading of cost–volume–profit analysis (e.g. Lynch 1967: ch. 5; Drury 1996: ch. 9). For a more finance-based view of breakeven analysis, see Brigham (1992: ch. 11).

he already enjoyed from being a dealer for a major multinational computing company. He said: "We're an [X][17] dealer – our risk is with them. We try and get them to take the risk if there is one." In representing his potential to an investor, $\mathbf{A}_G$ did try to communicate to $\mathbf{P}_G$ the level of risk to which he was subject. Though he felt that his business was inherently low risk, and that he communicated this fairly to $\mathbf{P}_G$, $\mathbf{A}_G$ felt that $\mathbf{P}_G$ went too far in minimizing the significance of risk for him. He pointed out that although he had a dealership with a large multinational company [X], he was in difficulty "if they decide they don't want to deal through dealers"; then, put simply, "you may not have a business". It is clear that the upstream multinational needed to retain a power of 'market sanction' over its dealers, and this would tend to stimulate their efficiency.[18] Indeed, this multinational provider of the relevant generic hardware and software was a principal to $\mathbf{A}_G$ as agent, in exactly the same way as the venture capital provider of outside equity ($\mathbf{P}_G$) was a principal to $\mathbf{A}_G$ as agent.

In seeking to conclude a deal with the investor, $\mathbf{A}_G$ thought that the fact risk could be shared with the investor was important. Indeed, he considered that, "They took all the risk on financing". He was attracted to the idea of being paid a fixed sum by the principal, rather than a proportion of the value at exit, and felt he had become more relaxed in the running of his business since the investor began bearing part of the risk. Of this latter effect, he said, it was true "especially when you've got a firm like [$\mathbf{P}_G$] behind you". All of this is to suggest considerable risk aversion on the part of $\mathbf{A}_G$. He did not think that motivation was an issue, either before or after venture capitalists started to share risk with him, though this view was coloured by the fact that the deal struck was a management buyout (MBO), and "I only joined at the buyout".

10.7 INFORMATION-HANDLING ($\mathbf{A}_G$)

The chosen methods for assessing performance within $\mathbf{A}_G$'s firm were net profit, cash flow and the wage bill. These had all been newly adopted since agreeing a deal with $\mathbf{P}_G$, and they were all reported to $\mathbf{P}_G$. Further, setting financial budgets, costing the output produced, producing information to motivate the business, controlling staff numbers (e.g. by headcount), reporting on margins and on sales were all new since $\mathbf{P}_G$ became involved, and were all reported to $\mathbf{P}_G$. In other words, there had been a radical overhaul of information provision and procedures as a result of venture capital intervention: monitoring and control had become very tight. Indeed, in some aspects – for example, the time sheets enumerating

17 [X] stands for the name of a major multinational computing firm.

18 That is to say, [X] had developed the capacity to avoid hold-up or tough bargaining tactics by the dealership network by simply bypassing this network on a selective basis and dealing with customers directly.

hours worked, which were a part of the process of costing the output produced – $\mathbf{A}_G$ thought the procedures had become "too detailed".

The purpose of the above requirements set by $\mathbf{P}_G$ is, of course, to resolve information asymmetry, and hence, indirectly, better to direct the agent $\mathbf{A}_G$ along the lines desired by him. A very wide information set was thought to be relevant to the running of this business, and over most of this set, $\mathbf{A}_G$ felt he was more knowledgeable than $\mathbf{P}_G$. This included knowledge about technology, markets, managerial staff, budgets, capital structure, business strategy, management accounts, financial accounts and supply sources. Knowledge was thought to be evenly distributed between $\mathbf{P}_G$ and $\mathbf{A}_G$ as regards capital structure and capital investment. Only in the areas of "venture capital for business" did $\mathbf{A}_G$ think $\mathbf{P}_G$ was more knowledgeable than himself. In this area, the strengths of $\mathbf{P}_G$ were thought to lie, not surprisingly, in "reporting structure and systems". A consequence of this instigation of extensive and detailed monitoring and control systems was that $\mathbf{A}_G$ could truthfully say that he had "no interference from the investor", presumably because 'interference' was associated with arbitrary or unsystematic intervention. By contrast, his experience was that $\mathbf{P}_G$ was very "hands-off", this being possible because so much was known about $\mathbf{A}_G$ through the formal reporting protocol.

Concerning the forms that budgets took, a wide range was relevant: profit and loss account, cash flow, balance sheet, headcount and capital budget. The cash flow and capital budgets were originally set annually, and the rest monthly. After venture capital intervention, the cash flow target was also set monthly, and was based on a forecasting model. A new form of analysis, undertaken monthly, concerned the use of manpower. This looked in detail at hours spent working and hours not worked (e.g. through sickness, holiday, non-productive administrative work, etc.).

The attribution of elements of cost to products involved direct materials, direct labour and distribution costs. Of sales and administration costs, $\mathbf{A}_G$ said: "We don't fill in time sheets, so we can't find the true cost." Presumably their new form of manpower analysis was intended precisely to address information needs like this. The product costs used were actual, and a distinction was made between fixed and variable costs. Referring to his capacity as financial director, $\mathbf{A}_G$ said: "The fixed overheads relate to us, the variable overheads to people who fill in the time sheets." He said that accountants would not be involved in costing at the design stage, and that "salesmen basically do the costing". It appeared that the overall management of costs was going through a transformation, some of which – especially the detailed consideration of time spent by personnel on specific tasks – was not being embraced with any enthusiasm.

When it came to capital investment, $\mathbf{A}_G$ behaved in a particularly clear fashion. The only method $\mathbf{A}_G$ used was qualitative assessment. Strictly speaking, $\mathbf{A}_G$ argued, "Capital investment is not really relevant". As regards fixed plant and equipment he said, "Most of the time we are re-cycling machines". This side of the business he regarded as relatively unimportant, as strictly his concern was "investment in people". A_G was not able to give information on discount rates and payback periods because all investment appraisal was qualitative.

In reporting back to the venture capital investor, A_G thought that, for reported information, distortion or error in reporting was scarcely relevant, in that he only had an interest in imparting reasonably accurate information. He thought that financial data were perhaps "slightly distorted" in reporting. Of other information, he illustrated his views with a few examples, saying of markets, "We don't know our market share, so we don't really report it"; and of production, "It's difficult to know till somewhere down the line what your profit is". Personnel data were hard to provide on a basis suitable for reporting because, "for example, we take on a couple more people during the year". A_G was aware that, in a sense, he was conveying that he encountered considerable reporting difficulties, and put it down to time lags. He said, "There are delays in putting systems in", presumably because the bespoke features involved in every installation take time which is hard to anticipate. This delay in installation had knock-on consequences for the rest of his firm's operations because "we trade by putting a third down, with the balance being paid on installation and delivery". Given the distortion in reporting that would arise from these very unpredictable features of business operations, A_G's reluctance to report more fully was understandable.

10.8 TRADING RISK AND INFORMATION (A_G)

Unusually, A_G thought he was better equipped to handle risk than the venture capital investor. As he had fewer opportunities for diversification, this seemed a strange conclusion to reach. However, it appeared to arise from his strict decoupling of market and financial risk. Of product and market risk, he said: "We know more than he does about risk analysis." The investor's risk skills would be relevant if "for example, we wanted to borrow some money from the bank".

Despite the fact that very detailed budget returns to the venture capital investor were required, A_G felt that the flow of information to P_G was "limited", though "he gets the same as us", which is "adequate for their needs". Perhaps because of P_G's strict adherence to contractual obligation for information provision, and no more, A_G claimed that "nothing is requested" (presumably beyond this) and that "no formal reporting structure is required". A_G did have a desire to generate more information about the business, but "not specifically for [P_G]", presumably implying that he desired superior management accounts for monitoring and control within his business.

Though his approach to information provision appeared equivocal, A_G claimed he did not feel he retained any right of confidentiality over aspects of running the business. He thought this issue would only become important "when people approach you to buy the business". Then, he thought, "conflict of interest comes in". He thought that in determining areas of confidentiality he "couldn't achieve more – and less doesn't really matter". His view of his reporting overall was, "It's very open".

Business operations were thought to be an area in which $\mathbf{A_G}$ had a natural advantage, compared to $\mathbf{P_G}$. $\mathbf{A_G}$ said, "It's always useful to know what's going on", and perceived this as conferring bargaining advantage over $\mathbf{P_G}$. He said, "It gives us the upper hand", but also conveyed his sense of not always knowing what $\mathbf{P_G}$ was doing because he asked himself, "What are they planning?"

$\mathbf{A_G}$ thought that he brought many attributes to his relationship with the investor. However, he felt that effort, finance and commitment to the business were important in terms of $\mathbf{P_G}$'s contribution. On balance, he thought that his own most important attribute was "knowledge of the product or service" and that $\mathbf{P_G}$'s was "financial expertise". Although this does not suggest trading risk for information, it is to be recalled that $\mathbf{A_G}$ decoupled business and financial risk, his concern being the former, and presumably $\mathbf{P_G}$'s being the latter. It certainly is reasonable to assume that $\mathbf{P_G}$'s "financial expertise" did include the management of financial risk.

The proportion of equity held in the firm by $\mathbf{A_G}$ was stated to be 70 per cent.[19] $\mathbf{A_G}$ had been party to a performance-linked equity scheme with $\mathbf{P_G}$, but was reluctant to elaborate on its detailed structure, though he described it as "basically a 'buy-back' of shares". He certainly thought it had been a good motivator for him, and was glad that it had given him the opportunity, as he put it, to "shake off the venture capitalist" at an agreed price. He was unaware of any need to compete with other investees for more favoured treatment from $\mathbf{P_G}$. He said: "Unless you know their aim or goal in a particular business, you can't assume that."

It was remarkable that $\mathbf{A_G}$'s perception of the relationship he had with the investor was one of "trust and understanding" rather than being tightly legally defined. I say 'remarkable' because the latter view (i.e. 'tightly legally defined') was the one taken by $\mathbf{P_G}$. What seems to have happened is that $\mathbf{P_G}$'s insistence on contractually agreed behaviour, *but nothing more*, was interpreted by $\mathbf{A_G}$ as implying a high level of trust. Indeed, because there was little discretionary intervention by $\mathbf{P_G}$, the perception of $\mathbf{A_G}$ was that "in reality, there isn't much control". As a consequence, the relationship with the investor seemed to offer little scope for improvement, and was thought by $\mathbf{A_G}$ to be "close to the optimum".

10.9 CONCLUSION

This concludes the last of the three full 'within site' case studies of this book. The method is intensive, indeed so much so that, for reasons of space, this concludes

19 $\mathbf{A_G}$ qualified this by saying, "It depends on how you classify the preference shares because they're non-voting". In other words, a 70 per cent equity holding may not confer full power to control the business.

the case study section, though I hope to return to the case studies again in print at a later date. But now, turning first to Case G before reviewing Part 3 of the book as a whole, the following comments are appropriate.

The investor clearly pursued a careful portfolio diversification policy, so almost inevitably he would be regarded as approximating to risk neutrality. In fact, he expressed a range of risk-averse sentiments, which might be interpreted as suggesting he was highly motivated to diversify risk, should the means be available. Of course, constructing a portfolio is perhaps the perfect means to that end. The investee regarded his business as essentially low risk, but this partly arose from his substantially shifting the risk burden towards two of his principals, the upstream provider of computer supplies and the provider of external finance capital (the VCI himself).

The investor and investee were strongly oriented towards attaining maximal performance. There was considerable information asymmetry between investor and investee in Case G. $\mathbf{A}_G$ was very much more knowledgeable than $\mathbf{P}_G$ about the MSF's operations, including its technology, staff, strategy, budgets, supplies and accounts. To resolve this, and the attendant incentive impediments it can create, the investor required extensive and detailed monitoring and control systems at the time of concluding a contract with the investee. This was strongly buttressed by explicit clauses in the subscription agreement. The investor's strengths lay in the provision of venture capital, knowledge of reporting structures and systems, and financial expertise. Although the investor was manifestly an experienced risk specialist, the investee laid claim to considerable risk-handling skills as well. Given the nature of the MSF's business, with much risk deliberately spread onto the broad shoulders of principals, this is not implausible. However, this does not imply that the comparative advantage of the investee in Case G lay in his being a risk specialist, because his detailed knowledge of products and markets was a far more important source of comparative advantage.

In interacting with one another, principal and agent in Case G seemed liberated by having such a clearly defined relationship. Thus the investor felt his risk exposure was greatly reduced because he had become well informed about the running of the MSF, and the investee felt that beyond strict contractual conditions very little discretionary control would be exerted. As a consequence, implicit contracting features were emerging, and very much governed day-to-day operations. The contracting nexus was perceived to be close to optimal.

Taking the three case studies as a whole, their diversity is apparent. For example, they differ considerably by size, investment involvement, source of funding, mission and specialization. They were chosen partly to illustrate the rich morphology of investor/investee relations. An incidental benefit is that they examine in detail some exciting deals. In their diversity the cases provide a good test of the categories, relationships and behaviour specified in principal–agent analysis, for they are designed to show how good the 'fit' is between theory and evidence.

Despite this diversity of cases in Part 3, it is even more apparent that there is common ground between them. The main features of this are as follows:

1 Both **P** and **A** functioned in risky environments. In general, the **P**s created sufficiently large portfolios that, on available expert opinion (e.g. Fama 1976; Statman 1990), they might be considered as almost fully diversified and therefore approaching risk neutrality. The **A**s displayed varieties of attitude to risk, but were always averse to highly risky situations. Though they might attempt diversification across projects in the MSF, this generally did not offer opportunities for complete diversification. They therefore were motivated to seek risk-sharing arrangements with **P** – and, on occasion, with other principals. The willingness of **P** to share all the risk with **A** was limited, and **P** was inclined to leave **A** bearing some risk as an incentive for effort.

2 There was by nature an acute information asymmetry between **P** and **A**. Such signals as **A** provided to **P** about his MSF were typically noisy, and this concealment of **A**'s effort could be used strategically by **A**. As a consequence, **P** insisted on quite tightly specified explicit contracting, and required frequent, detailed and wide-ranging information from **A**. Typically, this involved a sea change in the generation and provision of information by **A**. As a consequence of this improved information flow, moral hazard and adverse selection effects were attenuated, and **P** was thereby able to manage risk to better enhance the performance of the MSF, and might increase his equity stake as a consequence. Flexible equity arrangements, including ratchets, were used by **P** to maintain an incentive for effort on the part of **A**.

3 **P** and **A** differed considerably in the attributes which they brought to the contract, and this marked difference in comparative advantage provided a superior basis for gainful contracting. **P** and **A** shared common attributes like commitment and willingness to bear risk, but in most other respects they were very different. The skills in risk management possessed by **P** extended so far beyond those possessed by **A** (which were largely confined to business risk management) that there was a qualitative difference: of the two, **P** was the risk specialist. To this skill, **P** added other special attributes in terms of high financial expertise, knowledge of reporting structures and systems, and, of course, the provision of what for the MSF was a large volume of private equity capital. The latter was by no means exogenously given. The capacity of **P** to raise money from clients to create funds that could finance entrepreneurs depended on his reputation. This, in turn, hinged on the success with which **P** was able to interact productively with **A**: reputation was based on the perceived quality of the deal flow. The most important attributes of **A** were knowledge based. They related to markets, products, suppliers and technology.

4 Contracting between **P** and **A** involved seeking optima at several levels: risk distribution, effort, capital structure, information provision and so on. In seeking favourable contracts, there was a dovetailing of the different specialized attributes of **P** and **A**, as noted in item 3 above. The form of contracting

> was continuous, initially based closely on explicit contracting, often with close reference to the subscription agreement, but increasingly based on implicit contracting as new procedures were adopted by mutual consent, and strict conditions which had become defunct were held in abeyance. As this process developed, trust and cooperation became more evident than control and compliance. From a subjective standpoint, these contracting relations were regarded as optimal, or near optimal, by **P** and **A** alike.

These conclusions have been based on just three cases, but they all provide a good 'fit' with the agency model. The purpose of Part 4 is to engage in much more detailed cross-site analysis of the investor–investee dyads, seeking to discover whether the provisional conclusions of Part 3 are capable of further generalization.

Part 4

ANALYSIS

11

RISK MANAGEMENT

with Nicholas G. Terry and Julia A. Smith

11.1 INTRODUCTION

This chapter provides an empirical analysis of the forms of risk management arrangements which are adopted in the relationship between the venture capital investor (VCI) and his investee (MSF). As elsewhere in this book, the underlying theoretical framework is that of principal–agent analysis.[1] In using this framework, the investee is viewed as a risk-averse, but relatively well-informed, agent who is entering into a risk-sharing contract with a risk-neutral, but relatively poorly informed, principal, the venture capital investor. The asymmetry of information between investor and investee, and their different attitudes to risk, provide the basis for mutually beneficial contracting.

The analysis proceeds by looking first at risk relevance and the perceived value of risky projects to the investor and the investee. Then the extent to which portfolio balance is sought by (especially) the investor is considered. This is followed by an examination of screening devices for evaluating new projects, and their significance for both investor and investee. Finally, risk-sharing between investor and investee is considered from the standpoint of risk-spreading, effort elicitation, and alternative payoff schemes.

11.2 EXPECTED RETURNS

While outcomes were typically thought by investors to involve some measure of chance, its exact extent was not always easy to quantify and might only be expressed in qualitative terms. When exact quantification was used, this was typically associated with broader professional judgement. The data presented in Table 11.1 relate to the following question:

1 See Chapter 3 for an introduction, and Chapter 4 for a fairly detailed account.

> Suppose a project you were contemplating backing would give rise to a return almost immediately, or not at all. For example, a geophysical company may take test drillings for a precious ore which may yield an immediate return if evidence of the ore is found, or a zero return if not. Suppose the value is £10m. if drilling is successful. Suppose further that previous geophysical evidence indicates that only one in ten drillings give positive results. I should like to know how you would evaluate the worth of the project. Assume drilling costs are negligible.

Investors were then asked how relevant to the evaluation of the worth of this project was the fact that drillings may or may not be successful. Then they were asked what best represented the approximate value of the drilling project before the results came in. If the investor were able to appeal to a frequency limit principle, contemplating many similar independent repetitions of this situation, and were risk neutral, he would be inclined to value the project at its actuarial value, that is, at its mathematical expectation = (0.10)(£10m.) = £1m. However, if the investor treated this as a one-shot situation, with considerable downside risk exposure, and worried that his own reputation for investment acumen hinged on a high success rate, the value of the project might be perceived to be far less. In fact, when confronted with this £10m. project with only a 1/10 chance of success, most investors said they would not get involved. Their comments were often forthright: "Not interested" (A); "Not worth anything" (D); "Not worth its mathematical expectation" (I); "We wouldn't touch this type of investment" (R). Table 11.1 summarizes responses to questions about risk relevance and a risky project. For 78 per cent of investors who responded (14/18), the chance element was very important in reaching an evaluation of the project (see column 3 of Table 11.1). For 75 per cent (12/16) of the responding investors, the chance of failure was so high that the project was evaluated as worthless (see column 4 of Table 11.1). Only 12.5 per cent (2/16) placed the value of the project at its actuarial value of £1m., and just two investors again (12.5 per cent = 2/16) put it at half its actuarial value. This suggests risk aversion in very risky situations. However, given the choice between £1.2m. for certain and a lottery or gamble giving £1m. with chances 9/10 or £3m. with chances 1/10, 59 per cent (10/17) of investors expressed a preference for the risky alternative and 35 per cent (6/17) a preference for the sure thing. Thus on single investment risk exposure, investors frequently expressed a love of risk, presumably expressed against a background confidence that moderate risk could be managed. Just one investor (6 per cent = 1/17) was indifferent between the investments. In the situation where downside risk is attenuated (investors could not get less than £1m.) and upside risk is attractive (investors have a reasonable chance, 1/10, of getting £3m.) the actuarial value may seem a less plausible reference point than in the previous example with extreme downside risk (i.e. 9/10 chance of getting nothing). Of course, individual agent risk aversion is consistent with a desire to diversify risk,

Table 11.1 Risk relevance and value of risky project

Investor	*(1)* *Not at all*	*(2)* *Moderately*	*(3)* *Very*	*(4)* *£0*	*(5)* *£$\frac{1}{2}$m.*	*(6)* *£1m.*
A			✓		✓	
B	✓					
C			✓	✓		
D			✓	✓		
E			✓	✓		
F			✓	✓		
G			✓	✓		
H			✓	✓		
I			✓		✓	
J			✓	✓		
K			✓	✓		
L	✓					✓
M			✓	✓		
N	✓			✓		
O	✓					
P						
Q			✓	✓		
R				✓		
S			✓			✓
T			✓	✓		

Notes:
a Table relates to questions on a drilling project which can yield £10m., with probability $\frac{1}{10}$, or zero, with probability $\frac{9}{10}$.
b Columns 1 to 3 relate to relevance of the riskiness of the project to its perceived worth to the investor.
c Columns 4 to 6 represent the approximate value of the project before the results come in.
d Further columns (up to £12m. by increments of £1m.) could be nominated, but were not.

should the means be at hand. In the case of the investor, it is through portfolio diversification.[2]

Investees were fairly unanimous (88 per cent = 14/16) in regarding their involvement with the investor as having an element of luck or chance in it. While comments like, "Luck plays a large part", "It's luck in some ways", "There's always an element of luck", "You take a gamble" feature strongly with investees, these are usually modified by statements like, "I certainly don't rely on luck" and "It's [i.e. the gamble] limited by your own knowledge". This is rather in contrast to investors, who emphasize right from the start that luck is not a blind force, that uncertainty can in some measure be controlled (by risk categories, structuring, risk/reward profile, sensitivity analysis, etc.). With the investor there is a

2 Further, it is known from the work of Khaneman and Tversky (1979) that anomalous responses can be given by agents to specific forms of gambles.

lesser sense of risk being irremediable; while with the investee there is a sense that there may be no remedy for risk – it is just there.

When investees were asked the same question as that addressed to investors about choosing between (a) £1.2m. for sure and (b) a lottery with £1m. mostly (9/10) and £3m. occasionally (1/10), a somewhat higher proportion went for the sure thing (44 per cent = 7/16, compared to 40 per cent) and a somewhat lower proportion (56 per cent = 9/16, compared to 53 per cent) went for the risky alternative.[3] Seventy-five per cent (= 12/16) of investees thought that the profitability of a new project was partly a matter of chance, and 75 per cent (= 9/12) attached a risk discount to profit for that reason. When confronted with a potential sale of £1m. which only had a 50/50 chance of coming off, most investees (59 per cent = 10/17) evaluated the worth of the order as zero, but a surprisingly high proportion (35 per cent = 6/17) evaluated the worth at its actuarial value of £$\frac{1}{2}$m. This compared with just 14 per cent of investors nominating the actuarial value. However, in the latter case, the probability of no net reward was much higher (at 9/10). It is also possible that in the latter case the risk-situation might have been viewed as a 'one-off', whereas in the former (investee) case the connotation is of a repeated risk.

The overall picture that emerges is of investors who are more experienced at risk management than investees; more inclined to want to 'handle' or 'manage' risk; and less inclined to view risk – especially downside risk – as something that must be borne or suffered. In high-risk situations individual agents on both the investor and investee side display strong risk aversion. In low-risk situations, the response is much more equivocal.

11.3 PORTFOLIO BALANCE

Now the way in which good outcomes were offset against bad by investors seeking to manage their risk will be considered. This was addressed in three ways. First, the investor was asked, for a set of investee involvements, about the extent to which uncertain good and bad outcomes could be balanced by directly influencing the chances of success or failure. Further, the extent to which this process had limits, and thus chance was irreducible, was probed. Second, the actual methods used to bring about an offsetting of good outcomes against bad were investigated, probing especially on devices like the avoidance of single-sector or single-technology involvements in a given fund. Third, the least number of investees the investor would contemplate in a fund, regarded as a portfolio, was

3 As mentioned earlier, this 'experiment' with investees may not be a good measure of attitude to risk, as it was carefully chosen to be a borderline example, and indeed has generated revealing responses. The response on the potential sales question is less equivocal.

investigated, with particular emphasis on the anticipated effect that investee numbers had on risk management.

In approaching investees, initial interest was on the investee's perceived risk class. Their perceived risk classes were as follows: high 33 per cent (= 5/15); medium 13 per cent (= 2/15); and low 53 per cent (= 8/15). A surprisingly high proportion reported a self-appraised low-risk category, suggesting investors face a problem of adverse selection. Investees were then asked whether they could undertake actions to limit or modify their exposure to risk, and if so, what they were. Of the twenty investors asked, nineteen answered the question which enquired whether they used methods to offset bad against good outcomes. Of these, the majority (68 per cent = 13/19) said they did use such methods. Of the investors who replied, most (71 per cent = 10/14) said they avoided single-sector involvements and most (71 per cent = 10/14) said they would also avoid single-technology involvements. Some who would avoid single-technology involvement might not avoid single-sector involvement. The converse was also true, but uncommon (one example only). In the latter case, the investor (H) said that while he was willing to have one cider company in his portfolio, he was not willing to confine his portfolio to alcoholic beverages.

As well as single-technology avoidance per se, there was also a tendency to high-technology avoidance. This was not just a matter of perceived higher risk, but also because, "We don't have the expertise to handle them" (A), "Technology gets obsolete" (C), and "[Experience of] bad outcomes" (R). In such cases, fear of adverse selection led to this decision rule. Stage of investment was also important for portfolio balance, with a tendency to avoid early-stage and start-up investments. In these cases, avoidance of risk, rather than of adverse selection, was the rationale. In this context the computer software industry (E), gambling and property development (Q) and building (T) were regarded as too risky.

Many investors explicitly used the language of portfolio balance in explaining how a fund would be composed. Thus B said, "Yes, [we] spread the portfolio risk"; D said, "[We] try to balance out areas, see how it goes before taking another one in that area"; G said, "Sectoral balance is something we do take into account"; H said, "You wouldn't want the portfolio balanced very heavily to companies which had one chance of success"; I said, "We try not to get overweight on any one sector"; K said, "[We] have one or two very high-risk investments out of 15 to 20 in any one portfolio"; and T said, "We stratify by area of activity".

To the extent that the canons of portfolio balance were defied, the existence or acquisition of especially detailed information was usually the reason. In the spirit of Mark Twain's famous statement, "Put all your eggs in one basket – and watch that basket", investor L said, "I stay pretty close in touch with the investees and talk to some almost daily on the phone. I wouldn't avoid single sector or single technology involvements." In a similar vein, investor F said, "Because of where we come from, we tend to invest in things that are manufacturing related". Investor N, who did not claim to balance his portfolio by sector or technology, said, "We check that they [the investee] have the experience they say – due diligence is important. We check they do stay where they say [they will] and have the experience they claim."

Considered overall, no investors literally used a portfolio balance model.[4] Many, indeed most, did think in portfolio balance terms, but at differing levels of formality. In doing so, this perspective was often modified by a variety of considerations, of which the depth and scope of information on investees were the most important. Thus investor E said he did "no arithmetical or statistical analysis. We use our own feelings and judgement"; I said, "We're not very scientific on this", and J said that portfolio balance is used, "but only in a limited way", it being modified "by judgement of the management involved".

Regarding portfolio size, the average size was twenty-eight investees. The modal size-class was ten to fifteen and the size range was from one (P said "one is OK") to 200 (O said he "may be overdiversified").[5] Putting aside the house style reflected in P's response ("each [investee] is treated on its own merits"), the very small fund of A (five only) made sense in the context of his use of "relatively safe assured tenancy based property investments under BES [business expansion scheme]". A widely used rule of portfolio composition was to hold no more than 10 per cent of the portfolio in any one company. A related, but not identical, rule that was commonly used was to have no less than ten investees in a portfolio. A distinction must sometimes be made between a fund and a portfolio. In the early stages of creating a new fund, the number of investees included in it may be small. At this stage such a fund is not truly a portfolio. Sometimes such new funds are created by repacking a few younger investees from a more mature fund into a new fund, and adding to these further new investees by appeal to portfolio balance principles, combined with broader judgements, as outlined above.

In describing how investee numbers were determined, many investors provided further insight into issues of portfolio balance. Three gave quite detailed accounts of risk management of a portfolio:

1 Investor C explained that the absolute size of the fund made a difference to risk management. In the case of C, as with most investors in the sample, the number of venture capital executives was quite limited. One of his funds had a value of £70m. This was best portrayed as 35 × £2m. investment involvements rather than 140 × £0.5m. investment involvements. For C, the main criteria for portfolio construction were: likelihood of success; prospective return; and portfolio balance.
2 In the case of investor F, a model was built of a desired portfolio, which

4 E.g. a Markowitz (1959) quadratic programming model.

5 This is slightly less than the figure of thirty investments that work by Statman (1990) suggests is required for a fully diversified portfolio. However, some of the earlier finance literature gives figures as low as fifteen investments for full diversification. The modal figure suggests many investors operated with portfolios this size or even lower.

originally had fifty investees in it. Several funds of different maturities were run simultaneously, and a house rule was that no more than 20 per cent of any one fund should be invested in a single firm. The aim was to spread the cash in each fund over different sectors, and then to further partition this cash among different companies, so as to "put a limit on the ultimate risk we take with any one company".

3 Investor N typically had 10 to 20 investees in a portfolio. He paid attention to size distribution within the portfolio and saw a place for balancing large against small investee involvements. One investment was too low, and twenty (worth, say, £0.25m. each on average) was probably just too many. Monitoring was known to be costly ("problems take a lot of time"), so N favoured getting into a syndicate agreement with lead investors who would do the controlling. He saw there being a trade-off between larger numbers for superior risk management and smaller numbers for tighter monitoring and control. This was a common finding.

Overall, size of portfolio was dictated both by considerations of risk management and by limits to the span of control of venture capital executives. Very often, investors contemplated investee numbers in a portfolio which looked well below what is required for fully diversifying risk.[6] Investor T made a comment which encapsulates most experience: "We prefer smaller numbers, closely monitored, to a large portfolio where risk is more diversified." Although this need not imply that monitoring is proactive, it is at least widespread.

11.4 SCREENING

The third area of interest in this chapter focuses on the use of risk-return analysis, and more generally on ways of evaluating the chances of new investees doing well, rather than badly, in relation to the returns they promise. This was addressed in two ways. First, investors were asked about the screening methods that they used to decide which propositions to evaluate, and subsequently the type of investment selection procedures they employed. Second, the way in which investees may attempt to modify risk were explored, as well as ways in which risk exposure was communicated to investors.

The use of risk-return analysis for investment was accepted if not universal practice among investors.[7] Some undertook this informally. For example, investor L said, "I don't write down the probabilities. I do it intuitively." Others

6 Though note earlier remarks (Chapter 5, fnn. 8, 12) to the effect that rather few investees in a portfolio can lead to considerable risk diversification.

7 Only investor S said categorically, "No, we don't do this". Methods used ranged from, "It's the key to our investment" (K) to "There is no statistical analysis, it's just a hunch" (I).

were more formal, and in some cases highly sophisticated. For example, investor J said: "We want to know the whole range of rates of return across the probabilities from 0 per cent to 100 per cent – that is, a complete probability distribution of IRRs." Pushing the formality of this analysis further, the concept of risk-return analysis was recognized by venture capitalists when they were engaged in investment selection. As two investors (D and H) stated, "The greater the risk, the greater the return required"; and, "The higher the projected return, the higher the chance of them doing badly". However, within the context of venture capital investment, the progression between levels of risk and the compensatory levels of return required was probably not proportional, but rather increasing. This was evidenced by the generally accepted minimum target rates of return being typically set at no less than 25 per cent, and up to 40 per cent to accept any risk at all. This implies that the risk-return locus starts at a base level of 25 per cent or more, rises rapidly, and quickly reaches a level of risk for which the required upside gain to accept it is probably without limit. The dominant view among venture capital investors was that without the prospect of significant upside gains in all situations of non-trivial risk the deal was not worth doing. This was exemplified by the statement of investor G that, "[We] will only make the investment if we feel a very high level of confidence that the plan will succeed". It is this expectation on the part of investors that is one of the most likely explanations of why business plans, submitted by potential investee firms, contain an overestimate of what can be achieved. As investee N put it, "We were bullish as we were desperate to do this [i.e. the deal]".

Given these investor expectations, how do they evaluate the chances of new investees doing well rather than badly in relation to the returns promised? The business plan is the platform from which information is taken to begin the process of investment selection. The evidence indicated that the evaluation by the venture capital investor (VCI) started from the proposition that the information provided in the plan was optimistic, especially within the timescale and for the type of exit route preferred by the investor. A typical view was that, for example, of investor N: "We look at the realism of the assumptions underlying the [business] plan. We test projections heavily, analyse markets and check that costs are reasonable for sales levels." This was not surprising given that the business plan was likely to have been prepared by an accountant who would intend it to be seen by a range of potential financial backers. Of these, bankers, for example, may well be more ready to accept optimistic predictions about cash flow generation, profitability and growth because they often protect themselves against unfulfilled promises with devices such as covenants to the lending agreement (see the subscription agreement or investment memorandum used in venture capital investment transactions). Covenants could include the requirements that regular interest cover calculations be prepared for the bank during the life of the loan (to protect against interest default risk); and that security taken against assets can be exercised if the bank felt that the loan was under threat (from principal default risk). Conversely, the venture capital investor, in the absence of an active secondary market into which the investment could be traded, sees the deal as more than just getting the money back plus some fixed interest margin. Venture capitalists can be seen, therefore, as that class of investors which takes on high-risk investment propositions, in the expectation of high returns. Despite the commitment to this type of financial intermediation, the venture capital investor must still take a realistic view of what the investee firm might achieve. This does not mean, however, that 'unexciting' returns (in other words, those close to, or just below, the target), or returns available to other classes of investor, will be acceptable. Investors were aware of the need to be protected from the behaviour of investees who, as in the case of investee Q, would argue that, "I don't think we would communicate a downside [risk] unless specifically asked".

This introduces the role of trust between the investor and investee (Sapienza and Korsgaard 1996). Two investors (Q and R) expressed this notion in the following terms: "We are more interested in how we think they will perform, rather than what they say. We do require plans, but also assess the people involved"; and, "If you have confidence in the people, then you tend to accept their projections". This approach was recognized by some investees, who said they were willing to "talk openly about the whole business" (for example, investee P).[8]

However, the general premise remains that investors looked at propositions with some degree of suspicion, especially with regard to the promised performance. In the SSI, this led to a consideration of particular approaches to screening. The expected 25–40 per cent range of rates of return mentioned already represents a type of filtering device. In setting such 'hurdle' IRRs, many conventional lending propositions will be excluded, as will equity-based transactions that can be done reasonably easily and in a straightforward manner by traditional corporate finance departments of banks. This can mean that many propositions sent to venture capitalists will have been turned down by more traditional forms of financial intermediation. As one investor (T) explained, either "they come to us because they need the money and the bank has refused", or they are "the 'cherries' – those who have . . . [an already] successful business . . . [which they] wish to grow, . . . [but who need to] obtain additional funding to expand". In these cases, the expansion plans may have been considered by the banks to be too risky.

To this extent, the venture capital investor's role was confirmed as offering a specialist type of financial intermediation. Indeed, his skills and expertise could be seen to be directed towards refining this role, as witnessed by the following comment by investor J: "An experienced venture capitalist can only hit [that is, choose successful ventures] slightly more than the inexperienced. I am good at managing the downside risk." In other words, what distinguished the activities of

8 See also the paper by Hatherley *et al.* (1994), which emphasizes mutual interest and cooperation.

a venture capital investor from other forms of financial intermediation was not the ability to spot 'winners'; this ability, it seems, was accepted as being reasonably equally distributed across different types of finance houses. Rather, it was the ability of the venture capital investor to turn an underperforming investment into another 'winner' (at least within the context of the funding structure employed and the methods of realization available). One investee (F) summarized the reason for this approach as, "When things get tough, it concentrates his [the investor's] mind".

Overall, in order for venture capital investors to consider an investment proposition, the evidence is that it must initially appear to be capable of satisfying a rather high minimum rate of return. About 25 per cent appears to be the industry norm, though higher rates were frequently mooted. The sampled investors received, on average, 550 proposals a year of which 35 per cent passed this threshold test. More detailed consideration will now be given to those propositions that passed the first 'test'. This concentrates upon the 'realism' of the projections contained within the business plan submitted by the hopeful investee. These projections are subjected to extensive scrutiny by both the venture capital house representatives and by other 'independent' specialists invited by the potential investor. For our sample of investors, of the 550 proposals received on average per year, just fifteen, only 3 per cent, led to investment involvement. There appeared to be a generally accepted view that the promises and the paths to deliver them, described by investees in their plans, were likely to be overoptimistic. This resulted in a recalibration of both the likely returns and the risks present. There was also a recognition that, once involved in the investment, the venture capital house had a stake in making the transaction work, according to the revised and agreed plan. This could take the form of providing managerial and technical assistance, or of making clear that additional finance could be made available, or both.

11.5 RISK-SHARING

In this, the final, substantive section, several aspects of the investor–investee relationship are highlighted, centring upon the issue of sharing risk. First, the possible motivation of investees in seeking risk-sharing positions with this type of investor is considered. Second, the willingness of the investor to bear the larger part of the risk is explored, extending to full risk acceptance, in which case the investee is given a fixed, rather than an uncertain, payoff at exit. Third, the investor's use of risk management to elicit investee effort is considered. And fourth, the investee's own perception of the consequences of reduced risk exposure on effort are explored, including the attractiveness of a fixed, rather than an uncertain, payoff.

Although investee firms recognized the optimistic nature of the business plans submitted to potential financial backers, about 56 per cent (9/16) of investees persisted with the view that venture capitalists tended to overestimate the risk inherent in the particular business. As one investee (D) put it, "They have to overestimate, to safeguard themselves". Moreover, investees recognized that this tendency existed both because investors "require a high return on their funds" (investee F) and because they "are much more worried about . . . their ignorance" (investee H). This supposed 'ignorance' could arise from deliberate attempts by the investee to disguise or hide risk, or simply from investors bringing a limited body of technical knowledge to investment appraisal. In the words of investee R, "It depends on the background of the person within the venture capital company". Whatever the reason, investors tried to reduce ignorance. Thus investor K stated: "We do an appraisal – it's the key to our investment – a fundamental part of the job."

Given this difficulty of fully resolving information asymmetries, and the use of risk assessment in the face of a less than full understanding (and incomplete revelation) of both the nature and type of the risks, it is perhaps surprising that deals are concluded at all. That they are, in practice, concluded indicates that investors are willing to bear risk, even if their knowledge of it may be incomplete, and they may feel its extent has been understated. Further, there is a motivation for investees to seek a risk-sharing position, knowing that once the deal is concluded they are going to rely on investors not only for finance but also to 'troubleshoot' company problems. For the majority of investee firms (9/16 = 56 per cent), the fact that the venture capital investor would be sharing in some of the business risk with them was considered important. As investee K clearly stated, "It was vital [for the deal to be done]"; and investee G admitted that a realization that the investor was taking "all the risks on financing" was also an important and attractive aspect of the deal. For the investors, the relationship was viewed rather differently. While investor M made it clear that, "If they don't share risk, we don't do the deal", many others saw it as varying according to the type of transaction under consideration, be it management buyout, expansion, reconstruction or whatever. In addition, investors perceived a resistance on the part of the investee firms to share ownership. As investor G quipped, "His desire is to fulfil his dreams with our money".

One way in which such dreams can be fulfilled is by retaining a significant part of the equity in the business. Therefore, the investee is motivated to raise the maximum amount of capital by giving away the minimum amount of equity. This could be achieved through getting the venture capital investor to accept a greater amount of the risk than they think they are accepting for any given amount of funding supplied. Although this presents the unlikely picture of the investor being a victim of adverse selection, the reason why he may accept such a position at the outset is because of what investor O calls "commonality of interest with management". That is, if things go wrong, as a result possibly of the overly optimistic picture presented by the investee, then the venture capitalist becomes the most likely rescuer and will extract a bigger ownership stake.

An alternative way of arriving at a subscription contract would be to offer the investee firm a fixed sum in return for the venture capitalist's involvement, rather than receiving a proportion of the value of the firm at exit. Of the sixteen investees questioned, 38 per cent (= 6/16) said 'yes' to this idea. While the fixed sum needed to be sufficiently attractive, its main advantage was complete risk elimination: that is, "knowing exactly what you are working for", as investee D put it. Compare this with the view of investee firm M, which typified that of those *not* attracted to this idea, who said it would be "a disenchantment for me . . . they [the investor] need me committed to the end result [the exit value]". As far as the investors were concerned, the idea of a fixed payoff to the investee firm appealed to 15 per cent (= 3/20), while the rest said 'no' with varying degrees of distaste. According to investor E, "We wouldn't even contemplate a fixed sum"; while investor T explained, "No – it is perceived as a criterion or requirement to have a focused and motivated management". Thus the majority view was that offering fixed payoffs had the potential for disturbing the incentive mechanism used to avoid or mitigate the effects of moral hazard. Interestingly, the three investors who responded positively to the suggestion of fixed payoffs did so in terms of a percentage of equity (e.g. a payoff of 25 per cent of equity, to be agreed at the time of signing the subscription agreement). The *value* of this stake, however, was not fixed at the time of the financing deal. In this way, the prospect of a share in the exit value provided investees with an incentive for effort throughout the contract.

The incentive issue was pursued further by investigating the extent to which the investee firms felt that having a venture capital investor to bear some of the business risk resulted in their relaxing more in the running of the business. Only 15 per cent (= 3/16) felt able to say 'yes' to this suggestion. The strongest views were held by those investees who rejected this notion. For example, investee K reported, "It is not a very relaxed life". Moreover, 77 per cent (= 10/13) of those who said that they had not relaxed since becoming involved with a venture capitalist thought they now worked harder or much harder than before the financing deal. As investee D stated, it "keeps you on your toes because of a second party [the venture capital investor] to answer to". In addition, as investee N put it, "Because we have part of the cake [we have an incentive to see the cake grow]".

The investors had more diverse reactions to the suggestion that their involvement could lead to less effort on the part of the owner-managers. A significant proportion of investors (47 per cent = 9/19) felt that there were positive incentive (and effective control) benefits to be gained from ensuring that owner-managers retained a sizeable stake (up to 75 per cent was quoted) in the business. Further, their ability to cash in this stake was inextricably bound up with the overall success of the business and the exit plans of the venture capital investor. As investors E and R expressed it, "We tend to find that effort increases because there is a new shareholder to whom they are responsible"; and, "To ensure management effort we like them to have a big equity stake". Nonetheless, there existed a significant (20 per cent = 4/19) group of investors who were uncomfortable with this idea of using an exit-based financial bribe to avoid a reduction in management effort. This view can be best summarized using the words of investors L and S who said, "I think mostly they're not influenced by financial considerations"; and, "We weed out early on in our assessment of management [which would include those thought likely to reduce post-investment effort]". That leaves a third group of investors who considered that the resulting impact of their involvement on management effort could go in either direction. According to investor Q: "Sometimes personality is such that their motivation won't change – some people are there to win. In some it has an effect . . . [what is important here] is to build a relationship in advance of any funding being given."

At least in the minds of owner-managers, their involvements with venture capitalists had as much to do with gaining access to funds as sharing risk. However, the reason for other, more traditional, backers having refused to become involved needs to be considered before taking this view at face value. It is likely that the cause of refusal by a bank, for example, to fund entirely a particular deal will be linked to risk. Therefore, perhaps without being fully aware of it, investees who seek a partner prepared to fully or partially fund their firms are in effect looking for a partner in risk. In such circumstances owner-managers and investors may hold differing views on the nature and impact of risk. Managers live with business risk as part of being a manager, while investors see risk as something that can be moulded in some way, or at least clearly reflected in anticipated rates of return.

11.6 CONCLUSION

This chapter has examined the sample of investor–investee dyads, with a view to analysing how risk was managed. As elsewhere, this involved analysing risk management under four headings: *expected returns*, *portfolio balance*, *screening* and *risk-sharing*. The following conclusions have emerged, under each of these headings.

Expected returns

1 Both investors and investees perceived themselves to be exposed to significant levels of risk.

2 Investees were inclined to consider their risk exposure to be irreducible; investors were more inclined to feel risk could be managed.

3 Investees took it for granted that risky situations involved an upside and a downside; investors were more inclined to seek means of enhancing the upside (e.g. by incentives) and attenuating the downside (e.g. by screening).

Portfolio balance

1 Investors sought to construct a balanced portfolio, offsetting good outcomes against bad, by avoiding single sector and single technology investment involvements.

2 The average portfolio size (28) fell short of that suggested by diversification considerations because of organizational features (e.g. the span of control of venture capital executives, and their conscious management of risk).

Screening

1 Risk-return analysis was widely used by investors.

2 Progression between perceived risk classes of investors was not proportioned. It could be subject to jumps (e.g. 20 per cent target IRR for a *range* of low risks; 30 per cent target IRR for the next range, of medium risks, etc.).

3 At high levels of risk, many projects were unfundable, even to venture capitalists, as required IRRs were perceived to be unbounded.

4 Investors assumed investees would overstate returns and understate risks. They attempted to limit adverse selection by rigorous screening (only 30 per cent of proposals being reviewed) and careful due diligence, leading to just 3 per cent of proposals being backed.

5 Investees knew investors screened with a fine filter and set high hurdle IRRs. They responded by overoptimism in formulating their business plans. This partly sustained investors' expectations of adverse selection.

Risk-sharing

1 Investees overestimated potential rewards to investors, and investors overestimated risks of investees.

2 Investors sought risk-sharing benefits from their relationships with investors.

3 Both investors and investees disliked fixed payoff arrangements for investees, feeling they disturbed incentives on both sides.

4 Investees were sufficiently exposed to risk post-contract to sustain effort.

The general picture that emerges is of skilled risk-handling by investors to limit adverse selection pre-contract, and to attenuate moral hazard post-contract. The former is achieved by using a fine filter on proposals, high hurdle rates of return, and by being strongly resistant to permitting downside risk exposure. The latter is achieved by tight monitoring and an unwillingness to bear all risk. Investee behaviour is governed in fair measure by investor procedures. The tendency of investees to overstate returns and to understate risk is partly driven by a desire to conclude a deal that relieves their finance capital scarcity. But it is also motivated by the desire to share the risk, especially the downside, with a specialist like the investor.

12

THE DEMAND FOR INFORMATION BY INVESTORS

with Falconer Mitchell and Nicholas G. Terry

12.1 INTRODUCTION

This chapter explores the venture capital investor's (VCI's) demand for information after initial investment funds have been committed to the investee (MSF). Within the book's principal–agent framework, the role of information has been seen to be crucial (see Chapter 4). Following this theoretical lead through to empirical analysis, the focus of this chapter is on data, in the sense of the information gathered in accounting form by investors. Such accounting data clearly reflect the information requirements of this increasingly important specialist investor. It is known from Chapter 5 that the forms in which data were gathered provide a unique opportunity to study the methods that these sophisticated users of investees' accounting information deploy to meet their information needs.

In the discussion that follows, the main concern is with the individual practices used by investors in obtaining and processing information as a basis for investment decisions. The approach is in the tradition of research which attempts to directly investigate investor behaviour. For example, in the UK, studies by Lee and Tweedie (1981), Arnold and Moizer (1984) and Day (1986) have respectively utilized interview, questionnaire and process-tracing methods to gather data on: institutional investors' perceptions of the relative importance of accounting information; the types and mechanics of the information analyses which they undertake; their comprehension of financial information; and their views on how information provision could be improved. This research has, in general, confirmed the high degree of importance attaching to the financial statements provided in interim and annual shareholder reports, both in the sense of confirming previous estimates and in the sense of serving as inputs to future financial forecasts.

While the above work emphasizes stock market investments, this chapter examines the demand for accounting information by investors in a less restrictive context. It is concerned particularly with the accounting portions of the information flows to venture capitalist investors (VCIs) from their investee firms (MSFs). This provides the opportunity to investigate the institutional investor's demands for information in a situation where their demand for information can directly influence supply. The VCIs can negotiate their own terms of access to financial information as part of the investment deal struck with the individual investee.[1] Information provision in itself can therefore be variable; but it can also extend considerably beyond that contained in conventional shareholder reports. In this less regulated situation, examination of the practices developed by UK VCIs in obtaining and using accounting information will provide additional and novel insights into the information needs of the institutional investor.[2] This chapter explores the pattern of demand for accounting information by the VCI and examines how these demands may be influenced by the nature of the relationship between the two parties to the investment, viewed from a principal–agent (or simply 'agency') perspective. Results are presented under the headings of accounting information flows, information asymmetry and moral hazard safeguards.

12.2 ACCOUNTING INFORMATION FLOWS

Types of information

Despite the existence of a variety of contacts and information sources in investee firms (e.g. client meetings, board membership), accounting information was a universal requirement of the VCIs. Indeed one said that: "We won't invest in a company unless they have a good accounting system." Four respondents remarked on the value of receiving the annual audited accounting report, and

1 According to the VCI interviewees in this study, their formal rights to accounting information are enshrined in the subscription agreement, which provides the legal basis of the investment relationship. While interviewees were willing to discuss the nature and implications of this subscription agreement, there was extreme reluctance to provide examples on the grounds, first, of confidentiality to clients, and secondly, on commercial grounds because the subscription agreement is a key source of their competitive advantage. With few exceptions (e.g. Chapter 10) data gathered in this study were therefore restricted to the oral information provided to the researchers in interviews. Where direct speech by an investor or investee is being presented, double quotation marks are used.

2 It must, however, be borne in mind that there are significant differences in the nature of established stock market and venture capital investments. The latter will typically involve smaller firms and possibly more novel products or services. Their risk levels and the information needs of investors might therefore be considered greater. Thus, the evidence of this study may also reflect partly the impact of increased risk on the institutional investors' demand for information. However, the existence of portfolios of investments and the larger equity stakes normally held by the management team may be viewed to some extent as risk-limiting factors.

in the main, the accounting information requested and obtained by VCIs was of a fairly conventional composition. Central to the information flow were the three core financial statements: balance sheet; profit and loss account; and cash flow statement. The importance of the cash flow statement for assessing an investee's performance was particularly emphasized by over half of the interviewees.

Although these three financial statements are all a required part of the content of the annual shareholders' report, the actual form of disclosure to the VCI extended significantly beyond statutory requirements in six distinct ways:

1 The frequency of their provision was considerably increased from the statutory one of once or (in the case of interim reports) twice a year. Twelve VCIs obtained them monthly and five at least monthly. They were actively used to monitor investees' performance over these short time periods. For the most part they were, in fact, the key components of the investee firms' management accounting package, and were therefore readily available for distribution to the VCI. The other three VCIs also utilized the management accounting information of their clients, but did not specify exactly the time period requirement for its provision.
2 As a part of the management accounting package these statements were expressed in a much more detailed form than those provided to shareholders. For example, the profit and loss account would disclose the components of cost of sales, identify all overheads, and possibly show profitability segmented by product line and by corporate division.
3 In one quarter of the cases it was specifically mentioned that these financial results were assessed within the context of the firm's budgeted performance. In many cases this provided a direct link to the forecasts on which investment decisions were made. Variance from budget provided an important 'attention directing' signal to the VCI.
4 In a small number of cases (two) it was indicated that all of this information had to be provided within a strict time limit from the end of the reporting period.
5 The supplementation of the financial information by a qualitative explanatory summary of performance by the management team was specified by a significant minority (six) of VCIs.
6 Further types of information were highlighted by several VCIs as being an important part of information disclosure by investees. These comprised: capacity utilization levels (one investee); further non-financial measures of performance (one); capital expenditure analysis (two); order book position (two); and the auditors' management letter (one). While important, these additions merely modify, but do not challenge, the primacy accorded to the conventional accounting reports.

Variability of information requirements

The degree of detail, content and frequency of information all represented sources of possible variation in the nature of information required and received by VCIs. They were specifically asked whether their information flow varied over time (longitudinally) or at a point in time (cross-sectionally) for investees in their portfolios. Table 12.1 summarizes their responses.

Over a third of the VCIs had fixed requirements for information provision. They did not permit variation from them for any reason. In four cases the inability of the investee to produce information up to the standard normally expected was the main way in which information flow was constrained. Such investees were typically small, start-up businesses. However, the capabilities of investees to generate a good quality of financial information did develop over time. One VCI suggested that as investees developed their skills in information provision, information overload could become problematic, saying: "Information varies by firm capability – sometimes it's too detailed and sophisticated." Deviations from the expected performance levels by the investee also prompted changes in the requests for information provided. Two VCIs increased the requirement for information when the investee's performance dipped below target. They considered tighter monitoring was necessary in such circumstances. On the other hand, two VCIs reduced their information demands when performance was better than expected. Direct comments by VCIs on each of these responses to negative and positive variations were: "Yes, there can be fundamental change if there are problems, for example with customers or new projects"; and, "As it gets better and the more we feel comfortable, the less we want to stress them in this area". The maturity of investees' projects also influenced the need for information for seven of the VCIs. This was evident in two contrasting ways. Three venture capitalists accepted that less information would be available on new investees, particularly when they were small and at or near start-up. These VCIs appeared to appreciate that other factors might require priority. One said:

> "I expect very little when they start out. I like to get the cash book balanced. Often I don't even get that and I don't press for it too much. I

Table 12.1 Information variation

	N^1
No variation in information provision	7 firms
Variation caused by investee's inability to provide required information	4 firms
Variation caused by changing circumstances of investee (e.g. new projects, poor performance)	4 firms
Variation by maturity of investee's projects	7 firms

Note: [1] Two venture capitalists indicated two influencing factors

think it's a waste of time. They're working to build a business. As they develop, accounting information becomes more important."

The other four VCIs were of the opinion that information flows could be reduced over time as the client became established. An exception to this would be if refinancing were required, where the control aspect would be expected to be more significant once more. This aside, more information was required in the early years where investors had less familiarity with investees and there was more risk associated with the investments. However, for one of the four, the lighter information burden on more mature investees was due to a more liberal policy on information provision having been adopted when drawing up subscription agreements in previous years. A tightening of information requirements since then had resulted in more recent investees being required to provide more information.

Information cost

Only two investors indicated that cost was a critical factor in influencing their information-gathering activities. Both had found it impractical to access all the information which they would ideally have liked, and were prepared to compromise on cost grounds. For example, one VCI would have liked to take comprehensive soundings from all its customers on investee performance, but restricted this to the 'occasional one or two'.

All of the others did not consider cost to be a serious constraint on obtaining relevant information. The typical views of these VCIs are reflected in the following statements:

> "[It is] very important to get information and if it does cost more so be it. There is no greater crime than to report back 'don't know'."
>
> "[We] are conscious of the cost of information but this does not deter us from getting it if we need it."
>
> "I'm not ever aware of having used cost as a basis for not getting information."

Several VCIs argued that the cost of information provision was mainly borne by the investee, and in that sense was not an investor's problem. While it was true that investees were required to provide the information asked of them by investors, many VCIs observed that the costs had already been borne in meeting the information demands which any normal firm would find being generated routinely by the investees' own senior management. The incremental (i.e. marginal) cost of providing the data to investors was therefore negligible.

The costs to the venture capitalist of processing the information provided by investees was only raised as an important issue by two investors. They were trying to avoid 'information overload'. If it were threatened, they required curtailment of the information supplied:

> "Processing it is the problem. You can only absorb so much data and information. We occasionally shout 'Stop!'."
>
> "We like to think we don't ask for information we can't process. It is important to home in on one of the key variables. We are not into information overload."

12.3 INFORMATION ASYMMETRY

Investee informational advantage

All VCIs accepted that their investees had some informational advantage over them. Indeed, several remarked that the absence of such advantage would be good reason for not investing in the managerial team concerned. In other words, part of the gain to be obtained from entering into a contract with the investee was in sharing this expertise. Investees were expected to be experts in the type of business which they ran. The nature of the informational advantage was perceived as having different aspects to it. Central was the sectoral technical expertise and the operational knowledge of the specific firm which management was inevitably assumed to possess. Their more direct exposure to the business situation and their participation in day-to-day decision-making typically imbued them with a unique knowledge of their firm's current affairs and prospects. Being positioned at the 'sharp end' ensured that they certainly obtained information on problems *before* the VCI (one respondent). Another VCI attributed the inevitability of informational advantage in part at least to the existence of a portfolio of investments which all required attention by him. The size and diversity of the portfolio precluded the development of a particularly detailed familiarity (matching that of management) with any of them.

Investors (five) held that investees may attempt to hide operational problems or delay reporting bad news, even though this information was needed by VCIs at the earliest opportunity. It was emphasized that a VCI did consider it an obligation of investees to "put all their cards on the table from the start", with one suggesting that, "If we suspected we weren't getting full answers we wouldn't continue the relationship". In addition to investees hiding problems, another VCI suggested that those with a particularly good performance might mask it to allow the management team to achieve a preferable exit deal by changing backers. It is difficult to judge how serious a comment this was, as there is not yet an active secondary market in venture capital investments in the UK. Therefore, it would be difficult for management to operationalize this without raising the suspicions of the existing backers.

Three factors were also cited as *limiting* the adverse effects of management's informational advantage. First, the nature of the investee's line of business could be kept simple (one respondent) with complex businesses such as biotechnology and micro-electronics being excluded. In fact only four out of the twenty VCIs expressed an exclusive preference for high-technology involvements. Second, the relationships established were based on trust. "We buy integrity not information" was how one venture capitalist expressed this idea. Another said: "We have faith in the people. If we didn't, we shouldn't have invested." Third, a congruence in the interests of both venture capitalist and investee was considered to exist, centred on the substantial ownership of shares in the firm by both parties. Therefore, the personal attachment of management to the company and the cost of perquisite consumption ('perks') would be greater than normally found in the stock-market context. The investee's informational advantage was also thought to be limited by the tendency of VCIs to have development-stage and sectoral specializations.

Selective information

Most investors (seventeen) considered their investees to be selective in the information they provided. The three who did not thought that their rigorous selection procedures limited adverse selection. This ensured that only those who would be "open with us" were chosen for investment. All of the others accepted that full disclosure did not occur. One remarked that they have "a rational motivation to misrepresent" and another that they "give you what you want to hear". Most respondents (eleven) felt an optimistic bias did tend to pervade reported information. In particular, aspects of poor performance, a deterioration in the market, or a decline in customer relations, were not fully communicated, and only reported when it became unavoidable.

Information conformity with reality

We have seen that monitoring may be hampered by the deliberate manipulation of information by the investee. It is also possible that monitoring is handicapped by the intrinsic inability of accounting information to reflect the reality of performance. Seventeen investors considered that this was an additional problem affecting the usefulness of the accounting information provided to them by investees. The most prominent contributory factor was the time lag with which accounting statements reflected reality. This was not merely associated with the delay in producing financial statements. Several VCIs mentioned that an accrual accounting-based profit figure could indicate an apparent level of success at the time of reporting which was not matched by corresponding cash generation. Thus conflicting signals of reality were often conveyed by the information. There was also some appreciation that performance could not be properly assessed from accounts in the short run. As one VCI remarked: "In the first two years we don't really know how the investee is doing." Others suggested that monthly information has to be accumulated in order to allow trends to become apparent.

Other less classifiable problems of matching information with reality included the following. In one case the investee's accounting information was used to translate physical product reality into financial terms. This obscured the fact that the investee's firm was not actually selling the product for which they were financed. It was also noted that errors could be made in the construction of management accounts and these could mislead investors. Moreover, accounting reports may not include vital contextual information on the market situation which may affect an investee's performance (e.g. a tripling of a competitor's capacity output). Serious problems or 'disasters' were often not adequately represented in accounts. Indeed two VCIs noted that they had needed to "send someone in" in these circumstances to find out what was happening. Finally, one VCI reported that accounting policy changes by an investee created an inconsistency in translating events into reported information, which had the potential to result in misleading assessments of their progress.

12.4 MORAL HAZARD SAFEGUARDS

Vetting investees' accounting systems

All but one of the VCIs vetted the systems of their clients. The one VCI who did not was in the process of developing a means of so doing. Seven VCIs observed that their vetting tended to be done as a one-off exercise at the time of making the investment. This was done to ensure that a reasonable information flow would be forthcoming in the post-investment period and also to ensure that management were able to control and make decisions on an informed basis. The vetting tended to cover key business systems (e.g. sales, credit control and product costing). Where deficiencies were identified changes were required as a condition of investment. To illustrate, in one case a VCI imposed basic cash control systems on many of his small investees.

In some cases vetting was not done directly by the investor. Five of the venture capitalists, at least on some occasions, hired firms of professional accountants to produce formal reports (incorporating recommendations for improvement) on the investees' accounting systems. A further five consulted the investees' auditors. As one VCI put it, by depending on the auditors' familiarity with financial systems he could "get comfort that the information which is produced will be reliable and accurate".

Investee audit

The statutory audit of investee companies was of considerable interest to the venture capitalist. All but one VCI claimed to have an impact on the audit process. The nature of any influence exerted varied. It could be both direct and indirect. Most commonly it took the form of participating in the selection of the auditor.[3] Six venture capitalists imposed their choice of audit firm, often as a condition of investment. The change to a 'large respectable' auditor (usually one of the 'big six') was what they required of the investee. However, the VCI's influence extended beyond auditor selection in a number of ways. One venture capitalist met with the appointed auditor at an early stage to "let them know we are investors and that we are relying on their report".[4] Another discussed the investee's accounting policies with the auditor, and had influenced them in one case by having the levels of provision raised to ensure that "there would be no skeletons in the cupboard to hinder improvement when recession ends". The results of the audit were also of interest, with six of the venture capitalists monitoring the auditors' feedback through membership of the investee audit committee and by scrutiny of the management letter.

Direct access to the investees' accounting system

There was an almost even split among the VCIs sampled on this issue. Eleven had no direct access to their investees' accounting systems. However, several of these venture capitalists made the point that they could request any accounting information they wished, and one mentioned that he could instigate a third-party investigation. Another with no direct access did use the client's auditor as a surrogate source of information. Again, the requirement to trust the investee was mentioned by one of the venture capitalists. Of the nine venture capitalists claiming direct access to investees' accounting systems, three achieved this through directorships, while one stated that such access was a condition in the subscription agreement. The others gave no specific justification for their right of access.

12.5 DISCUSSION OF RESULTS

The analysis of this chapter prompts the following observations on the use of accounting information by institutional investors of the venture capital variety. In this investment sector the absence of stock-market (and arguably 'efficient')

3 This does indicate a greater than normal shareholder involvement in the appointment of the auditor. In practice it is common for the appointment and the reappointment of the auditor to be simply approved by shareholders at an AGM on the basis of a nomination by the company directors.

4 The nature of the auditors' liability to shareholders has long been a contentious issue (Gwilliam 1987). This type of behaviour could be construed as an attempt to establish a relationship which could facilitate litigation by the VCI in the event of business failure. In effect, it may be viewed as another means of confronting the problem of moral hazard.

prices for shares precludes the use of both technical and beta analysis. The investor has to rely on fundamental analysis. Fortunately, this is facilitated by the absence of stock-market-like restrictions on information access. This allows VCIs to effect a more liberal expression of their information needs.

It was clear from the analysis above that accounting information is a key requirement of this type of investor. Superficially, their information demands are centred on the same three financial statements as those which are conventionally provided to stock-market shareholders. However, there was considerable evidence that their information needs extended well beyond those generated by traditional external financial accounting methods. Although conventional accounting statements remained the centrepiece of the accounting information flow, they had to be provided more *regularly* (typically monthly) and in a *more detailed form* (as per the management accounts). Moreover, they usually had to be set in the context of agreed budgets and narrative explanations, and were subject to regular query. The monitoring behaviour of these sophisticated information users revealed a keenness to maintain as current a financial information flow as possible.

This greater intensity of scrutiny of the investee's performance was important in motivating the agent to act in accordance with the principal's objectives. It also ensured that the investor was well placed to react promptly to any deviations from plan. In the absence of a stock market the VCI is unable to effect an exit in the short term. As a result of this 'lock-in' effect, the VCI's main reaction to difficulties experienced by the investee has to be constructive. Thus VCIs can bring to bear their financing expertise, can utilize their network of business contacts and, *in extremis*, can exercise their powers to replace management. Their main concern appeared to be to ensure that losses were disclosed promptly, and that difficulties were thereby contained rather than being allowed to intensify because they were unidentified. The avoidance of operational 'disasters' (the occasional outcome of extreme downside risk) that could seriously affect the value of the investment appeared to be a primary concern underlying the monitoring behaviour of the VCIs. They were certainly keen to identify perquisite consumption ('perks') by their agents, but their perception of the main threat of moral hazard was that it lay mainly in the investee's ability to delay the disclosure of serious problems that could threaten their firm's survival. While procrastination could bring short-term benefit to the agent (e.g. in terms of continued remuneration, avoidance of loss of face and the opportunity autonomously to 'turn things round'), it did heighten the risk of ultimately experiencing a substantial loss.

The *existence* of moral hazard is a common problem across different situations. It is intrinsic to risk-sharing situations with information asymmetry. However, the *response* to moral hazard (generally governed by its severity) varies across investor–investee involvements. Among the VCIs interviewed there was little experience with start-up and early-stage investment where proactive policies are common. Rather, the emphasis was on development capital and buyouts. These differ mainly by adverse selection (a pre-contract problem of information asymmetry and risk classification) rather than moral hazard (with its post-contract problems of efficient risk-sharing and effort elicitation). This chapter gives an account of variations, to be found in practice, in treatment of moral hazard problems through monitoring policies.

While the nature of the financial information flow provided by investees was generally similar, there was evidence to suggest that variations were allowed. These permitted variations to be rewards for good performance or recognition of a sound track record. In such cases a reduction in reporting frequency was permitted, although no VCI would allow information to be received at less than quarterly intervals. This pattern of behaviour indicated that, for investees who were perceived by VCIs to be in a relatively low-risk category, a more conventional approach to information provision was often deemed acceptable, taking the stock-exchange disclosure protocol as a benchmark. This behaviour is as would be predicted for VCIs subject to moral hazard of the sort described above.

The constructive role of the VCIs extended to their proactive influence in the development of management accounting systems in the investee firms. For example, they were prepared to design some of their clients' systems and would buy-in consultancy expertise to improve their investees' situation. The emphasis on budgeting and cash flow analysis reinforces the VCIs' prime concern for the viability of their investees' enterprises. Their contractual involvements can therefore guarantee that no less than the basic level of information necessary for operational effectiveness is available to the investee firm's management. Indeed, this is probably one of the more beneficial consequences of venture capital involvement.

This chapter suggests that information asymmetry is ubiquitous in investor–investee relations in the UK venture capital industry. This was generally recognized and was considered particularly serious if it delayed the identification of deteriorating situations. These were the particular province of proactive or interventionist actions by VCIs. Even the high degree of information access accorded to VCIs did not completely remove this problem. Indeed, in some situations, it was felt that conventional accounting methods could compound the difficulties of a crisis situation because of their susceptibility to 'managerial masking' of the real, current financial position of the investee. While there was no suggestion that the comprehension of the information provided constituted a significant barrier to communication between the two parties, masking or selection of information could degrade the quality and volume of communications.

12.6 CONCLUSION

The results presented above confirm that a number of the key concepts of principal–agent analysis are mirrored in the financial communication process between VCIs and their investees. They reveal VCIs' appreciation of the dangers of ***moral hazard***, against which some safeguard is sought through their ***bonding*** arrangements to establish a sound supply of accounting information. This contributes to their ***monitoring*** of investees' performance, which is typically maintained on a regular short-term basis. A concern with ***information asymmetry*** is also evident in their doubts about the completeness and reliability of this information, particularly because of its managerial origins.

However, in a context in which the VCI has the power to influence information supply fairly directly, there has been no pressure applied to MSFs to make them diverge from conventional accounting procedures. Traditional financial statements remain at the centre of the reporting process.[5] A marked increase in the frequency of their provision, and the incorporation of considerable management accounting detail in their construction, appear to be the main differences from the regulated accounting supply.

5 These findings tend to confirm the preoccupation of institutions with the short-term performance of investments. This occurs even when the option of a short-term decision to sell is not commonly available and it therefore suggests that close monitoring is indeed viewed by the VCI as a means of combating moral hazard. Further, these findings suggest that VCIs, in their role as institutional investors who use accounting information, do not represent a radical force for change in financial reporting. This lack of desire for change in the substance of accounting procedures is probably unconnected with the perceived relevance or otherwise of information flowing to them, for user studies show that institutional investors as a class are enthusiastic users of financial statements. Thus their apparent acceptance of the status quo should simply be regarded as indicating a substantial degree of satisfaction with conventional financial statements. VCIs are certainly practised in their use, and this facility with them undoubtedly enhances the quality of investees' attempts to monitor, to the end of uncovering (and, if need be, rectifying), the consequences of moral hazard.

13

THE SUPPLY OF VENTURE CAPITAL AND THE DEVELOPMENT OF INVESTEES' ACCOUNTING INFORMATION SYSTEMS

with Falconer Mitchell and Nicholas G. Terry

13.1 INTRODUCTION

One of the most important events in the early life cycle of any entrepreneurial firm which harbours serious growth ambitions is the infusion of external capital (Reid 1996a). This event can lead to significant changes in the firm's ownership composition, and affects its subsequent rate of growth and, consequently, its size and organizational structure. It is within the context of such changes that the managerial demand for information about the firm is stimulated. This chapter examines the origins and characteristics of developments in the accounting information systems (AIS) of firms which are going through this stage. It does so by investigating the consequences of venture capital[1] intervention for the entrepreneurial firm (MSF), particularly as regards the characteristics of its accounting information system (AIS).

13.2 THEORY AND METHOD

As before, the overarching framework within which the evidence is explored in this chapter is principal–agent analysis which, in an increasing body of literature,

1 Originally, influenced by US practice, referring to high-risk, high-return unquoted equity involvement, but increasingly, in a UK context, having the connotation of development capital (see Chapter 2). An emerging term is 'private equity', which emphasizes the highly incentivized arrangements agreed between investor and investee.

is used to represent the relationship between the venture capital investor (VCI), as principal, and the entrepreneur (MSF), as agent. For example, Gompers (1995) uses this approach to emphasize the role that monitoring plays at various stages of venture capital investment; and Lerner (1995) investigates the incentive effects of monitoring venture-backed firms through having venture capital representation on the board of directors. However, in this predominantly US literature, questions are rarely asked about the nature of information systems, and the issues that arise in their development. This chapter aims to address this deficiency of the extant literature.

The significance of positive increments in the firm's supply of external capital for the development of its accounting system depends on characteristics of the evolving circumstances which confront both the owners and managers of the firm. The venture capital investors (VCIs) have put their invested funds at risk, but both at the time of negotiating the subscription agreement,[2] and also subsequently through their ownership stake, they can take steps to 'manage' their risk by making direct and effective demands on the investee for regular information. This can be seen as an attempt to improve contractual efficiency between the investee and investor. Recent studies have shown that VCIs do expect that the power they possess, which arises from their investor status, allows them to make effective their demands for information from investees as regards its type, quality and frequency (Sweeting 1991a; Mitchell *et al.* 1995; Wright and Robbie 1996). Indeed, at the pre-investment stage, special investigations of the capacity of the investee's systems to meet the post-investment requirements of the VCI are frequently undertaken. Any upgrading which is thought to be necessary is then made a condition of the investment. Thus changes in the flow of information from the firm to its new investors have the potential to influence the form of the internal accounting system. Moreover, as decision-making is a central facet of entrepreneurship, it also influences the in-house provision of accounting information. In an uncertain world, the efficacy of decision-making is heavily conditioned by the quality of information available to the entrepreneur. Indeed, information inadequacy is often associated with business distress and failure in small and medium-sized enterprises (SMEs) (e.g. Storey *et al.* 1987). Conversely, better quality information has been associated with success and survival (e.g. Hutchison and Ray 1986).

For firms which are classed as relatively risky investment opportunities, one would expect their providers of capital to take an interest in information provision. Specifically, one would expect investors to take steps to ensure that investees are well served by information which is of relevance to their managerial

2 Although many such agreements are standardized, an opportunity exists for customization (e.g. by type and frequency of accounting information requested). To this extent, the chapter casts some light on the sort of provisions that are likely to be found in this essentially confidential document.

decisions. It is also probable that this external pressure for the development of the AIS, which is an indirect influence, is reinforced by those who can more directly influence the supply of information, namely, the entrepreneurs or owner-managers of the investee firms. Their motivation to enhance internal accounting methods is strengthened by two specific factors. The first is that appropriate 'decision support' for the allocation of new or existing funds to their most productive uses is needed, such that both *ex ante*, on the basis of projections, and *ex post*, on the basis of outcomes, an improvement is demonstrable. The second is that growth in corporate size, which is contingent upon the planned use of the venture capital provided, is often perceived to reduce or eliminate that personal involvement of the entrepreneur in many aspects of his business from which he may have derived satisfaction ('psychic income'). Thus increased size creates a problem of control and may lead to a growth/profitability trade-off (Reid 1998). The need to monitor and report remains, but if it cannot be achieved so readily by direct personal supervision, the entrepreneur satisfies the need for involvement and superintendence directly through the generation of relevant information on performance. The AIS of the firm is one important source of such relevant information for control, and it typically requires modification to cope with those new and more extensive demands placed upon it which arise when the firm grows.

The focus of this chapter is therefore on the impact of finance capital supply and ownership change on internal information provision. Broader consideration of the determinants of an appropriate AIS is contained in the literature on the contingency theory of management accounting.[3] This work suggests that key contingent variables influencing the AIS and its appropriate development are features of: the firm's environment (normally to be conceived of in terms of uncertainty); its technology (normally conceived of in terms of complexity); and its organizational structure (normally conceived of in terms of flexibility). It may be that the VCI influence will run counter to contingency theory, which suggests that industrial sector characteristics, like market competitiveness and technology, will be key formative influences on internal accounting.

The VCI, in contrast, is more immune to these, and is likely to provide a standard influence independent of these factors. Jones (1995) has used a contingency theory approach to assess the importance of these features as determinants of internal accounting systems in merger situations where ownership has changed. He concluded that 'overall management accounting systems tended to bear the characteristics of the Universalist theory', that is, practical management accounting procedures remain similar despite differing contexts in terms of contingent variables. This chapter extends this research by examining one of the factors which, for some firms, may exert a universalist influence on the AIS. The

3 See Otley (1980) and Ezzamel and Hart (1987) for reviews.

presumption of part ownership by the VCI, and the institutionalization of 'standard' information demands on investees, may represent strong formative influences on the genesis of AISs for MSFs going through an important stage of development. Also of relevance is the work of Jones (1992) on MBOs (which are predominantly VC backed). His work emphasizes accounting control systems (ACS), and he shows that they are modified to facilitate changes which will enhance profitability, along lines which are consistent with contingency theory.

While the theoretical backdrop of principal–agent analysis has allowed a wide range of questions to be addressed in earlier chapters, the concern here is more narrowly focused on the information system. As a consequence, there is less evidence to work with than before. However, the quantitative evidence that is available, allied to the 'thick' qualitative data of the case studies, enables the undernoted propositions to be put forward for substantiation by the evidence. This chapter is therefore exploratory and should be viewed as an initial step in establishing the propositions empirically. It aims to provide both weight of evidence in support of them, and a platform on which further research ideas, related to their verification, can be built. In the sequence of five propositions reported on below, earlier propositions are embedded in later propositions: thus the empirical argument assumes an increasing level of generality.[4]

> *Proposition 1*
> Considerable monitoring demands in the form of accounting provision requirements will be imposed by the VCI.

Supporting evidence for this proposition would come from affirmative replies to the following questions. Are the VCI's information demands met both pre- and post-investment? Is compliance with the VCI's information demands enforceable? Can the VCI impose change in the form of the investee's provision of information? Are cost impediments to the implementation of such change absent? Does the VCI have direct access to the investee's information system? Can the VCI influence the investee's audit? Is the frequency of information provision and its level of detail, as imposed by the VCI, in excess of statutory requirements?

> *Proposition 2*
> The fulfilling of monitoring demands by accounting information (Proposition 1) and other sources (e.g. the VCI having representation on the board) stimulates the need for internal accounting change within the investee firm.

4 This methodology of treating propositions as emerging from evidence is well established. See Yin (1984) for background and Cable and Shane (1997) for an application.

In addition to the evidence for Proposition 1, Proposition 2 requires that obvious information development, after VCI involvement, should have occurred. This would be expected in terms of both performance measurement (profit and loss, financial ratios, etc.), and accounting control (monitoring reports, setting of financial budgets, reporting of budget components).

> *Proposition 3*
> Not only will increases in the variety and extent of the procedures adopted occur to meet increased monitoring demands (Proposition 2), but also increases will occur in the frequency of provision of accounting information.

In addition to the evidence for Proposition 2, support for Proposition 3 requires an examination of the frequency of reporting over wide budgetary categories (profit and loss, cash flow, balance sheet, capital expenditure, headcount, etc.) on a frequency spectrum which extends from daily, weekly, monthly, to annual. Pre- and post-VCI situations need considering to confirm both increased incidence of reporting at specific intervals and increased incidence of reporting at more frequent intervals.

> *Proposition 4*
> The development of more varied, extensive and frequent information flows (Proposition 3) will lead to the development of accounting information support for internal decision-making.

In addition to the evidence for Proposition 3, this evidence requires for its support that main categories of decision types (operating, strategic and capital investment) should be more widely supported after VCI involvement with the investee than before. Evidence of the perceived importance to investees of any one of these categories (e.g. capital investment) would further increase the weight of evidence for this proposition.

> *Proposition 5*
> The capital supply from the VCI has a strong and universalist influence on internal accounting systems in investee firms.

This proposition builds on the previous four propositions, and makes reference to the universalist theory of management accounting of Jones (1995). It requires support from a complete overview of AIS development after the VCI has started to infuse capital into the investee firm. It needs to be established that typically a *range* of AIS developments occur after VCI involvement, and that these may be extensive.

While these propositions cannot be put into a classical hypothesis-testing framework, they have been formulated in a way that permits a significant and persuasive body of qualitative evidence to be adduced in their favour. We turn now to a consideration of this 'weight of evidence'.

13.3 THE EVIDENCE ON INFORMATION

Because of the narrower focus of this chapter on the investee's AIS, fewer dyads (twelve only) are available than previously for analysis. A summary of key sample characteristics[5] of these investor–investee dyads is given in Table 13.1. It is to be noted that this subsample of twelve cases displays considerable variation by size measures (e.g. funds managed, turnover), structure (e.g. ratio of venture capital executives to investees, venture capital stake) and sectoral activity. It represents well the larger body of investor–investee relations in the UK venture capital industry analysed in earlier chapters, so far as individual (rather than paired) investor and investee data indicate. Such sample bias as exists is likely to be by investment stage, and by performance. The typical investment stage was development (45 per cent) followed by buyout (40 per cent). These are close to the industry figures reported in Reid (1996a: 5) for development (43 per cent, 38 per cent) and buyout (21 per cent, 32 per cent) in the years 1990 and 1992 respectively. Arguably, these figures overrepresent buyouts. As regards performance, we have no complete post-exit data to give an authoritative view, but it is possible that the subset who provided investees have, on average, higher performance than those which do not.

Establishing the information source

All of the VCIs interviewed made effective demands on their investees for accounting information, not only at the time of making the investment – in part, having drawn lessons concerning system shortfalls in the execution of their original due diligence – but also subsequently, in the light of the evolving investor/investee relationship, to ensure a regular flow of monitoring information. The requirements which VCIs placed on the investees to report externally therefore set a minimum standard of systematic accounting information provision within the investee companies. To ensure compliance, the establishment of an appropriate system was a normal condition of investment. Every VCI interviewed (with one exception) undertook a vetting of the investee's AIS. Even the single one which did not was at least positive about the idea, saying:

5 The figure of 99 per cent for the venture capital stake of Case J is correct, but refers to a development company with multiple VCI involvement.

Table 13.1 Key characteristics of the subsample

Case	*Venture capital investor (VCI)*				*Investee (MSF)*			
	Venture funds under management (£m.)	*Number of venture capital executives*	*Number of investees*	*Average value of investment made (£000s)*	*Industrial sector (SIC)*	*Turnover (£000s)*	*Number of employees*	*Venture capital stake (%)*
B	200	16	25	2,000	n.a.	n.a.	n.a.	n.a.
D	28	8	11	400	95	279	8	36
E	45	2	2	300	22	4,000	55	n.a.
F	29	3	13	245	21	7,000	193	n.a.
H	175	9	n.a.	n.a.	47	90,000	840	75
J	50	8	12	1,000	48	1,700	50	99
K	60	6	5	4,000	34	33,800	735	n.a.
L	2	1	5	25	25	275	7	28
M	100	7	n.a.	700	94	2,750	35	n.a.
N	8	3	6	400	34	1,800	27	n.a.
P	88	7	33	n.a.	13	13,500	97	55
Q	150	16	61	500	64	6,500	35	n.a.

Note: In the cases of multiple investees (J, N, P, Q) the investees chosen are J1, N2, P1 and Q1 respectively.

> "We want to do this, but haven't in the past. In the past we haven't looked at their accounting but we realize the investees need good information not just for me, but also for their own decision-making."

Most of the other eleven VCIs (n = 9) assessed the investee's AISs themselves. Of these, two also used auditors' findings (e.g. the reviewing of recent letters by managers and the reactions of clients to them).[6] For another two, one relied on the auditor to judge the system in use, and the other commissioned special investigative reviews by independent accountants. In seven cases, the VCIs indicated that they regularly required changes to be made. They cited examples of improvements in various aspects of internal accounting which had been made at their insistence (e.g. the development of the sales system, the creation of an effective credit control system, the creation of a costing system). Moreover, one VCI assessed the quality of staff involved in operating the accounting systems, and prompted the recruitment of better staff where necessary. In one case, involving smaller investors, the VCI was even more proactive in influencing internal accounting, saying:

> "Sometimes I set them up to begin with . . . I show them my accounting system and several of them use it until they grow."

Thus the concern of VCIs for the availability of reliable and relevant accounting information was manifested primarily in their readiness to examine and improve the underlying system. However, it was also apparent in three other facets of their behaviour towards investees.

First, in most cases (n = 9), the deterrent effect of extra costs of generating and/or processing information was not considered to impose a constraint on obtaining what the VCI wanted to know. Indeed, several saw the pursuit of information needs through to their provision as a central facet of their role. Illustrative quotes are:

> "This is a very real issue. It is very important to get information, and if it does cost more, then so be it. There is no greater crime than to report back, 'Don't know.'."

> "The trend which I've seen over the last 12 years is to be more and more

6 Such letters may signal to the VCI the sort of information that needs to be sought, or areas where the system can be improved. This role in the development of the AIS is an incentive arrangement permitted by VCIs, allowing investees to go beyond the reporting uses of information (e.g. to proactive decision-making and strategic planning). Viewed in this way, the AIS plays a role in the trajectory to investment realization, and begins to play a management information system (MIS) function.

> cautious on financial information, to gather more and more information to balance against the price of a deal."[7]
>
> "Information gathering is an essential cost. We are paid a management fee by our clients to monitor our investments."

Although the information which was perceived as necessary would apparently be gathered with little regard to its total cost, a number of VCIs did also express the view that the incremental cost to them of information was seldom high. In view of this, they would ensure that the investee firm had established a system to produce all that was needed. They would not be perturbed at the prospect of imposing any new requirements, for their implementation would, in any case, be funded by the investee. The VCIs' information demands were, however, selective (see following section) and attempts were made to contain the volume of information received, so that overload did not become a problem. This is illustrated by the comments:

> "Processing it [data] is the problem. You can only absorb so much information. We occasionally shout 'stop'."
>
> "We like to think we don't ask for information we can't process. It is important to home in on key variables."

Second, over half (n = 7) of the VCIs had obtained direct access to their investees' internal accounting systems, in the sense of first-hand exposure to internally generated data and reports. This access had enhanced their capacities both to monitor and to verify the information provided. Finally, ten of the twelve VCIs specifically influenced the audit of the investee company. Six did so by an involvement in the selection of the auditor, with a strong preference being expressed for 'big, reputable' firms. The remaining four were prepared to initiate additional audit work, where problems were apparent that required more external visibility. The two VCIs who did not exert any audit influence did, however, request and study the annual management letter from the auditor.[8]

Information required

All twelve VCIs required their investees to return fairly conventional packages of accounting information every month, and they used this as the basis for monitoring their investees' performance. These data were frequently referred to as the

7 This is a significant comment. It emphasizes that the higher the value of the equity at the time of investment, the greater will the MSF's performance have to be to raise the value at exit to a level which will enable the target IRR to be realized.

8 See findings on MBOs in Wright *et al.* (1992).

'monthly management accounts'. They typically consisted of three financial statements: the balance sheet; the profit and loss account; and the cash flow statement. These are described as 'conventional', because of the commonness of this type of information, both for internal and external reporting.

These statements also constitute the core financial content of the statutory shareholders' report. However, the VCIs' package differed from this report, not only in terms of reporting frequency, but also in several other significant respects. In particular, the level of detail disclosed was greater than that which was statutorily required for external reporting. For example, the profit and loss account supplied would normally incorporate the segmentation of turnover by product line, expenses would be detailed to show the make up of cost of sales and overheads, and a similar breakdown of cash flows would be available. In addition, five of the VCIs specifically mentioned that these financial results would be presented within the context of the MSF's budget to provide a clear comparison of budgeted against actual magnitudes. Two VCIs also requested the investee company's management to provide a written commentary or narrative on the results contained in the monthly information package. While these figures for reporting variances, and returning narratives, may seem low, it must be borne in mind that some VCIs may discuss results orally with the firm, or may be present at board meetings where they are discussed. The budget will, of course, be in the possession of VCIs, so, in other cases, they may check budget variances for themselves. To provide some further indication of investees' future prospects, another two VCIs required a report on their order book positions. Finally, various forms of supplementary information, all directly or indirectly linked to performance, were requested in the light of specific needs of individual VCIs. These included measures of product quality, and capacity utilization, as well as capital investment proposals and gearing ratios.

Information requirements were, in the main, set and enforced in a fairly standard manner. In all cases, investees had, at some stage, to meet the basic demands for information described above, and five of the VCIs allowed no variation in these information demands. The others did allow a measure of flexibility. Four allowed some relaxation in the regularity of reporting (from monthly to a quarterly or half-yearly basis). This required that the relationships they had with investees were well established, and that investees had generated satisfactory track records over this time. Another VCI did not require reports from MSFs before trading operations had started, and yet another allowed MSFs to report on differing bases, depending on how reporting demands had evolved over the 1980s.

13.4 THE INVESTEE'S AIS: PRACTICE AND CHANGE

The sample of twelve representative investees provided information on both the nature of their AISs and the developments which had occurred therein subsequent to VCIs' involvements with them. Their responses are presented in the three sections below (i.e. performance measurement, budgetary control and decision-making).

Performance measurement

This aspect of the study focused on the operating performance of the investee. Key components of the profit and loss account (e.g. turnover, labour costs, profit), cash flow, and some financial ratios (linking the profit and loss account to the balance sheet) were all specifically discussed. In addition, the investees were requested to identify any other important means by which they assessed their MSF's progress and performance. Table 13.2 summarizes the responses. The general picture is of a rich flow of information from investee to investor, as would be expected in situations of relatively high risk, in which risk can be 'managed' by attenuating the information asymmetry between investee and investor.

Turnover, profit and cash flow information were used within all of the investee companies and with only two exceptions (on cash flow) these types of information were also reported to the VCI. Cash flow information did reflect some potential degree of VCI influence in its generation. In four cases its development had only occurred after VCI involvement. The utilization of the profit and loss account and balance sheet information to derive commonly used financial ratios occurred in roughly half of the firms, and, if desired, they were typically reported to the VCI. However, only in the case of the return on equity capital employed (a 'shareholder' ratio) was there an indication of a significant number of investees developing the measure in response to requests from their VCIs. The 'other' key performance measures used by investees had largely been associated with the VCI

Table 13.2 Performance measurement information used by investees (n = 12)

	Information used internally by investee	*Information reported to VCI*	*Information developed since VCI involvement*
Profit and loss components			
Turnover analysis	12	12	1
Labour cost analysis	8	8	1
Net profit	12	12	2
Financial ratios			
Return on equity employed	6	5	3
Return on assets	6	6	1
Sales/assets invested	3	3	1
Other aspects			
Cash flow	12	10	4
Other (see discussion in text)	11	11	8

link. They included market share analysis (n = 1); stock turnover (n = 1); profit margin (n = 1); order situation (n = 1); debtor analysis (n = 1); headcount (n = 1); overtime volume (n = 1); research milestones (n = 1); and proof of bank covenant compliance (n = 1).

Budgetary control

To ascertain details of the accounting control system within investee firms, interviewees were asked whether they: (a) produced information to allow them to monitor their business operations; and (b) set financial budgets. If relevant, they had to identify the key components of their budgets, and the basis on which they were reviewed over time (e.g. monthly, quarterly, etc.) and used for control purposes. Each was also requested to indicate if the control information produced had been developed since becoming involved with their VCI. The responses are reported by the class of control information in Table 13.3 and by the frequency of budgetary reporting in Table 13.4.

For all classes of control information reported in Table 13.3, the information generated internally by the investee is typically reported to the VCI. In just one case, the monitoring report, this was not done. Generally, the VCI played a significant role in ensuring that its demand for information was met by the investee. Thus, for most classes of control information, about a quarter of this provision had occurred after the VCI had become involved. The one exception to this was in the setting of financial budgets – a crucial class of control information even for independent MSFs – in which case the influence of the VCI was less.

Table 13.4 emphasizes another aspect of information provision, namely, its time basis, flow rate or frequency, as opposed to its volume or variety. Six forms of budgetary reporting are identified, covering a wide range of types from profit and loss account, through balance sheet, to head count. The frequency of

Table 13.3 Control information used by investees

	Used internally by investee	*Reported to VCI*	*Produced since VCI's involvement*
(1) Use of monitoring reports	11	10	3
(2) Financial budgets set	12	12	1
(3) Budget components			3
Profit and loss account	12	12	3
Cash flow	12	12	3
Balance sheet	12	12	3
Capital expenditure	10	10	3
Headcount	11	11	3
Other	2	2	—

Table 13.4 Frequency of budgetary reporting by investee

	None	*Annual*	*Biannual*	*Quarterly*	*Monthly*	*Weekly*	*Daily*
(a) Profit and loss account							
Before VCI involvement	3	5	—	1	3	—	—
After VCI involvement	—	6	1	2	3	—	—
(b) Cash flow							
Before VCI involvement	3	3	1	—	2	2	1
After VCI involvement	—	4	—	—	5	2	1
(c) Balance sheet							
Before VCI involvement	3	5	—	—	4	—	—
After VCI involvement	—	4	1	1	6	—	—
(d) Capital expenditure							
Before VCI involvement	5	6	—	—	1	—	—
After VCI involvement	2	8	—	—	2	—	—
(e) Headcount							
Before VCI involvement	4	4	—	2	2	—	—
After VCI involvement	1	6	—	1	4	—	—
(f) Other							
Before VCI involvement	10	1	—	—	1	—	—
After VCI involvement	10	—	—	1	1	—	—

reporting is then indicated, both before (first row) and after (second row) VCI involvement with the investee.

Overall, annual and monthly reporting are the typical frequencies. For all classes of budgetary reporting, the effect of VCI involvement is almost always to raise the frequency of reporting, in two senses. First, more investees are involved in reporting at any given interval (e.g. annual) after VCI involvement, as compared with before. Second, additional intervals for reporting may also be required (e.g. biannual as well as annual) after VCI involvement, as compared with before. For example, biannual reporting emerges for the profit and loss account and balance sheet, and quarterly reporting emerges for the balance sheet. Thus the general picture of increased frequency of reporting as a result of VCI involvement is substantiated. In the sample of Jones (1992), involving more mature firms, in which monthly accounts were already commonplace, this effect was less obvious. However, there was increased frequency of performance forecast updates, and marked increase in frequency of cash flow reporting. Further, the importance of reporting, the greater emphasis in Jones (1992), was considerably increased following an MBO.

To conclude our analysis of control, we find that monitoring reports and budgetary control systems were widely used within the investee firms, to an extent which was positively affected by their VCIs. Financial control through budgetary targets was an important aspect of operations and one that was used with differing degrees of flexibility, as the following qualitative evidence indicates:

> "We know what we have in the bank and what we should have next month in the bank. Everything is looked at virtually daily. We're locked into a six-month cycle: . . . We're on a treadmill that doesn't stop."
>
> "The budget is set annually and we phase it month by month. We might reset the budget depending on the circumstances prevailing at the time."
>
> "We set the budget every 12 months if the Tables run in line with the budget. But if they deviate we review the results, which leads to a new budget."

Decision-making

The investees were asked about the accounting information produced within their organizations for decision-making. Once again they were requested to indicate if this type of information was reported to their VCI and whether or not it had been developed subsequent to the VCI involvement with them. Some exploration of the type of information produced was also made. The results on decision types are presented in Table 13.5. The decision types identified are: operating, strategic and capital investment.

The results indicate the widespread development of AIS support for internal decision-making. Moreover, in a substantial number of cases this type of information was reported to the investee's VCI. This pattern was most marked in the case of capital investment analysis. Indeed, particularly with regard to longer-run decisions on strategy and investment, the VCI's involvement was linked with the new development of accounting information.

Two information types for decision-making were investigated: output costing and capital investment. Of four output costing procedures considered, it was found that full costing (including a non-production element), which has enjoyed increasing advocacy, particularly for decision-making in recent years, was in predominant use (two-thirds of the firms).[9] The results on capital investment techniques are displayed in Table 13.6.

They broadly mirror the pattern of usage found in more general surveys of practice in larger firms (e.g. Pike 1982). Payback (in all users) and qualitative assessments (in eight of the nine users) are both widely used and generally influential in investment decisions. Accounting rate of return is used by half of

Table 13.5 Decision-making information in investee firms

Decision type	*Information used internally*	*Information reported to VCI*	*Information developed only since VCI involvement*
Operating decisions	11	5	1
Strategic decisions	12	5	5
Capital investment	9	8	4

Table 13.6 Importance of capital investment techniques

	Number of firms	*Importance of technique within firms*		
		Low	*Medium*	*High*
Payback	9	2	2	5
Internal rate of return	5	—	1	4
Net present value	4	1	1	2
Accounting rate of return	6	1	3	2
Qualitative assessment	8	1	—	7
No response	1	—	—	—

9 Kaplan and Shank (1990), Shank and Govindarajan (1989).

the investees, but is typically not regarded as highly important, while both of the main discounting techniques (IRR, NPV) are used in less than half of the subjects. The four net present value users also used the internal rate of return. When use of the IRR is favoured (typically, as computed with Lotus 123 software at the time of the study), it is regarded as important. It is worth noting here that the contrast between the VCI's typical predilection for IRRs and the fact that for many projects, especially those involving an outflow followed by fairly uniform annual inflows, the inverse of the payback approximates to the IRR. In this sense, the two approaches provide the same decision signals. More generally, requests by VCIs for NPV information on capital projects that have been envisaged by, or committed to, by either potential or invested-in firms, may represent an example of one of the ways in which the VCI 'tests' for management awareness. This relates both to the DCF technique as a guide to management decision-making, but also to its indicating that management has given thought to alternative expenditures. Reciprocally, VCIs may wish to use capital expenditure appraisal as a useful lesson, or issue, through which to demonstrate a concern for how firms select projects.

13.5 OVERVIEW OF FINDINGS

Tables 13.7 and 13.8 contain summaries of our results, highlighting the key aspects of VCIs' involvements in developing AISs. Table 13.7 considers six VCI policies. The ticks indicate by their presence an interest by the VCI (as evidenced by the adherence to the stated policies/requirements) in the capabilities their investees have in supplying accounting information. They also indicate considerable variation across cases in the policies underlying the VCIs' demand for accounting information. Half of the VCIs exhibited a relatively comprehensive approach to accessing information by pursuing five of the six policies investigated in this chapter. By investor types, these were independent investment management companies or (one case) a subsidiary thereof. By contrast, a distinct third of the VCIs appeared to adopt a more laissez-faire attitude, and only pursued three or less of the six policies. All the investors in this group were subsidiaries of banks. Thus the institutions which specialized most in investment management appeared to set more comprehensive information requirements for investees.

The representative investees considered in Table 13.8 also exhibit considerable variation in the nature of AIS developments after their VCIs' involvement in terms of performance measurement, after control and decision-making. While the overall extent of change was just over 25 per cent of the cells in this table, only two cases (B, Q1) experienced no change, most experienced some change (over several AIS features), and one (F) experienced extensive change.

Of those companies enjoying relatively great AIS development, as indicated by Table 13.8 – namely, investees F, H and M – the following comments may be made. Company F had received the attention of a company turnaround specialist

Table 13.7 VCI policies on information

VCI policies	*Cases*												
	B	*D*	*E*	*F*	*H*	*J*	*K*	*L*	*M*	*N*	*P*	*Q*	*Total*
Reporting requirements extend beyond financial statements	—	✓	✓	—	—	—	✓	—	✓	✓	✓	—	6
Access to investee AIS required	✓	✓	—	—	—	✓	✓	✓	✓	✓	—	—	7
No variation allowed in information provided	✓	—	—	✓	✓	✓	—	✓	—	—	—	—	5
AIS vetted	✓	✓	✓	✓	—	✓	✓	✓	✓	—	✓	✓	10
Influence exerted on investee audit	✓	✓	✓	✓	✓	✓	✓	✓	✓	—	—	—	9
No cost deterrent in obtaining information	✓	✓	✓	✓	—	✓	✓	✓	✓	✓	—	—	9
Total number of policies	5	5	4	4	2	5	5	5	5	3	2	1	46

Table 13.8 AIS developments subsequent to VCI involvement

AIS developments subsequent to VCI involvement	*Cases*												
	B	*D*	*E*	*F*	*H*	*J*	*K*	*L*	*M*	*N*	*P*	*Q*	*Total*
Performance measurement													
Profit and loss account components	—	—	✓	✓	—	—	—	—	—	—	—	—	2
Financial ratios	—	✓	—	—	—	—	—	—	—	—	✓	—	2
Cash flow	—	—	✓	✓	✓	—	—	—	—	—	✓	—	4
Control													
Use of monitoring reports	—	✓	—	✓	—	—	—	—	✓	—	—	—	3
Setting finance budgets	—	—	—	—	—	—	—	—	—	—	—	—	0
Increasing budget components	—	—	—	✓	—	✓	—	✓	✓	—	—	—	4
Increasing frequency of budget interval for some aspect of the budget	—	—	✓	✓	✓	✓	—	✓	✓	—	—	—	6
Decision-making													
Operating decision information	—	—	—	✓	—	—	—	—	—	—	—	—	1
Strategic decision information	—	—	—	✓	✓	✓	—	✓	—	✓	—	—	5
Capital investment information	—	✓	—	✓	✓	—	✓	—	✓	—	—	—	5
Total number of changes	0	3	3	8	4	3	1	3	4	1	2	0	32

Note: In the cases of multiple investees (J, N, P, Q) the investees chosen are J1, N2, P1 and Q1 respectively.

nominated by the investor. The firm was a manufacturer of combustion equipment and refractors, described as having 'world-beating' products which were patent protected. The firm had its roots in an MBO, when personnel recognized that the engineering ideas were good, but the firm was populated by "people with no commercial knowledge". The VCI insisted on increased reporting frequency (especially to monthly), and instituted many new reporting activities (on budgets, capital investment, costs) after involvement. The investor drew on deep financial expertise and controlled a wholly commercial fund which was ultimately owned by five local authorities. The investor conceived its role as that of 'company developer' and became very involved in investees, especially in the first three months.

Investee H had also been created by MBO, and produced specialist papers and board. It was required to produce a cash flow financial performance indicator after VCI involvement and also financial information for strategic decisions. Budget setting was at more frequent intervals, after VCI involvement, for cash flow, head count and promotional advertising. Further, after VCI involvement, capital investment appraisal had four new elements: the use of internal rate of return; net present value; accounting rate of return; and sensitivity analysis. The general picture was of a major overhaul of the types and frequencies of information provision to the VCI. The investor was a subsidiary of a bank with a development capital specialization, which managed about £175m., of which £86m. was available for investment at a required IRR in the range of 30–39 per cent. The investor could draw on very high levels of financial expertise, but was not a specialist in the investee's technology. The VCI insisted on playing a role in auditor selection and also sat on the audit committee.

Investee M had been in business for ten years, and supplied environmental services on a one-stop basis, combining survey, scientific analysis and investigation services along with remedial, reinstalment and maintenance work, where necessary. The investee's typical activity was in problem areas like effluent and pollution control, water quality, soil contamination and asbestos removal. Performance assessment was largely unaffected by VCI involvement, save in the introduction of 'receivable days' (a debtor/creditor performance measure). As regards managerial actions, several new requirements were imposed after VCI involvement: information for business monitoring; appraisals of capital investment; production of financial information for strategic decisions; and use of a financial software model for six-monthly projections. The flow of information to the VCI was perceived to be 'extensive' (i.e. full and detailed). The investor specialized in growth markets in the environmental, healthcare and information technology areas. Their sponsors were: a leading UK merchant bank and stockholder; the oldest investment bank in the USA; and the UK's leading investment capital company. They had the right to appoint auditors, and had done so in cases which were described as 'terminal'.

The relatively high levels of initial investor involvement, and consequent modification of the investee's AIS, for cases F, H and M, can be contrasted with the lower involvement and lesser change in cases K, N and P. In case K, the investee was a manufacturer of printed circuit boards and the company had been created by MBO seven years earlier. There was limited modification required by the investor to what was already fairly extensive and frequent information provision. For financial performance, the VCI required new information on the return on investment, net profitability and compliance with bank covenants. The new managerial actions required by the VCI were: the appraisal of capital investment; the production of financial information for strategic decisions; and detailed sales analysis. While the investor was unwilling to directly influence audit, it is clear that VCI involvement was considerable, and of an extent which is somewhat understated by the categories adopted in Table 13.8.

While all budget intervals were unchanged after VCI involvement for the investee of case N (a specialist in oilfield operations, service and repair), changes were required elsewhere. Specifically, these changes applied to measuring firm performance (return on investment and cash flow), and managerial actions (finance for strategic decisions and headcount). The investor, a subsidiary of a bank, did not directly influence audit, but did see audit letters.

Finally, case N displayed rather low levels of change in type and frequency of information provision after VCI involvement. The investee was a new retail motor business and the investor was a bank. Before VCI involvement, the investee already had complex and high-frequency information, as is common in this line of business. The VCI did not require modifications to attributable costs or capital investment procedures, and only slight change in the form of budgets. While the investor would not influence audit, it specifically would "make suggestions as to which type of performance segmentation might be relevant" and would use auditor feedback "to highlight system weakness".[10]

These references to case notes help to 'flesh out' the story being told by Table 13.8. The incidence of AIS modification appears tightly aligned to requirements for an enhanced relationship between investor and investee. Table 13.8 tends to understate a richer qualitative picture of AIS modification post-investment, in which there is considerable 'fine-tuning' in the light of specific investor–investee features.

10 While levels of audit involvement vary, it appears that all of the firms exhibiting the highest levels of MAS change were among the group where the VCI had exerted influence on the audit process. This highlighted the VCI's strong interest in the audit and, given the potential legal liability of auditor to shareholder, could have stimulated auditor proactivity and so enhanced their role as agents of change.

13.6 CONCLUSION

In terms of VCI monitoring behaviour and investee AIS change (post-VCI involvement), the study does provide considerable support for the five propositions developed in section 13.2 on theory and method. In addition to providing this validation, a basis for identifying a number of opportunities for extending the research has been established, and some implications for practitioners can be derived.

The results of this chapter indicate that VCIs view the capabilities of their potential investees' AIS as endogenous to their own decisions as to whether or not to back the firms. This view may, in part, reflect their desire to see the management of investee firms supplied with appropriate information for operational purposes, but it is also a function of their own needs for regular information flows for monitoring purposes. The VCIs' power to influence the investees' internal accounting systems has its basis both in their ownership stake, and in the conditions negotiated (and incorporated into) the initial subscription agreement. Thus VCIs can exert this power to influence significantly both the content and the frequency of accounting reports. Their specific information demands do tend to be both conventional and similar, and are typically based on a monthly package of traditional financial statements. However, particularly where problems exist, more information may be demanded on an even more regular basis.[11]

In many cases, the AISs of investees do change when VCIs become involved, not only with respect to performance measurement, but also with respect to control and decision-making functions. In this process, the role of the VCI is important, especially as his involvement occurs in the relatively early stage of AIS development, at which point the potential exists for him to have a strong formative impact. Thus the sources and forms of VCI influence contrast noticeably with the variables identified by contingency theorists as being important in their explanations of management accounting practices. The latter emphasize the demands of firm and/or industry specific effects (e.g. market environment, organizational structure and technology), while VCIs emphasize demands based on in-house standards which are applied to all investees, irrespective of their particular operational circumstances.

While investees are free to adopt their own approaches to internal accounting, the burdens and costs of more than one system might well be impractical for

11 When problems occur with investees, the normal procedure is to put them into so-called intensive care. This entails a much greater degree of VCI involvement in the day-to-day operations of the business. The AIS must be sensitive enough to provide early warning of such problems, yet robust enough to allow for an expansion of the role of information beyond simple monitoring. It should extend to control of the sort emphasized by Jones (1992: 163), as well as *indicating* (by area of responsibility) and *prescribing* (by diagnosis of fault, error or malfunction).

MSFs. This encourages the VCI-driven system to dominate, and thus it tends to determine the path of future development for the MSF. This adaptation of procedures indicates the movement to an improved match between important components of the accounting control system and the changing organizational context, here relating to various forms of venture capital intervention, and, in the case of Jones (1992), relating specifically to the MBO.

The chapter also adds weight to the argument for attaching importance to accounting information in managing the investment contract between investor and investee. Moreover, the AIS adopted must be capable of handling periods of difficult, or off-target, trading conditions. The strengths of the AIS become most relevant when there is a requirement for unforeseen additional funds or 'refinancing'. Such an event would probably imply some degree of contract renegotiation, involving issues such as: the realignment of equity stakes; and the further refinement of the information interchange represented by the AIS.

Turning now to practitioners, our research findings highlight for them the operational significance to VCIs of collecting and interpreting information supplied or controlled by investee firms. The ease of access, the making sense of, and the imputed reliability of such information will be directly influenced by the appropriateness and efficiency of the AIS/MCS. This set of factors is important to practitioners in terms of the investment selection decision, as it attenuates adverse selection, and in terms of investment monitoring, as it helps to ameliorate the consequences of moral hazard. Thus there is an incentive for the investor to become involved in designing and developing such systems. To illustrate, the VCI can derive benefit beyond the enhancement of quality and frequency of information by seeking to enhance its reputation among potential investee firms and financial intermediaries, thereby improving its deal flow. Similarly, it can use its commitment to improving this aspect of investee firms' operations as an additional way of justifying fees and carried interest. To further illustrate, an effective AIS can aid the VCI in deriving a clearer picture of alternative routes and possible timings for the exit arrangement. Thus early indications of features such as the 'burn rate' of cash, and the requirement for additional funding, are vital to effective investment management. In sum, it is hoped that the above chapter is of interest to those concerned with investment management from either the academic or the practical standpoint.

14

SEEKING OPTIMALITY THROUGH THE EXCHANGING OF RISK AND INFORMATION

14.1 INTRODUCTION

A systematic approach has been adopted to examining investor–investee relations in the venture capital world. In the framework established, the venture capital investor (VCI) is the prime mover in contract formulation. However, the deal which is ultimately agreed with the mature small firm (MSF) is mutually voluntary. It is driven by the quest for serving their self-interest on the part of both VCI and MSF. As a consequence, the negotiating and concluding of a contract to give and receive equity capital in return for committing to certain obligations and providing certain services is by itself the seeking of optimality in exchange between VCI and MSF.

In considering what each party brings to this exchange relationship, the conclusion proffered has been that risk management and information-handling have been the predominant categories, with the VCI being more specialized in the former activity and the MSF in the latter. Exactly how these forces impinge upon one another has not been considered in a combined fashion, except in the 'within site' case study expositions of Part 3. The purpose of this concluding chapter is to examine, by 'cross-site' analysis across dyads of investors and investees, what trades are effected between these parties, and the extent to which they reflect optimality-seeking behaviour.

In pursuing this goal, the analysis considers first the trading of risk and information from the perspective of both the investor and investee. In doing so for the investor, it examines: the extent of risk and information-sharing with investees; the exchanging of information for risk-bearing; the effect of risk-sharing on effort; the effect of size of equity stake on effort; discriminating between investees on efficiency grounds; and the designing of contractual relations with the investee to achieve efficiency. The format for examining the trading of risk and information from the perspective of the investee is somewhat different for the investee compared to the investor. Much of the latter evidence is qualitative, whereas the former evidence is a mix of the qualitative and quantitative.[1]

1 Being based as it is on the evidence from the AQ as an instrument, rather than the SSI.

In considering the trading of risk and information from the perspective of the investee, the following will be examined: the comparative advantage in risk-handling between investor and investee; the flow of information from investee to investor; the extent of rights to confidentiality that the investee possesses; the advantages in running the MSF were the investee to become better informed about the operations of the investor; the attributes the investee brings to the relationship with the investor; the attributes which the investor brings to the relationship with the investee; the highest and lowest proportion of equity held; the use of performance-linked equity; the competition among investees for the investor's attention; the extent to which contracting is based on trust, rather than on contractual clauses; the scope for moving towards contract optimality; and the ideal form of the relationship with the investee.

In developing the argument of this chapter, the VCI and MSF will generally be considered together under a sequence of headings, rather than treating the investor and the investee separately, as the goal is to see how they interact. These headings, which form the basis for the ensuing sections, are: the sharing of risk; the sharing of information; exchanging information for risk-bearing; incentives and effort; and the pursuit of contract optimality. The approach adopted entails a largely cross-site qualitative analysis, with this being heavily supported, for the purposes of illustration, example, and indeed empirical support, by direct reference to the views of investors and investees.[2]

14.2 THE SHARING OF RISK

The starting point of this area of enquiry was to ask investors whether they thought they were better able to handle risk than their investees (SSI 3.1.0). Of particular interest here was whether the VCI's risk-handling went beyond the more mechanical advantages deriving from diversification, to wider skills of risk management, conceived of as a cultivated ability. The great majority of investors (18/20 = 90 per cent) considered they had superior capabilities, compared to their investees, in risk management. Only two investors (G and R) thought investees had superior capabilities but, as it turns out, in rather a narrow sense. The

2 The views expressed, or answers given, were usually in response to questions which are contained in the instruments in the appendices to this book. These are noted in the text in brackets; e.g. (AQ 3.6) means question 3.6 of the administered questionnaire in Appendix B. These views have sometimes been expressed in the form of 'yes' or 'no' answers. However, more commonly, a judgement or view was expressed. These utterances were transliterated, with minimal editing, in the form of the quotes which are appealed to extensively in this chapter. They are often couched in demotic terms. Wherever such direct speech is reported, double quotation marks are used, and the quote is followed by a letter denoting the case to which it applies. For each such quote, it is indicated whether the investor or investee was speaking.

investor in Case G emphasized the importance of returns, saying: "We have one objective in mind – to maximize our return from the portfolio. He wants to maximize the return from his business" (G). Though this investor was inclined to overlook the point, this maximization of portfolio return itself assumes advanced risk management skills.[3] But beyond that, more complex, qualitative judgements concerning risk management come into play. Thus this VCI could say, "We're very good at assessing risk for them; but so are our investee companies at assessing risk for their type of business" (G). This appraisal is borne out by the corresponding investee in the dyad for Case G, who said, "We know more than he does about risk analysis, unless, for example, we wanted to borrow some money" (G). What is emerging here is an acceptance by VCI and MSF alike, that skill in risk management can be specialized according to a specific risk class, with, for example, the VCI having a comparative advantage in the handling of financial risk, and the MSF having a comparative advantage in the handling of business risk. This is echoed in the comment of the VCI in Case C. Here, another investor was reluctant to claim complete comparative advantage over investees in risk management skill, saying they were: "No better, no worse. They and we have risks re our respective businesses. They know more about *their* risks, and we about *ours*" (C).[4]

For the majority of VCIs who thought they were the better at handling risk than MSFs, portfolio diversification was usually mentioned, but by no means to the exclusion of other risk-bearing considerations. On the former point, the comments which VCIs made about their skills are well illustrated by: "Due to diversification" (A); "We're able to handle risk by diversification" (B); "We are in the risk business" (E); "We have a risk-handling experience advantage – it's like falling off a log" (I); "The investee's got all his eggs in one basket . . . risk pooling is a function of what we do" (K); "We can diversify our portfolio more easily than a firm can diversify its products" (S). It was common to qualify this view, on the advantages of VCIs, in the narrow sense of diversification, with remarks about comparative advantages in specific risk categories, and also about the role of both experience and training in cultivating the skills of risk management. To illustrate, the VCI in Case E said, "It's what we are set up to do. There's an on-the-job learning curve" (E); and, in Case F, the VCI said skills came "through involvement with the company. We look at our resource capabilities and ask whether we can use them in other sectors. Half of the companies have to do an

3 In the sense that it can be viewed in terms of solving a type of mathematical programme in which the standard deviation (risk) of the portfolio rate of return is minimized subject to a required rate of return (see Vickers 1987: 138).

4 A related approach to that adopted in this paragraph, where different risk classes are distinguished, is contained in the work of Fiet (1995) who regards entrepreneurs as protecting business angels from market risk, and business angels as specializing in handling the agency risk.

internal review – the ones that are riskier or not doing so well. We review that as a team. We put quite a lot of effort into some, to alter the profile of the company" (F).

When investees, rather than investors, were asked about which partner in the VCI/MSF relationship was better equipped to handle risk (AQ 3.1), their responses did not exactly mirror those given by investors. This was largely because investees, arguably being more typically risk exposed compared to investors, and almost certainly having fewer diversification options, simply had to deal 'head on' with the vagaries which risk created for their MSFs. Thus an appreciable minority of investees thought they could handle risk better than investors (10/22 = 45 per cent), though some favoured the investor (5/22 = 23 per cent), and some had no clear view (6/22 = 27 per cent). Three investees who emphasized their own risk-handling capabilities did not so much emphasize risk management as what might be called 'living with risk'. The latter attitude is exemplified by diverse comments from investees explaining why they could live with risk: "We've been in manufacturing situations – have seen what can go wrong" (A); "Me, because I have the knowledge of the business, industry, market, product and competitors" (H); "We do it all the time" (P2); "We have more knowledge of what's going on out there" (R). This was not necessarily thought to be inconsistent with the VCIs being superior risk analysts. Thus in one of the further remarks made by the investee in Case P, it was admitted that: "He's probably better at analysing it [that is, risk]" (P1). The generalizations suggested by the evidence are, first, that investors were confident of their risk management skills, which were deployed both to achieve risk-spreading by diversification and to exercise broader judgements about risk incidence for qualitative assessment. Secondly, investees had confidence in their abilities to function in the face of risk, even if it should prove to be undiversifiable.

14.3 THE SHARING OF INFORMATION

I turn now to the extent to which information is shared between investor and investee. Given that contractual efficiency is generally facilitated by information-sharing, there is a presumption that openness and transparency in contracting is desirable. However, there are counter-forces at work which prevent the complete sharing of information, even if both parties are aware of its potential desirability. For example, one party may be trying to protect its intellectual property. This could be wrapped up in detailed descriptions of new products which have not yet been patented. Yet another may be protecting the rights of employees to confidentiality because of personnel considerations like equality, equity, affirmative action, or social inclusion.

When investors were asked (SSI 3.2.1) whether they regarded all information as being open to investees, or whether they kept some information confidential, opinions were very mixed, though it was clear overall that confidentiality was rarely entirely absent, often tangible, and sometimes intense and extensive. A narrow majority (13/20 = 65 per cent) of investors at least espoused an open system, but, of them, seven admitted to the existence of some pockets of confidentiality. Few had completely open systems, though some talked as though they did have, saying: "It's all pretty open" (H); "We attempt to be transparent" (I); "I'm very open and tell everybody everything" (L); "This has never been a problem" (R). Typically, however, this apparent information openness was qualified. A good example is provided by the investor in Case M who said: "Ninety per cent of information is open, but it may be selective. We share views on the internal management team with the chief executive – if he can take it, and it will do some good. We hold back to keep deals together" (M). The later part of this quote illustrates the sort of qualification on openness that was common. Clearly, restrictions on openness can be quite severe in sensitive circumstances. A representative set of qualifying remarks on the notion of openness would include the following: "They can access our accounts, but our own plans for future developments are confidential" (A); "Normally, all valuations are open to investees, and are published on an annual basis. The situation could arise in which I need to keep some information confidential . . . this might occur when some of my investees are actual rivals" (B); "I don't think there's much we would hold back on, except at a time of wishing to manoeuvre at exit" (J); "Investees would like to know how they perform versus the rest of the portfolio – but we can't share confidential information about other firms" (O); "We don't pass along confidential, cooperative information; though we would share industry information, and also anecdotal information; for example about how Hong Kong is difficult just now" (P),[5] "Yes, we have confidential information we won't pass along – about relative performance, and potential customers, and pricing" (Q). In sum, the VCI as principal always seemed to retain a measure of control over information. This could be extensive. Indeed, it would usually be complete, or absolute, were it 'deal sensitive'.

The investees too were asked about the openness of information (AQ 3.2). Of the sixteen responses received, to a question about the flow of information to investors, most investees (11/16 = 69 per cent) said that they thought the best characterization of the flow of information was that it was extensive, in the sense of being full and detailed. Amplifying comments included: "We didn't want to hold anything back" (H); "We are obligated to give minutes of our monthly board meetings, and monthly financial figures" (K); "They are given our monthly figures and our views on the marketplace. They are told whether our cash is coming in or not" (Q). Other investees (4/16 = 25 per cent) thought the information supplied to investors was 'measured' in the sense of being related to requests, and only one investee thought it was 'limited', in the sense of being

5 This remark by the VCI in Case P predated the changeover in Hong Kong in 1997.

severely edited. For this investee (Case G), it was said that "he gets the same as us – adequate for their needs". In fact, few investees thought that they provided either too much or too little information to their investors (AQ 3.2.1). The general view (13/16 = 81 per cent) was that the supply of information was now appropriate, indeed perhaps even at a proper or equilibrium level. Comments suggesting this included: "We don't see a need to alter our pack . . . experience suggests the right amount of information is being given" (A); "We produce a lot already – it's very detailed – any more wouldn't be read" (F); "What we've done was about right. We've kept them well-informed on the state of the business" (H); "We've cut down from monthly to quarterly accounts statements. It's reasonable what he gets now. We've reached a kind of equilibrium. I think what we thought we should give him was too much at the start" (L); "I think we've got it about right" (M); "They're our partner, so we want to share as much information as they need to make the correct business decisions. We think we've got the balance right" (P); "The balance we have is right. I wouldn't want to give them any more" (R). To summarize, investees certainly provided extensive information to investors, but they were satisfied that, after some adjustment, this was an appropriate level of provision.

In terms of retaining a right to confidentiality (AQ 3.3) over certain aspects of the running of their businesses (e.g. patent rights, personnel records), most (10/15 = 67 per cent) investees felt they did have certain rights. These largely involved matters relating to manpower, like disciplinary procedures, internal managerial problems, and personnel problems. There was a tendency too, to be sensitive about technological issues. The investee in Case F referred to caution about information provision concerning a patent for energy conservation which he referred to as "a world beating product" (F). In a similar vein, the investee in Case J said he would retain confidentiality over "a technology before we file for patents" (J), adding that "we're trying more and more to protect the identity of customers and the products they're interested in" (J). Even when the general level of information provision was high, some investees retained areas of confidentiality, often with the consent of investors. To illustrate, in Case P1 the investee said, "Because our investor invests in us and one of our main competitors, we have the right to retain confidentiality where it's in conflict with the good of our business"(P1).[6] A common view was that certain types of provision of confidential information would not be relevant to the VCI anyway. Thus remarks were made like: "Yes, I retain confidentiality, not to keep it secret, but because it's not relevant to them. They're entitled to know about anything relating to the well-being of the company" (Q); "There would be situations in which we would say 'That's not of interest to you' [the VCI], and we would have to say no" (R). It

6 This remark was also made from the perspective of a VCI when reference was made above to Case B.

seems, therefore, that investees and investors alike tend to retain rights of confidentiality over information, and that it can be quite extensive. These restrictions are often not dictated by narrow commercial concerns: for example, they are often related to the internal relations between personnel. However, commercial sensitivity is by no means absent from wide classes of information, which creates taboo areas of high confidentiality, especially where valuable intellectual property is concerned.

VCIs generally seemed to require extensive information about MSFs, and this was usually willingly given. By contrast, investees did not tend to think they would gain a great deal, in terms of running their own MSF, from being better informed about the operations of their investors (AQ 3.4). A majority (11/16 = 69 per cent) thought there was little to be gained from such explorations. The investee made comments like: "We're informed as much as we'd wish to be" (K); "It would be just nosiness" (Q); "I'm not sure it would make any difference at all" (R). All of this strongly supports the appropriateness of regarding the investor as the principal and the investee as the agent. As regards information, one might expect the investee to be much more demanding about the affairs of the investor, if she were more of a principal, or even if there were reciprocal principal–agent features.[7] In fact, the latter features were generally absent. The VCI tended to call the shots in information provision, and the MSF tended to go along with these demands (see Chapter 12), and indeed seemed to regard them as fitting to the VCI/MSF relationship.

I conclude this section on the sharing of information by looking at the investors' attitudes to a full and free exchange of information. They were asked if this was practical and desirable, or whether they would stop short of this (SSI 3.2.3). They were probed about potential advantages arising from such extensive information, and asked to comment on possible limits to going so far. In view of the apparently expressed desire by VCIs to retain confidentiality over at least some classes of information (SSI 3.2.2), it was surprising how frequently a commitment to 'full and free' exchange of information was expressed. Some VCIs displayed a strong desire for full and free information, saying: "There is no reason not to have a good two-way flow" (A); "Full and complete information is essential rather than desirable – the relationship is one of trust and openness – rather like a marriage" (B); "We expect a full and frank exchange of 'need to know' information" (E); "There is full and free exchange of information" (H); "Yes – anything less means trust is lacking" (N); "Yes, and we achieve this to a large extent" (Q); "We do business on the basis of full and frank exchange of information" (S); "Yes, we should be free" (T). Although this view was held by a

7 There were occasional, but not frequent, hints of reciprocal principal–agent relations. For example, the investee for the MSF of Case N said: "The investor makes too much of getting a deal done. Not enough is said about the downside and options. We have more knowledge of them and we could approach the investor for extra finance more competently."

majority (11/20 = 55 per cent) of VCIs, many of them qualified their opinions. For example, in Case E, the investor referred only to 'need to know' information. Typical of these caveats which were stated to the need for 'full and free' information were: "We stop short . . . There's room to ask for more if you need to" (D); "Over all matters, it's impossible" (G); "Not practical because of cost, time, irritation, lack of ability to process" (I); "It takes too much of our time to talk about it" (K); "It's not practical for everything – there isn't enough time" (L); "Within reason – he holds back more than we do" (M); "Too much cost in monitoring everything. We want edited information" (P).

To summarize this section, the main conclusions drawn were as follows:

1 Both the VCI and the MSF retained areas of confidentiality in reporting, but usually they were isolated from 'deal-sensitive' areas, unless there was a conflict of interest (e.g. over rivals).
2 There was much freedom in the provision of information by both the VCI and the MSF, but the great bulk of the information flow was from the MSF to the VCI, emphasizing the role of the MSF, as agent, to the VCI, as principal.
3 After some time, the pattern of information provision settled down to a kind of equilibrium, which was to the satisfaction of both the VCI and the MSF.
4 The full and free exchange of information was uncommon and generally impractical, for reasons which were both operational (e.g. too costly) and confidential (e.g. disturbing to staff relations) in character.

14.4 EXCHANGING INFORMATION FOR RISK-BEARING

The extent of information provision having been fully explored, including its relationship to ideal information provision, attention now turns to the scope for trading risk and information. Investors, as principals in the VCI/MSF relationship, are particularly examined, as it is they who are likely to be the initiators of contractual propositions about exchange relationships. In examining investors there are two matters of especial interest: the willingness of the VCI to bear more risk if the MSF provides more information; and the extent to which this provides a sort of risk/information menu or trade-off. The corresponding concern, in looking at investee behaviour, will be somewhat different. It emphasizes those special features or attributes that each party to the VCI/MSF relationship brings (e.g. effort, finance, commitment) to the contract, and their relative importance for efficiency in a contractual sense.

Starting first with investors, they were asked whether their willingness to bear greater risks for investees, other things being equal, depended upon better information being supplied about their MSFs (SSI 3.3.1). Of particular interest was the form that better information might take. For example, was it more speedily returned, produced in a form which was more easily assimilated, or was it especially revealing about insider knowledge or trade secrets? The majority of VCIs (14/20 = 70 per cent) were indeed willing to increase their risk-bearing if they received a superior information flow concerning the MSF's operations, either in volume or quality. Dissenting voices of investors largely arose from their emphasizing their leading positions as principals in the VCI/MSF relationship, and therefore concluding, perhaps erroneously or overconfidently, that they could fully control both risk and information on both sides of the contract. Representative of this view held by a significant minority (6/20 = 30 per cent) of investors was the remark made by the investor in Case A, who said: "No, we have a minimum level of information we must get, and wouldn't invest if we didn't get it. The extent of our stake is not dependent on information" (A).

However, the predominant view was that more information helped the investors in risk management. There were two forms this view took: in the first, it was that there was a simple inverse relationship at work – more information, less risk; the second, was that more information clarified the framework for risk assessment, making it more precise or better targeted. Representative of the former view were comments like: "The more information we have, the lower we perceive our risk to be, so the more likely we are to invest" (D); "We definitely *are* willing. If he is not willing to provide us with better information it's a turn-off" (F); "Yes, we are. It influences our judgement if it can be more easily assimilated. Assimilation of information about what is going on in business is our real problem" (H); "Definitely more. If I think information is being withheld, I get very negative about the business. I don't mind so much about the form it takes – they know what's needed" (L); "Yes, we'd take a higher equity stake in future rounds if we got high-quality information . . . there is a learning effect and we do get more confidence in them" (S). From these quotes, among others, one concludes that improved information flows enhance the investor's confidence in the MSF's operations, increasing trust and commitment and leading to tangible signs of willingness to bear greater risk, like, for example, investing more heavily in the MSF, and increasing the equity stake in future financing rounds.[8]

Representative of the latter view, that risk assessment on the part of the VCI is improved by better information about the MSF, are the following comments by investors: "More information won't encourage us to take more risk, but it does let us assess risk more closely. More information on a production process doesn't reduce risk, it just clarifies it. The entry price is influenced by risk" (C); "It would

8 In the work of Sapienza and Korsgaard (1996), timely feedback of information from investee to investor is shown to promote positive relations between them. As they would put it, effort of this sort establishes a protocol with the property of 'procedural justice', which makes the investor more likely to feel committed to the entrepreneur and more tolerant of bad states of the world.

be like any other investment appraisal . . . We would be prepared to increase our exposure if there were an opportunity offered by the company" (G); "It's not so much information that I judge it on as opportunity. If it increases – new business, new or bigger dimensions – we'll invest more. But it has to be really solid, good news" (M); "Information itself is not a guide . . . it aids our assessment, but doesn't determine it" (R). To summarize the position of investors, it seems that better information does improve their ability to engage in accurate risk assessment, and that this may, but will not inevitably, lead to a willingness to take up a more risky position in the MSF. Even if the latter does not occur, contractual efficiency may be enhanced in terms of better monitoring of the MSF, and more considered appraisal of actions like funding rounds and exit routes.

To amplify the discussion about exchanging information for risk-bearing, investors were asked if there was a sense in which they confronted a kind of 'menu' or trade-off between risk-bearing and their investees' provision of information (SSI 3.3.2). They were probed, if they admitted to such a menu, on whether one point on it was mutually perceived to be the most efficient. The respondents found this quite a difficult question to answer, and some of the responses were oblique, or even obtuse or evasive. A minority of those who expressed a clear view (6/15 = 40 per cent) were persuaded by the menu analogy. Some quite bluntly rejected it, saying: "No, I don't think the minds of either party work that way" (G); "No, it's not as easy as that. It's a very subjective business" (I); "No, I can't conceive of this happening" (P).

However, many other comments seemed to allow for a less structured form of trade-off relationship. While not being expressible so conventionally as a one-to-one, negatively sloped locus between an information variable and a risk variable, it nevertheless assigned an assessment of lower risk to fuller information provision by the MSF.[9] Comments made on this level included rather direct views on the possibility of a trade-off, like: "Yes, there must be, between our risk-bearing and the quality and honesty of the information provided by the investee" (J); "We are prepared to take greater risk where we are better informed. You can manage risk much better if you are aware of it, than if you are not" (F). More sophisticated comments on forms of trade-off between risk and information included: "Yes, we would put more money in [if information were better]. We would go further if the information was 'what you see is what you get', rather than if the situation was fuzzy" (K). A quite refined approach was also adopted by some investors, of which the following is a good example: "I expect them to tell me all the things they regard as being of major importance to the business and, provided they do tell me, if the business needs more funds I would be more likely to invest.

9 And an assessment of higher risk to sparser information provision by the MSF. Although this does not define a simple mathematical relationship, its systematic pairing of sets of situations can certainly be regarded as having a coherent mathematical form.

Willingness to provide information is more important than the form it takes. A lot of my investments are science oriented – accounts are not their thing" (L).[10]

Although the investors were typically resistant to, or even resentful about, being treated as theorists of their own trade, the explanations they provided had a coherence which did cast some useful light on analytical issues. While the notion of a trade-off locus between risk and information was rejected, in a simple sense, for not being obviously descriptive of investor practice, it was clear from responses in the interviews that something of this sort was not uncommonly behind certain real patterns of investment behaviour.

More generally, this section on the exchanging of information for risk-bearing has enlarged the analysis of information demands in Chapter 12, and provides a bridge to the treatment of risk management in Chapter 11. The demand for information and the willingness to bear risk are clearly related, on the evidence considered. The main senses in which that seems true are as follows:

1 Greater information flow from MSF to VCI helped the investor's risk management capability.
2 Greater information flow from MSF to VCI also enhanced trust and commitment, and increased the willingness of the VCI to hold, or enlarge, the equity stake in the MSF.
3 While there was little evidence supporting a strict risk/information trade-off, investors were able to associate higher- and lower-risk classes of investment, respectively, with lesser and greater richness in information provision by investees.

14.5 INCENTIVES AND EFFORT

The main concern of this chapter so far has been with the structural features of information and risk, and how they affect the process of decision-making (e.g. the direction and level of investment). However, as the theoretical framework of Chapter 4 emphasized, in situations involving both unseen actions being taken by investees (MSFs) and states of the world that are uncertain and thus mask investee effort levels, the incentives and risk distribution (e.g. via equity share) created by the principal (VCI) and agreed with the agent (MSF) have an important bearing on the efficacy of contracting.

To examine this further, investors were first asked the following about risk and effort: whether risk or uncertainty per se affected the effort of investees

10 This assessment echoes that noted by Sapienza (1992), who emphasized, especially in high-technology contexts, the value of open communications and the minimization of conflict. Frequency of communication was also found to be important.

(SSI 3.4.1); whether a risk-sharing arrangement reduced the investee's effort (i.e. adverse selection) (SSI 3.4.2); and whether there was a best level of risk the investee should bear (SSI 3.4.3). They were then asked about their equity stake in the MSF, in terms of: how its extent was determined (SSI 3.5.1); whether equity participation was flexible (SSI 3.5.2); and whether equity involvement was incentive-based (SSI 3.5.3). This section goes beyond the mere structure of risk and information to questions of effort and outcomes, thus preparing the ground for ultimate consideration of contract optimality.

The starting point of this part of the enquiry looked at the bearing of risk and uncertainty on investees' efforts, with a particular emphasis on whether investees used chance outcomes systematically to mask their effort levels, thus producing biases in favourable directions. There was almost unanimous agreement (19/20 = 95 per cent) that this did occur, and even the sole VCI dissenting from this view (Case A) indicated by his words that he was defending MSFs against this generic classification, saying: "Managers aren't poor in a recession and good in a boom. Results are a function of market conditions as well as management" (A). This reply did not simply 'turn around' the logical content of the question, which suggests the answer is itself constructed, from a new perspective, as a kind of defence. Other investors made comments which ranged from the blunt to the complex and sophisticated, but all amounted to the observation that it was difficult to disentangle the consequences of effort from the actual outcomes which are partly a consequence of chance, and that this effect was sometimes used strategically, to his advantage, by the investee.

At one end of the scale, blunt remarks were made of the following sort: "If there is good news, he did it; bad news, it wasn't him" (D); "I think it's a quirk of human nature . . . people look for credit when things go well, and look to apportion blame when they're doing badly" (E); "It definitely happens – it's part of human nature" (I); "It is inherent in the relationship – all good news is down to them, not us. Bad news is due to someone else" (K); "They claim success comes from their efforts. One terrible management team produced great results – the *assets* did the work!" (O); "Yes, they do make this claim, and everyone does it" (Q).

These basic behavioural generalizations are valuable in that they suggest, in an unadorned fashion, that investees are inclined to seek benefit from the random component of performance arising from the 'draw' which is the state of nature. If trust and honesty were the predominant pattern, then the use of a principal–agent perspective would be limited.[11] However, clearly unforced revelation of true effort by the agent is not the norm. This point is reinforced, rather than diminished, when more sophisticated views are considered, such as the following:

11 Though it is certainly true that agency relationships can be used to support trust. Their presence, *ab initio*, with trust and honesty being universal, is, however, subject to doubt.

"When I talk of lack of effort, I feel I have misjudged management. This could be hard to disentangle from a poor outcome by bad luck, for example an investment has gone well in itself, but the timing is wrong. If the timing went well by luck, then I would say this is good, even if I have misjudged management" (B); "Yes, this is human nature. We do have to 'help' some investees and assess performances as they come in as to whether bad luck has caused problems" (R); "Yes, behaviour of management changes when we get involved. Some people do say bad outcomes are bad luck and good luck is good management. I'd refuse to invest in someone who said all poor decisions were down to bad luck. But management do have bad luck sometimes, for instance the Gulf War – you need to assess each situation" (S).

In short, the agency perspective seems to be based on a view of behaviour that is well grounded in reality, so far as the relationship between VCI and MSF is concerned. Because MSFs as agents appear inclined to behave in this way, VCIs as principals are willing to invest in information systems which monitor effort, even if imperfectly. Chapter 12 indicated how complex these information systems can be, and emphasized that their purposes extended very much beyond mere monitoring of effort, to embrace control and decision support functions (see Siskos and Zopoundis 1987). Even these arrangements may not provide investees, as agents, with complete motivation for effort. This will also depend on the extent to which investees create problems of adverse selection. In the face of them, VCIs as principals attempt to create a framework which will stimulate commercial alertness and awareness within the MSF, rather than inducing merely perfunctory compliance with monitoring and control requirements.

Insofar as VCIs are aware of these problems, they will, for example, aim to keep investees somewhat risk exposed in order to put some part of their potential rewards 'at hazard', thus generating the motivation for effort.[12] It has already been seen in Chapter 4 that when conditions of incomplete observability prevail, the desired contractual form for inducing efficiency will typically not involve the investor bearing all the risk. To examine this analytical insight empirically, investors were asked whether investees were tempted to reduce effort once they had agreed a contract that pushed the risk towards the investor (SSI 3.5.3). Further, were this to be the case, what actions did the investor take to attenuate the effect, and how successful were they? Almost all investors were aware of this sort of effect, but only a limited number (11/20 = 55 per cent) were willing to say that they had direct experience of the effect, largely because they felt that an important duty of investors was to detect the possible incidence of effort reduction within the MSF at the stage of screening investees. Thus the investors make comments

12 This does not entirely address the problem of effort elicitation, as work by Gupta and Sapienza (1992) emphasizes that not only effort level but also the direction of effort may be important. In my sample, I did not frequently encounter mention of this difficulty, although admittedly the instrument design did not aim to detect such effects directly.

like: "Yes, they can reduce effort. If they do, we have been poor judges" (A); "In that case you have misjudged" (B); "No, screen these out" (S); "We don't invest if it will affect his effort" (I). There was a general tendency to regard rigorous screening pre-investment as the best way of attenuating adverse selection.

There was therefore a widespread impression created that only the good, hardworking entrepreneurs were selected for the portfolio of VCIs. This may be a reflection of the considerable resources which VCIs put into due diligence, and the fine sieve which was used at the selection stage. Thus investors generally had very positive views about entrepreneurial energy, tending to regard it as unflagging. A typical expression of this was: "Entrepreneurs, when in full flight, work very hard. You can say to yourself, he'll kill himself. They are a very active type, not idle" (D). One interpretation of the evidence is that the tendency to effort reduction when risk is spread (by sharing it with a new equity holder) is almost universal, and a key feature of the VCI's approach is to find the investee who is not inclined to this behaviour. Almost inevitably, even with severe screening, some VCIs do fail in this endeavour, and have subsequently confronted problems of eliciting the necessary effort within the MSF. One of the most insightful comments by an investor came in Case M, where it was said of diminished investee effort that: "There is that potential – you've got to eliminate it. We have a direct confrontation on it. Why are you not working? What's going on? We want an entrepreneur to be highly visible – that is a real issue. Among the worst things you can find is that he's bought himself a new car. Another one is that he's 'inaccessible' – you can't get hold of him. He's 'doing business' – in Henley, Ascot or Wimbledon! The worst indicator of all is that he's at home 'working'. There's got to be 150 per cent commitment, working long hours, like fourteen hours a day. I'd say that if *they* are poncing about, *everyone* in the business is poncing about" (M). Other cases of neglect were also illustrated, as in: "Coming to the stock market . . . running the company is problematic. They do neglect the running of the firm to obtain funds" (R); "If people have not known wealth before, they may coast. If they come from a wealthy family, then that's not usually a problem" (Q); "If management 'fall out' or one dies, then loss of control can cause problems. In one case, a director had been exposed as incompetent, but had been sheltered by colleagues because he had a key share-holding" (T). There is a reluctance to deal with performance default on the part of the investee by reference back to strict, explicit contractual clauses. As the VCI in Case S said: "If you have to rely on an agreement, then you've probably lost your money" (S). In a similar vein, the VCI in Case T said: "The subscription agreement is a necessary evil. It's only used when problems arise – it's a safeguard" (T). A number of VCIs thought it prudent to avoid the extreme measure of having recourse to strict contractual terms (see Fried and Hisrich 1995: 106–8). Instead, they considered how incentives could be put in place for sustaining effort. Two of the most thoughtful comments along these lines by investors were as follows: "We try very hard to structure the deal so that the energy increases, as he has more to gain. We say 'don't let the chief executive get rich when you enter the deal'. We had an example with a high-tech start-up in which more people turned up to put in money than was available for shares. So he sold half of his! He had £60m. in the bank, and lost most of it over six years, through things like taking out £$\frac{1}{4}$m. salary each year" (J); "It does happen. Most of his reward will come late. He has the facility to get it, but he has to convert it. You realize at that time if you've backed a good manager – whether he's interested in capital gain or not. We reward these people at the time we get our reward. We give ordinary shares, ratchets, option schemes, and a fairly low basic salary, with a bonus equal to a percentage of profit" (K). This last comment anticipates a consideration which will be elaborated upon shortly, namely, the consequences for effort of the scale and structure of equity holdings. But to conclude on the issue of how risk affects effort, it seems to be unanimously acknowledged that there is a tendency within the MSF for investees to reduce effort if the environment becomes 'safer' (i.e. less risky). The main route which VCIs adopt to avoiding this is rigorous screening of MSFs, but even this is not foolproof. Incentive structures of a financial variety are created to sustain effort when risk is relatively lower.[13] When this is itself of limited effect, investors must ultimately have recourse to strict contractual requirements. However, when this occurs, it seems to be a last resort, and in all probability the deal has failed.

The comments made by the investor in Case K suggest that equity can play a significant role in effort elicitation, even though VCIs much prefer investees who are naturally inclined to work, whatever their stake, the risk or state of the world. Investors were asked what factors governed the equity stake they were willing to take in an MSF (SSI 3.5.1). They also were asked whether this equity participation was used in a flexible way to affect effort (SSI 3.5.2), and whether they had implemented an incentive-based equity involvement with investees which pushed ownership towards the VCI in bad outcomes, and towards the MSF in good outcomes (SSI 3.5.3). They were probed further on issues like the importance of eliciting investee effort, the implementation of performance-linked equity and options, and the mechanics of incentive-based equity involvements.

It was very clear that 'house styles' differed quite markedly, and this was reflected in views taken about equity stake and effort. A useful encompassing statement was made by the investor in Case A, concerning the factors governing the VCI's equity stake, which he neatly expressed as: "Prudence, diversification and getting a satisfactory level of motivation" (A). This was a statement made by a VCI who had been rather cautious about even admitting that investee effort varied. It has already been apparent from Chapter 7 that the form which equity stakes take can vary widely, which suggests that there is no simple general rule concerning the best equity stake. A few investors felt that size of equity stake was unimportant, an example of this view being: "Size of equity stake is not a relevant

13 If risk is relatively high, low effort may cause control to be transferred to the VCI.

factor. The only issue we have is whether we are a minority or a majority player. Whatever it takes, we'd do it. We prefer minority stakes. If they have a quality management team, we take a minority stake" (M). However, most investors saw their equity stake as affecting investee motivation, and had quite highly developed – but usually singularly different – views as to how to proceed. House negotiation guidelines played a large part in limiting the variety of equity arrangements implemented.[14] The rules which they applied were widely varying, some of them being of the following form: "We are limited to taking zero to 49 per cent; very seldom less than 10 per cent; and typically between 10 per cent and 30 per cent – it has to do with the value of the company upon investment" (E); "Maximum is up to 50 per cent. It's a house negotiation guideline" (G); "In the past we took 25 to 30 per cent – influence without control . . . Now we'd rather have a big influence through a syndicated deal" (N); "We are flexible. We will give them 51 per cent but restrict them and get control in other ways, for example through loan conditions" (O); "How big should our stake be as an organization? I would be uncomfortable with less than 10 per cent . . . too much effort for us; I might go down to 5 per cent if it's a very big, growing company; and I prefer 15 to 35 per cent" (J). It seems the likely reason that these rules are so different is that they reflect major firm-specific differences across VCIs. These features can vary widely and reflect numerous factors, including founders and their mission; current personnel; current fund composition; sectoral specialization; target IRRs; specialization by stage of finance; and desire for control. An example of how VCIs can have a distinctive view on the factors governing the equity stake is given by the following contrasting views: "Potential of business, money required, size of opportunity, management assessment, competition strength, potential outcomes (flotation etc.), motivation of man" (P); "How much money they're looking for, size of company, our funds available, our current portfolio structure" (T).

The wide variety of factors which account for size of equity stake, and the different proportional stakes taken, should not disguise the possibility that there may yet be a common motivation for influencing effort. The investors were asked about the extent to which equity finance was used in a flexible way to influence effort (SSI 3.5.2), and thus performance, for example by the use of performance-linked equity and options.[15] The great majority (16/20 = 80 per

14 More is said about this in section 14.6 below, especially in Table 14.5, and the discussion attaching to it. However, this is from the investees' perspective, many of which have multiple-investor involvements. Thus the MSFs may be more heavily invested in than the following comments in the main text suggest.

15 Performance-linked equity is equity assigned to various parties depending on the performance of the MSF. A particular form is the ratchet or earn-out which structures the deal in a way which gives the investee a higher stake in the MSF, subject to at least attaining a performance goal. An option confers on its holder the right to buy a financial instrument like an

cent) of investors used equity in a flexible way for incentive purposes. Ratchets were used by half the investors, these being devices for giving the investee a higher stake in the MSF if certain performance targets are met; but there was a distinctly divided body of opinion as to their usefulness. When ratchets were used, their precise form was often not divulged. Comments by VCIs ran along the following sorts of lines: "Yes, we use ratchets, but the documentation is confidential" (H); "Yes, ratchets are the usual arrangement. They are usually tailor-made, though they might start out standard" (K); "We do use them – positive and negative are used" (T). Perhaps precisely because of their variety of forms, ratchets were not always popular with investors. Discontent was often strongly expressed: "The ratchet is a better psychological than economic tool" (O); "Winners like to have ratchets, but they cover a multitude of sins" (Q); "Ratchets are a disaster. We find things never work out as expected, and the time and costs of ratchets being set up and amended for acquisitions, and so on, is more bother than they're worth. Simplest deals are best" (R). This disillusion with ratchets was not typical, but criticism was widespread. It also reflected a trend away from their use within the venture capital industry. Perhaps the opinion of the investor in Case E was prophetic: "While we are keen for management teams to be rewarded with occasional bonuses and options, ratchets are a thing of the past" (E).

Although ratchets were viewed with caution by some, and tentatively embraced by others, varieties of forms of flexible equity participation were in common use. Many arrangements were customized to the particular investee. Thus the investor of Case F said of flexible equity participation: "The expectation is that you are going to use it. There is no standard way of doing it – it is customized to suit each company. We say, if the business is worth X, our impact is Y – we are entitled to Z" (F). The investor can be willing to bargain very freely with the investee. A good example of this is the investor in Case L. He said: "If they're very concerned about the equity stake, I give them the chance to buy back equity. I think it's a good motivator. For example, I just gave a £5,000 loan. If it's not paid back by Christmas it reverts to shares and redeemable preference shares. I have no standard documentation, and I don't use lawyers" (L). If the equity participation is performance related, a number of performance indicators might be used. The investor for Case K explained: "Targets have changed in recent years. It always used to be a profit target. Now, we would do most of our deals on a cash flow basis – I think that's peculiar to us. We like to take redemptions of our preference shares along the way. Equity is our incentive device – we link it to alternatives" (K). The clear conclusion to be reached is that equity can

ordinary share. For example, the investee may have the right to buy a certain number of shares from the investor within a certain time at a certain price (which is satisfactory to the investor in terms of rate of return).

be used in many forms to influence incentives: there is almost no situation that fails to be amenable to modification by this route.

A final feature of such arrangements which is to be considered is that of equity involvements which push ownership towards the investor in bad states of the world, and towards the investee in good states of the world (SSI 3.5.3). Investors were asked whether they used such arrangements, and if so, how they worked. A majority (14/20 = 70 per cent) of investors used this technique, and views varied considerably as to both its desirability and efficacy. Fairly typical expressions of qualified approval were the following remarks: "Yes, we like to start low and win high. Vice versa is a demotivator" (H); "Yes, we do have it, and I don't like them. We're going to phase it out" (I); "Yes, we never write them downwards if they do badly. If they do better than the plan, we're happy to write in that they get more shares" (M). There clearly are dangers to the investor's interest in an arrangement of this sort, though it strongly motivates investees. Aware of the dangers, some investors viewed the structure in negative terms. Thus the VCI in Case A said: "No, it's usually the other way round. We start with the biggest stake, put up 60 per cent of the cash, and get what they think is a disproportionate share of the equity. They are in a weak bargaining position" (A). However, the most balanced view expressed was probably by the VCI in Case K, who said: "Yes, we're not keen on it, but it invariably happens. We would rather have a positive incentive than a disincentive. We have two investments where that is the case. We start at the midpoint. Cash flow is a downside ratchet. We start at 60 per cent/40 per cent. Each time you don't deal in preference shares, we get more. It has been negotiated as the involvement has evolved. We're happy with a 60/40 split" (K). Although there was a clear awareness of responsibility towards the investee as agent in the settled form of VCI/MSF relationship, in very bad outcomes investors would limit their losses. For example, the VCI in Case B said: "At the outset you have your ratchets. But if there are problems, then it's a different ball game. If you have to put money in out of weakness, then you have to sack the management. This is not enshrined in the contract, because, if such a default clause were in, it would look like lack of confidence. However, you can't sack anyone unless you have control" (B). A similar point was made by the VCI in Case E, who said, more briefly: "We protect ourselves with the potential to take some greater control" (E).[16]

So far, the investee side of the VCI/MSF relationship has not been directly discussed in this examination of the flexible use of equity, and it is to this that attention now turns. Of the sixteen investees who answered questions about equity (AQ 3.9), a half (8/16 = 50 per cent) admitted to being party to a

16 These rewards are very much in line with the financial modelling in the seminal paper of Chan *et al.* (1990). In that paper, the entrepreneur has to demonstrate a certain threshold level of competence in order to retain control.

performance-linked equity scheme with investors. A slightly larger proportion (10/16 = 62 per cent) thought that this was a good motivator for investees. One of the respondents, the investee of Case G, had previously had such an arrangement and said: "It gives you the chance to shake off the venture capitalist at an agreed price. Basically, it's a buy-back of shares" (G).

Even those subject to performance-linked equity schemes were vague about the specific performance criteria to which they were subject (AQ 3.9.1.1). Sales, profit, cumulative profit and capital value at exit were all mentioned. There were significant incentive aspects to the holding of equity, which could vary considerably depending on performance (AQ 3.9.1). Again, some investees were vague, in Case F even saying, "I can't remember – there might have been some mechanism" (F). But several investees were quite specific, as for example in Case H: "Originally, 20 per cent of equity, which by ratchet we could take up to 37 per cent. The baseline went up by 5 per cent (fixed), we repaid our preference shares earlier and went up to 42 per cent." Two-thirds of investees thought these arrangements were good motivators, representative comments being: "The whole purpose of being involved is wealth creation – harder work, more money" (B); "It was central" (H); "It's a good motivator. Both management and VCs are interested in increasing the value of the shares" (J). But there were significant criticisms, such as: "I have enough in-house motivation without that" (D); "I'm ambivalent about this one. I found shareholders' meetings a pain . . . A money incentive rather than ownership is a better idea" (F); "I'm not sure it's in the best interests of the business. It drives hard in the short term, possibly to the detriment in the long term" (P).[17] Overall, there are mixed views on what are, in effect, state-contingent income or profit allocations to VCI and MSF, especially if benefits accrue mainly to the investee in good states. However, these arrangements *are* used, though clearly they have their dangers. Although they strongly motivate the investees as agents to apply effort to try to increase the probability of the good state of the world, they diminish the enthusiasm of investors in some measure if they feel as though all they are there for is to share in the downside. In extreme cases, this may encourage precipitate reversion of control to the investor, seeking to protect his interest if bad states of the world occur.

The complete picture of incentives and effort is complex, but some key features have emerged:

1 Because it was hard to disentangle the investee's effort from states of the world, this was used strategically by investees to present a favourable impression of their effort.

17 This reference to long-term goals confirms the 'clinical' rather than statistical evidence adduced by Roberts (1991). This suggests that an entrepreneurial attitude which is shaped towards long-term directions rather than short-term goals is to be preferred by VCIs.

2 Investors installed information systems both to monitor the investee's effort and to control the MSF, but the working assumption was that the rigorous screening of entrepreneurs tended to select out those likely to inflict moral hazard problems on the VCI/MSF relationship post-contract.
3 If investee performance default did occur, post-contract, informal rather than formal methods of redress were favoured.
4 Many factors governed the way in which VCIs used their equity stake to affect investees' effort, leading to marked differences in 'house style' across investors.
5 Equity finance was used successfully in a flexible way to assist in achieving performance goals, but judgements varied about such schemes, and some were considered more efficacious than others (e.g. in terms of motivating investees, or of subordinating short-term to long-term goals).

14.6 THE PURSUIT OF CONTRACT OPTIMALITY

The overall objective of concluding contractual arrangements between VCI and MSF is to seek to move both parties to preferred points from their current positions. Although the structure of the principal–agent relationship puts the principal in a leading position as regards contract formulation in the investor–investee case, this does not deny the voluntary nature of any subsequent contract engagement by the investee. The purpose, therefore, of the detailed consideration of risk, information, exchange, incentives and effort in this chapter has not only been to examine these issue for their intrinsic interest, but also to understand better and explain how these various features of contracting under uncertainty coalesce to create best contracting practice. The focus of this last substantive section of this chapter is on this central point, and again the method of exploring it appeals to evidence from both investors and investees.

The first issue to be explored is how investors allocate time and attention over investees. In only a few cases were multiple investees available in the dyadic relationships.[18] Therefore evidence on interactions with other investees is indirect. Despite this, such evidence is both extensive and revealing. From the viewpoint of investees, to start with, opinions were pretty clear cut. When asked whether, in their relationship with the investor, they felt they had to compete with other investees for more favoured treatment (AQ 3.10), the answer was resoundingly in the negative (13/14 = 93 per cent). It was clear that here was an instance in which confidentiality restrictions by investees (see section 14.3 above) were effective, and had important implications for securing trust and harmony in VCI/MSF relations. Few further comments were made on this issue, apart from

18 Presumably more felicitously described as 'triadic', when two investees are matched with one investor.

the perfunctory "You can't answer that" (G), "I don't have a view on that" (K), and "We don't know investees" (N). Only two investees were willing to comment on whether they would put on a 'good show' for the investor to attract more attention (AQ 3.10.1). One said "yes" and the other "no", but the only extended utterance made was, "We give them expensive biscuits at the AGM!"

Although investees appeared universally to feel they had even-handed treatment from the investors, the latter's perspective could well be different. In contemplating the allocation of effort over a portfolio or fund, the investor could feel inclined to follow up on investees who were proportionately more rewarding for a day of attention allocated. To explore this issue, investors were asked if they gave more favoured treatment to the more efficient investees (SSI 3.6.1), and if so, what form it might take (SSI 3.6.2). The result was that a majority of investors (12/20 = 60 per cent) said that they did not favour more efficient investees. In fact, even those who said they did were aware of alternative considerations. Thus, for example, the investor in Case P said, "Most attention is given to extremes" (P), the implication being that non-normal investees, high-flying or struggling, were the ones that received most attention. A number of investors made the point that it was exactly the underperforming firms that offered the most potential for improvement: "We tend to spend most time on companies who are underperforming" (E); "We actually spend a lot of time with the least efficient, bringing them up to scratch" (F); "They would probably get more visits if they are underperforming" (G); "We want to buy companies that are inefficient and offer 10 per cent if they get out of it" (H); "What makes a good portfolio is converting the losses into midstream" (K). What these comments emphasize is the positive role that investors can play in unlocking the potential for performance in a company, a potential that the MSF itself may not recognize.

Given that a significant minority of investees clearly did enjoy relatively favoured treatment, the logical next step is to enquire into what consequences follow on from this, both in terms of the favoured investees and the non-favoured investees. There is a general awareness among investors that confidentiality is important to the harmonious handling of multiple investee relationships. In this sense, the investor in Case I put the matter most simply when he said of his investees: "They are all isolated" (I). Similar remarks along these lines from other investees included: "I don't suppose they're aware they're more favoured – they're not aware of the others" (L); and "It's so segmented that they can't see the difference" (M). In short, there did not seem to be a major problem arising through investees in a portfolio jockeying for most favoured position with the investor.[19] This aligns very accurately with investees' perceptions that they receive even-handed, or at least appropriate, treatment from their investor.

19 In a limited way this has already been suggested by the 'within site' analysis of Case J, for which there were two investees, in Chapter 8.

Although principal–agent relationships have been portrayed as alternative modes to relationships of reciprocity or trust, they can in fact support trust, and indeed they may thereby function more effectively. The use of confidentiality to build trust, as illustrated above, provides a good example of this, within what seems a fairly strict principal–agent relationship, in terms of its attention to details of monitoring, risk-bearing, information, motivation and effort. When asked whether the contract they had agreed with the VCI was largely based on trust or understanding, or was largely tightly legally defined, a majority of investees (9/17 = 53 per cent) declared it was based on trust (AQ 3.11). This was despite the fact that they were well aware of the importance of formal contractual arrangements. Even when investees said they regarded the legal arrangement as predominant, they mollified their views in various ways: "To protect both partners" (B); "Both" [i.e. trust and legally tight] (F); "We put it [the contract] in a drawer and get on with the business" (H); "There is no sense of humour that comes into a contract" (Q). Those investees who emphasized trust were also aware of the formal legal underpinning, as illustrated by the following epithets from the investees in Cases J and N: "Trust, in practice, legal form, in theory" (J); "Tightly defined agreement at first, but trust is crucial" (N).

In a similar fashion, investors were asked about the extent to which the contracts agreed with their investees were based on understandings or trust (so-called implicit contracts) or based on formal legal documents (so-called explicit contracts (SSI 3.7.1)). In the discussion that followed, investors were probed further about explicit contracts as regards their costs and their litigability. The potential vagueness of implicit contracts and problems arising in enforcing them were also explored. Where possible, copies were obtained of formal documentation, like subscription agreements.

By contrast to the investees, the majority of investors (14/20 = 70 per cent) generally thought of their contracts with their investees in formal, explicit contracting terms. Even the minority who made primary reference to implicit contracting and trust had a healthy admixture of more formal contracting in their dealings with investees. But it is also true that those investors who emphasized explicit, formal contracting distinguished between different phases of investment involvement, with the early phase being largely driven by an explicit contract, but trust, loyalty and commitment being developed as the VCI/MSF relationship matured, bringing with it more implicit forms of contracting based on understandings, experience and mutual respect. Those who favoured a hard-nosed explicit contracting approach made the following sorts of comments about VCI/MSF relations: "All are based on contracts – always formal. Implicit factors are also important – you must feel empathy between yourself and the investee. Our contract is very standard" (A); "Initially, it is mostly formal legal documentation. There has always been a lot of debate about this – do we have too much? It alters slightly later, and moves towards trust" (F); "I'm afraid too much the latter [that is, explicit contracting]. I think it's to do with enforcement and litigability. Any corporate finance does need lots of paperwork. It's about protecting your rights.

We have standard documentation, articles, subscription agreement, contract of employment, etc." (G); "They're all bolted to the ground. There is a draft of the subscription agreement and a pre-completion legal checklist" (H); "It's totally formal, legal documents. Underlying it is the explicit contract. You know it's there – a bit like Terry Venables.[20] Now and again you have to get the contract out. Then it's failure, not exit – you're looking to shut down the business" (M); "We do try and make clear what our requirements are. We aren't trying to hide requirements, and hope they hire a solicitor too. It is in everybody's interest to have things spelt out in black and white" (N).

Many of the strong views were particularly expressed with the early stages of contracting in mind. Even investors who were strongly committed to an explicit contracting protocol were prepared to admit that as the VCI/MSF relationship developed, so alternative contractual forms became apparent, with a more evolutionary, implicit contracting mode emerging. These views are well represented by the following comments of investors: "We have to have an element of control, for example, to say don't sell assets, and change articles, do insure: and problems with these formal items determine how the relationship will be. Sensible negotiations give a good foundation for the relationship. A banker may be risk-maximizing. This pushes us to be progressive and constructive" (C); "There has to be both. Every case has formal legal documents which set out the parameters for everyone. There is also an understanding between us of the working relationship. We are hands-on, with a level of trust, and work as a partnership. There is a standard purchase agreement, for example. Although there is no 'pro forma' there is a lot in common between the investees" (E); "Ninety per cent written, formal; 10 per cent implicit. In practice, far more implicit than you would imagine. Explicit conditions are broken. The same applies to the position with management. There is an explicit understanding that, if he goes, he loses all his money before we lose ours. Take the example of ratchets – most are negotiated" (J).

Finally, there are the views to be considered of those investors who espouse very much an implicit contracting mode. Despite their nailing their colours to the mast in this respect, it will be observed that explicit contracting considerations rarely fade entirely from view. Examples of the mode of operation of these investors are provided by the following comments: "The whole success of the investment is implicit. In our legal process it is frightening for a lot of people when they first come to it – everything's in there. We work in practical terms, and would never write 'in accordance with Clause X . . .' . Vagueness is always on the cards. Efficiency is governed by the implicit contract" (K); "Very largely the former [that is, implicit contracting]. But I do write a letter and we both sign it. It's just two pages long, but contains everything. I positively refer to it – both

20 For readers outside the UK, a noted English soccer player who went on to a high profile and successful career in soccer management. However, he was also a victim of business failure.

parties understand it. If it came to court, it would be able to be understood easier than long litigation, which is often internally contradictory. I'm pretty explicit about key things: shares, salaries, how I'll get my money back. It covers all the major points, and costs nothing" (L); "Our relationships are based on trust. Subscription agreements allow us to get initial information and clarify what they should be consulting us on. However, we can't use it as a straitjacket" (R); "Trust gets us to the subscription agreement. Managers can change and we need control. We must tailor agreement to the particular circumstances of the investee. For example we might set a ceiling on directors' emoluments in a small company with a board remuneration committee. The agreements differ. How we work three years later may not be as per the agreement" (S); "Most important is the trust in the relationship. If you have to rely on the rules, you're in trouble" (T).

It seems that, despite the apparently formalistic nature of the principal–agent framework, a mixture of contracting modes is present in the VCI/MSF relationship. From the standpoint of the investor, the explicit contract is important and is clearly designed to provide incentives for effort on the part of the investee, and to limit the scope for moral hazard. In the limit it also protects the investor's interest, especially in bad states of the world, and thereby helps to sustain the investor's reputation. It also controls the relative risk exposure of VCI and MSF and (not unrelated) the size and split of the equity in the MSF. As the VCI/MSF relationship evolves, the explicit contracting mode is partially replaced by a mode which places less emphasis on formal procedures and monitoring and more emphasis on trust and harmonious communication. However, it is rare for the formal contracting features to be suppressed entirely, and even in high-trust, long-lived relationships, the formal contract underpins such activity, and not only in the sense that it provides a safety net, or determines a security level for investors.

From the investee perspective, the formal aspects of contracting are less apparent. They may involve numerous state-contingent features, for example relating to performance default in any of several areas (e.g. cash flow, profits, management). Some of these states (e.g. those leading to control reversion) only occur with low probability. Thus the investee may never observe in practice how many of the contractual features operate. Further, because investor confidentiality effectively isolates one investee from another, there is little opportunity for learning, either by imitation or by doing, in what is essentially a one-shot situation for the investee. Thus the investee must perforce take more on trust than does the investor. Despite this relatively informal nature of the investee's contracting preferences, quite strict performance requirements set by the investor keep her on her toes, and ensure incentives for effort and profit-seeking remain intact.

Having put together the relevant building blocks it is now possible to construct the final qualitative empirical analysis of contract optimality. This requires a consideration of what both investor and investee seek to achieve in contracting, the means they have of achieving it, and the extent to which they do actually achieve it. The starting point for this final discussion is how the investee views the investor from the standpoint of potentially useful characteristics and their place in an 'ideal' contract, however defined.[21] Investees were asked how important the following were, in terms of what they brought to the VCI/MSF relationship: knowledge of the product or service; knowledge of markets; risk-bearing; effort; financial expertise; commitment to the business; and the supply of finance capital (AQ 3.5). They were asked to rank each factor on a three-point scale. The results are displayed in Table 14.1.

These evaluation counts clearly put four factors – knowledge of the product or service supplied by the MSF (a), the knowledge of markets (b), effort (d) and commitment to the business (f) – into a combined set of 'high capabilities' that the investee brings to the contracting nexus.[22] There is little to choose between these four categories, though commitment to the business (f) should probably be regarded as the most important on this evidence. However, it is perhaps more sensible to regard (a), (b), (d) and (f) in Table 14.1 as together constituting the core abilities or competencies of the investees. It is also worth noting that risk-bearing (c) and financial expertise (e) were generally ranked as being of importance, and they, as a combined group, may be considered as the second-string abilities which the investee brings to the contract. Generally ranked as unimportant by investees is the supply of finance capital (g).

In a symmetrical way one may now ask what the investor brings to the VCI/MSF relationship (AQ 3.6).[23] The relevant preference counts are displayed in Table 14.2. There is really only one dominant attribute, the supply of finance capital (g), this being the only one that is widely regarded as very important. Also of importance are risk-bearing (c) and commitment to the business (f), of which (c) is ranked above (f) if a lexicographic method of ranking is used.[24] Surprisingly, financial expertise (e) is only ranked fourth, though clearly it is also important.[25] Effort (d) is ranked next, followed by knowledge of markets (b) and knowledge of product or service (a). It will be observed that there is a neat dovetailing of VCI attributes and MSF attributes if Table 14.1 and Table 14.2 are considered together.[26] There is an additional body of evidence, outside that of the dyad

21 The standard reference point for the ideal contract, so far as the economist is concerned, is Pareto-optimality (see especially Chapter 4).

22 In Chandler and Hanks (1994: 334) a 'capability' in the context of an MSF is defined as 'the capacity for a coordinated set of resources to perform some task or activity'.

23 This is not, however, entirely symmetric as the respondent is the investee in each case. A similar question design is not available for the investor, partly because the instrument used was of interview rather than questionnaire form.

24 That is to say, ranking first by the highest category, then by the next category, and so on.

25 Were rankings for this case done by the investor, rather than by the investee, this probably would have come out higher.

26 This form of outcome is also anticipated in the theoretical work of Cable and Shane (1997: 143) who say, 'Entrepreneurs and venture capitalists each specialize in the development and contribution of different types of knowledge, allowing each party to exploit its comparative advantage'.

Table 14.1 Importance of attributes that investee brought to the VCI/MSF relationship

Case	*Attributes* (*a*) *Knowledge of product or service*	(*b*) *Knowledge of markets*	(*c*) *Risk-bearing*	(*d*) *Effort*	(*e*) *Financial expertise*	(*f*) *Commit-ment to the business*	(*g*) *Supply of finance capital*
A							
B	v	v	v	v	v	v	
C							
D	v	v	i	i	i	v	u
E	i	i	i	u	v	v	i
F	i	i	i	i	i	v	u
G	u	u	i	u	i	i	u
H	v	v	i	v	i	v	u
I							
J1	i	i	i	v	v	v	u
J2	v	i	i	v	i	i	u
K	v	v	i	i	i	i	v
L	v	v	i	v	i	v	v
M	i	i	i	u	i	v	u
N	v	v	i	v	v	v	u
O							
P1	v	v	u	v	i	v	i
P2	v	i	i	i	i	v	u
Q	v	v	v	v	v	v	i
R	v	v	i	v	u	v	u
S							
T							

Notes:
1 u = unimportant; i = important; v = very important.
2 No data were returned for Cases A, C, I, O, S and T.

Table 14.2 Importance of attributes that investor brought to the VCI/MSF relationship

Case	*Attributes*						
	(a) Knowledge of product or service	*(b) Knowledge of markets*	*(c) Risk-bearing*	*(d) Effort*	*(e) Financial expertise*	*(f) Commitment to the business*	*(g) Supply of finance capital*
A							
B							v
C							
D	u	u	i	u	i	u	i
E	u	u	i	u	u	i	v
F	u	u	i	i	i	i	i
G	u	u	u	i	i	i	u
H	u	u	v	i	i	v	v
I							
J1	i	i	i	u	u	i	v
J2	i	i	v	i	i	i	v
K	u	u	u	i	i	v	i
L	u	u	v	i	i	v	v
M	i	u	i	u	i		u
N	u	i	i	u	i	u	v
O							
P1	u	u	i	i	v	i	v
P2	u	u	i	i	i	v	v
Q	u	u	i	u	u	u	i
R	i	i	v	u	v	u	v
S							
T							

Notes:
1 u = unimportant; i = important; v = very important.
2 No data were returned for Cases A, C, I, O, S and T.
3 For Case B, only one response provided.

evidence to which this chapter is confined, which has been referred to in Chapter 7, and this further strengthens the pattern displayed in these two tables.[27] That is to say, the VCI has, pre-eminently, comparative advantage in the supply of finance capital (which presumably cannot be done without considerable skill in fund acquisition and management), and also in commitment to the business, risk-bearing and financial expertise. The MSF has comparative advantage in knowledge (of products, services, markets), effort and commitment.

To further simplify the picture it is reasonable to treat effort as partly endogenous, being created by the incentive structure of the contracting nexus. Further, commitment is in a sense a foregone conclusion in that both parties have sought to agree a contract in a challenging situation in which 'many are called, but few are chosen'. Thus commitment might well be taken for granted. Stripping down the preference orderings in this way, one can now characterize the VCI as having a comparative advantage in supplying finance capital (presumably with expertise) and bearing risk. The MSF can now be regarded as having a comparative advantage in knowledge (of products, services and markets). This brings the empirical picture quite close to that anticipated in the theoretical and methodological framework delineated in Chapter 3, a framework which was established, incidentally, before any structured fieldwork had been undertaken.

Addressing this issue more inductively, reference can be made to Table 14.3. The data summarized there are responses to a question posed to all investees in the dyads about the single most important attribute that the VCI and MSF, respectively, brought to the contrasting nexus (AQ 3.7). Quite clearly, the supply of finance capital (g) is thought to be the most important for the VCI and commitment to the business (f) is thought to be most important for the MSF.[28] There is an almost tautological feeling to this conclusion, which is clearly correct, but yet lacks context. After all, the VCI is *the source* of finance capital and the investee is *the owner* of the MSF. Therefore, while Tables 14.1 and 14.2 are more empirically revealing, it is comforting to observe that Table 14.3 so clearly displays what is most important about the VCI and the MSF is *what they are*, in a functional sense, namely: that the one is a supplier of outside finance; and the other is a supplier of ownership and entrepreneurial services. There is a clear disjuncture by function, which is a useful reminder of the separateness by function of VCI and

27 This is what I have called the extraneous sample of investees, which provided a further set of fourteen cases, using telephone interview methods. For these additional investees, commitment (43 per cent) was marginally rated ahead of knowledge (36 per cent) for the MSF, and these were well ahead of the rest; and finance capital was completely dominant (71 per cent) in rankings for the VCI.

28 These results have support from the literature too. For example, Gorman and Sahlman (1989) find that the most frequently performed service of the VCI was the provision of additional funding; and Tyebjee and Bruno (1984) found that two important aspects of the contracting process were the market and the management quality (arguably provided by knowledge, commitment, etc.).

Table 14.3 Most important attribute of investor and investee, respectively, brought to the VCI/MSF relationship

Case	*Attributes*						
	(a) Knowledge of product or service	*(b) Knowledge of markets*	*(c) Risk-bearing*	*(d) Effort*	*(e) Financial expertise*	*(f) Commitment to the business*	*(g) Supply of finance capital*
A							
B						MSF	VCI
C							
D						MSF	VCI
E		MSF					VCI
F						MSF	VCI
G	MSF				VCI		
H		MSF				MSF VCI	VCI
I							
J1						MSF	VCI
J2	MSF						VCI
K	MSF						VCI
L	MSF						VCI
M						VCI	
N						MSF	VCI
O							
P1						MSF	VCI
P2	MSF						VCI
Q					VCI	MSF	
R					VCI	MSF	
S							
T							

Notes:
1 Case M had MSF selected for an ‘other’ attribute (h), not shown.
2 No data were returned for Cases A, C, I, O, S and T.
3 Case H had double responses for ties.

MSF. Though both may bear risk, and both have financial expertise, only one owns a firm and only one has a deep purse of finance capital.

Moving on now from best attributes of investors and investees, final consideration has to be given to the ideal contractual form in the light of all the considerations broached so far. In order to reduce the dimensionality of this complex problem, investees were asked how important a set of six key characteristics was to *their* ideal relationship with the investor (AQ 3.13).[29] As before, these characteristics were evaluated on a three-point scale. The characteristics were: (a) appropriate capital structure; (b) efficient risk-sharing; (c) free sharing of information; (d) maximum rate of return; (e) enhancement of reputation; and (f) increase of motivation. Each of these characteristics itself denotes a bundle of attributes, as has been illustrated in section 14.2 when free sharing of information was discussed in detail. A similar point could be made about motivation, when considered in the light of discussion in section 14.5. However, the point of proceeding in this way is precisely to reduce the dimensionality of the problem, as proposed, so that sharp, summary conclusions can be obtained despite an apparent wealth of qualitative information.

Table 14.4 presents responses, on the three-point scale of intensity, to these questions posed to investees on the importance of six attributes (risk, IRR, motivation, etc.) for ideal contracting. What is particularly interesting about Table 14.4 is the relationship it bears to previous tables in this chapter. Recall that a point had been reached (in Table 14.3) at which is was argued that what was most important in what the VCI and MSF brought to the contract was what they were, in the sense of functions they performed. However, this was thought best treated as a tautology, though perhaps one that it was timely to affirm. Stepping back from this to Table 14.2 and Table 14.1, behind the tautology one discovered a collection of attributes. Their remarkable characteristic was that they were almost disjoint attributes in terms of the rankings for the VCI and the MSF. The results in Table 14.4 resonate well with previous results, in that appropriate capital structure (a) is thought to be the most important characteristic in determining the ideal relationship between VCI and MSF.[30] Interestingly, it is not maximum rate of return (d), which might be very much an investor's view. Nor is it free sharing of information (c) or increasing MSF motivation (f), both of which are identically ranked. These two both loomed large in earlier analysis in this chapter concerning investee behaviour. The revealing point suggested by the choice of 'appropriate capital structure' as the principal determinant of the ideal

29 The word 'their' is italicized because, for example, reputation and motivation refer to the MSF. Investor views will be considered next.

30 This is also true for the extraneous sample of fourteen investees reported upon in Chapter 7. For this sample, capital structure was ranked most important by far (37 per cent on 'very' important), followed by efficient risk-sharing and the free sharing of information (16 per cent each on 'very' important), which tied by ranking of importance across the scale.

Table 14.4 Importance of investee attributes to the ideal contractual relationship with investor

Case	*Attributes*					
	(a) Appropriate capital structure	*(b) Efficient risk-sharing*	*(c) Free sharing of information*	*(d) Maximum rate of return*	*(e) Enhancement of your reputation*	*(f) Increasing of your motivation*
A						
B	v	u	i	v	u	u
C						
D	v	i	v	v	v	v
E	v	v	v	i	i	u
F	v	i	i	i	v	i
G	v	u	u	u	i	i
H	v	v	i	i	u	i
I						
J1	i	i	i	i	u	v
J2	v	i	u	i	u	i
K	v	v	i	i	i	u
L	i	i	i	v	i	v
M	u	u	i	i	u	i
N	i	i	v	i	v	u
O						
P1	i	i	v	v	u	i
P2	v	u	u	i	u	i
Q	i	not an issue	not an issue	u	i	u
R	v	i	u	u	v	v
S						
T						

Notes:
1 u = unimportant; i = important; v = very important.
2 No data were returned for Cases A, C, I, O, S and T.

relationship is that it is, in a sense, prior to many of the other characteristics in Table 14.4. Thus capital structure plays a major role in distributing risk between investor and investee (e.g. through split of equity), in motivating the investee (e.g. through options), in determining the flow of information (e.g. according to management and financial accounting conventions) from the investee to investor, and in determining the internal rate of return (e.g. through the financial engineering of the deal).

The investor too has views on what the ideal relationship with an investee should look like, and VCIs were asked what they aimed to achieve in this ideal relationship. They were probed about capital structure, risk-sharing, information-sharing, rate of return and effort elicitation. In the same way as house styles differed markedly among VCIs on financial arrangements, so also did the 'ideals' proffered by them concerning their relationship with the MSFs. It is for this reason that comments were made like the following for the investors of Cases P and Q: "We are pragmatic – each situation is different" (P); "Structure is evolutionary and changeable – not optimal" (Q). Considering that the venture capital world is widely regarded as epitomizing the market mentality, it is surprising how often more of a stakeholder view of the VCI's purpose was expressed, rather than a profit- or return-maximizing view. It was remarkable how often investors referred to affiliative needs, peer group approval, reputation, partnership norms and other types of social reference points. Their views reflect an emerging venture capital literature which analyses these attitudes (e.g. Sapienza and Korsgaard 1996). The following examples of investors' remarks illustrate this point, by reference to their need for a good reputation: "Reputation – the ability to raise more funds depends on it. Important!" (D); "Reputation – we like to think we are friendly, in partnership, flexible, undemanding, supportive when things are not going as well as planned, 'nice guys', who foster anti-contentious board meetings" (E); "Reputation – that we always treat him reasonably, treat him well. We recognize that reputation is in the eye of the beholder" (J); "Our reputation is known in general terms in the venture capital industry, but not in the world at large. Our reputation is implied, in that we've done some good deals" (K). The reason why reputation is so important is simple: it is that reputation determines the VCI's ability to raise money from upstream investors (sometimes called 'clients'). To illustrate, in addition to the quote above for the investor in Case D, consider the remarks of the investor for Case L: "The entrepreneur should value my input – should trust and support me when the need arises. It is vital, because as the company grows, I'm not otherwise in a good position to provide the next sum of capital" (L).[31] In turn, reputation will hinge on financial performance, but

31 Cable and Shane (1997) put forward a repeated Prisoner's Dilemma argument for the emergence of more cooperative arrangements and higher levels of trust, the greater the longevity of the VCI/MSF relationship.

it will be damaged if it is bought at the price of poor interpersonal relations. Of course, good interpersonal relations sustain stable contracting, promote efficiency and foster harmony, so there is no necessary trade-off between good conduct in this sense and financial performance.

A fairly realistic description of how a pragmatic VCI proceeds is in the following quote: “We look at a deal, its sector, how the company’s going to perform. It governs the way we put the deal together. For example, we might decide we’d like cash, or loan stock redeemed first. It’s normally equity. It may be loan stock, but it behaves as equity. We won’t make an investment if the company shows less than 40 per cent IRR on the business plan we’re backing” (G). The quote illustrates a diversity of approach and a flexibility of perspective. Here is a VCI who wants to make money, but knows there is no unique magic formula. A similarly well-grounded view, though on an entirely different tack, was taken by the investor in Case N: “There are four main factors: (1) the ability to control management, for example capital expenditure, selling firms/ buying firms; (2) reward factors – ratchets, exit options; (3) capital structure – a lot will be in the articles; put the confidential factors in the subscription agreement; (4) management accounts structure – the problem here is what we can do if they don’t deliver. We don’t have a standard agreement – we would use lawyers” (N). Here the emphasis is on process and procedures and how they can best be deployed. There is not even a mention of IRR, the presumption being that if you do the best, you perform the best.

Although house styles varied enormously, the prevalence of reputation as a goal was notable. It suggests that ‘nice guys’ can have fun and still make money, but that without a sufficiently high performance, reputation is lost and hence the capacity to raise money from upstream investors (‘clients’) is lost. It was also apparent that in discussing their ideal relationship with the MSF, investors were not averse to an injection of humour. Thus the investor in Case H said: “We would want a hugely profitable investment, the business to prosper after our involvement, and to be perceived by the investee to have offered him value” (H). An ideal indeed! The investor in Case I put it even more briefly when he said, “We have it” (I). Fortunately humour and good reputation go hand in hand.

The role that equity plays in the VCI/MSF relationship is crucial, so it is natural to turn next to give consideration to the best, ideal or optimal equity involvement with the investee. Matters of interest include whether the optimum changes over time, whether there may be many optima, and whether the optimum can be considered in isolation from other considerations such as risk, incentives and monitoring. When the investors in the dyads were asked about these matters (SSI 3.7.2), again the replies were diverse, reflecting wide differences in house style. Many investors mentioned there was no unique best equity involvement, examples of how they expressed this being: “It can vary from 2 per cent to 70 per cent or 80 per cent – it’s very subjective and flexible” (A); “It’s in hand” (H); “A range – can’t be specific on that” (I); “There are many optima. You can never say in any one situation where it may be. But we do have optima. That, for example, is why we feel uncomfortable with non-optima, like IRR less than 10 per cent" (J); "The optimum is a long-term relationship" (M); "We might have an ideal for each specific investment, . . . but things are changeable. There is no optimal structure" (Q); "We have *differing* relationships. 'Best' is a difficult word, though what I like best is 'return'. 'Best' is a funny term" (S). The idea of a non-unique optimum is actually very familiar to economists, and neither puzzling nor surprising. In the Edgeworth boxes of Chapter 4, the contract curve maps out a locus of infinitely many optima. However, this is still a valuable thing to do, for it rejects many more allocations than it accepts at the optimum. To use an analogy, there are an infinity of optima in the path described in the sawdust by a clown poised on a unicycle in the circus ring, but the path so traced by his unicycle is unique, and excludes far more than it includes.

One way of looking at the ideal equity involvement between investor and investee, from the investor perspective, is at the level of a single deal or investment. This is clearly expressed by the investor in Case Q: "We might have an ideal for each specific investment . . . things are changeable" (Q). As investments vary so much, involving different features of 'time and place' information, they are in a sense unique; they are always a 'one-off'.[32] This will be true even from the perspective of a single investor, following a specific investment 'house style'. This explains the sort of comment made by the investor in Case P: "Yes, we vary it. Each company is different, and reactions to competitive market conditions change them over time" (P). Another comment reinforcing this view was made by the investor in Case O: "Our documentation is situationally based. It is in part determined by our assessment of them" (O). Thus a combination of unique investment house styles makes it difficult to characterize the best or ideal equity involvement. While it is known that the typical minimum and maximum equity stakes, in an average sense, for VCIs are 6 per cent and 60 per cent respectively,[33] this makes for a great diversity in practice – from 0 per cent and 30 per cent (N) to 10 per cent and 100 per cent (M), with even quirky conventions like 2 per cent and 55 per cent (A). The only discernible pattern for the VCI is a tendency *not* to seek a majority stake.[34] As the investor in Case G put it: "We are seeking to support, not to control" (G).

When the experience of investors in terms of equity involvement is matched up with that of investees, the specific 'time and place' feature remains. They are well displayed in Table 14.5, which provides more than the usual detail on maximum and minimum equity, and also some narrative. There has, of course, been a stage at which the investee has held a 100 per cent stake in the MSF, this implying

32 The term 'time and place' information is taken from so-called Austrian economics. For a summary account, see Reid (1987: ch. 6).

33 See Table 7.3, in Chapter 7, on the main characteristics of investors.

34 This is what gives a modal (min, max) value of (1 per cent, 49 per cent) (E, O, P, Q, R, T) for the sample of investors.

Table 14.5 Highest and lowest equity held in the MSF by investor

MSF	*Highest*	*Lowest*
A		
B	15% to 17% × 2 partners (30%–40% in total).	5% to 6% × 3 partners (15%–18%)
C		
D	100% (50% each partner).	62%
E	55% £400k capital put in from start. It is a limited company.	55%
F	100% (original proprietor).	51%. Two had 49% between them. Most institutions do not want control or to be majority shareholders because they do not want to consolidate the results, whether good, bad or indifferent.
G	70%	70%. It depends how you classify the preference shares because they are non-voting.
H	42% (just before the float).	20%
I		
J1	1%	1%
J2	Slightly > 0. Always been nominal.	0%
K	16%	14%
L	72% – same all the way along.	72%
M	$33\frac{1}{3}$%	23%
N	117/275 (i.e. 43%). Our holding has gone up.	107/275 (i.e. 39%)
O		
P1	29%. 43.5% now (just gone up in the last week).	Nil, pre-buyout.
P2	100%	60%
Q	100%	50.9% (sold the company, went to zero, bought it back).
R	74% (as it is now).	46%
S		
T		

ownership. But since that point, experience has clearly been very diverse. In some cases the maximum has gone down from 100 per cent and subsequently the investee has returned to it. Similarly, the lowest equity holding may have gone from zero back to a majority holding (Case Q). One also gets development companies like the MSF of Case J1, where the ownership stake has scarcely got off the floor – by design – at any point. This table also emphasizes the precedence of complicating special factors like partnership splits of equity, syndicate holdings of equity, the classification of preference shares, company sale, and flotation. In short, there is no general rule for equity holdings.

To conclude this substantive part of the chapter, reference will be made to the views of investees on whether they were at, or close to, an optimum in their relationship with investors, or whether there was scope for moving further towards an optimum (AQ 3.12). Most investees (10/15 = 67 per cent) felt that they were close to an optimum. In explaining this feeling, some remarks were unconditional, like those of the investee in Case J2, who said the optimum had been achieved "because of the support the venture capitalists have provided to the company" (J2). However, most investees modified the opinion they had reached, on balance, with specific comments, as in: "There is scope for improvement – working closer together on strategy and company acquisitions (in terms of helping to value). I need professionals that won't charge me through the nose" (M); "We have a good relationship – they have had a 'hands off' approach" (N); "There is always scope for any improvement. There are subtle differences in the attitudes of investors and investees. Some companies have a very low equity holding, and have more business problems. There's a completely different relationship there" (Q).

All this suggests a moving optimum, that is, being constantly adapted to changing features. When these changes overran the company, then the investee could feel that he or she was in a far from optimal relationship with the investor. Expressions of discontent about not being close to the optimum by the minority of investees included: "It's a great deal better than it was, but I would like them to think in a much broader way about what's best for the company as a whole, rather than just what's best for them" (J); "It was much less than the optimal – we ran out of funding in the middle of the recession – not an ideal arrangement" (K); "It's a very good relationship, but I'd like to have more of their time to discuss issues. They're in Edinburgh. With a local institution you're more casually in touch" (P); "It's a function of time. We're only in our second year, and we need time to build up that trust and exploit it more fully" (P2). Overall, a close to optimum appearance was presented of VCI/MSF relations, with most qualifying statements being about adjustments required for moving from an old to a new optimum, or closer to an identified optimum. There seemed no difficulty in thinking of optimum relationships, nor in seeking them, or indeed in recognizing when they had last been achieved.

14.7 CONCLUSION

This is both a long and a complex chapter, and the last one in the book. It has focused very much on cross-site qualitative methods, and these have been used to explore and draw together all the major themes discussed earlier in the book. In doing so, I have paid particular attention to illustrating points with explicit verbatim comments made by investees and investors. Most of these are highly informative, some are very witty, and some even a little sad. However, taken together, they very much enrich the fine fabric of the discussion.

Each section has its own summary, so further encapsulation of ideas need not be extensive, but a review of principal results may prove useful. Probably the most important general conclusion is that the evidence points to the appropriateness of using the categories of analysis deployed in principal–agent analysis. Thus the functions of the VCI as principal and of the MSF as agent: (a) are sharply delineated, with the VCI providing finance capital, and the MSF market knowledge and business commitment; (b) are clearly distinguishable, with the skill sets of each being almost disjoint; and (c) offer considerable opportunities for mutually beneficial contracting, with a rich flow of information going from investee to investor, and the investor taking on greater risk from the investee.

Of the many detailed conclusions, the following ten are worthy of a reprise:

1 The VCI was the risk specialist in a general sense, but the MSF had highly developed specific risk-bearing skills. Briefly, the VCI recognized risk and dealt with it, whereas the MSF recognized risk and had to live with it.
2 Although open information was widely espoused, significant areas of confidentiality persisted. For VCIs, it mainly protected other investees, for MSFs, it mainly protected intellectual property.
3 A rich flow of information, by scope and detail, went from MSF to VCI, especially post-investment, but the flow from VCI to MSF was much less extensive. Both parties were mutually satisfied with information flows in both directions: a kind of optimal position was recognized as having been reached.
4 The fuller the information – by frequency, type, detail, etc. – provided by the MSF to the VCI, the better able was the VCI to manage risk. This led to a higher level of trust, a more productive relationship, and a greater willingness on the part of the VCI to increase his equity stake.
5 Moral hazard problems were widespread and well recognized, but attenuated by a variety of means. Information systems helped, as did placing a measure of risk on the MSF. Flexible equity participation schemes were widely used to provide incentives for MSFs post-contract, and were regarded as generally successful.
6 The explicit contracting mode was omnipresent at all stages of the VCI/MSF relationship, but particularly evident at the earliest stage. As the relationship developed, implicit contracting features emerged, with higher levels of trust, but formal features of contracting were never very far below the surface.
7 In terms of the comparative advantage of each party in the contracting relationship, those of the VCI resided largely in the supply of finance capital (presumably with the associated skills of fund raising and allocation), and those of the MSF largely resided in knowledge (e.g. markets, products, rivals), effort and commitment.
8 The most crucial feature of contract optimality was perceived to be the right choice of capital structure. As this established ownership entitlement, created incentives for effort, and apportioned risk, its pivotal role was very evident.

9 Optimality in the VCI/MSF relationship was widely perceived to have been achieved, or to be a goal towards which progress was being made. Optima were varied and specific to individual investor/investee dyads.

10 The specific 'time and place' nature of optima went hand in hand with highly individual 'house styles' on the part of investors. Their reputations very much hinged on the efficacy of their house styles, which in turn had considerable leverage over their ability to raise funds from upstream investors or clients, hoping to use the financial intermediation skills of VCIs in the high-risk/high-return investment arena.

Thus, in seeking a satisfactory contracting nexus, the roles of risk and information were central. States of the world were unpredictable, creating problems for the VCI and offering opportunities for dissimulation by the MSF, which posed challenges of business management. The VCI as principal sought to attenuate the negative incentive consequences of uncertainty, and indeed aimed to use uncertainty in a positive way to promote the better performance of the MSF, and to better align the interests of the investee with his own.

The investee as agent sought to acquire sufficient finance capital from the VCI to support mutually agreed growth and development plans for the MSF. In doing so, as part of the *quid pro quo* of the VCI sharing risk, the investee provided detailed and extensive information. This provision was fluid, and developed over time.

Not surprisingly, the settled contracting relationship between VCI and MSF embodied much specialized 'time and place' information, so the notion of a typical or representative optimal contract was meaningless. Instead, one saw how the fine detail of information provision, monitoring, control, risk-bearing and incentivization came together to create for each VCI/MSF dyad a unique contracting outcome. This blended skilfully both implicit and explicit contracting features, according to the stage of development of the relationship.

EPILOGUE

A significant purpose of this work has been methodological. It has been to apply qualitative methods systematically and carefully to a well-defined institutional arrangement: the provision of outside financial backing for the promising mature small firm. In doing so, a well-rounded theoretical perspective has always governed the progression of the argument, that of principal–agent analysis. As we have seen, this approach, sometimes called simply agency analysis, focuses on the relationship between two parties – in my case, the investor and investee – who can, in principle, engage in favourable trades. It is the principal, here the investor, who typically initiates the writing of a contract that will describe the terms on which this trading will take place. However, the agent, here the investee, is not passive. She may have been the first to approach the agent, and may have a significant input in the drafting of the contract. This is indeed probable, because the essential nature of the contracting relationship is that it is voluntary. In agreeing to this contract, both parties do so by an act of conscious volition, and no doubt both expect tangible benefits from so doing.

The contract, of course, is more than a sheaf of paper. This is only its explicit form, and when we talk of writing a contract the language used is partly metaphorical. Even from the start, much of a contract is implicit, involving tacit understandings and agreements that are not written down, but which powerfully govern conduct because of convention, societal norms, taboos and ethical and moral presumptions. As the contracting relationship develops, so does the implicit contract, until a point is reached at which the practice of contracting has more operational significance than the clauses of a written contract. Further, as this contract develops, given the desire of both parties to promote their own interests, the relationship between them more closely approximates to its desired, ideal or even optimal form.

The qualitative analysis of this volume has examined in considerable microeconomic detail how this contracting process takes place. The qualitative methods deployed are particularly well suited to looking at relationships. Thus matters of judgement, opinions, motivations, attitudes, drives, personality, and much more besides constitute the raw materials of the analysis. These data have to be elicited by a person-to-person social transaction. Thus the research procedures have involved extensive fieldwork. In analysing these data with the intention of conveying meaning, seeking understanding, providing explanation, and illustrating theory, the raw materials I have used are these attitudes and opinions themselves. For that reason, within this book they have been handled as formally as one would handle numbers in quantitative analysis. Although quantitative measures have by no means been abandoned, they are part of the qualitative analysis itself. To illustrate, my interest is not so much in what the target rate of return is, considered as a quantitative measure, but rather in how decisions are made about how to reach a target, how intermediate outcomes are used to modify targets, and how final outcomes are used to create a distribution of payoffs.

Although no stranger to either theories of industrial organization (Reid 1987) or the econometric analysis of small business units (Reid 1993), it seems to me that both approaches, while valuable, and indeed perhaps of central importance, are incomplete. They fail to grapple with the microeconomic fine structure which governs relationships at the level of single individuals and single firms. Principal–agent analysis itself has theoretical categories, like 'information', 'risk', 'effort', etc., which scarcely meet scientific standards of mensuration. Further, the extant statement of the theory is a collection of special cases that are very sensitive to assumptions about information asymmetry, monitoring and attitude to risk, giving it the appearance of irrelevance to any realistic empirical context. The purpose of this volume, following the methodological precepts of Yin (1984, 1993), is to take measurement issues seriously, to embed them in the behavioural relationship between investor and investee, and thereby to treat applied principal–agent analysis at some level of generality, using solidly grounded evidence.

When I first embarked upon this endeavour, the research agenda was adjudged impossible or too ambitious by many of the expert opinions I plumbed. It was felt that ports of entry into the field would be closed to me; that deal sensitivity would be so acute that investors and investees would be unwilling to talk; that principal–agent analysis was a purely mathematical exercise, not suited to empirical contexts; that qualitative methods gave one negligible empirical leverage over data compared to quantitative methods; and that, even if all these proved not to be true, it would be an impossible task to deal with the complex data so generated in a sufficiently coherent fashion that it would demonstrate how principal–agent relationships worked in the real world.

It is for others to judge whether I have fully achieved my research goals, but it is self-evident that there has been more than a measure of success. I discovered willing and kindly 'gatekeepers' or 'high communicators' who were effective as facilitators of field contacts; investors and investees spoke freely and fully, trusting me to publish only when deal sensitivity was long spent; the principal–agent approach proved amenable to instrumentation along social science lines, thanks to the important lead given by the work of Sapienza (1989); qualitative data became the principal form of evidence, and were readily integrated with quantitative evidence using a new database methodology (Reid 1992); and the vast body of evidence gathered, much of it textual, proved amenable to analysis, though not without a considerable intellectual struggle, in both 'within site' and 'cross site' forms, thanks largely to the design of both the instrumentation and the database. I was fortunate, in bringing all this to conclusion, in having knowledgeable co-workers, excellent research assistance, and uncommonly generous cooperation from all whom I met in the venture capital industry.

The value of what has been achieved within the covers of this book, as judged against the research agenda set out above, is, to be faithful to my methodology, very much in the mind of the reader. However, I should like to conclude by highlighting the features of this book that, as it unfolded in the surprising way that such products of the mind do, struck me as both distinctly less than obvious to those who have not trodden my research path, and also of evident usefulness in achieving a better understanding of real contracting relationships within the 'social laboratory' of the venture capital industry. If this might stimulate further analysis, so much the better; but even if no more than superior understanding of investor and investee relations has been achieved, I would think I have obtained much the better of the 'research bargain'.

The first feature of note is, I think, the close attention to what is meant by information in an agency context. This book suggests that the management accountancy perspective on information (see Ezzamel and Hart 1987) is valuable, and provides a rich and highly organized 'information set' upon which economic agents can predicate their decision-making. The second is that classical and judgemental evaluations of risk can be usefully combined in risk assessment for decision-making, of which investment appraisal is an important example. The third is that the seeking of optimality by economic agents operating with incomplete information in risky environments is a practical as well as theoretical goal, which is often achieved, but usually in a unique fashion. In that sense, there is no one best configuration of investor and investee. It would not be paradoxical to summarize this third point by saying that the way best to proceed is to proceed to the best. The fourth is that monitoring and control devices do have a practical edge, which promotes efficiency in the way predicted by agency analysis. But they also support the emergence of efficient non-incentivized behaviour as the implicit contracting mode takes over from the explicit, and relationships based more on trust and affiliation emerge (see Sapienza and Korsgaard 1996). This book started with a quote from John Reid's *The Scot's Gard'ner* (1683). Let me finish with another, equally appropriate to the venture capital world: 'By right contrivance, whereby you do your works both orderly and cheap, you may improve your estates to best advantage both in Profite and Pleasure.'

APPENDICES ON INSTRUMENTATION

APPENDIX A

SEMI-STRUCTURED INTERVIEW (SSI) SCHEDULE FOR INVESTOR (**P**)

UNIVERSITY OF ST ANDREWS

DEPARTMENT OF ECONOMICS
ST SALVATOR'S COLLEGE
ST ANDREWS
FIFE KY16 9AL
SCOTLAND UK

CRIEFF
Centre for Research into Industry,
Enterprise, Finance and the Firm
Professor Gavin C. Reid (Director)

Telephone: St Andrews (xxxx) xxxxx ext: xxx
Fax: (xxxx) xxxxx

Date

Dear

We are jointly involved in a study of the relationship between venture capital investors and those of their investees who are mature small firms. Our main focus of interest is on risk management and information-handling. We will be using a framework known as agency analysis, which is a new way of looking at commercial contractual relationships. We believe it is both fruitful for research, and for practitioners like you who are no doubt keeping an eye open for new ideas that may be useful in improving the conduct of your business.

We would seek to conduct an interview of an hour or so with you, which examines the nature of your business, and the way in which you structure relationships with investee firms. We would also wish to interview a sample of your investee firms. In this way we can piece together the jigsaw of risk management and information-handling from both points of view. This will enable us to reach new and useful conclusions about efficient contracting.

We think you and your investees will find that this new structured way of looking at your business gives you fresh insights. At the end of the study we would provide you with a summary report. At all times confidentiality will be respected. No individual identities will be revealed, and conclusions reached are based on average tendencies for the sample as a whole, rather than specific cases.

For your information, I am attaching two items. First, a list of agenda items to be used in the interview we would hope to conduct with you. Secondly, a list of basic data which it may help you to have close at hand at the time of interview. We do very much hope you are willing to agree to this interview. One of us will be contacting you by telephone in the near future.

Yours sincerely

CRIEFF
Department of Economics
University of St Andrews

AGENDA OUTLINE

1. Risk management

1.1 Chance outcomes and sure prospects
1.2 Offsetting good outcomes against bad
1.3 Effects of new investee on overall risk management
1.4 Sharing risk with the investee

2. Information-handling

2.1 Information types relevant to investee relationship
2.2 Differences in information between investor and investee
2.3 Ways of aligning information of investor and investee
2.4 Ways of reducing information selection
2.5 Correspondence of information with reality
2.6 Effects of costs on information acquisition

3. Trading risk and information

3.1 Extent of risk-sharing with investee
3.2 Extent of information-sharing with investee
3.3 Exchanging information for risk-bearing
3.4 Effects of risk-sharing on effort
3.5 Effects of size of equity stake on effort
3.6 Discriminating between investees on efficiency grounds
3.7 Designing contract with investee to achieve efficiency

APPENDIX A

BASIC DATA

It would help us in our interviewing if you made available to us the following data. They are probably contained in your firm's current documentation, so if it would save your time, we could transcribe the data if you could provide us with the documents. Many thanks for your cooperation.

1. Type of business (e.g. subsidiary of bank or corporation) ....
2. Industry preference (e.g. biotechnology) ....
3. Geographical preference (e.g. USA, Europe) ....
4. Date established ....
5. Number of proposals received per year ....
6. Number of proposals reviewed per year ....
7. Number of proposals accepted (i.e. invested in) per year ....
8. Number of employees ....
9. Number of full-time venture capital executives ....
10. Value of venture capital funds managed ....
11. Value at cost of total funds invested ....
12. Value at valuation of total funds invested ....
13. Value of funds available to invest ....
14. Value of minimum investment considered ....
15. Smallest, largest and average investment made ....
16. Per cent of investees who are start-ups, developments, buyouts ....
17. Minimum and maximum equity stake ....
18. Type and level of fees ....
19. Preferred exit route ....
20. Timescale for investment ....
21. Per cent of investments as sole, lead, consortium ....
22. Degree of involvement by frequency of reporting ....
23. Degree of involvement by representation on board ....
24. Required internal rate of return on investments ....
25. Per cent of investments in which equity stake can be bought back ....
26. Weeks from proposal to completion of investment ....

[N.B. Many of these questions are answered in standard directories like the VCR guide: your entry may be of help.]

UNIVERSITY OF ST ANDREWS

DEPARTMENT OF ECONOMICS
ST SALVATOR'S COLLEGE
ST ANDREWS
FIFE KY16 9AL
SCOTLAND UK

CRIEFF
Centre for Research into Industry,
Enterprise, Finance and the Firm
Professor Gavin C. Reid (Director)

Telephone: St Andrews (xxxx) xxxxx ext: xxx
Fax: (xxxx) xxxxx

Frontpiece

VENTURE CAPITAL PROJECT

SEMI-STRUCTURED INTERVIEW SCHEDULE FOR VENTURE CAPITAL INVESTOR

Company code

Name of interviewer ____________________

Company code ____________________

Date of interview ____________________

Time interview started ____________________

Time interview concluded ____________________

Signature of interviewer at conclusion of case ____________________

Preamble

[Before proceeding to this preamble, the interviewer should have completed the Basic Data sheet. Once this has been accomplished the content of this preamble should be explained to the respondent.]

INTERVIEW PREAMBLE

Thank you for helping us with the Basic Data and now for agreeing to this interview. It is conducted on the basis of strict confidentiality. It will work through an agenda, or list of headings. This outline agenda should help give you a general idea of how the interview will proceed.

[Hand respondent the agenda outline overleaf.]

As the agenda outline indicates, we are concerned with your relationship with investee firms within a principal/agent framework. You, as principal, can determine aspects of your relationship with an investee firm, as agent. I wish to look at this relationship in terms of risk management, information-handling, and the trading of risk and information.

SSI SCHEDULE FOR INVESTOR

(Respondent's copy: may be left with respondent)

AGENDA OUTLINE

1. Risk management

1.1 Chance outcomes and sure prospects
1.2 Offsetting good outcomes against bad
1.3 Effects of new investee on overall risk management
1.4 Sharing risk with the investee

2. Information-handling

2.1 Information types relevant to investee relationship
2.2 Differences in information between investor and investee
2.3 Ways of aligning information of investor and investee
2.4 Ways of reducing information selection
2.5 Correspondence of information with reality
2.6 Effects of costs on information acquisition

3. Trading risk and information

3.1 Extent of risk-sharing with investee
3.2 Extent of information-sharing with investee
3.3 Exchanging information for risk-bearing
3.4 Effects of risk-sharing on effort
3.5 Effects of size of equity stake on effort
3.6 Discriminating between investees on efficiency grounds
3.7 Designing contract with investee to achieve efficiency

(Administrator's copy:
retain during interview)

AGENDA OUTLINE

1. Risk management

1.1 Chance outcomes and sure prospects
1.2 Offsetting good outcomes against bad
1.3 Effects of new investee on overall risk management
1.4 Sharing risk with the investee

2. Information-handling

2.1 Information types relevant to investee relationship
2.2 Differences in information between investor and investee
2.3 Ways of aligning information of investor and investee
2.4 Ways of reducing information selection
2.5 Correspondence of information with reality
2.6 Effects of costs on information acquisition

3. Trading risk and information

3.1 Extent of risk-sharing with investee
3.2 Extent of information-sharing with investee
3.3 Exchanging information for risk-bearing
3.4 Effects of risk-sharing on effort
3.5 Effects of size of equity stake on effort
3.6 Discriminating between investees on efficiency grounds
3.7 Designing contract with investee to achieve efficiency

SSI SCHEDULE FOR INVESTOR

SECTION 1

RISK MANAGEMENT

1.1 Chance outcomes and sure prospects

To what extent do you judge possible outcomes of your investment involvement to be more or less likely?

[Probe on: possible exit route categories; e.g. investee firm does well, does badly or just survives, with an idea of the chances of each of these outcomes.]

I should like you to look at this card, which asks how you compare chance outcomes with sure prospects.

[Hand respondent Card 1, and ask for a choice to be made.]

Now I should like to enquire into the extent to which you use expected values or 'certainty equivalents' in project evaluation. Could you look at this card.

[Hand respondent Card 2, and ask for a choice to be made.]

1.2 Offsetting good outcomes against bad

If you have a set of investee involvements, to what extent do you think that chance good outcomes with some of them, can be balanced against chance bad outcomes with others?

[Probe: Do you think actions can affect the chances of success in some measure? To what extent is chance irreducible?]

Are there methods you adopt to try and bring about the offsetting of good outcomes against bad?

[Probe on: avoidance of many single sector or single technology involvements.]

What is the least number of investee firms you would wish to have in your portfolio?

[Probe on: effects that investee numbers are likely to have on risk management.]

1.3 Effects of new investee on overall risk management

In your acquiring of new investees, to what extent do you evaluate their chances of doing well rather than badly in relation to the returns they may promise?

In screening potential new investees, do you have in mind how they will fit in with your existing portfolio of investees?

[Probe on their consequences for overall risk management, in terms of: mix of modest-return/low-risk investees and high-return/high-risk investees; sectoral and regional composition, with a view to approximating to zero correlation across sectors or regions.]

1.4 Sharing risk with the investee

To what extent do you consider your investees are motivated to have you involved in their businesses through their desire to share risk with you?

[Probe on: (a) you as a possessor of a diversified portfolio, with (b) your investee as less diversified and hence more exposed to risk.]

How far would you be willing to go in bearing risk for the investee?

[Probe on: willingness to pay a fixed payoff to the investee in place of a random payoff at exit.]

To what extent do you think that your willingness to bear risk for the investee affects his effort level?

[Probe on: extent to which requiring investee to continue to bear some risk maintains his enthusiasm for the business; e.g. if investee bore no risk, having a guaranteed sum on exit, would you largely assume control, on the assumption that without this action, effort may be low?]

APPENDIX A

SECTION 2

INFORMATION-HANDLING

2.1 Information types relevant to investee relationship

What accounting information do you receive from investees?

[Probe on: availability of advisory documentation for investees on this; if possible, seek copies.]

How does this information received from investees differ over time (e.g. by longevity of relationship) and among investees (e.g. by sector of activity, or by perceived efficiency)?

[Probe on: how and why such differences arise.]

Do you have direct access to your investees' accounting systems?

[Probe on: the form this access takes; e.g. in terms of frequency, detail, type of accounts involved.]

Do you vet your investees' accounting systems?

[Probe on: forms this vetting takes, purposes for which it is done, and factors which limit its scope.]

2.2 Differences in information between investor and investee

What informational advantage, if any, do you think the investee has over you?

[Probe on: specific types of advantage; e.g. production, markets.]

What informational advantage, if any, do you think you have over the investee?

[Probe on: specific types of advantage; e.g. capital restructuring, investment appraisal.]

2.3 *Ways of aligning information of investor and investee*

When you meet with investees, do you discuss what types of information would be useful for both of you to share freely?

In some sense, do you trade your information or knowledge (e.g. on best forms of capital structure) with investees' information or knowledge (e.g. of emerging best practice technologies)?

2.4 Ways of reducing information selection

Preamble [*spoken*]: Information, even if it corresponds with reality, may be presented selectively. Thus only parts of it may be passed on, and hints about logical connections between components of data may be omitted. There may be reasons for doing this (e.g. control) or a protocol that dictates this (e.g. only supply information on a 'need to know' basis).

To what extent is there selection, in the above sense, in the information that you provide to investees?

[Probe on: types of information most subject to selection (e.g. timescale of involvement, required rate of return); and on omitted logical connections (e.g. between riskiness and required rate of return).]

To what extent do you think that investees provide you with information which is selective, in the above sense?

[Probe on: types of information most subject to selection (e.g. technical know-how, labour relations, market prospects); and on omitted logical connections (e.g. between pricing or marketing strategies and market penetration).]

2.5 *Correspondence of information with reality*

Preamble [*spoken*]: The previous section looked at problems of deliberate selection in information. By contrast, the interest now is in the lack of correspondence between information used and the reality they are meant to reflect.

To what extent do you encounter problems in using your current information sources to get to grips with the reality that governs the relationship with your investee?

[Probe on: the difficulties of matching up accounting data on profitability, cash-flow, etc., with actual performance.]

To what extent do you find that the information an investee returns to you fails to convey what the investee intends?

[Probe on: extent to which investee may use unfamiliar reporting conventions (e.g. engineering or production based, rather than economic or accounting based), or unfamiliar 'trade practice' jargon.]

To what extent are you willing to influence the audit of your investees' accounting systems?

[Probe on: ways in which this influence might be brought to bear.]

2.6 Effects of costs on information acquisition

Preamble [*spoken*]: As a general rule, no information is available at zero cost. However, some types of information are more costly than others. One has to balance the value of extra information against the costs of getting it.

To what extent are you deterred from more extensive information gathering by the costs of acquiring it (e.g. more frequent attendance at board meetings) or of processing it (e.g. analysing managerial accounts at monthly, rather than quarterly, intervals)?

SSI SCHEDULE FOR INVESTOR

SECTION 3

TRADING RISK AND INFORMATION

3.1 Extent of risk-sharing with investee

Given your diversified structure, do you feel you are better equipped to handle risk than your investees?

[Probe on: whether investor feels his advantage goes beyond mere diversification to wider skills of risk management, conceived of as a cultivated ability.]

3.2 *Extent of information-sharing with investee*

Do you regard all information as open to investees, or do you as principal keep some information confidential?

[Probe on: types of information kept confidential.]

To what extent does the investee retain the right to confidentiality over certain types of information to which it has access (e.g. production techniques, market and sales forecasts)?

Would you regard a completely full and free exchange of information as practical and desirable, or would you stop short of this?

[Probe on: advantage of full information, or on advantages of stopping short of a full and free exchange of information.]

3.3 Exchanging information for risk-bearing

To what extent are you willing to bear greater risk for your investee, other things being equal, if your investee is willing to provide you with better information?

[Probe on: the forms that better information might take. For example, is it more speedily returned, produced in a form which is easily assimilated, or of an inside knowledge or trade secret form?]

Do you have a sense that for any given investee there is a sort of menu or trade-off between your risk bearing and your investee's information provision?

[Probe on: extent to which, should such a menu exist, one point on it is mutually perceived to be the most efficient.]

3.4 *Effects of risk-sharing on effort*

To what extent does the fact that both you and your investee face risky or uncertain prospects have a bearing on your investee's effort?

[Probe on: propensity of investee to attribute lucky good outcomes to his own effort and unlucky poor outcomes to bad luck.]

In your experience, is there a temptation for the investee to reduce his effort once he has agreed an arrangement with you that spreads his business risk?

[Probe on: specific examples of such effects, if any; whether investor has put in place mechanisms to mitigate this possible effect, and if so, how successfully.]

Would you say there was an ideal, or optimal, level of risk that you should let your investee bear?

[Probe on: how risk-bearing should be distributed if there is no such ideal; or how it is distributed, and why, if there is such an ideal.]

3.5 Effects of size of equity stake on effort

What are the main factors governing the equity stake you are willing to take in an investee?

[Probe on: Does the elicitation of the investee's effort come high on your list of important factors?]

Do you use your equity participation in a flexible way to affect effort?

[Probe on: the use of performance-linked equity and options. Obtain detail, and documentation if possible.]

Do you have incentive-based equity involvement with investees which may push ownership towards you in bad outcomes and towards the investee in good outcomes?

[Probe on: How does this scheme work? Do you have documentation on it?]

3.6 Discriminating between investees on efficiency grounds

To what extent do you give most favoured treatment to your most efficient investees?

[Probe on: the nature of this favoured treatment, how it is modified by efficiency, and how efficiency of investees is measured.]

To the extent that some investees are more favoured than others, how does this affect the behaviour of your investees?

[Probe on: extent to which investees may try to circumvent differential treatment. If they did, would you resist this?]

3.7 Designing contract with investee to achieve efficiency

To what extent are the contracts you agree with investees based on understandings or trust (so-called implicit contracts) and to what extent are they based on formal legal documents (so-called explicit contracts)?

[Probe on: costs of explicit contracting and litigability of explicit contracts; potential vagueness of implicit contracts and problems of enforceability. Ask for copies of agreements, if possible.]

To what extent do you aim to get a best, ideal or optimal equity involvement with your investee?

[Probes: does this optimum change over the duration of the relationship; are there many optima; can such an optimum be considered in isolation from other factors (e.g. risk, incentives, monitoring)?]

What do you aim to achieve in terms of the ideal relationship with an investee?

[Probe on: capital structure, risk-sharing, information-sharing, rate of return, reputation, effort elicitation.]

CONCLUSION

That concludes the interview. Thank you for assisting us. I should stress that all information provided is treated in the strictest confidence. The specific identities of investors or firms is of no importance to our study. We shall send you a summary account of our research at a later date.

In order to further develop our research in a way that I think you could find illuminating, it would very much help us if you would provide us with a sample of one or more of your investees. They should be chosen to be representative of your investee base, and we would wish to approach them with a view to looking at the other side (i.e. agent side) of the principal/agent relationship. Your assistance in this matter would be much appreciated.

I hope this outline schedule of the sorts of issues we would wish to pursue with investees will encourage you to help us in this respect.

[Hand respondent attached outline]

[*Please leave with investor after interview*]

AGENDA OUTLINE FOR INVESTEE

1. Risk management

1.1 Defining risk
1.2 Modifying risk
1.3 Communicating risk
1.4 Risk-sharing and motivation

2. Information-handling

2.1 Methods of performance evaluation
2.2 Budgetary intervals
2.3 Capital investment appraisal
2.4 Costing
2.5 Reporting error

3. Trading risk and information

3.1 Advantages in risk-handling
3.2 Flow of information
3.3 Important attributes of parties to contract
3.4 Performance criteria and ownership

4. Business characteristics

4.1 Size measures
4.2 Capital structure
4.3 Desired returns
4.4 Expected exit

CARD 1

Suppose a project that you were contemplating backing would give rise to a return almost immediately, or not at all. For example, a geophysical company may take test drillings for a precious ore which may yield an immediate return if evidence of the ore is found, or a zero return if it is not. Suppose the value is £10m. if drilling is successful. Suppose further that previous geophysical evidence indicates that only one in ten drillings give positive results. I should like to know how you would evaluate the worth of this project. Assume drilling costs are negligible.

(a) How relevant to your evaluation of the worth of this project is the fact that the drillings may, or may not, be successful:

Not at all	[ ]
Moderately	[ ]
Very?	[ ]

[*Please tick as appropriate*]

(b) Which of the following do you think best represents the approximate value of the drilling project, before the results come in:

£0 (i.e. zero)	[ ]
£500,000	[ ]
£1m.	[ ]
£2m.	[ ]
£3m.	[ ]
£4m.	[ ]
£5m.	[ ]
£6m.	[ ]
£7m.	[ ]
£8m.	[ ]
£9m.	[ ]
£10m.	[ ]
£11m.	[ ]
£12m.?	[ ]

[*Please tick as appropriate*]

CARD 2

We saw in Card 1 that *chance outcomes* do not happen inevitably: they may or may not happen. For example, a project may promise a good return in its first year, if all goes well, but may yield a poor return if luck runs against it. One can attach *chances*, or a *probability*, to chance outcomes. For example, there may be chances of 7/10 of getting a good return on a project and of 3/10 of getting a poor return.

Sure prospects happen inevitably. For example, a government may promise to redeem a bond at a certain value, and you know there is no question of default: you are sure you will receive that value.

Suppose, then, that you had to choose between two situations, A and B:

(a) Situation A offers either £1m. or £3m.: with a 9 in 10 chance of getting the £1m. and a 1 in 10 chance of getting the £3m.
(b) Situation B offers £1.2m. for sure.

Which would you prefer?

A to B	[ ]
or	
B to A	[ ]
Indifferent between A and B?	[ ]

[*Please tick as appropriate*]

APPENDIX B

ADMINISTERED QUESTIONNAIRE (AQ) FOR MATURE SMALL FIRMS (A)

UNIVERSITY OF ST ANDREWS

DEPARTMENT OF ECONOMICS
ST SALVATOR'S COLLEGE
ST ANDREWS
FIFE KY16 9AL
SCOTLAND UK

CRIEFF
Centre for Research into Industry,
Enterprise, Finance and the Firm
Professor Gavin C Reid (Director)

Telephone: St Andrews (xxxx) xxxxx ext: xxx
Fax: (xxxx) xxxxx

Date

Dear

We are jointly involved in a study of the relationship between venture capital investors and those of their investees who are mature small firms. Our main focus of interest is on risk management and information-handling. We will be using a framework known as agency analysis, which is a new way of looking at commercial contractual relationships. We believe it is both fruitful for research, and for businessmen like you who are no doubt keeping an eye open for new ideas that may be useful in the more effective running of your business. We would seek to conduct an interview with you at your place of work which examines the nature of your business, and the relationship it bears with your venture capital investor. It has been suggested to us by your venture capital investor, whom we have already interviewed on this topic, that you might be willing also to give us an interview. We think that you and your investor will find this new structured way of looking at your business gives you fresh insights. At the end of the study we would provide you with a summary report. No individual identities will be revealed, and conclusions reached are based on average tendencies for the sample as a whole, rather than specific cases. For your information, on the reverse side of this letter you will find two items. First, a list of agenda items to be discussed in the interview we would hope to conduct with you. Secondly, a list of basic data which it would help you to have close at hand at the time of interview. The interview itself will only take about an hour, and we very much hope that you will agree to participate. One of us will be contacting you by telephone in the near future to arrange the interview with you.

Yours sincerely

CRIEFF
Department of Economics
University of St Andrews

AGENDA OUTLINE

1. **Risk management**
2. **Information-handling**
3. **Trading risk and information**
4. **Business characteristics**

BASIC DATA REQUIRED

1. How many years have you been in business?...
2. Define your main line of business...
3. At what time intervals do you recalculate your key budgets? ....
4. What discount rate do you use in capital investment appraisal?....................
5. What payback method do you use in capital investment appraisal? ....
6. How many full-time employees do you have?...
7. What are your annual sales? ....
8. What are your net assets (i.e. fixed assets + current assets – liabilities)? [Here, a range or rough figures will do.]...
9. What were your net profits after tax in the last tax year? [Here, a range or rough figures will do.]...
10. What is your recent history of equity holding in the firm (e.g. high, low and current values)?...
11. What has been your debt/equity ratio before and after involvement with the venture capital investor?..
12. What proportion of share capital do you own? ....
13. What is your current rate of return (i.e. net profit after tax divided by total owners' capital employed, including reserves and retained profits)?............
14. What was your rate of return to be by the time of exit from your relationship with the venture capital investor? ....

APPENDIX B

Code number

VENTURE CAPITAL PROJECT

ADMINISTERED QUESTIONNAIRE FOR MATURE SMALL FIRMS

Interviewer's name ______________________________

(Please PRINT)

Date and time of interview ______________________________

NAME OF RESPONDENT ______________________________

(Please PRINT)

FIRM (if relevant) ______________________________

____

____

Telephone number ______________________________

FIRM'S TRADE ______________________________

Interviewer's signature and date ______________________________

Date when case complete ______________________________

A. PREAMBLE

Good Morning/Afternoon. My name is .... I shall be conducting the interview today, with my colleague taking notes. Our earlier letter explains our purpose. Put briefly, our main focus of interest is on risk management and information-handling. We will be using a framework known as agency analysis, which is a new way of looking at commercial contractual relationships. We believe it is both fruitful for research, and for businessmen like you who are no doubt keeping an eye open for new ideas that may be useful in the more effective running of your business.

At the end of the study we will provide you with a summary report. At all times confidentiality will be respected. No individual identities will be revealed, and conclusions reached are based on average tendencies for the sample as a whole, rather than specific cases. May we now proceed with the interview?

0.1 How many years have you been running your business?

0.2 How would you define your main line of business (e.g. provision of nursing home care, supply of printed circuit boards)?

B. RISK MANAGEMENT

1.1 Do you think that the outcome (e.g. in terms of the value of your firm at exit) of your relationship with your investor has an element of chance or luck in it (i.e. it might work out well if the luck runs with you, or it might work out badly if luck runs against you)?

Yes [ ]
No [ ]

1.2 I should like you to look at this card, which asks how you compare chance outcomes with sure prospects.

[*Hand respondent Card 1.2 and ask for a choice to be given*]

1.3 When you contemplate a new project, do you consider the possibility that whether or not it gives you a net profit is partly a matter of chance?

Yes [ ] *Go to Question 1.3.1*
No [ ] *Go to Question 1.3.2*

1.3.1 Would you adjust your net profit figure by a certain amount (i.e. would you attach a risk discount to it) to take account of this chance element?

Yes [ ]
No [ ]

1.3.2 I should like you to look at this card, which asks how you would value an order which is subject to chance.

[*Hand respondent Card 1.3.2 and ask for a choice to be made*]

1.4 Do you think you are a high-risk or a low-risk type of business venture?

High-risk [ ]
Low-risk [ ]

1.4.1 Do you think there are things that you can do to limit or modify your exposure to risk?

Yes [ ] *Go to Question 1.4.1.1*
No [ ] *Go to Question 1.5*

1.4.1.1 If *Yes*, could you give some brief examples:

____

____

____

1.5 In representing your firm's potential to an investor do you attempt to communicate to him the level of risk that your business is subject to?

Yes [ ]
No [ ]

1.5.1 Do you think that the potential investor tends to underestimate or overestimate the risk inherent in your business?

Under [ ] *Go to Question 1.5.1.1*
Over [ ] *Go to Question 1.5.1.2*
Neither [ ] *Go to Question 1.6*

1.5.1.1 If *Under*: Why do you think this is so?

____

____

____

____

1.5.1.2 If *Over*: Why do you think this is so?

____

____

____

____

1.6 In seeking to become the investee of a venture capital investor, was the fact that he would share some business risk with you:

Important [ ]
Unimportant [ ]
Irrelevant? [ ]

1.7 Would you find it attractive for an agreed fixed sum to be paid to you by the venture capitalist in return for his involvement, rather than to receive your proportion of the value of your firm at exit?

Yes [ ]
No [ ]

1.8 Do you feel that, having had the venture capital investor bear some of your business risk with you, you now find yourself relaxing more in the running of the business?

Yes [ ]
No [ ]

1.9 What do you think has happened to your motivation within the business since the venture capital investor began sharing your business risk? Has it:

Greatly increased [ ]
Increased [ ]
Stayed the same [ ]
Decreased [ ]
Greatly decreased? [ ]

C. INFORMATION-HANDLING

2.1 I should like you to look at this card, which asks you about how you assess your firm's performance.

[*Hand respondent Card 2.1 and ask for a choice to be made*]

2.2 Thank you. Now I should like you to look at this next card, which asks you about the managerial actions you take and which actions you report back to the venture capital investor.

[*Hand respondent Card 2.2 and ask for a choice to be made*]

2.3 Next, would you look at this card which compares the state of your knowledge to that of the venture capital investor.

[*Hand respondent Card 2.3 and ask for a choice to be made*]

2.4 Now I should like to identify the form your budget takes. For each, I should like to know your normal interval (in months) between setting the relevant budget, both *before* and *after* your involvement with a venture capital investor.

Form of budget	*Original interval (in months)*	*New interval (after VCI contract)*
(a) Profit and loss account	______	______
(b) Cash flow	______	______
(c) Balance sheet	______	______
(d) Head count	______	______
(e) Capital budget	______	______
(f) Other (please specify) ______	______	______

2.5 Which of the following elements of costs do you attribute to products? Could you say which are new since venture capital involvement?

	Attributable cost		*New since VCI contract*
(a)	Direct material	[ ]	[ ]
(b)	Direct labour	[ ]	[ ]
(c)	Production overhead	[ ]	[ ]
(d)	Distribution costs	[ ]	[ ]
(e)	Sales costs	[ ]	[ ]
(f)	Administration costs	[ ]	[ ]
(g)	Other (please specify)	[ ]	[ ]

____

2.5.1 Are product costs actual, or are they standard?

Actual [ ]
Standard [ ]

[*Prompt: predetermined estimates of what costs should be*]

2.5.2 Do you distinguish between fixed and variable costs?

Yes [ ]
No [ ]

2.5.3 Are accountants involved in costing at the design stage?

Yes [ ]
No [ ]

2.6 Could you look at this card, which enquires into the capital investment techniques you use?

[*Hand respondent Card 2.6*]

If (b) or (c) checked on Card 2.6:

2.6.1 What discount rate do you use in your capital investment appraisal? ____

____

[*Prompt: You may give a range, or a 'guesstimate' if a precise figure is hard to produce.*]

If (a) checked on Card 2.6:

2.6.2 Could I also ask you what payback period you use?________________

[*Prompt: Again, a range or 'guesstimate' would do, if you have no exact figure.*]

2.7 To what extent are the following classes of information subject to distortion or error in reporting them back to the venture capital investor?

Class of information	*Not at all*	*Slightly*	*Markedly*
(a) Product or service	[ ]	[ ]	[ ]
(b) Market	[ ]	[ ]	[ ]
(c) Production	[ ]	[ ]	[ ]
(d) Financial data	[ ]	[ ]	[ ]
(e) Personnel data	[ ]	[ ]	[ ]

2.7.1 If for any of these you have replied '*Markedly*', could you say briefly why this is so and what implication this may have?

Why?

____

____

____

____

Implication:

____

____

____

____

D. TRADING RISK AND INFORMATION

3.1 Which partner to the contract you have with the venture capital investor is, in your view, better equipped to handle risk?:

(a) Yourself [ ]
(b) The venture capital investor [ ]

3.1.2 Briefly, why do you think this is so?

____

____

____

____

____

3.2 What would you say best characterizes the flow of information which you provide to the venture capital investor? Is it:

(a) Extensive (i.e. full and detailed) [ ]
(b) Measured (i.e. related to requests) [ ]
(c) Limited (i.e. severely edited) [ ]
(d) Sparse (i.e. without scope and detail) [ ]
(e) Non-existent? [ ]

3.2.1 Would you wish to provide more or less information than you have just indicated?

More [ ]
Less [ ]
Neither [ ]

3.2.2 Could you explain briefly why this is so?

____

____

____

____

3.3 In your relationship with the venture capital investor do you feel you retain the right of confidentiality over certain aspects of the running of your business (e.g. patent rights, personnel records)?

Yes [ ] *Go to Question 3.3.1*
No [ ] *Go to Question 3.4*

3.3.1 Briefly, without divulging their contents, what are the areas in which you feel you retain such rights?

____

____

____

3.3.2 Would you desire these areas of confidentiality to become more, or less, extensive?

More [ ]
Less [ ]

3.4 Would you think it advantageous to the running of your business that you became better informed about the operations of your venture capital investor?

Yes [ ] *Go to Question 3.4.1*
No [ ] *Go to Question 3.5*

3.4.1 Briefly, why do you think this would be advantageous?

____

____

____

3.5 I should like you to complete the following card, which asks about the attributes that you think you bring to your relationship with the venture capital investor.

[*Hand respondent Card 3.5*]

3.6 Now could you fill in the next card, which looks at the same attributes from the viewpoint of the venture capital investor.

[*Hand respondent Card 3.6*]

3.7 Finally, as regards attributes, I should like you to complete this next card, which asks you to identify the single most important attribute which you think you bring, and the venture capital investor brings, to your relationship.

[*Hand respondent Card 3.7*]

3.8 What has been the highest and lowest proportion of the equity that you have held in the firm?

High ....
Low ....

[*Prompt: Give a range or 'guesstimate', if precise estimates unavailable.*]

3.8.1 When your equity share was higher in the firm was your commitment to it *more* or *less* than when your equity share was lower?

More [ ]
Less [ ]
The same [ ]

3.8.2 Briefly why do you think this was so?

____

____

____

____

3.9 Are you party to a performance-linked equity scheme with your venture capital investor?

Yes [ ] *Go to Question 3.9.1*
No [ ] *Go to Question 3.9.2*

3.9.1 What proportion of the authorized share capital, which has not yet been issued, might you eventually be able to hold, subject to performance?

....

[*Prompt: Give a range or 'guesstimate' if you cannot give an exact answer.*]

3.9.1.1 Briefly, what performance criterion must your firm meet to bring this about?

___

___

___

___

3.9.2 Do you think that a performance-linked equity scheme would be a good motivator for you?

Yes [ ]
No [ ]

3.10 Do you feel that, in your relationship with the venture capital investor, you have to compete with the other investees for more favoured treatment?

Yes [ ] *Go to Question 3.10.1*
No [ ] *Go to Question 3.11*

3.10.1 Do you, therefore, attempt to put a 'good show' on for your venture capital investor, or do you think the facts speak for themselves?

Good show [ ]
Facts speak [ ]

3.11 In your opinion is the contract you agreed with the venture capital investor largely based on trust or understanding, or is it largely tightly legally defined?

(a) Trust or understanding [ ]
(b) Tightly legally defined [ ]

3.12 In your opinion, is the relationship you currently have with your venture capital investor already close to, or at, a kind of optimum, or is there scope for moving further towards an optimum?

(a) Close to optimum [ ]
(b) Scope for moving towards optimum [ ]

If (b), explain briefly why this is so:

____

____

3.13 I should now like to know what you think are the features of an ideal relationship with your venture capital investor.

[*Hand respondent Card 3.13 and ask for a choice to be made*]

BUSINESS CHARACTERISTICS

We have now come to the last section of the questionnaire. Thank you for bearing with me. I should like to conclude by asking you about characteristics of your business.

4.1 What is the size of your business in terms of:

(a) Full-time employees ....

(b) Sales (annual) ....

(c) Net assets ....

[*Prompt: Fixed assets + current assets – liabilities*]

(d) Net profits (after tax)? ....

[*Prompt: Rough figures, or a range will do*]

4.2 What is your current debt/equity ratio (i.e. your debt or loan capital divided by your equity or share capital)?

....

4.2.1 What was your debt/equity ratio before the involvement of a venture capital investor?

....

4.3 What proportion of the share capital do you own? ....

4.3.1 Has this been deliberately chosen at a level which confers control of the company on you?

Yes [ ]
No [ ]

4.4 Did you receive any 'sweat equity' (i.e. equity received for your effort in getting the business up and running)?

Yes [ ] *Go to Question 4.4.1*
No [ ] *Go to Question 4.5*

4.4.1 What proportion of the total equity was this? ....

[Note to Interviewer: The following question (i.e. 4.5 below) is very important and we seek a response in all cases, even if only a guess]

4.5 What is the current rate of return earned by your business on an annual basis?

....

[*Prompt: Net profit after tax divided by total owners' capital employed, including reserves and retained profits.*]

[*Prompt: You may give a range if you wish or provide a 'guesstimate' if you lack hard facts.*]

4.5.1 And what was your rate of return before involvement with the venture capital investor?

....

4.6 What do you expect your rate of return to be by the time of exit from your relationship with the venture capital investor?

....

4.7 What form do you expect your exit from the relationship to take? Will it be:

(a) Listing on a stock market (e.g. over the counter, unlisted securities market) [ ]
(b) Sale of the company [ ]
(c) Sale of the investor's share to outside purchaser [ ]
(d) Sale of investor's share to you [ ]
(e) Voluntary liquidation [ ]
(f) Receivership [ ]
(g) Other (please specify)? [ ]

....

4.8 How would you rate the importance of the venture capital investor to the fortunes of your business? Was the investor:

Very important [ ]
Moderately important [ ]
Slightly important? [ ]

That completes the interview. May I make a further request for documentation, if possible (e.g. the firm's most recent set of annual accounts, descriptions or histories of it, financial PR). Thank you very much for helping us. Again I can assure you that your replies will be treated with confidentiality. In due course we will send you a general summary of our results.

Thank you again. Goodbye.

CARD 1.2

Suppose you had to choose between two situations, A and B, as follows:

(a) Situation A offers either £1m. or £3m.: with a 9 in 10 chance of getting the £1m. and a 1 in 10 chance of getting the £3m.
(b) Situation B offers £1.2m. for sure.

Which would you prefer?

A to B	[ ]
B to A	[ ]
Indifferent between A and B	[ ]

Thank you. Could you now return this card to the interviewer.

CARD 1.3.2

Suppose you have a customer who might place an order for £1m. either with you or with one of your rivals. He can't decide which firm to choose, so he will toss a coin: heads you win the order; tails your rival wins the order. Before the coin is tossed, what is the value to you of this prospective order?

Is it:

£1m.	[ ]
£$\frac{3}{4}$m.	[ ]
£$\frac{1}{2}$m.	[ ]
£$\frac{1}{4}$m.	[ ]
Zero?	[ ]

Thank you. Could you now return this card to the interviewer.

CARD 2.1

I should like to know which of the following methods of assessing your firm's performance you use, whether this is new since your involvement with the venture capital investor, and whether its results are reported back to the venture capital investor.

	Method of Assessment	*Used*	*New since VCI involved*	*Reported to VCI*
(a)	Sales	[ ]	[ ]	[ ]
(b)	Ratio of sales to investment (i.e. 'investment turnover')	[ ]	[ ]	[ ]
(c)	Return on investment	[ ]	[ ]	[ ]
(d)	Net profit	[ ]	[ ]	[ ]
(e)	Ratio of net profit to assets (i.e. 'net profitability')	[ ]	[ ]	[ ]
(f)	Cash flow	[ ]	[ ]	[ ]
(g)	Wage bill	[ ]	[ ]	[ ]
(h)	Other (please specify.)......................	[ ]	[ ]	[ ]

[*Tick for positive response*]

Thank you. Could you now return this card to the interviewer.

CARD 2.2

Which of the following managerial actions do you take, and for each action (a) is this new since your contractual involvement with the venture capital investor, and (b) do you report the results back to the venture capital investor?

	Action	*Used*	*New since VCI involved*	*Reported to VCI*
(a)	Set financial budgets	[ ]	[ ]	[ ]
(b)	Cost output produced	[ ]	[ ]	[ ]
(c)	Produce information to monitor business	[ ]	[ ]	[ ]
(d)	Make appraisals of capital investments	[ ]	[ ]	[ ]
(e)	Produce financial information for operating decisions	[ ]	[ ]	[ ]
(f)	Produce financial information for strategic decisions	[ ]	[ ]	[ ]
(g)	Control of staff numbers (i.e. headcount)	[ ]	[ ]	[ ]
(h)	Other (please specify)	[ ]	[ ]	[ ]

[*Tick for positive response*]

Thank you. Could you now return this card to the interviewer.

CARD 2.3

You will find below a list of the categories of information that may be relevant to the running of your business. For each that is relevant to you, I should like you to rate the relative extent of the venture capital investor's knowledgeability compared with your own. The scale used runs from 'less' to 'more'.

Category of information	*VCI's knowledge compared to yours*			
	Less	*The same*	*More*	*Not applicable*
(a) Technology	[ ]	[ ]	[ ]	[ ]
(b) Markets	[ ]	[ ]	[ ]	[ ]
(c) Managerial staff	[ ]	[ ]	[ ]	[ ]
(d) Technical staff	[ ]	[ ]	[ ]	[ ]
(e) Budgets	[ ]	[ ]	[ ]	[ ]
(f) Capital structure	[ ]	[ ]	[ ]	[ ]
(g) Business strategy	[ ]	[ ]	[ ]	[ ]
(h) Management accounts	[ ]	[ ]	[ ]	[ ]
(i) Financial accounts	[ ]	[ ]	[ ]	[ ]
(j) Capital investment	[ ]	[ ]	[ ]	[ ]
(k) Supply sources	[ ]	[ ]	[ ]	[ ]
(l) Other (please specify)	[ ]	[ ]	[ ]	[ ]

....

Thank you. Could you now return this card to the interviewer.

CARD 2.6

Which of the following techniques do you use in deciding upon your capital investments? I should also like to know how important they are, and whether they are new since your involvement with venture capital.

Technique		*Importance*				*New since VCI contract*
		Used	*Low*	*Moderate*	*High*	
(a)	Payback	[ ]	[ ]	[ ]	[ ]	[ ]
(b)	Internal rate of return	[ ]	[ ]	[ ]	[ ]	[ ]
(c)	Net present value	[ ]	[ ]	[ ]	[ ]	[ ]
(d)	Accounting rate of return	[ ]	[ ]	[ ]	[ ]	[ ]
(e)	Qualitative assessment	[ ]	[ ]	[ ]	[ ]	[ ]
(f)	Other (please specify)	[ ]	[ ]	[ ]	[ ]	[ ]

....

Thank you. Could you now return this card to the interviewer.

CARD 3.5

How important are the following attributes in explaining what you bring to the relationship with the venture capital investor? I should like you to evaluate them in terms of the undernoted categories:

		Unimportant	*Important*	*Very important*
(a)	Knowledge of product or service	[ ]	[ ]	[ ]
(b)	Knowledge of markets	[ ]	[ ]	[ ]
(c)	Risk-bearing	[ ]	[ ]	[ ]
(d)	Effort	[ ]	[ ]	[ ]
(e)	Financial expertise	[ ]	[ ]	[ ]
(f)	Commitment to the business	[ ]	[ ]	[ ]
(g)	Supply of finance capital	[ ]	[ ]	[ ]

[*Please tick where appropriate*]

Thank you. Could you now return this card to the interviewer.

CARD 3.6

How important are these same attributes in explaining what the venture capital investor brings to the relationship with you? Again, the same categories of evaluation are used:

		Unimportant	*Important*	*Very important*
(a)	Knowledge of product or service	[ ]	[ ]	[ ]
(b)	Knowledge of markets	[ ]	[ ]	[ ]
(c)	Risk-bearing	[ ]	[ ]	[ ]
(d)	Effort	[ ]	[ ]	[ ]
(e)	Financial expertise	[ ]	[ ]	[ ]
(f)	Commitment to the business	[ ]	[ ]	[ ]
(g)	Supply of finance capital	[ ]	[ ]	[ ]
(h)	Other (please specify if possible)	[ ]	[ ]	[ ]

[*Please tick where appropriate*]

Thank you. Could you now return this card to the interviewer.

CARD 3.7

Now by reference to this same list of attributes I should like you to single out the most important *single one* that you think you bring to the relationship, and the most important *single one* that you think the venture capital investor brings to the relationship.

		Most important attribute of:	
		You	*Venture capitalist*
(a)	Knowledge of product or service	[ ]	[ ]
(b)	Knowledge of markets	[ ]	[ ]
(c)	Risk-bearing	[ ]	[ ]
(d)	Effort	[ ]	[ ]
(e)	Financial expertise	[ ]	[ ]
(f)	Commitment to the business	[ ]	[ ]
(g)	Supply of finance capital	[ ]	[ ]
(h)	Other (please specify if possible)	[ ]	[ ]

Thank you. Could you now return this card to the interviewer.

CARD 3.13

How important are the following factors in determining the ideal relationship with your venture capital investor?

		Unimportant	*Important*	*Very important*
(a)	Appropriate capital structure	[ ]	[ ]	[ ]
(b)	Efficient risk-sharing	[ ]	[ ]	[ ]
(c)	Free sharing of information	[ ]	[ ]	[ ]
(d)	Maximum rate of return	[ ]	[ ]	[ ]
(e)	Enhancement of your reputation	[ ]	[ ]	[ ]
(f)	Increasing of your motivation	[ ]	[ ]	[ ]

Thank you. Could you now return this card to the interviewer.

APPENDIX C

TELEPHONE QUESTIONNAIRE (TQ) FOR MATURE SMALL FIRMS (**A**)

UNIVERSITY OF ST ANDREWS

DEPARTMENT OF ECONOMICS
ST SALVATOR'S COLLEGE
ST ANDREWS
FIFE KY16 9AL
SCOTLAND UK

CRIEFF
Centre for Research into Industry,
Enterprise, Finance and the Firm
Professor Gavin C Reid (Director)

Telephone: St Andrews (xxxx) xxxxx ext: xxx
Fax: (xxxx) xxxxx

Date

Dear

We are jointly involved in a study of the relationship between venture capital investors and those of their investees who are mature small firms. Our main focus of interest is on risk management and information-handling. We will be using a framework known as agency analysis, which is a new way of looking at commercial contractual relationships. We believe it is both fruitful for research, and for businessmen like you who are no doubt keeping an eye open for new ideas that may be useful in the more effective running of your business.

We would seek to conduct a telephone interview with you which examines the nature of your business, and the relationship it bears with your venture capital backer. We think that you and your investor will find this new structured way of looking at your business gives you fresh insights. At the end of the study we would provide you with a summary report. No individual identities will be revealed, and conclusions reached are based on average tendencies for the sample as a whole, rather than specific cases.

On the back of this letter, you will find three items which illustrate the sorts of questions you will be asked in the interview. It may help you to fill in these items before the interview. It would also help if you had at hand during the interview basic data on your firm like sales and number of employees. The interview itself will only take about twelve minutes, and we very much hope that you will agree to participate. One of us will be contacting you by telephone in the near future to arrange the interview.

Yours sincerely

CRIEFF
Department of Economics
University of St Andrews

Figure 1

Suppose you had to choose between two situations, A and B, as follows:

(a) Situation A offers either £1m. or £3m.: with a 9 in 10 chance of getting the £1m. and a 1 in 10 chance of getting the £3m.
(b) Situation B offers £1.2m. for sure.

Which would you prefer?

A to B	[ ]
B to A	[ ]
Indifferent between A and B	[ ]

Figure 2

By reference to the following list of attributes I should like you to single out the most important *single one* that you think you bring to the relationship, and the most important *single one* that you think the venture capital investor brings to the relationship.

		Most important attribute of:	
		You	*Venture capitalist*
(a)	Knowledge of product or service	[ ]	[ ]
(b)	Knowledge of markets	[ ]	[ ]
(c)	Risk-bearing	[ ]	[ ]
(d)	Effort	[ ]	[ ]
(e)	Financial expertise	[ ]	[ ]
(f)	Commitment to the business	[ ]	[ ]
(g)	Supply of finance capital	[ ]	[ ]
(h)	Other (please specify if possible)	[ ]	[ ]

Figure 3

How important are the following in determining the ideal relationship with your venture capital investor?

		Unimportant	Important	Very important
(a)	Appropriate capital structure	[ ]	[ ]	[ ]
(b)	Efficient risk-sharing	[ ]	[ ]	[ ]
(c)	Free sharing of information	[ ]	[ ]	[ ]
(d)	Maximum rate of return	[ ]	[ ]	[ ]
(e)	Enhancement of your reputation	[ ]	[ ]	[ ]
(f)	Increasing of your motivation	[ ]	[ ]	[ ]

Code number

VENTURE CAPITAL PROJECT

TELEPHONE INTERVIEW SCHEDULE FOR MATURE SMALL FIRMS

Interviewer's name ______________________________

(Please PRINT)

Date and time of interview ______________________________

NAME OF RESPONDENT ______________________________

(Please PRINT)

FIRM (if relevant) ______________________________

____

____

Telephone number ______________________________

FIRM'S TRADE ______________________________

INTERVIEW STATUS

Call complete [ ]
Call incomplete [ ]
No reply [ ]
No time now – call back [ ]
Not available now – call back [ ]
Interview refused [ ]
Untraceable [ ]

Status notes:

Interviewer's signature and date ______________________________

Date when case complete ______________________________

A. PREAMBLE

Good Morning/Afternoon. My name is .... I am conducting a study with colleagues from the Universities of St Andrews and Edinburgh, which is concerned with the relation between venture capital investors and their investees. Did you receive the letter we recently sent you, explaining our work?

If *Yes*: I wonder then if you would be willing to proceed with the interview that we requested in that letter? It should only take about ten minutes, and of course your replies will be treated in strict confidence. At the end of the project we will post you a summary of our results, which may be useful in appraising your own business. It will help if you have by you the letter we sent, which has Figures 1, 2 and 3 on the back. We shall refer to them shortly.

Go to Question 0.1

If *No*: I am sorry, perhaps there has been a hitch in the mailing. Let me explain to you then what the letter said:

Explain content of letter, then go to rubric under 'Yes' above

0.1 How many years have you been running your business?

___

0.2 How would you define your main line of business (e.g. provision of nursing home care, supply of printed circuit boards)?

___

B. RISK MANAGEMENT

Generally, I shall refer to the venture capital investor as simply, 'the investor'.

1.1 Does the success of the relationship you have with the investor depend on pure chance?

A lot	[ ]
To some degree	[ ]
Not at all	[ ]

1.2 Could I now refer you to Figure 1 on the back of your letter from us. It referred to two situations, A and B. Could I ask you how you replied to this?

[*Prompt: Respondent should have the undernoted before him as Figure 1; if not, you will have to read this to him*]

Suppose you had to choose between two situations, A and B, as follows:

(a) Situation A offers either £1m. or £3m.: with a 9 in 10 chance of getting the £1m. and a 1 in 10 chance of getting the £3m.
(b) Situation B offers £1.2m. for sure.

[*Prompt: I can repeat this for you if you wish*]

Which would you prefer?

A to B	[ ]
B to A	[ ]
Indifferent between A and B	[ ]

1.3 Do you adjust your expected net profit from a project to take account of riskiness?

[*Prompt: Would you attach a risk discount to your net profit?*]

Yes	[ ]
No	[ ]

1.4 Do you tell your investor how risky your business is (e.g. high, low, moderate)?

Yes [ ]
No [ ]

1.4.1 Do you think that the potential investor tends to **under**estimate or **over**-estimate the risk inherent in your business?

Under [ ]
Over [ ]

1.5 In seeking to become the investee of a venture capital investor, was the fact that he would share some business risk with you:

Important [ ]
Unimportant [ ]
Irrelevant? [ ]

1.6 Would you find it attractive for an agreed fixed sum to be paid to you by the venture capitalist in return for his involvement, rather than to receive your proportion of the value of your firm at exit?

Yes [ ]
No [ ]

1.7 Do you feel that having had the venture capital investor bear some of your business risk with you, you now find yourself relaxing more in the running of the business?

Yes [ ]
No [ ]

C. INFORMATION-HANDLING

Again, by 'investor', I mean the venture capital investor.

2.1 I should like to know which of the following types of information you use in assessing your firm's performance.

Type of information	*Used*	*New since VCI involved*	*Reported to VCI*
(a) Profit and loss account	[ ]	[ ]	[ ]
(b) Balance sheet	[ ]	[ ]	[ ]
(c) Cash flow statement	[ ]	[ ]	[ ]
(d) Other (please specify).......................	[ ]	[ ]	[ ]

[*Tick for positive response*]

2.2 I am now going to ask you which of the following managerial actions you take?

Action	*Used*	*New since VCI involved*	*Reported to VCI*
(a) Set financial budgets	[ ]	[ ]	[ ]
(b) Cost output produced	[ ]	[ ]	[ ]
(c) Make appraisals of capital investments	[ ]	[ ]	[ ]
(d) Produce financial information for operating decisions (e.g. which products to sell)	[ ]	[ ]	[ ]
(e) Control of staff numbers (i.e. 'headcounts')	[ ]	[ ]	[ ]
(f) Other (please specify).......................	[ ]	[ ]	[ ]

[*Tick for positive response*]

2.3 Do you think you have greater knowledge than the investor in respect of the following aspects of your business?

		Yes	*No*
(a)	Technology	[ ]	[ ]
(b)	Markets	[ ]	[ ]
(c)	Capital structure	[ ]	[ ]
(d)	Financial performance	[ ]	[ ]
(e)	Future prospects	[ ]	[ ]

2.4 How frequently do you currently set your budget (e.g. monthly, 3 monthly, etc.)?

____

2.4.1 Could you also say how frequently it was done before venture capital involvement?

____

2.5 Which of the following techniques do you use in deciding upon your capital investments?

[*Prompt: For subsidiary questions you may give me a range or guesstimate.*]

Technique	*Used?*	*New since VCI?*		
(a) Payback	[ ]	[ ]	What payback period do you use?	__
(b) Internal rate of return	[ ]	[ ]	What discount rate do you use?	__
(c) Net present value	[ ]	[ ]	What discount rate do you use?	__
(d) Accounting rate of return	[ ]	[ ]		
(e) Qualitative assessment	[ ]	[ ]		
(f) Other (please specify) …………………	[ ]	[ ]		

2.6 I am going to ask you the extent to which the following types of information are subject to error or inaccuracy when you report back to the investor?

Information	*Subject to error?*	*A lot*	*Not much*
(a) Product or service	[ ]	[ ]	[ ]
(b) Market	[ ]	[ ]	[ ]
(c) Production	[ ]	[ ]	[ ]
(d) Financial data	[ ]	[ ]	[ ]
(e) Personnel data	[ ]	[ ]	[ ]

D. TRADING RISK AND INFORMATION

Again, by 'investor', I mean the venture capital investor.

3.1 Which partner to the contract you have with the venture capital investor is, in your view, better equipped to handle risk?

(a) You [ ]
(b) The investor [ ]

3.2 What would you say best characterizes the flow of information which you provide to the investor? Is it:

(a) Extensive (i.e.full and detailed) [ ]
(b) Measured (i.e.related to requests) [ ]
(c) Limited (i.e.severely edited) [ ]
(d) Sparse (i.e.without scope and detail) [ ]
(e) Non-existent? [ ]

3.2.1 Would you wish to provide *more* or *less* information than you have just indicated?

More [ ]
Less [ ]
Neither [ ]

3.3 Do you think it would be advantageous to the running of your business if you became better informed about the operations of your investor?

Yes [ ]
No [ ]

3.4 Could I ask you now to refer to Figure 2 attached to your letter from us? It referred to the most important attributes of both you and the venture capitalist. Could I ask you how you answered that question?

You? ________ [**one** of (a) to (h)]
Venture capitalist? ________ [**one** of (a) to (h)]

[*Prompt: Respondent should have the undernoted before him as Figure 2; if not, you will have to read this to him*]

By reference to the following list of attributes I should like you to single out the most important *single one* that you think you bring to the relationship, and the most important *single one* that you think the venture capital investor brings to the relationship.

		Most important attribute of:	
		You	*Venture capitalist*
(a)	Knowledge of product or service	[ ]	[ ]
(b)	Knowledge of markets	[ ]	[ ]
(c)	Risk-bearing	[ ]	[ ]
(d)	Effort	[ ]	[ ]
(e)	Financial expertise	[ ]	[ ]
(f)	Commitment to the business	[ ]	[ ]
(g)	Supply of finance capital	[ ]	[ ]
(h)	Other (please specify)	[ ]	[ ]

3.5 What has been the highest and lowest proportion of the equity that you have held in the firm?

Highest..

Lowest..

[*Prompt: Give a range or 'guesstimate', if precise estimates are unavailable*]

3.5.1 When your equity share was higher in the firm, was your commitment to it *more* or *less* than when your equity share was lower?

More [ ]
Less [ ]
The same [ ]

3.6 Are you party to a performance-linked equity scheme with your venture capital investor?

Yes [ ] *Go to Question 3.6.1*
No [ ] *Go to Question 3.6.2*

3.6.1 By what percentage can your existing stake be raised through good performance?

____

[*Prompt: Give a range or 'guesstimate' if you cannot give an exact answer*]

3.6.2 Do you think that a performance-linked equity scheme is a good motivator?

Yes [ ]
No [ ]

3.7 In your opinion is the contract you agree with the venture capital investor largely based on trust or understandings or is it largely tightly legally defined?

(a) Trust or understanding [ ]
(b) Tightly legally defined [ ]

3.8 Could I ask you to refer to Figure 3 attached to your letter from us? It referred to determinants of the ideal relationship with your investor. Could I ask you how you answered that question?

[*Prompt: Respondent should have the undernoted before him as Figure 3; if not, you will have to read this to him*]

How important are the following in determining the ideal relationship with your venture capital investor?

	Unimportant	*Important*	*Very important*
(a) Appropriate capital structure	[ ]	[ ]	[ ]
(b) Efficient risk-sharing	[ ]	[ ]	[ ]
(c) Free sharing of information	[ ]	[ ]	[ ]
(d) Maximum rate of return	[ ]	[ ]	[ ]
(e) Enhancement of your reputation	[ ]	[ ]	[ ]
(f) Increasing of your motivation	[ ]	[ ]	[ ]

BUSINESS CHARACTERISTICS

We have now come to the last section of the questionnaire. Thank you for bearing with me. I should like to conclude by asking you about characteristics of your business. Again, when I refer to 'investor', I mean the venture capital investor.

4.1 What is the size of your business in terms of:

(a) Full-time employees ....

(b) Sales (annual) ....

(c) Net assets ....

[*Prompt: fixed assets + current assets – liabilities*]

(d) Net profits (after tax) ....

[*Rough figures, or a range will do*]

4.2 What is your current debt/equity ratio (i.e. your debt or loan capital divided by your equity or share capital)?

....

4.2.1 What was your debt/equity ratio before the involvement of a venture capital investor?

....

4.3 What proportion of the share capital do you own? ....

4.3.1 Has this been deliberately chosen at a level which confers control of the company on you?

Yes [ ]
No [ ]

[Note to interviewer: The following Question (i.e. 4.4 below) is one to which we seek a response in all cases, even if only a guess]

4.4 What is your current rate of return earned by the business on an annual basis?

....

[*Prompt: Net profit after tax divided by total owners' capital employed, including reserves and retained profits*]

[*Prompt: You may give a range if you wish or provide a 'guesstimate' if you lack hard facts*]

4.5 And what was your rate of return before involvement with the venture capital investor?

....

4.6 How would you rate the importance of the investor to the fortunes of your business? Was the investor:

Very important	[ ]
Moderately important	[ ]
Slightly important?	[ ]

That completes the interview. Thank you very much for helping us. Again I can assure you that your replies will be treated with confidentiality. In due course we will send you a general summary of our results.

Thank you again. Goodbye.

REFERENCES

Admati, A.R. and Pfleiderer, P. (1994) 'Robust financial contracting and the role of venture capitalists', *The Journal of Finance* **49** (2): 371–402.

Amit, R., Glosten, L. and Muller, E. (1990) 'Entrepreneurial ability, venture investments and risk sharing', *Management Science*, **36**: 1232–45.

Arnold, J. and Moizer, P. (1984) 'A survey of the methods used by UK investment analysts to appraise investments in ordinary shares', *Accounting and Business Research*, summer.

Arrow, K.J. (1985) 'The economics of agency', in J.W. Pratt and R. Zeckhauser (eds), *Principals and Agents: The Structure of Business*, Boston, Mass.: Harvard Business School Press.

Baiman, S. (1982) 'Agency research in managerial accounting: a survey', *Journal of Accounting Literature*, **1**: 154–209.

Ballweiser, W. (1987) 'Auditing in an agency setting', in G. Bamberg and K. Spremann (eds), *Agency Theory, Information and Incentives*, Berlin: Springer-Verlag, 327–46.

Bamberg, G. and Spremann, K. (eds) (1987) *Agency Theory, Information and Incentives*, Berlin: Springer-Verlag.

Barney, J., Busenitz, L., Fiet, J. and Moesel, D. (1989) 'The structure of venture capital governance: an organizational economic analysis of relations between VC firms and new ventures', *Academy of Management Proceedings*, 64–8.

—— (1994) 'Determinants of a new venture team's receptivity to advice from venture capitalists', in B.A. Kirchoff, W.A. Long, W.E. McMillan, K.H. Vesper and W.E. Wetzel, Jr. (eds), *Frontiers of Entrepreneurship Research 1994*, Wellesley, Mass.: Babson College.

Bowden, R.J. (1994) 'Bargaining, size and return in venture capital funds', *Journal of Business Venturing*, **9**: 307–30.

BPP (1997) *Financial Reporting*, CIMA Study Text, London: BPP Publishing.

Brealey, R.A. and Myers, S.C. (1991) *Principles of Corporate Finance*, 4th edn, New York: McGraw-Hill.

Brigham, E.F. (1992) *Fundamentals of Financial Management*, 6th edn, Fort Worth, Tex.: Dryden Press.

Burgess, R.G. (ed.) (1982) *Field Research: A Source Book and Field Manual*, London: Allen & Unwin.

—— (1984) *In the Field: An Introduction to Field Research*, London: Allen & Unwin.

BVCA (1994, 1995, 1996a) *Directory*, London: Jeffrey Pellin.

—— (1996b) *A Guide to Venture Capital*, London: Jeffrey Pellin.

Bygrave, W.D. and Timmons, J. (1992) *Venture Capital at the Crossroads*, Boston, Mass.: Harvard Business School Press.

Bygrave, W.D., Fast, N., Khoylian, R., Vincent, L. and Hue, W. (1988) 'Rates of return on venture capital investing: a study of 113 funds', in B.A. Kirchoff, W.A. Long, W.E. McMillan, K.H. Vesper and W.E. Wetzel, Jr (eds), *Frontiers of Entrepreneurship Research 1988*, Wellesley, Mass.: Babson College.

Cable, D.M. and Shane, S. (1997) 'A prisoner's dilemma approach to entrepreneur–venture capitalist relationships', *Academy of Management Review*, **22** (1): 142–76.

Carlsson, B. (1987) 'Reflections on "industrial dynamics": the challenge ahead', *International Journal of Industrial Organization*, **5**: 135–48.

Cary, L. (1989) *The VCR Guide to Venture Capital in the UK*, 4th edn, Henley-on-Thames and London: Venture Capital Report/Pitman.

—— (1991) *The VCR Guide to Venture Capital in Europe*, 5th edn, Henley-on-Thames and London: Venture Capital Report/Pitman.

—— (1993) *The VCR Guide to Venture Capital in the UK and Europe*, 6th edn, Henley-on-Thames and London: Venture Capital Report/Management Today.

—— (1995) *The VCR Guide to Venture Capital in the UK and Europe*, 7th edn, Henley-on-Thames: Venture Capital Report.

Cary, L. and Mallinson, J. (eds) (1997) *The VCR Guide to Venture Capital in the UK and Europe*, 8th edn, Henley-on-Thames: Venture Capital Report.

Chan, Y.-S. (1983) 'On the positive role of financial intermediation in allocation of venture capital in a market with imperfect information', *The Journal of Finance*, **38** (5): 1543–68.

Chan, Y.-S., Siegel, D. and Thakor, A.V. (1990) 'Learning, corporate control and performance requirements in venture capital contracts', *International Economic Review*, **31** (2): 365–81.

Chandler, G.N. and Hanks, S.H. (1994) 'Market attractiveness, resource-based capabilities, venture strategies and venture performance', *Journal of Business Venturing*, **9**, 331–49.

Clarke, R. and McGuiness, T. (1987) *The Economics of the Firm*, Oxford: Blackwell.

Cohen, S.I., Loeb, M.P. and Stark, A.W. (1992) 'Separating controllable performance requirements from non-controllable performance: the case of optimal procurement contracting', *Management Accounting Research*, **3**.

Cooper, I.A. and Carleton, W.T. (1979) 'Dynamics of borrower–lender interaction: partitioning final payoff in venture capital finance', *The Journal of Finance*, **34** (2): 517–33.

Curran, J., Stanworth, J. and Watkins, D. (eds) (1986) *The Survival of the Small Firm*, Aldershot: Gower.

Day, J.F.S. (1986) 'The use of annual reports by UK investment analysts', *Accounting and Business Research*, autumn.

Dixon, R. (1991) 'Venture capitalists and the appraisal of investements', *OMEGA International Journal of Management Science*, **19** (5): 333–44.

Drury, C. (1996) *Costing: An Introduction*, 3rd edn, London: International Thomson Business Press.

Edgeworth, F.Y. (1881) *Mathematical Psychics: An Essay on the Application of*

Mathematics to the Moral Sciences, London: Kegan Paul; reprinted (1967) New York: Augustus M. Kelley.

Eisenhardt, K.M. (1989a) 'Agency theory: an assessment and review', *Academy of Management Review* **14** (1): 57–74.

—— (1989b) 'Building theories from case study research', *Academy of Management Review*, **14** (4): 532–50.

Ezzamel, M. and Hart, H. (1987) *Advanced Management Accounting: An Organizational Emphasis*, Gillingham: Cassell.

Fama, E. (1976) *Foundations of Finance*, New York: Boric Books.

Fiet, J.O. (1995) 'Risk avoidance strategies in venture capital markets', *Journal of Management Studies*, **32** (4): 553–74.

Flaherty, M.T. (1984) 'Field research on the link between technological innovation and growth: evidence from the international semiconductor industry', *American Economic Review* (*Papers and Proceedings*), **74**: 67–72.

Frank, L. (1984) *Database Theory and Practice*, Reading, Mass.: Addison-Wesley.

Frey, J.H. (1983) *Survey Research by Telephone*, Beverly Hills, Calif.: Sage.

Fricke, F. (1987) 'Asymmetric information between investors and managers under the new German accounting legislation', in G. Bamberg and K. Spremann (eds), *Agency Theory, Information and Incentives*, Berlin: Springer-Verlag.

Fried, V.H. and Hisrich, R.D. (1995) 'The venture capitalist: a relationship investor', *California Management Review*, **37** (2): 101–13.

Friedman, M. (1953) *Essays in Positive Economics*, Chicago: Chicago University Press.

Gifford, S. (1995) 'Endogenous opportunity costs and first-best outcomes in a principal–agent model of venture capital', working paper, Boston University.

Gladstone, D. (1988) *Venture Capital Investing: The Complete Handbook for Investing in Small Private Businesses for Outstanding Profit*, New Jersey: Prentice-Hall.

Glaser, B.G. and Strauss, A.L. (1967) *The Discovery of Grounded Theory: Strategies for Qualitative Research*, New York: Aldine.

Gompers, P.A. (1994) 'Optimal investment, monitoring, and the staging of venture capital', mimeo, Harvard Business School.

—— (1995) 'Grandstanding in the venture capital industry', mimeo, Harvard Business School.

Gompers, P.A. and Lerner, J. (1994) 'An analysis of compensation in the US venture capital partnership', Working Paper No. 94–009, Harvard Business School.

Gordon, L.A., Loeb, M.P. and Stark, A.W. (1990) 'Capital budgeting in the US venture capital partnership', *Journal of Political Economy*, **98**.

Gorman, M. and Sahlman, W.A. (1989) 'What do venture capitalists do?', *Journal of Business Venturing*, **4**: 231–48.

Gravelle, H. and Rees, R. (1981) *Microeconomics*, London: Longman.

Green, B.M. (ed.) (1991) *Venture Capital: International Comparisons*, London: Routledge.

Grinyer, P., McKiernan, P. and Mayes, D. (1988) *The Sharpbenders: The Secrets of Unleashing Corporate Potential*, Oxford: Blackwell.

Gupta, A.K. and Sapienza, H.J. (1992) 'Determinants of venture capital firms' preferences regarding the industry diversity and geographic scope of their investments', *Journal of Business Venturing*, 7: 347–62.

Gwilliam, D. (1987) *A Survey of Auditing Research*, Research Studies in Accounting Series, ICAEW: Prentice-Hall.

Harrison, R. and Mason, C. (1992) 'The roles of investors in entrepreneurial companies: a comparison of informal investors and venture capitalists', *Venture Capital Research Project*, Working Paper No. 5, University of Southampton.

Hatherley, D., Innes, J., Macandrew, J. and Mitchell, F. (1994) 'An exploration of the MBO–financier relationship', *Corporate Governance*, **2**: 20–9.

Hey, J.D. (1979) *Uncertainty in Economics*, Oxford: Martin Robertson.

Hoffman, H.M. and Blakey, J. (1987) 'You *can* negotiate with venture capitalists', *Harvard Business Review*, March/April, 16–24.

Holmström, B. (1979) 'Moral hazard and observability', *Bell Journal of Economics and Management Science*, 10: 74–91.

Holmström, B. and Tirole, J. (1989) 'The theory of the firm', in R. Schmalensee and R. Willig (eds), *Handbook of Industrial Organisation*, Amsterdam: North-Holland, ch. 2.

Hutchison, P. and Ray, G. (1986) 'Surviving the financial stress of small enterprise growth', in J. Curran, J. Stanworth and D. Watkins (eds), *The Survival of the Small Firm*, Aldershot: Gower.

Jensen, M.C. and Meckling, W.H. (1976) 'Theory of the firm: managerial behaviour, agency costs and ownership structure', *Journal of Financial Economics*, **3**: 305–60.

Jones, C.S. (1992) 'The attitudes of owner-managers towards accounting control systems following management buyout', *Accounting, Organizations and Society*, **17**: 151–68.

—— (1995) 'An empirical study of the evidence for contingency theories of management accounting systems in conditions of rapid change', *Accounting Organizations and Society*, **10** (3): 303–28.

Kaplan, R.S. and Shank, J.K. (1990) 'Contribution margin analysis: no longer relevant – strategic cost management: the new paradigm', *Journal of Management Accounting Research*, fall, 2–15.

Khan, A.M. (1987) 'Assessing venture capital investments with noncompensatory behavioural decision models', *Journal of Business Venturing*, **2**: 193–205.

Khaneman, D. and Tversky, A. (1979) 'Prospect theory: an analysis of decision under risk', *Econometrica*, **47**: 263–91.

Kirchoff, B.A., Long, W.A., McMillan, W.E., Vesper, K.H. and Wetzel, W.E., Jr (eds) (1994) *Frontiers of Entrepreneurship Research 1994*, Wellesley, Mass.: Babson College.

Kirk, J. and Miller, M.I. (1985) *Reliability and Validity in Qualitative Research*, London: Sage.

Kozmetsky, G., Gill, M.D., Jr and Smilor, R.W. (1985) *Financing and Managing Fast-Growth Companies: The Venture Capital Process*, Lexington, Mass. D.C. Heath.

Kreps, D.M. (1990) *A Course in Microeconomic Theory*, New York: Harvester Wheatsheaf.

Lam, S. (1991) 'Venture capital financing: a conceptual framework', *Journal of Business Finance and Accounting*, **18** (2): 137–49.

Lambert, R.A. (1986) 'Executive effort and selection of risky projects', *Rand Journal of Economics*, **17** (1): 77–88.

Landström, H. (1990) 'Co-operation between venture capital companies and small firms', *Entrepreneurship and Regional Development*, **2**: 345–62.

—— (1992) 'The relationship between private investors and small firms: an agency theory approach', *Entrepreneurship and Regional Development*, **4**: 199–223.

Lawson, T. (1985) 'Uncertainty and economic analysis', *Economic Journal*, **95**: 909–27.

Lee, T.A. and Tweedie, D.P. (1981) *The Institutional Investor and Financial Information*, London: Institute of Chartered Accountants in England and Wales.

Leland, H.E. and Pyle, D.H. (1977) 'Information asymmetries, financial structure and financial intermediation', *Journal of Finance*, **33**: 371–87.

Lerner, J. (1994a) 'The syndication of venture capital investments', *Financial Management*, **23** (3): 16–27.

—— (1994b) 'Venture capitalists and the decision to go public', *Journal of Financial Economics*, **35** (3): 293–316.

—— (1995) 'Venture capitalists and the oversight of private firms', *Journal of Finance*, **50** (1): 301–18.

Loasby, B. (1995) 'The organisation of capabilities', paper read to EMOT Workshop, University of Reading, UK.

Lorenz, T. (1989) *Venture Capital Today: A Practical Guide to the Venture Capital Market*, 2nd edn, New York: Woodhead-Faulkner.

Lynch, R.M. (1967) *Accounting for Management: Planning and Control*, New York: McGraw-Hill.

Macmillan, I.C., Kulow, D.M. and Khoylian, R. (1988) 'Venture capitalists' involvement in their investments: extent and performance', *Journal of Business Venturing*, **4**: 27–47.

Macmillan, I.C., Siegel, R. and Subba Narashima, P.N. (1985) 'Criteria used by venture capitalists to evaluate new venture proposals', *Journal of Business Venturing*, **1**.

March, S.G. and Simon, H.A. (1958) *Organizations*, New York: Wiley.

Markowitz, H. (1959) *Portfolio Selection*, New York: Wiley.

Masey, A. (1993) *The Adventurers: A Year in the Life of a Venture Capital House*, London: BBC Books.

Mason, C.M. and Harrison, R.T. (1991a) 'Venture capital, the equity gap and the "North–South divide" in the United Kingdom', in M.B. Green (ed.), *Venture Capital: International Comparisons*, London: Routledge.

—— (1991b) 'The small firm equity gap since Bolton', in J. Stanworth and C. Gray (eds), *Bolton Twenty Years On: The Small Firm in the 1990s*, London: Paul Chapman.

— (1994) 'The role of informal and formal sources of venture capital in the financing of technology based SMEs in the United Kingdom', in R. Oakey (ed.), *New Technology-Based Firms in the 1990s*, London: Paul Chapman.

Miller, D.H. and Myers, S.C. (eds) (1991) *Frontiers of Finance: The Battermarch Fellowship Papers*, Oxford: Blackwell.

Mirrlees, J. (1971) 'An exploration in the theory of optimum taxation', *Review of Economic Studies*, **38**: 175–208.

—— (1976) 'The optimal structure of incentives and authority within an organization', *Bell Journal of Economics*, 7: 105–31.

Mitchell, F., Reid, G.C. and Terry, N.G. (1992) 'Some agency aspects of venture capital investment behaviour', working paper, Centre for Financial Markets Research, University of Edinburgh.

—— (1995) 'Post investment demand for accounting information by venture capitalists', *Accounting and Business Research*, **25** (99), 186–96.

—— (1998) 'Venture capital supply and accounting information system development'. *Entrepreneurship Theory and Practice* (forthcoming).

Murray, G. (1995a) 'Managing investors' risk in venture capital financed new technology based firms', paper presented to an ESRC conference on Risk in Organisational Settings, The White House, London, mimeo.

—— (1995b) 'A synthesis of six European case studies of successfully-exited, venture capital financed, new technology based firms', paper presented to seminar on Financing SMEs, NUTEK, Brussels, September, mimeo.

—— (1995c) 'Evolution and change: an analysis of the first decade of the UK venture capital industry', Warwick Business School, mimeo.

Murray, G. and Lott, J. (1995) 'Have UK venture capitalists a bias against investment in new technology-based firms?', *Research Policy*, **24**: 283–99.

Otley, D.T. (1980) 'The contingency theory of management accounting: achievements and prognosis', *Accounting, Organizations and Society*, **5**: 413–28.

Pike, R. (1982) *Capital Budgeting in the 1980s: A Major Survey of Investment Practices in Large Companies*, London: Chartered Institute of Management Accountants.

Porter, M.E. (1980) *Competitive Strategy: Techniques for Analyzing Industries and Competitors*, New York: Free Press.

Pratt, J.W. and Zeckhauser, R.J. (1985a) 'Principals and agents: an overview', in J.W. Pratt and R.J. Zeckhauser (eds), *Principals and Agents: The Structure of Business*, Boston: Harvard Business School Press.

—— (1985b) *Principals and Agents: The Structure of Business*, Boston: Harvard Business School Press.

Rees, B. (1990) *Financial Analysis*, New York: Prentice-Hall.

Reid, G.C. (1987) *Theories of Industrial Organization*, Oxford: Blackwell.

—— (1992) 'A note on the design and structure of a small firm's relational database', *Small Business Economics*, **4**: 9–14.

—— (1993) *Small Business Enterprise: An Economic Analysis*, London: Routledge.

—— (1996a) 'Fast growing small entrepreneurial firms and their venture capital backers: an applied principal–agent analysis', *Small Business Economics*, **8**: 1–14.

—— (1996b) 'Mature micro-firms and their experience of funding shortages', *Small Business Economics*, **8**: 27–37.

—— (1998) 'Limits to a firm's rate of growth: the Richardsonian view and its contemporary empirical significance', in B.J. Loasby and N.J. Foss (eds), *Economic Organisation, Capabilities and Co-Ordination: Essays in Honour of G.B. Richardson*, London: Routledge.

Reid, G.C. and Anderson, M.E. (1992) 'A new small firms database: sample design, instrumentation, and summary statistics', Discussion Paper No. 9207, Centre for Research into Industry, Enterprise, Finance and the Firm (CRIEFF), Department of Economics, University of St Andrews.

Reid, G.C., Jacobsen, L.R. and Anderson, M.E. (1993) *Profiles in Small Business: A Competitive Strategy Approach*, London: Routledge.

Reid, G.C., Terry, N.G. and Smith, J.A. (1997) 'Risk management in venture capital investor–investee relations', *European Journal of Finance*, **3** (1): 27–47.

Reid, John (1683) *The Scots Gard'ner: Published for the Climate of Scotland*, first published (1683) by David Lindsay in Edinburgh, and reprinted (1988) in facsimile form with a new introduction by Annette Hope, Edinburgh: Mainstream Publishing.

Ricketts, M. (1986) 'The geometry of principal and agent: yet another use for the Edgeworth box', *Scottish Journal of Political Economy*, **33**: 228–48.

—— (1987) *The Economics of Business Enterprise*, New York: Harvester Wheatsheaf.

—— (1994) *The Economics of Business Enterprise*, 2nd edn, New York: Harvester Wheatsheaf.

Robbie, K. and Wright, M. (1995) 'Managerial and ownership succession and corporate restructuring: the case of management buy-ins', *Journal of Management Studies*, **32** (4): 527–49.

Roberts, E.B. (1991) 'High stakes for high-tech entrepreneurs: understanding venture capital decision making', *Sloan Management Review*, **37** (2): 9–20.

Ruhnka, J.C. and Young, J.E. (1987) 'A venture capital model of the development process for new ventures', *Journal of Business Venturing*, **2**: 167–84.

—— (1991) 'Some hypotheses about risk in venture capital investing', *Journal of Business Venturing*, **6**: 115–33.

Ryan, R., Scapens, R.W. and Theobald, M. (1992) *Research Method and Methodology in Finance and Accounting*, London: Academic Press.

Sahlman, W.A. (1990) 'The structure and governance of venture-capital organizations', *Journal of Financial Economics*, **27**: 473–521.

Sapienza, H.J. (1989) 'Variations in venture capitalist–entrepreneur relations: antecedents and consequences', unpublished PhD thesis, University of Maryland at College Park, UMI Dissertation Services, Ann Arbor, Michigan.

—— (1992) 'When do venture capitalists add value?', *Journal of Business Venturing*, **7**: 9–27.

Sapienza, H.J. and Korsgaard, M.A. (1996) 'Procedural justice in entrepreneur–investor relations', *Academy of Management Journal*, **39**: 544–74.

Sappington, D.E.M. (1991) 'Incentives in principal–agent relationships', *Journal of Economic Perspectives*, **5**: 45–66.

Schatzman, L. and Strauss, A.L. (1973) *Field Research: Strategies for a Natural Sociology*, Englewood Cliffs, NJ: Prentice-Hall.

Schmalensee, R. and Willig, R. (eds) (1989) *Handbook of Industrial Organisation*, Amsterdam: North-Holland.

Sekaran, U. (1992) *Research Methods in Business: A Skill Building Approach*, 2nd edn, New York: Wiley.

Shank, J.K. and Govindarajan, V. (1989) *Strategic Cost Analysis*, Boston: Irwin.

Simon, H.A. (1982) *Models of Bounded Rationality*, vols 1 and 2, Cambridge, Mass.: MIT Press.

Siskos, J. and Zopounidis, C. (1987) 'The evaluation criteria of the venture capital investment activity: an interactive assessment', *European Journal of Operational Research*, **31**: 304–13.

Stacey, N. (1990) 'Should venture capitalists be more intrepid?', London: Foundation for Business Responsibilities.

Statman, L. (1990) 'How many stocks make a diversified portfolio?', in D.H. Miller and S.C. Myers (eds), *Frontiers of Finance: The Battermarch Fellowship Papers*, Oxford: Blackwell.

Steier, L. and Greenwood, R. (1995) 'Venture capitalist relationships in the deal structuring and post-investment stages of new firm creation', *Journal of Management Studies*, **32**: 337–57.

Storey, D.J. (1994) *Understanding the Small Business Sector*, London: Routledge.

Storey, D., Keasey, K., Watson, R. and Wynarczyk, P. (1987) *The Performance of Small Firms*, Beckenham: Croom Helm.

Strong, N. and Walker, M. (1987) *Information and Capital Markets*, Oxford: Blackwell.

Strong, N. and Waterson, M. (1987) 'Principals, agents and information', in R. Clarke and T. McGuiness (eds), *The Economics of the Firm*, Oxford: Blackwell.

Sweeting, R.C. (1991a) 'Early-stage new technology-based businesses: interactions with venture capitalists and the development of accounting techniques and procedures', *British Accounting Review*, **23** (1).

—— (1991b) 'UK venture capital funds and the funding of new technology-based businesses: process and relationships', *Journal of Management Studies*, **28** (6): 601–22.

Terry, N.G. (1994) 'Some thoughts on trends and maturity patterns in UK venture capital 1985–1993', Working Paper 94.3, Centre for Financial Markets Research, Department of Business Studies, University of Edinburgh.

Tucker, A.L., Becker, K.G., Isimbabi, M.J. and Pogden, J.P. (1995) *Contemporary Portfolio-Theory and Risk Management*, St Paul, Minn.: West Publishing.

Tyebjee, T.T. and Bruno, A.V. (1984) 'A model of venture capitalist investment activity', *Management Science*, **30**: 1051–66.

Varian, H.R. (1990) *Intermediate Microeconomics: A Modern Approach*, 2nd edn, New York: Norton.

Venture Economics (1986) 'Human resources of the UK venture capital industry', *UK Venture Capital Journal*, March.

Vickers, D. (1987) *Money Capital in the Theory of the Firm*, Cambridge: Cambridge University Press.

Webb, R.K. (1980) *Modern England: From the 18th Century to the Present*, 2nd edn, London: George Allen & Unwin.

Williams, H.P (1985) *Model Building in Mathematical Programming*, 2nd edn, New York: Wiley.

Williamson, O.E. (1975) *Markets and Hierarchies*, New York: Free Press.

Wilson, J.W. (1985) *The New Venturers: Inside the High-Stakes World of Venture Capital*, Reading, Mass.: Addison-Wesley.

Wozniak, G.D. (1987) 'Human capital, information, and the early adoption of new technology', *Journal of Human Resources*, **22** (1): 101–12.

Wright, M. and Robbie, K. (1996) 'Venture capitalists and unquoted equity investment appraisal', *Accounting and Business Research*, spring.

Wright, M., Thompson, S. and Robbie, K. (1992) 'Venture capitalist and management-led leveraged buy-outs: a European perspective', *Journal of Business Venturing*, 7: 47–71.

Yin, R.K. (1984) *Case Study Research*, Beverly Hills, Calif.: Sage.

—— (1993) *Applications of Case Study Research*, Newberry Park, Calif.: Sage.

AUTHOR INDEX

SUBJECT INDEX

Note: page numbers in italics refer to figures or tables where these are separated from their textual reference